Learning jQuery

A Hands-on Guide to Building
Rich Interactive Web Front Ends

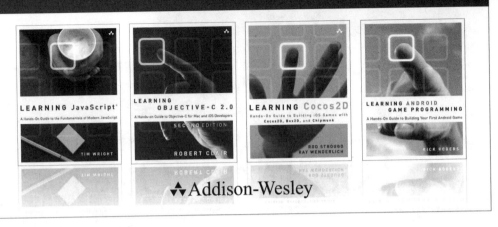

Learning jQuery

A Hands-on Guide to Building Rich
Interactive Web Front Ends

Ralph Steyer

♦♦Addison-Wesley

Upper Saddle River, NJ • Boston • Indianapolis • San Francisco
New York • Toronto • Montreal • London • Munich • Paris • Madrid
Cape Town • Sydney • Tokyo • Singapore • Mexico City

Learning jQuery: A Hands-on Guide to Building Rich Interactive Web Front Ends

Trademarks

All terms mentioned in this book that are known to be trademarks or service marks have been appropriately capitalized. Pearson cannot attest to the accuracy of this information. Use of a term in this book should not be regarded as affecting the validity of any trademark or service mark.

Warning and Disclaimer

Every effort has been made to make this book as complete and as accurate as possible, but no warranty or fitness is implied. The information provided is on an "as is" basis. The author and the publisher shall have neither liability nor responsibility to any person or entity with respect to any loss or damages arising from the information contained in this book.

Bulk Sales

Pearson offers excellent discounts on this book when ordered in quantity for bulk purchases or special sales. For more information, please contact

U.S. Corporate and Government Sales
1-800-382-3419
corpsales@pearsontechgroup.com

For sales outside of the U.S., please contact

International Sales
international@pearsoned.com

Editor in Chief
Mark Taub

Acquisitions Editor
Mark Taber

Managing Editor
Sandra Schroeder

Project Editor
Mandie Frank

Copy Editor
Keith Cline

Indexer
Larry Sweazy

Proofreader
Megan Wade

Translator
Almut Dworak

Technical Editor
Brad Dayley

Publishing Coordinator
Vanessa Evans

Designer
Chuti Prasertsith

Compositor
Jake McFarland

Contents at a Glance

Table of Contents

About the Author

Ralph Steyer is a computer programmer, consultant, journalist, and book author with decades of experience in a wide variety of computer programming languages and technologies. He has a degree in mathematics from Frankfurt/Main University and is the author of several books on web programming, including *JavaScript Handbook* and *AJAX Frameworks* (Addison-Wesley).

We Want to Hear from You!

As the reader of this book, *you* are our most important critic and commentator. We value your opinion and want to know what we're doing right, what we could do better, what areas you'd like to see us publish in, and any other words of wisdom you're willing to pass our way.

You can email or write directly to let us know what you did or didn't like about this book—as well as what we can do to make our books stronger.

Please note that we cannot help you with technical problems related to the topic of this book, and that due to the high volume of mail we receive, we might not be able to reply to every message.

When you write, please be sure to include this book's title and author, as well as your name and phone or email address.

Email: feedback@developers-library.info

Mail: Reader Feedback
           Addison-Wesley Developer's Library
           800 East 96th Street
           Indianapolis, IN 46240 USA

Reader Services

Visit our website and register this book at www.informit.com/register for convenient access to any updates, downloads, or errata that might be available for this book.

Your purchase of this book includes access to a free online edition for 45 days through the Safari Books Online subscription service. Details are on the last page of this book.

1

Introduction

Rich Internet Applications (RIAs), with their somewhat vaguely worded *rich* opportunities, have significantly changed the way we use the Web over the past few years. And the speed of this change keeps increasing. The significance of classic desktop applications is being repositioned. Many types of programs that were traditionally used only as desktop application now suddenly appear on the Web, be it personal calendars, entire office programs, games, route planners, or communication programs. But apps for cell phones or smartphones are also increasingly based on web technology. This changes both the user behavior and the user expectation for Internet applications in general and the availability of services. As classic web applications, but with a certain extra value, RIAs are, on the one hand, always available if you have a halfway decent Internet access and a modern browser.[1] On the other hand, they are hardly distinguishable any more from classic desktop or mobile apps in terms of operation, performance, and visual appearance.

The most effective way to ensure that these rich opportunities are available usually involves using an appropriate web framework. Be aware, however, that if you use a framework, you become significantly dependent on a manufacturer or a project, and that you then no longer have complete control over the source code in your applications. In any case, using frameworks requires familiarizing yourself sufficiently with the relevant function libraries and working methods of the system. In contrast to grandiose advertising claims of some frameworks (and some tools), you can usually use them effectively only after you understand web programming concepts and have at least a basic knowledge of the underlying technology. Strictly speaking, you will profit most from frameworks the less you actually need them and the more you master the basics.

Regardless of these problems and disadvantages, however, there is much to be said for making use of frameworks and toolkits. They will certainly help you develop and maintain sophisticated websites much more quickly, effectively, and efficiently; and they enable you to offer a richer and more robust site.

---

1. The browser becomes a multifunctional access instrument for a specific task and thus replaces classic application types. In the future, users might only need a browser as application, or the operating system and the browser may merge so that they become indistinguishable.

> **Note**
>
> The preceding text included the terms *framework* and *toolkit* a few times. There is no standard definition for exactly what a framework is and how it differs from a toolkit. In fact, a reliable definition and differentiation is not very straightforward. But generally, the term *framework* implies a programming framework that already offers certain functionalities. A framework is not yet a finished program in itself, but merely provides a frame within which one or several programmers can create an application. A framework usually contains a library with useful predefined code structures, but also (in contrast to a pure library) specifies a certain control of the behavior patterns involved in using it (for example, a syntax or grammar). With a toolkit, the main focus is on a collection of programs (tools), but these can also be based on specific libraries or a syntax concept. Both a framework and, in particular, toolkits often provide widgets or components—in other words, elements that constitute a graphical user interface (GUI).

1.1   What Is This Book About?

This book provides an easy introduction to web programming with **jQuery, jQuery UI**, and **Mobile jQuery**. jQuery is a free and comprehensive framework built on top of the JavaScript language. It was originally developed by John Resig and released in January 2006 at BarCamp (NYC). It is now consistently developed further an open source project. jQuery UI is built on top of jQuery and extends the jQuery framework with UI specific components. Similarly, jQuery Mobile is also built on top of jQuery and extends the jQuery framework with mobile device-specific components.

The framework offers a whole range of very helpful features (for example, easy-to-use functions for DOM manipulation and navigation, as well as basic AJAX support). Beyond this, the framework offers support for Cascading Style Sheets (CSS), an expanded event system, impressive effects and animations, various auxiliary functions, and numerous free plug-ins.

But where jQuery particularly excels is the seamless integration of the framework in many web platforms by large industry providers or their official support. For example, Microsoft uses jQuery in the development environment Visual Studio in combination with the ASP.NET MVC framework and Microsoft Asynchronous JavaScript and XML (AJAX). For example, if you create a new ASP.NET project, you can also integrate jQuery automatically (although not necessarily in the latest version).

In an ASP.NET MVC 3 or later web application in Visual Studio, you can even choose to integrate some jQuery plug-ins (such as jquery.validate.js for validating user input).

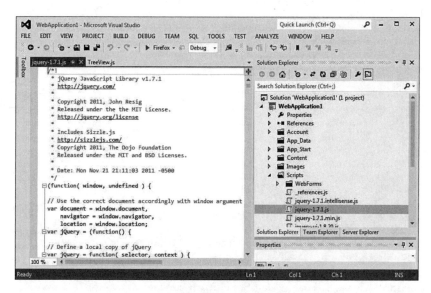

Figure 1.1   In an ASP.NET web application in Visual Studio 2010, you can also integrate jQuery.

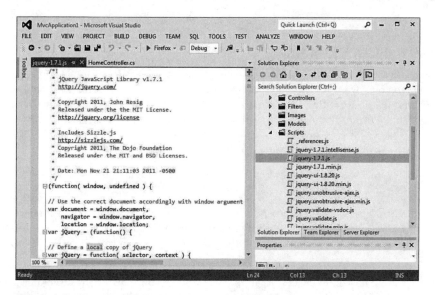

Figure 1.2   An ASP.NET MVC 4 web application with references to jQuery itself plus several jQuery plug-ins.

The links to the libraries are already created in the pregenerated source text and can be simply enabled by deleting the comment characters.

```
<html>
<head>
    <title>@View.Title</title>
    <link href="@Url.Content("~/Content/Site.css")" rel="stylesheet" type="text/css" />
    @*
    <script src="@Url.Content("~/Scripts/jquery-1.4.1.min.js")" type="text/javascript"></script>
    <script src="@Url.Content("~/Scripts/jquery.unobtrusive-ajax.min.js")" type="text/javascript"></script>
    <script src="@Url.Content("~/Scripts/jquery.validate.min.js")" type="text/javascript"></script>
    <script src="@Url.Content("~/Scripts/jquery.validate.unobtrusive.min.js")" type="text/javascript"></script>
    *@
</head>

<body>
```

Figure 1.3   In the generated code, you just need to enable the script references.

In addition to Visual Studio, various other web development tools offer jQuery. But even other suppliers with a different focus use jQuery (for example, the cell phone manufacturer Nokia in its Web Runtime platform, as well as Google, Dell, Mozilla, WordPress, Drupal, and Digg). The list of popular users reads like a Who's Who of the Web. The framework is also extremely popular on a wide scale, as many statistics prove. If you look at modern RIAs, more than 60% of them currently use jQuery and the jQuery UI, despite its powerful and impressive competitors.

1.1.1   What You Can Learn from This Book

In this book, you learn how to use jQuery for your own web applications—from simple websites to which you only want to add individual effects, right up to complex RIAs. This book is aimed at beginners, without starting right at zero, but it is not intended for an audience of freaks and programming experts either. You do not need to have lots of experience with AJAX or a framework or toolkit. But you should have a little bit of experience with web technology—more on this shortly when you read about the target audience.

The book follows the same basic structure in each chapter. A brief introduction precedes the more detailed topics, and a summary concludes the chapter.

The specific approach is this: After this chapter, which already provides all requirements for working with jQuery, we just jump in at the deep end and work through a few examples without much preparation. This is meant to give a feel for what you can do with jQuery.

We then cover some basic background information about the Web, JavaScript, AJAX, Extensible Markup Language (XML), JavaScript Object Notation (JSON), and so on. Then, we take a closer look at what working with jQuery involves. Next, we turn to selectors and filters. I believe that these options for selecting objects in the context of a website are one of the biggest highlights of the framework and form the basis for accessing the elements of a website. Many examples are provided to help you better understand what we mean.

Next comes the topic Dynamic Hypertext Markup Language (DHTML). In DHTML, the main focus is on changing websites based on certain events. Essentially (or at least in most cases), DHTML means the dynamic influencing of CSS properties. Once more, jQuery offers many options for making this task much easier and compensating for numerous browser incompatibility issues.

In the previous paragraph, I used the word *event*. Event handling on the Web is a bottomless pit with many browsers. jQuery provides a solution. In this book, you learn how.

For many visitors, effects and animations are an eye-catcher in a website. Again, jQuery has a whole range of horses in the stable that need not fear the competition in this race.

Then we explicitly venture into the Web 2.0. So, we turn to AJAX and look at what jQuery can offer in this respect.

That is really all on the topic of jQuery. But wait a sec, wasn't there something else? The jQuery UI! So far, I have hardly mentioned it when describing the topics contained in this book. You might now think that the jQuery UI is something like the ugly duckling in the jQuery universe. Or perhaps uninteresting. This is far from the truth. The jQuery UI is the beautiful swan. Purely in terms of visual appearance, the jQuery UI offers much more than jQuery itself, even though using it is much easier—as long as you understand jQuery. jQuery is the basis that makes life easier regarding source code and programming, whereas the jQuery UI builds on it as an independent framework and excels with visually advanced interface components and a CSS theme framework. Of course, we also take a closer look at the jQuery UI in this book and work through many examples with the various widgets it offers. In addition, you learn in detail how to use options, events, methods, and theming to adapt it further. The theme framework and the ThemeRoller of the jQuery UI are also covered in detail.

Then there are also plug-ins in jQuery, as extensions of the framework. You will learn how to use foreign plug-ins in case you cannot find a certain function in the jQuery and the jQuery UI core libraries, and you will learn how to create and publish your own plug-ins.

Last but not least, this book describes how you can create mobile apps based on jQuery. This involves using the mobile framework that is directly based on native jQuery (just as the jQuery UI is).

> **Note**
>
> To make things clearer, we often work with code examples in this book. You should type in the complete code examples yourself (and, of course, you can then also modify them and experiment with them if you like). However, you will also find the listings on the companion website for this book.

1.2   Writing Conventions

This book uses various writing conventions intended to help you keep track of things more easily. Important terms are **emphasized in bold**. Sometimes also in *italics*. Above all, you are meant to be able to see if it is normal text or `program code`. Keyboard shortcuts and some other special things are also highlighted. This formatting is used consistently throughout this book.

I also want to add a special comment on source text passages of complete listings. For all complete listings and some larger source code fragments, you will see **numbering** of the source text lines. The numbers are, of course, not part of the source text itself; they are only meant to make it easier for you to find your way around, to point out a new line in the source code, and to make it clearer which part of the source code I am referring to. In rare cases, it might be necessary because of technical reasons to split a source text line over several book lines. In this case, the numbering of the source code lines indicates which passages are to be written into one line in the editor. So long as you do not see a new line number in the book listing, you still have to type everything into a single line in the editor. This is particularly important for longer strings (texts in quotation marks) that must not be divided up into several lines.

1.3   Who Is the Target Audience for This Book?

It is always tricky to anticipate who may be interested in a particular topic. But I have certain ideas and by now quite a lot of experience from jQuery seminars about who will be interested in finding out more about creating RIAs in the context of jQuery, their potential reasons, and the most likely readership of this book. I assume that you have already created websites and have already been programming in one form or another. JavaScript would be a great basis, but other programming techniques are just as welcome, although your learning curve will be slightly steeper as you go along. Style sheets should also be a familiar concept to you. If you do not have any previous experience with creating websites or working with HTML or programming, this book will probably pose quite a challenge for you (but this should not discourage you from reading it). I also assume that you are tired of the limitations of a static HTML site. Perhaps you already have some experience with dynamic websites (at least as a user), and you would probably like to find an easy way to create such interactive modern sites. jQuery is a fantastic method for achieving this.

More and more programmers of powerful techniques and environments such as Java or .NET are pressing into the area of web programming. Correspondingly, I want to also address readers with this type of background knowledge. For programmers who switch over from such powerful and strict worlds, it is often hard to find their way in the seemingly trivial (but, in fact, rather distinctive) world of web programming.

1.4   What Do You Need?

Let's turn to the requirements you should meet for working with this book and jQuery.

1.4.1   Hardware and Operating System

We are dealing with the Internet. So, of course, you need to have a computer with Internet access. No special requirements apply as far as the computer itself is concerned, but your hardware should be at least reasonable quality. The requirements of modern operating systems already determine the minimum level of the required hardware. All graphic operating systems such as Linux, Windows, or OS X will work fine as long as they are relatively up-to-date. The exact type of the system you are using is not relevant for our purposes, just as in most cases on the Web.

1.4.2 jQuery and jQuery UI

Of course, you need to have jQuery itself so that you can re-create the examples in this book. You also need—in the later part of this book—the jQuery UI. You can download the most recent version of jQuery as well as past releases from the jQuery website: http://docs.jquery.com/Downloading_jQuery.

> **Tip**
>
> You can also download the current release from the project's home page at http://jquery.com/. You will see a large button that loads the JavaScript library directly. At the time of this writing, the current release is version 1.9.1.

You can download different variations, basically a minified version without comments and redundant spaces or line breaks that is used mainly in production or an uncompressed version that has comments in the source code and is easy to read but larger. The function of both versions is the same; they contain a JavaScript file that generally has the name jquery.js. This file, which will usually also have a version number in the filename and a description of its specific variant depending on its type,[2] is the central library of the framework that you integrate into your websites. If you download a variant with a zip archive from the Internet, simply extract it. You then just need to reference the JavaScript file in your website following the usual rules (more on this later).

> **Tip**
>
> If you click the link for downloading the jQuery file, most browsers just display the file, without first giving you the option to save it. After all, it is a JavaScript library, and as such is usually displayed as pure text. By contrast, if you click a zip file, you usually get the option to save it via the browser's download dialog that pops up when you click the file. In case of the jQuery library, you can display the code and then click the browser's option for saving the page to save the jQuery library locally.

Figure 1.4 The jQuery file is displayed.

2. For example, jquery-1.7.2.min.js indicates the minified version 1.7.2, and jquery-1.7.2.js is the uncompressed version 1.7.2.

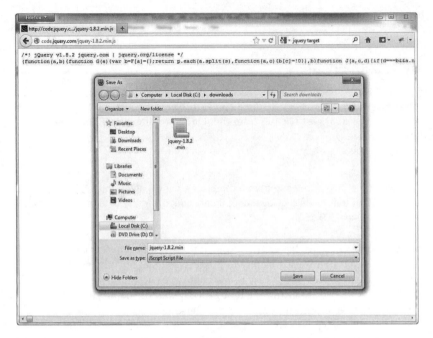

Figure 1.5   Use the browser's Save dialog to save the jQuery library locally.

If you want to use the jQuery UI, you need this framework, as well, because the jQuery UI is not contained in the normal jQuery JavaScript library. The jQuery UI is a separate project within the whole jQuery framework and contains other resources such as CSS files and graphics in addition to JavaScript files. You can find the home page of the project at http://jqueryui.com. There, you can load the framework via the **Download** link. Upon completion of the download, you get a compressed zip file that you can extract and make available on your server (just as with the jQuery library) and then integrate into your website via a central jQuery UI JavaScript file.

> ### Caution
>
> Regarding the versions, note that the jQuery UI versions always work with a specific version of jQuery itself and that incompatibilities can arise if the versions do not match. But the zip file always contains a version of jQuery, as well, the version that is the required minimum. There is more to be said about downloading the jQuery UI and its specific use, but I come back to this in more detail later in the chapters on the jQuery UI.

1.4.3   The Browsers

What you definitely need for programming with jQuery is, of course, a web browser that supports jQuery. After all, you want to be able to view your own sites so that you can test them. When using jQuery, you also need to take into account that the visitors of your websites have to comply with a certain minimum standard. As with most frameworks and toolkits, jQuery has anything but low requirements for the browser of a user who visits a website that works with jQuery. The minimum browser requirements may change with each new release of jQuery, but the following browsers are currently officially supported (you can check whether this still accurate at http://docs.jquery.com/Browser_Compatibility):

- Firefox[3]
- Internet Explorer
- Safari
- Opera
- Chrome[4]

Other browsers might work, but there is no official guarantee that they will. In the documentation, some browsers are officially listed as basically working, but with some known issues.

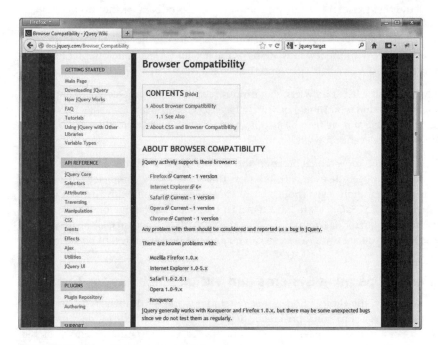

Figure 1.6   The officially supported browsers.

3. The same basically applies to all identical browsers, such as Netscape Navigator and Mozilla.

4. Including its safe and, in comparison with Google's data-gobbling habits, more reticent variant Iron.

> **Note**
>
> The version numbers are rather high, but users with older browsers hardly stand a chance in the current Web, even if we do not take jQuery into account. The situation has changed from what it was a few years ago. Now, more and more website creators no longer support as many browsers as possible. Instead, they explicitly set a minimum level. Certain functions cannot be realized at all in older browsers, or only with an exorbitant amount of effort, and hardly anyone is prepared to pay this price given that only a handful of users still have such old-timers. Some developers even cease supporting certain browser types, to give the impression that they are producing particularly modern websites. It seems to be almost a "mark of quality" if sites do not work with Internet Explorer or are not displayed correctly (as far as I can determine, this has almost become a national sport in the United States). This trend is essentially the opposite of what was going on about 10 years ago. Back then, you would find many websites with the note *Optimized for Internet Explorer*. Now, it seems that many websites want to demonstrate their exceptional quality by no longer working in Internet Explorer (at least in the really old versions, up to 7). Perhaps this is their motto: *We are making modern websites, and to use these, you need to have a modern and powerful browser.*

I believe that this is the wrong approach. I think that even though Internet Explorer 9 is now available and a really good browser, we should still offer a kind of protected-species support for versions 7 and 8 (and to a certain extent even version 6). After all, many users on the Internet are forced to use Internet Explorer[5] because of company politics or because they do not have sufficient knowledge to use an alternative browser or are just happy with a particular browser. I believe that jQuery is taking the sensible approach in supporting the older versions of Internet Explorer, and we can live with the few limitations of the jQuery UI regarding Internet Explorer; more on this in the relevant chapters later (and the explicit Microsoft support reflects this, too).

Unless you have one of the listed browsers, you cannot reliably test your jQuery web application. As a creator of websites, you should definitely have several browsers available. Because even when using a reliable and well-established framework like jQuery, you still need to test web applications in all relevant browsers.

And generally, you do not know which browsers the visitors of your websites are using. So, it is a good idea to test your website even with browsers that do not have completely guaranteed support for jQuery. For example, even though there are known problems with Firefox 1.0.x, Internet Explorer 1.0 to 5.x, Safari 1.0 to 2.0.1, Opera 1.0 to 9.x, and Konqueror, jQuery generally does work with Konqueror or Firefox 1.0.x. Just not with all components. Ultimately, it depends on the feature you are using, and you can go and test it in the relevant browsers.

1.4.4   Different Operating Systems and Virtual Machines for Testing

As mentioned previously, the choice of operating system for working with jQuery when creating a website is largely one of personal preference or any given constraints. This does not concern the choice of a test environment. Ideally, you have several operating systems available

---

5. Even still occasionally in the antiquated version 6, as I was appalled to realize in 2010/2011 during my seminars (and those were really big companies, too).

for testing your applications, because, after all, the visitors to your website will also be using different operating systems.

Of course, Windows is the reference system per se. The majority of users on the Web use this system. But Linux and OS X are also widely used, and there are different Windows versions, too. Sometimes it is very interesting to see how different web applications behave under different operating systems, although the differences should not really be significant. So, use different operating systems to test your applications if at all possible.

You do not need to have several computers or to install another operating system in parallel to your operating system. Especially for Linux, there are excellent live CDs or live DVDs from which you can launch the operating system directly without any changes being made to your hard disk. For readers with sufficiently capable hardware, it could also be interesting to have a closer look at a virtual solution (virtual machine [VM]) such as VMware (http://www.vmware.com), Virtual PC by Microsoft (http://www.microsoft.com/windows/virtual-pc/default.aspx), or VirtualBox (http://www.virtualbox.org/). These are available for free, at least for private use, and they simulate another operating system within the currently running operating system. For example, you can use these VMs to start a Linux system from within Windows or vice versa, or you can install another version of Internet Explorer under Windows parallel to your current Windows installation. With AJAX, the guest system (in other words, the system that runs in the VM) can act as server or client, and you therefore have two completely separate systems on one computer, enabling you to test a client/server relationship just as you would in reality.

1.4.5   The Web Server for Realistic Testing

With AJAX, data from a browser is requested from a web server and integrated into the website without reloading the site. Therefore, for practical use and for testing such applications, you must have access to a web server on the Internet and be able to execute programs and scripts on it. Ultimately, this is necessary for an AJAX project in practice, as well. However, in practice it is not usual to be working directly on a web server on the Internet while you are still developing a web application (especially if you just want to test a few things). But even without AJAX, to properly test a web application, you need to test it under realistic conditions on a web server.

For those reasons, you should create a test environment with a web server on a local computer or in a local network. Linux distributions, in particular, almost always contain one or more web servers. Different development environments for web applications also have an integrated web server. Then you are on the safe side. But even if you do not automatically have a web server available or simply want to make things as easy as possible, you can make use of an all-inclusive package such as XAMPP, which you can simply download for different operating systems from the Internet (at http://www.apachefriends.org).

This package is a collection of programs relating to the web server Apache, including the database management system MySQL (together with phpMyAdmin for administrating the database management system) and PHP support, the FTP server FileZilla, plus several other web technologies. You just install this package with a simple assistant, and then you have a fully functional web server in basic configuration at your disposal.

> **Caution**
>
> Note that in their default settings, these packages by XAMPP are for local testing purposes only. To make things as simple as possible, all security settings are at a minimum.

As soon as the installation of XAMPP completes, you can either launch Apache manually or set it up so that Apache is integrated as a service or process in your operating system and can even be launched automatically when the computer starts up. XAMPP offers a helpful and easy-to-use control panel.

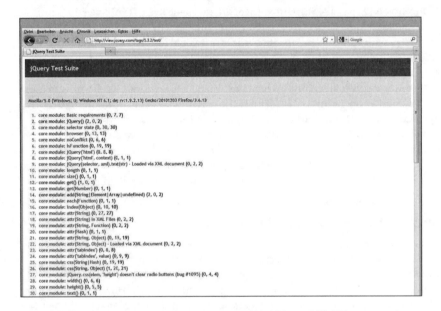

Figure 1.7   The XAMPP control panel: Apache, MySQL, and FileZilla are running.

> **Tip**
>
> Note that under XAMPP you have to follow the conventions commonly used on the Internet or Web regarding the path you specify. You cannot act as if you are working just under Windows (which, of course, means that you have to make sure that you work thoroughly and avoid potential problems right from the start). Under Apache, uppercase and lowercase is usually relevant. The best approach is to consistently use lowercase for directory names and filenames. And Windows users should note that you do not use a backslash for separating levels on the Internet, but instead use the slash.

1.4.6   The Development Tools

As backbone of an RIA, as for any website, you will almost always be using an HTML or XHTML frame. So, for creating the HTML source text and for all other techniques you use such as CSS, JavaScript, and so on, the minimum is a pure text editor, as included with any operating system.

In practice, though, you will probably use more powerful programming tools that support you in creating and analyzing the source text. Such programs may know some components of a programming or description language (such as HTML, CSS, or JavaScript) and support simple and sometimes even more complex standard processes, such as masking (the coded representation) of special characters, inserting source code templates, or aids for providing greater clarity by color-coding known commands. Some editors also offer the commands of a used language directly, which means the programmer can use menus or toolbars to choose them (sometimes with the mouse). Notepad++ (http://notepad-plus-plus.org/), for example, is an excellent editor offering this kind of support.

Another feature offered by some programs is different document views. This is often the case with pure HTML editors. You then have the choice of switching between the preview of a website (as it will look in the browser), a graphic editing mode, and above all a view of the HTML code itself.

Even in web programming, you can now make use of some proper integrated development environments (IDEs). These allow programming and executing from an integrated, common interface. A free yet very powerful IDE is Aptana (http://aptana.com/). It is based directly on the powerful development environment Eclipse (http://www.eclipse.org). Aptana offers a source code editor and has many features to directly support JavaScript, HTML, and CSS plus access to the DOM object model and even AJAX itself. The Code Assist function tries to autocomplete various user inputs, and syntax is marked with syntax highlighting (highlighting key terms and syntax structures in different colors). The option of displaying the properties and methods of objects is particularly interesting. The program even offers a debugger for JavaScript. Aptana also contains its own little web server (Jetty), via which you can test an AJAX application without installing an independent web server. If you create a project with Aptana, you will see that various popular JavaScript libraries are already integrated directly, among others jQuery, although there are usually more recent versions available on the Internet.

Figure 1.8   Aptana with direct support for jQuery.

Tip

Even if the version of jQuery available in Aptana for direct integration is not completely up-to-date, you should import the thus available (most recent, but potentially also outdated) jQuery library. You do not even need to use this outdated version. Instead, I recommend that you also download the most recent version separately and use this version in your web projects. But the import gives you the option of enabling in Aptana a code completion for the imported library (and this is not possible if you integrate the JavaScript file into a project via HTML alone). This code completion may then not be quite up-to-date, but is still immensely helpful.

Before you can use the code completion, you first have to complete the following steps:

1. Create a new web project via **File > New**.

2. Select **Default** from this list of available web project types.

3. After you have entered a name, you can either select a jQuery library directly (if it is already on offer), or you can click the **Install JavaScript Libraries** button. In the next dialog, you then choose **jQuery** under JavaScript Libraries. Where applicable, ensure that jQuery is also selected in the subsequent dialogs.

4. Under **Window > Preferences**, you can now go to the category Aptana Studio and open the subcategory **Editors** and then **JavaScript**. Here, you can select the code completion for jQuery under Code Assist. It is then available in all further default web projects. In other words, you need to complete these three steps only once, not for each and every project.

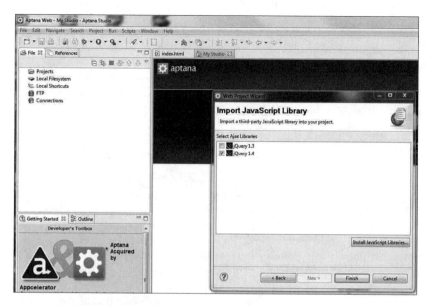

Figure 1.9   Enabling the code completion.

> **Note**
>
> The specific editor or IDE is not relevant for this book, although I am working mainly with Aptana.

As mentioned elsewhere, the big players in development also integrate jQuery into their tools; for example, Microsoft integrates it in Visual Studio from version 2008 onward. For creating web applications, the Web Developer integrated into Visual Studio is of particular interest. If your background involves ASP.NET, Visual Studio, which is also available as a free Express version (for example, as version 2012 under http://www.microsoft.com/visualstudio/eng/products/visual-studio-express-products), is an excellent development environment.

You can also expand the web browser Firefox with numerous extensions (add-ons) so that it offers many useful features for web development (for example, the DOM Inspector, Firebug, Live HTTP headers, and Web Developer). After installation, you can find the add-ons in the Extras menu. The simplest way of installing a Firefox extension is to go to the download page of the Mozilla project (https://addons.mozilla.org/), type the name of the add-on you want into the search field, and then click the installation hyperlink for your browser.

1.5   About the Author

To conclude this chapter, I give you a bit of information about myself. You will already know my name from the cover of this book or from reading the preface, but for the sake of politeness, allow me to introduce myself once more: My name is Ralph Steyer. I went to university in Frankfurt/Main (Germany) and studied mathematics (Diploma). I then spent several years working as a programmer and conceptual project member for a large insurance company in the Rhine-Main area, first with Turbo Pascal, later with C and C++. After 4 years, I spent 1 year working in database conception for a mainframe database under MVS. This experience was a great motivation for my step toward being self-employed because I realized that I did not want to do this long term.

Since 1995, I have been earning my living as a freelancer, switching on-the-fly between working as technical author, specialized journalist, IT lecturer, consultant, and programmer. In addition to these roles, I sometimes give lectures on web conferences, teach at various academies and one university, occasionally translate specialist books, and record online training videos. In my opinion, this makes quite a good mixture, preserves me from professional apathy, and keeps me close to the practice and at the forefront of development. In particular, I have the pleasure but also the burden of having to constantly stay current with new IT developments because the half-life of computer knowledge is rather short. Correspondingly, my job is sometimes tiring, but always exciting.

Summary

In this introductory chapter, you have found out who will guide you through this book, what this book is about, and who it is aimed at (in addition to its underlying structure). You now know what requirements you need to meet to start creating RIAs based on jQuery. And that is what we do next.

First Examples with jQuery

In this chapter, we make first contact with jQuery without any further preparations. In other words, we are jumping right into the deep end. I am anxious for you to get a feeling for what you can do with jQuery and what you can get out of this framework. Just accept for now that many questions regarding the source text have to remain open at this stage. Don't worry, though; these questions are answered over the next few chapters. The explanations on the listings also remain somewhat superficial at this stage, to avoid going off topic. We want to get into the practical application of jQuery as quickly as possible and just have some fun playing around, which means creating examples.

> **Note**
>
> For the examples in this chapter, but also most examples in the following chapters, it is not relevant which specific version of jQuery you are using. The examples in this book have been created with jQuery 1.8.2 or later, but often any version from 1.3 or at least 1.4.1 onward is sufficient.

2.1 Accessing Elements and Protecting the DOM

If you already have some basic knowledge of programming on the Web,[1] you already know that you can access the components of a web page via JavaScript or another script language in the browser via an object model with the name Document Object Model (DOM). For this type of access, there are several standard techniques,[2] each of which has its own weaknesses.

---

1. Given the target audience of this book, I assume you do.

2. For example, the methods `getElementById()` and `getElementsByTagName()` plus access via object fields or names.

In particular, you usually have to enter many characters when accessing just a single element of the web page (or a group). This involves a lot of effort and is susceptible to errors. Most frameworks therefore offer a system via which this access can take place with an abbreviated, unified approach. Plus the underlying mechanisms compensate for various weaknesses of the standard access methods, above all by compensating for browser-dependent particularities and supplementing various missing functions of the pure DOM concept. Particularly important is that this compensation has generally been tested on all officially supported browsers and therefore works rather reliably.

The following example demonstrates another extremely important function of jQuery—protecting the DOM. More on what this is all about later. For now, let's just say that different browsers process the web page differently on loading (parsing) the page, which can lead to a number of problems when the elements of the web page are accessed (especially if you try to access the elements of the web page too soon in a script—in other words, before the browser has correctly constructed the DOM). Here, jQuery offers a reliably method for mastering these problems.

The example also shows you in passing, as it were, how you can use jQuery as a standardized way of accessing contents of elements with text and reacting to events. But enough introduction. Here is our very first listing (ch2_1.html):[3]

Listing 2.1   **The First jQuery Example**

```
01 <!DOCTYPE HTML PUBLIC "-//W3C//DTD HTML 4.01 01
   Transitional//EN"
   "http://www.w3.org/TR/html4/loose.dtd">
02 <html xmlns="http://www.w3.org/1999/xhtml">
03   <head>
04     <meta http-equiv="Content-Type"
05       content="text/html; charset=utf-8" />
06     <title>The first jQuery example</title>
07     <script type="text/javascript"
08         src="lib/jquery-1.8.min.js"></script>
09     <script type="text/javascript">
10       $(document).ready(function(){
11         $("#a").click(function(){
12           $("#output").html("Boring :-(");
13         });
14         $("#b").click(function(){
15           $("#output").html("A nice game :-)");
16         });
17         $("#c").click(function(){
```

3. The quotations are from the movie *War Games*—one of the first movies about a hacker. I highly recommend that you watch it the next time it is on TV.

```
18              $("#output").html("A strange game. " +
19                  "The only winning move " +
20              "is not to play.");
21          });
22      });
23   </script>
24 </head>
25 <body>
26   <h1>Welcome to WOPR</h1>
27   <h3>Shall we play a game</h3>
28   <button id="a">Tic Tac Toe</button>
29   <button id="b">Chess</button>
30   <button id="c">
31      Worldwide Thermonuclear War</button>
32   <div id="output"></div>
33 </body>
34 </html>
```

Just create the HTML file in a separate directory and save it under the listed name.

In practice, you would usually save all your resources that are part of a project within a separate directory. For a web project, the best solution is to create these directories in the shared folder of your web server. In the case of Apache/XAMPP, this is usually the directory htdocs. This has the advantage that—if the web server is running—you can run the test directly via HTTP and a proper web call, not just load the file via the FILE protocol into the browser (in other words, the classic opening as file or simply dragging the file into the browser). The latter is not a realistic, practice-related test because later the pages also have to be requested by the visitor via a web server.

If you are working with an integrated development environment (IDE) such as Aptana or the Visual Studio Web Developer, you can usually display a web page directly from the IDE via an integrated web server. In Aptana, this is done via the **Run** command, and in Web Developer (a Firefox add-on) you can use the shortcut **Ctrl+F5**.

Note

In this book, all examples are sorted by chapter and listed accordingly on the companion website (http://jquery.safety-first-rock.de).

In lines 7 and 8, you see the reference to an external JavaScript file—the jQuery library that in this specific case resides in the subdirectory lib of the project directory where the website is saved. This structure has now become widely accepted in practice. This means that the jQuery library also has to be located in exactly that place. But, of course, you can instead choose to use a different path structure.

Figure 2.1   In this project, the jQuery library is located in the directory lib, seen from the perspective of the website.

Line 9 to 23 contains a normal JavaScript container. In it, the web page is addressed with $(document) (line 10). The function $() is a shorthand notation for referencing an element of the web page. You also see these shortened access notations in lines 11, 12, 14, 15, 17, and 18. But here, an element ID is used as a parameter.

> **Note**
>
> Note that an element (in terms of jQuery) as a parameter of $() is not enclosed in quotation marks, whereas an ID (or another selector) is enclosed in quotation marks.

Let's now take a quick look at the method ready() that starts in line 10 and goes up to line 22. This method ensures that the calls it contains are only executed when the web page has been fully loaded and the DOM is correctly constructed. As hinted at before and without going into too much detail, this is already a feature whose value cannot be appreciated highly enough.

> **Note**
>
> For readers with the corresponding knowledge and experience, the method ready() is an alternative for the event handler onload that you can write in HTML in the body of a web page or under JavaScript for the corresponding DOM object. But this event handler is seen as extremely *unreliable* because it is insufficiently implemented in various browsers. It is a good idea to avoid it wherever possible.

Within the `ready()` method, three event handlers each specify the reaction when clicking the listed elements. In our examples, these are three buttons marked with a unique ID.

> **Note**
>
> The method `click()` encapsulates (you probably guessed it) the function call of the event handler `onclick`.

The allocation to the correct function is achieved via the ID and triggering the function within the method `click()`. Note that we are using an anonymous function here (without an identifier).

It also gets interesting if a user clicks one of the buttons. This displays a specific text output in a section of the web page. We are again using `$()` and an ID for selecting the section (a `div` block) and the method `html()` for accessing the content.

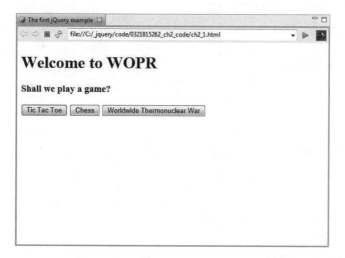

Figure 2.2   The web page with the three buttons; the user has just clicked the third button.

> **Note**
>
> In all following examples, we omit writing or using the DOCTYPE statement. For the sake of completeness, it does belong there, but omitting it does not have any effect for us, and because it is always the same, writing it down over and over again is just a waste of space in this book. In the examples on the companion website, the statement is included because it forms part of the correct standard.

2.2   Editing the Web Page with DHTML à la jQuery

Generally, you can design the visual appearance of a web page much better and more effectively with style sheets than with pure HTML. In particular, they make it easier to separate layout and structure of the site. These statements are probably old hat to you, as true as they are.

If you now change the style sheets of a site dynamically via JavaScript, we are talking about Dynamic Hypertext Markup Language (DHTML). But animation effects such as showing and hiding parts of a web page via other JavaScript techniques also form part of this. In the following example, we look at how you can carry out animated web page changes with jQuery quickly, simply, conveniently, and yet reliably in the various browsers. In this example, we change the Cascading Style Sheets (CSS) class of an element dynamically.

First, let's look at a little CSS file that should be integrated into the following web page and saved in the lib directory (ch2_2.css):

Listing 2.2   **The File with the External Style Sheets**

```
01 body {
02   background: lightgray;color: blue;
03 }
04 div {
05   background: white;font-size: 14px;
06 }
07 .mClass {
08   background: red; color: yellow; font-size: 24px;
09 }
```

Nothing much happens in the CSS file. It determines the background and foreground color of the entire web page and all elements of the type div, plus the font size for all elements of the type div.

Of primary interest is the class described in lines 7–9. It is not yet to be used on loading the following web page, but is to be assigned dynamically in case of a user action (ch2_2.html):

Listing 2.3   **Changing the CSS Class**

```
01 <html xmlns="http://www.w3.org/1999/xhtml">
02   <head>
03   <meta http-equiv="Content-Type"
04     content="text/html; charset=utf-8" />
05   <title>The second jQuery example</title>
06   <link type="text/css" rel="stylesheet"
07     href="lib/ch2_2.css" />
08   <script type="text/javascript"
09     src="lib/jquery-1.8.2.min.js"></script>
```

```
10  <script type="text/javascript">
11    $(document).ready(function(){
12      $("#a").click(function(){
13        $("#c").addClass("mClass");
14      });
15      $("#b").click(function(){
16        $("#c").removeClass("mClass");
17      });
18    });
19  </script>
20  </style>
21  </head>
22  <body>
23  <h1>Editing Style Sheets with jQuery</h1>
24  <button id="a">Add CSS class</button>
25  <button id="b">Remove CSS class</button><hr/>
26  <div id="c">He who knows all the answers
27    has not been asked all the questions.
28  </div><hr/>
29  <div id="c">Be not afraid of going slowly,
30    be afraid only of standing still.</div>
31  </body>
32  </html>
```

In the example, you can see two buttons below a heading and two texts within a div section that is separated by a separator in each case. This is pure HTML. Plus in lines 6 and 7 you can see the link to the CSS file.

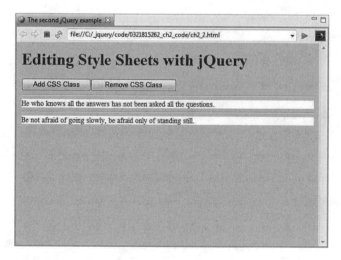

Figure 2.3   The site after loading

But now we want to use jQuery to manipulate the text below the buttons or the first `div` container. That is why the `div` container has an ID. The text below it is intended for comparison purposes.

For accessing the elements of the web page, the example uses jQuery mechanisms already mentioned in the first example. To react to the relevant click on a button, we again use the method `click()`. So far, there is nothing new.

Now you should notice that we do not yet assign the CSS class from the linked CSS file to an element on loading the web page. But take a look at line 13.

Listing 2.4   **Adding a CSS Class**

```
$("#c").addClass("mClass");
```

As the name of the method `addClass()` already implies, calling this method assigns the indicated style sheet class to the preceding element. This happens dynamically without the web page having to be reloaded in any way. The function is triggered when the user clicks the corresponding button, as you can see from the surrounding `click()` method.

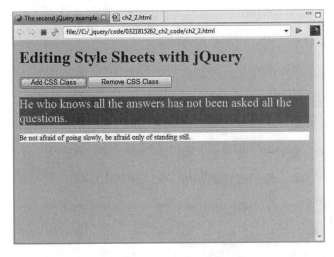

Figure 2.4   The CSS class has been assigned.

In line 16, you can see how the class is removed again following the same pattern. This time, we use the method `removeClass()`. If you test the example, you will see that font and background are changed accordingly.

> **Tip**
>
> Alternatively, you could use the method `toggleClass()` in this example. This removes or adds a CSS class, always depending on the state. If the class is already assigned, it is then removed, and vice versa.

2.3   Animatedly Reducing and Enlarging of an Element

Now we want to use jQuery to animatedly reduce and enlarge an element to hide or show it. First, let's look at the external CSS file in the subdirectory lib, in which a property is defined that has specific consequences for the following animation (ch2_3.css):

Listing 2.5   **The CSS File**

```
01 body {
02   background: lightgray;color: blue;
03 }
04 #i1 {
05   width:300px; height:225px;
06 }
07 #i2 {
08   height:225px;
09 }
10 #h2{
11   background: white; color:#0000FF; font-size: 18px;
12 }
```

The specification that is interesting for the following example is the width data in line 5. The ID used as selector references an image. The width specification influences the type of the animation that follows. But first, let's look at the web page itself. It basically contains two images and some text below. We want to animate all three elements (ch2_3.html):

Listing 2.6   **Reducing or Enlarging Two Images and Some Text**

```
...
06    <link type="text/css" rel="stylesheet"
07      href="lib/ch2_3.css" />
08    <script type="text/javascript"
09      src="lib/jquery-1.8.min.js"></script>
10    <script type="text/javascript">
11      $(document).ready(function(){
12        $("#toggle1").click(function(event){
13          $('#i1').slideToggle('slow');
14        });
15        $("#toggle2").click(function(event){
16          $('#i2').slideToggle('slow');
17        });
```

```
18          $("#toggle3").click(function(event){
19            $('#h2').slideToggle('slow');
20          });
21        });
22      </script>
23    </head>
24    <body>
25      <h1>Animated showing and hiding
26    of an image and text with jQuery</h1>
27      <button id="toggle1">Toggle Image 1</button>
28      <button id="toggle2">Toggle Image 2</button>
29      <button id="toggle3">Toggle Text</button><hr/>
30      <img src="images/i1.jpg" id="i1" />
31      <img src="images/i2.jpg" id="i2" /><hr/>
32      <h2 id="h2">A ski jump</h2>
33    </body>
34  </html>
```

At the core of this animation is the method `slideToggle()`. This name is also very telling. You can use this effect to show or hide objects depending on the current state, or to reduce or enlarge them. In other words, the current state is toggled to the opposite state. You can see it applied in lines 13, 16, and 19.

> **Tip**
>
> As you can probably see, a temporal interval is specified as a parameter. It determines how long the animation should take. You can pass such parameters for the speed in most animations in jQuery. Permitted parameters are `slow`, `normal`, `fast`, or a specification of time in milliseconds. The specification in milliseconds is not enclosed by quotation marks.

Figure 2.5   The original looks like this.

If you reconstruct the animation of the first image, you will see that reducing the image results in a reduction in image height and the image then disappears altogether. Vice versa, the image grows upward from that point if you enlarge it.

Figure 2.6   Here, the first image is squashed down.

Of massive importance for this behavior is that the width of this image is specified via the CSS rule for the ID i1. This prevents the width from also being reduced. The animation of the second image whose width is not specified shows what that looks like. You will see that on reducing the image, it shrinks into the lower-left corner of the image and then disappears altogether. Vice versa, the image grows outward from this point to the top right.

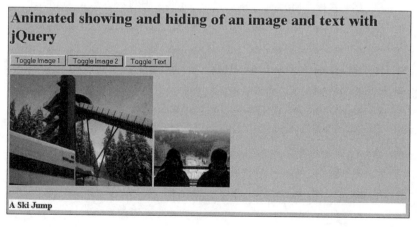

Figure 2.7   The second image shrinks animatedly in width and height.

But now observe what happens to the text if you click the third button. The heading also disappears but only in terms of height.

For the effect of `slideToggle()`, it matters to what type of element the animation technique is applied, and the CSS rules that have been previously applied to an element also play a role.

The animations in the example are basically independent from one another. If you set the interval for running the animation long enough, you can have the animations run in parallel.

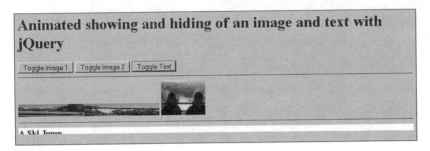

Figure 2.8   The three elements are animated in parallel.

In that case, note that the content positioned lower down is moved upward or could be repositioned vertically if a preceding element has disappeared completely. (In effect, it is removed from the text flow.)

But what happens in the example if you click the same button several times? This answer might surprise you: The events are cumulated. This means they are executed consecutively; the next event is executed only when the previous one has been fully processed. So, clicking the button again does not cause the current animation to stop and the next one to commence immediately. If that is what you want to achieve, you have to program it explicitly.

2.4   Changing Attributes Dynamically

This section shows how you can dynamically change attributes for an element of the web page. To this purpose, jQuery offers the extremely flexible and useful method `attr()`. With this, you can dynamically change one or several attributes of an element. In curly brackets, you set a value pair as parameter, first specifying the attribute, followed by a colon and then a string with the new value. Alternatively, you can also specify two string parameters. In this variation, the first parameter represents the attribute name and the second parameter the value. (In this case, you can change only one attribute.) If you only want to request the value of an attribute, you just enter the name of the attribute as a string parameter.

> **Note**
>
> For the sake of simplicity, we change only one attribute in the following example. If you want to change several attributes at once, however, you just need to write additional value pairs in the curly brackets, separated by commas.

For our example, we want to replace an image in the web page by changing the value of the attribute `src` of an `<img>` tag (ch2_4.html).

Listing 2.7 **Changing Attributes on an Element**

```
...
06    <script type="text/javascript"
07      src="lib/jquery-1.8.min.js"></script>
08    <script type="text/javascript">
09      $(document).ready(function(){
10        $("#toggle1").click(function(){
11          $("img").attr({
12            src: "images/i1.jpg"
13          });
14        });
15        $("#toggle2").click(function(){
16          $("img").attr(
17            "src", "images/i2.jpg"
18          );
19        });
20      });
21    </script>
22  </head>
23  <body>
24    <h1>Replacing an image</h1>
25    <button id="toggle1">Image 1</button>
26    <button id="toggle2">Image 2</button>
27    <hr/><img src="images/i1.jpg"/>
28  </html>
```

We change the value via the notation in the curly brackets once, and via the two string parameters once. As mentioned earlier, we replace the value `src` in each case.

Summary

This chapter provided just a few examples, but they already serve well to demonstrate central key facts of jQuery. In particular, you should memorize the function `$()` and the method `ready()`. But techniques for specifying reactions, such as the method `click()`, are also of elementary importance. And animation techniques such as `addClass()`, `toggleClass()`, `removeClass()`, and `slideToggle()` are also going to be helpful in practice later for DHTML effects. In this chapter, you also learned about changing attribute values (`attr()`). You will more fully understand these techniques as you work through other chapters of this book and have delved deeper into the overall concept of jQuery.

3

Basic Knowledge

In the preceding chapter, you worked through the first few examples with jQuery. Now it's time to turn to the underlying basics—not yet in the detail of jQuery itself, but in the world where jQuery is used and how the framework is anchored within it. This world is the Web with Hypertext Markup Language (HTML) or Extensible HTML (XHTML), Cascading Style Sheets (CSS), JavaScript, Extensible Markup Language (XML), JavaScript Object Notation (JSON), and Asynchronous JavaScript and XML (AJAX). After all, just as many other frameworks and toolkits in this area, jQuery is a JavaScript extension for websites that provides certain CSS features (in case of the jQuery UI, even custom CSS themes) and support for AJAX in addition to an independent syntax. Without elementary basic knowledge of the underlying technologies, you will hardly be able to use jQuery effectively and appropriately. In all our basic explanations, we focus, of course, on the jQuery aspect in this chapter as you learn how to integrate the jQuery library into your web page and what you need to look out for. Now let's get cracking so we can delve deeper into jQuery later.

> **Note**
>
> What this chapter cannot, should not, and does not do is to give you a complete introduction to the relevant techniques. Here you find only the basic information absolutely necessary in relation to jQuery. If you need to, use additional sources to find out more. The appendix contains more information about the most important basics of JavaScript as the core technology of jQuery.

3.1   The Web, Web 2.0, and the Client/Server Principle on the Internet

To start with, let's take a brief look at the World Wide Web (WWW); after all, you already know the basics facts about the WWW. At its core, the Web is based on the service protocol Hypertext Transfer Protocol (HTTP) for communication, the document description language HTML, and its strict XML-based twin XHTML plus the program types web server and web browser.

Just like all services available on the Internet, the Web is a classic client/server system, where each action consists of a cycle of requesting a service and providing the service. More specifically, this means that on the Web it is practically always a situation of a browser (the client) requesting a file (usually a web page or content that is to be integrated into a web page) and in some cases sending further requests for external resources referenced within this site (for example, graphics, videos, flash animations, or external JavaScript or CSS files). These are then displayed in the browser together with the web page or are otherwise processed. The central control mechanism is always the (X)HTML file.

3.1.1   Programming on the Web

Over the years, the Web has evolved into a system where you can program both on the server and on the client in terms of offering content. The hysteria about the dangers of client-side programming seems to have calmed down in recent years, and nearly all modern websites use client-side programming for that part of the business logic that should quite sensibly be taken care of in the client. After all these years, the only relevant representative of the client-side field that is still around is JavaScript, but by now it is used and accepted widely. Just take a look at some popular websites on the Internet. Not one of these sites can manage without JavaScript. And almost all users on the Web have JavaScript enabled in their browser. After all, who wants to do without the full and unlimited use of popular websites such as Google, Amazon, eBay, Facebook, Twitter, Wikipedia, or Yahoo! As a creator of websites, you can, in turn, assume that most clients have JavaScript plus its associated techniques.[1] This means that most arguments against using JavaScript frameworks such as jQuery or Dojo Toolkit, Prototype, YUI, and so on are no longer valid.

> **Note**
>
> As mentioned earlier in this book, various manufacturers are trying to establish proprietary techniques such as Silverlight in the client system to break through the limitations of JavaScript and web browsers as clients. But it will take some time before these are supported and accepted on a wide scale. It is unclear, at this point, whether these proprietary efforts will succeed.

1. According to the statistics I consulted, the support for JavaScript is fluctuating massively. Some statistics assume 99.9% availability, others perceive "only" 99.1% availability. I hope you are aware of the irony in my statementl to spell it out, you can currently assume that there is almost unlimited availability.

3.1.2   The Web 2.0

As ingenious and fundamentally simple as the concept of the Web is, there is a basic and serious problem with HTTP, HTML, and the concept of classic web browsers. When the browser requests new data from a web server, the latter always has to send a complete web page in response. Or to be more precise, the browser interprets the response in such a way that it completely replaces the site previously displayed in the browser with this new content. Obviously, this is very inefficient. This is where AJAX enters the stage. (You will read more about its technical background shortly.)

Generally, this is a procedure that ensures a reaction from a web application in (almost) real time, although new data is being requested from the web server. Instead of resulting in a complete web page with data that is in principle already present in the browser, an AJAX data request will result in only the really new data being sent by the web server and then using DHTML methods to "build it in to" the web page that is already loaded in the client. This does not usually even interrupt the normal user interaction with the web application by loading new data. Therefore, you can now create sites on the Web that are very much focused on interaction with the user. Thanks to Google, in particular, AJAX has now become established as standard procedure for such interactive websites. And since about 2005, the buzzword *Web 2.0* has been a collective term for most interactive websites. Often, Web 2.0 is also referred to as "participatory" or "interactive" web, because users are no longer just consumers but also contribute content themselves. Just think of blogs; tweets; wikis; or communities such as Xing, Facebook, MySpace, and so on. But even if users, for example, enter data in an online calendar, this will result in a different representation of the website (for example, the event is displayed—and, of course, also saved on the server). In this respect, that is also a form of participating in the Web 2.0.

3.2   JavaScript and Its Relationship to jQuery

Because jQuery is fundamentally a JavaScript library, we, of course, need to take a closer look at this language. Although marketing statements of jQuery and various other frameworks claim it will do many things with regard to JavaScript for you, to use jQuery you ought to have basic knowledge of JavaScript. And if you want to use jQuery really effectively (for example, to create plug-ins), you should even have good knowledge of JavaScript.

> **Note**
>
> The next few chapters lead you deeper into the world of JavaScript, where it is appropriate in connection with jQuery. For now, just a bit of basic information on JavaScript will suffice. For more basic concepts and information on JavaScript, see the appendix.

Generally, script languages on the Web are some of the most important extensions of HTML or XHTML and implement the client-side logic of a web application. These script languages are interpreter languages that are translated and executed within a host program (the browser) at runtime. This particularly applies to JavaScript.

> **Note**
>
> New browsers have a just-in-time compiler for JavaScript. This expands the interpreter principle for JavaScript with the option of keeping already translated code in the memory and making it available in a more performant way in case of a repeat execution. This is a key factor for Rich Internet Applications (RIAs) that are meant to behave in the same manner as desktop applications in terms of performance.

Essentially, jQuery is a JavaScript library. In other words, jQuery is based only on a function that every modern browser offers. You do not need a plug-in or another type of extension for the browser to have the functions in this library available. So, you are not adding it to the browser or even the operating system (as can be the case with competing technologies). This is, on the one hand, a great advantage, but on the other hand, you can only realize those things in the library that can be achieved with JavaScript or Dynamic HTML (DHTML) and Cascading Style Sheets plus Document Object Model (DOM) manipulation. But to be able to offer these exciting and powerful effects and services by jQuery using these simple basic technologies, they had to be stretched to their limits. As a consequence, not every browser can be fully supported (especially not older browsers).

If you are really good at programming with JavaScript, you could reproduce all the functionality of jQuery yourself. But that would involve quite some work and effort. The jQuery team has already invested many years of work in developing this library, and you can profit from this work for your own purposes.

3.2.1   The General Integration of JavaScript in Websites

JavaScript is to be seen as direct complement to and extension of HTML or XHTML and is intended for use as an integrated component of a corresponding website frame. Web scripts are directly written in plain text into a website or integrated and interpreted at runtime. Various techniques exist for connecting scripts to a website. Let's take a quick look at two of them.

The `<script>` Container in the Website

The connection of a JavaScript with a website can take place, for example, via a direct notation of the JavaScript in the website. The JavaScript statements are simply written as plain text into the corresponding (X)HTML file. The beginning of a script is marked via a separate control statement that is still part of HTML and forms with its matching end tag a container for the script instructions. Via the `<script>` element, you can specify that anything within the enclosed container is a script. So inside such a container, you are executing JavaScript.

Take a look at the following code snippet.

Listing 3.1   **A Code Snippet with the Direct Notation of JavaScript in a Website**

```
<body>
...
  <script>
```

```
... script statements
</script>
...
</body>
```

If you do not specify a language in the script tag, all known browsers use JavaScript as default—or in the case of Internet Explorer, its clone JScript. But you are then exploiting the very high tolerance level of browsers because really you should specify the script language you are using. You can use the parameter `language` or `type` to indicate which script language this is.[2]

Here you can see two alternative examples.

Listing 3.2   **Alternative Specifications of Script Language**

```
<script language="JavaScript">
<script type="text/javascript">
```

Although uppercase and lowercase is irrelevant when specifying the value of `language`, you need to use lowercase for specifying the MIME type[3] via `type`. For `language`, you can also specify the version of JavaScript—for example, as `JavaScript1.3` or `JavaScript1.5`. You simply add the appropriate version number to the token `JavaScript`—not separated by a space. This causes any browsers that do not yet master this version to ignore the script block.

> **Caution**
>
> Avoid using `type` and `language` in parallel. If you specify the `type` as well as the `language`, the `language` data will be ignored. This means that any version you may want to specify via `language` has no effect.

In the past, we used to write HTML comments into the script container (`<!-- ... -->` or even `<!-- ... //-->`) to prevent browsers that do not know JavaScript from simply displaying the instructions. Today, this is completely unnecessary because such browsers last came on the market in around 1996 and are therefore no longer existent in practice. Note that this comment does not refer to browsers where JavaScript is simply disabled.

When integrating a `<script>` element into a website, the question arises where it should go. There is no clear answer to this question. Basically, the element belongs in the header of a website.

But in practice, you will find `<script>` elements in any place within a website. In principle, such an element can even stand after the website itself. The script statements are simply processed by a browser when the website is loaded into the browser and parsed from top

---

2. Officially, the specification of the MIME type is required.

3. A MIME type determines the type of content. It first specifies a main category such as `text` or `image` and then (separated by a slash) a subcategory such as `html`, `css`, or `javascript`.

to bottom. So, obviously, the script statements (functions) that are written further down in a website will be available only after the site has been loaded up to that point. A common approach is therefore to place a `<script>` container before the body and embed the declarations of important functions into it. These functions are then available for the entire document.

In practice, it has become clear that there are many situations in programming with JavaScript where the position of the `<script>` element massively influences the execution. Many web pages, for example, force you to place the `<script>` container not into the header but in other areas of the web page. Even highly professional and modern concepts such as projects by Google or Microsoft, or AJAX frameworks, have to make use of this to compensate certain behaviors by various browsers.

> **Note**
>
> Remember the method `ready()` that came up in the last examples? It compensates for exactly these problems and so it is no longer necessary to use tricks.

Basic Information on External JavaScript Files

With the method described earlier, you can write the scripts directly into the (X)HTML file. But for using JavaScript, it is generally preferable to place the script directly in an external file. At least if you are dealing with subprograms (functions) and variable declarations. The external file with the collection of functions and variables then forms a library that you can link to any web page. This is what we are seeing with the reference to the jQuery library. This approach achieves a separation of structure and functionality, and this is highly important in practice. The external JavaScript file (as a general rule with the extension .js) contains, in an ideal case, your entire JavaScript code with the exception of explicit calls of JavaScript functions and a few statements.

To integrate an external JavaScript file into a web page, you just need to add the attribute `src` to the `<script>` tag. This specifies the URL of the external JavaScript data. The usual rules for URLs apply when referencing separate JavaScript files.

The Reference to the jQuery Library

The jQuery library is an external JavaScript file. Listing 3.3 shows three alternative code snippets with two variations for referencing an external JavaScript file that reference the jQuery library.

Listing 3.3   **Integrating the External jQuery JavaScript Files**

```
01 <script language="JavaScript"
      src="jquery-1.8.2.min.js"></script>
02 <script language="JavaScript"
      src="lib/jquery-1.8.2.min.js"></script>
```

```
03 <script type="text/javascript"
      src="lib/jquery-1.8.2.min.js"></script>
```

> **Caution**
>
> You should leave the `<script>` container empty in any case (it must not contain any spaces or line breaks either) because some browsers cause problems if it has content. (Purely formally, it must not contain anything; it is an empty element.) Other browsers ignore content in there under the principle of error tolerance. But do not use the XML syntax with the specification of an empty element `<script ... />` because then you run into trouble with, for example, Internet Explorer (although the syntax would be completely legitimate).

In the first variation, the JavaScript file is located in the same directory as the referencing web page, in the second case, in a subdirectory lib in relation to the website directory. In both cases, `language` specifies the type of the referenced script.

In the third case, the jQuery library is again integrated from the subdirectory lib (as in the second case), but the type of the referenced script is now specified with `type`.

Normally, you should write the reference to the jQuery library into the web page header. But the official documentation on jQuery points out that this should be avoided in certain cases. Once again, you will find that breaking the theoretical rules sometimes becomes necessary, as mentioned earlier.

Specifically, this applies to the case where the entire page with the reference to jQuery is integrated into a PHP script via the PHP functions `include()` or `require()`. The documentation states merely "because calling jQuery script file from inside the `<head>` tag doesn't work for some reason." In other words, even the jQuery team has no idea why it sometimes does not work. But that's just web programming. Due to the extremely varied behaviors of browsers and also server-side processes such as the work of an PHP interpreter, you sometimes just have to use tricks, break the rules, use workarounds, and so on. Google is a master at finding such practical solutions that often fly in the face of any official teachings. But other projects also simply focus primarily on the practical functionality. Of course, you cannot predict whether this trick for taking the reference out of the header is necessary in all versions of jQuery/PHP or for every browser. If a problem occurs, however, you should simply move the reference to the body of the web page and then try again. Web programming is sometimes simply trial and error. Even using a sophisticated framework does not change this fact.

3.3 AJAX and `XMLHttpRequest` (XHR)

As mentioned earlier, AJAX describes a method for ensuring a reaction of a web application in (almost) real time, even though new data is being requested by the web server. In concrete terms, AJAX only designates the interplay of long-established technologies, from HTML or XHTML and HTTP to JavaScript and CSS and even XML or JSON. The asynchronous requesting of additional data that is to be integrated in a web page has also already been around in principle since approximately the year 1998. Only the term *AJAX* is relatively new and became established around 2005, together with the buzzword *Web 2.0*.

Actually, AJAX could have been introduced as extension of the JavaScript object model. But I believe that with such a trivial marketing strategy, the concept would never have become as successful as with the buzzword AJAX. But purely regarding the concept, you could indeed describe AJAX in those terms.

To support this asynchronous communication, modern browsers offer a built-in interface for controlling HTTP transactions from client-side programming languages (mainly JavaScript) that run independently of the "normal" data requests of the web browser. This interface takes the form of the object XMLHttpRequest as an extension of the JavaScript object model. These XHR or XMLHttpRequest objects are oriented directly on the internal structure of HTTP and form the backbone of every AJAX request. And they are available in one form or another in all frameworks and toolkits that adorn themselves with the title AJAX:, of course, this also includes jQuery, which offers some very comfortable methods and, since jQuery 1.5, even an extension of the object itself.

For asynchronous communication between browser and web server, the object uses function references to allow the registration of callback functions that are then interpreted every time the transaction state changes.

Moreover, you can use an XMLHttpRequest object to access all HTTP header fields of an AJAX request or response.

The focus for data requests by AJAX is also on XML and JSON data in addition to plain text. I do not simply want to assume that you know all about these, and so instead briefly explain at least the most important details.

XML

XML describes a platform-neutral plain text standard based on Unicode for creating machine- and human-readable documents to exchange any kind of information. XML documents have a tree structure that allows navigating to the individual branches of the tree. Just like HTML, XML is a markup language for offering a structure of the information beyond the text information. The information contained in a document is structured via tags that are enclosed by pointed brackets both in HTML and XML. The elements in XML are not predetermined, unlike HTML. There is no ready-made, limited vocabulary of elements. There are no predetermined XML tags in the sense as most users know it for HTML tags. XML is merely a description of the syntax for elements and structures. Therefore, XML can be expanded indefinitely. The XML specification only describes the rules you need to follow in defining tags.

In contrast to HTML, XML is a strict language in terms of syntax, and no principle of error tolerance exists (whereas it is a central aspect in using HTML). The XML specification is strictly formal and does not permit any exceptions or unclear structures. But it means that XML can be easily and automatically validated and interpreted. So, XML is predestined for data exchange.

XML describes only a few, simple but very strict and absolutely clear rules as to how a document can be put together.

The building blocks of an XML document are what is referred to as components. The basic structure of an XML document consists of elements that—provided they are not restricted—can themselves contain subelements and represent the most important form of components. Elements themselves are structured as you basically already know from HTML. There is a start tag that would perhaps look like this:

Listing 3.4   **A Start Tag in XML**

```
<rjs>
```

The start tag in XML always requires a closing end tag that repeats the identifier behind a slash—unless a tag is marked as empty element. Any attributes in the start tag are never repeated in the end tag. In our case, the end tag looks like this.

Listing 3.5   **An End Tag in XML, Matching the Start Tag**

```
</rjs>
```

This should all be familiar to you from HTML, only there, the elements cannot be freely chosen.

Inside the element, you can write down any content—provided that no special rules apply. This can include further elements or text or a mixture of both.

XML allows declaring empty elements. These are mostly used in combination with attributes. An empty element is specified as follows.

Listing 3.6   **An Empty Element with Attribute**

```
<rjs url="www.rjs.de" />
```

Alternatively, you can use this form.

Listing 3.7   **An Alternative Notation for an Empty Element**

```
<rjs url="www.rjs.de"></rjs>
```

The container must not even contain a space. Spaces are regarded as proper content in XML and therefore as nodes in the tree. Sadly, certain browsers or the underlying XML parsers do not take this into account.

An XML document has to adhere to just a few syntax rules, but these are very strict. If a document fulfills these rules, it is referred to as well-formed.

XML documents are basically made up of Unicode symbols (16-bit character set). But you can save ANSI code when creating your XML document in an editor. The parser then interprets it as Unicode.

In XML, a strict distinction exists between uppercase and lowercase.

An XML document always starts with a prolog. The prolog must appear at the beginning of the XML document, and in its simplest form it currently looks like this.

Listing 3.8   **A Simple XML Prolog**

```
<?xml version="1.0" ?>
```

An XML document may contain only exactly one root element (also referred to as root tag or document element). Such a root element has to be present in any case and follows directly after the prolog, apart from comments.

Elements have to be cleanly nested.

Each element has to have an end tag or be written as empty element.

Attributes always have to be assigned a value, and the attribute value has to be enclosed in quotation marks.

Listing 3.9 shows a typical XML file (rjs.xml).

Listing 3.9   **A Typical XML File**

```
01 <?xml version="1.0" encoding="utf-8"?>
02 <rjs>
03    <business>
04      <name occupation="Dipl Math"
05        company="RJS EDV-KnowHow">Ralph Steyer</name>
06      <location>Eppstein</location>
07      <location>Bodenheim</location>
08    </business>
09    <websites>
10      <url>www.rjs.de</url>
11      <url>blog.rjs.de</url>
12      <url>www.ajax-net.de</url>
13    </websites>
14 </rjs>
```

Any browser can display XML files. Usually, the browser displays the file in a tree. You can usually click sensitive elements of the tree to expand and collapse the branches.

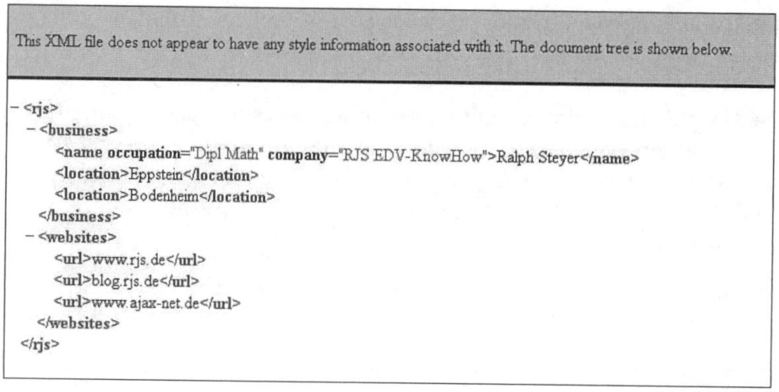

```
This XML file does not appear to have any style information associated with it. The document tree is shown below.

- <rjs>
  - <business>
      <name occupation="Dipl Math" company="RJS EDV-KnowHow">Ralph Steyer</name>
      <location>Eppstein</location>
      <location>Bodenheim</location>
    </business>
  - <websites>
      <url>www.rjs.de</url>
      <url>blog.rjs.de</url>
      <url>www.ajax-net.de</url>
    </websites>
  </rjs>
```

Figure 3.1   Most browsers represent an XML file as interactive tree; the lower branch of the tree has been collapsed.

> **Note**
>
> To put it briefly and succinctly, any XML file can be seen as DOM. This means you have all DOM methods and properties including the jQuery methods at your disposal. You may already grasp this statement if you are familiar with the DOM concept. If not, it will all make more sense when you read the section on the DOM concept.

JSON

In case of a request for additional data via AJAX, XML enables shifting a lot of logic into the transmission format, but it is very unwieldy and often oversized for AJAX requests. Also, various problems can arise during processing in different browsers, although jQuery does compensate for most of these problems. Yet there is an alternative in-between the two extremes, if pure plain text offers insufficient logic and XML is too complex and too heavy-weight. With JSON, you have a structure for the transmission format that is simpler than XML and above all gets processed more consistently in different web browsers.

Just like XML, JSON is a machine-readable plain-text format for data interchange that is considerably less flexible than XML but much more compact. And JSON contains data structures or data types that are directly based on JavaScript (objects, arrays, strings, numbers, the Boolean values `true` and `false`, plus the value `null`) that are nested and can be structured as needed with whitespace characters.

The concept of JSON is based on two central structures:

- **Name-value pairs:** Such combinations can be found in almost all modern programming languages. They are usually implemented as object, record, structure, dictionary, hash table, keyed list, or associative array.

- **An ordered value list as it appears in most languages:** It is implemented, depending on the programming language, via an array, vector, list, or sequence.

The basic concept of JSON is the description of universal data structures that are supported by practically all modern programming languages in one form or another. Based on these structures, JSON provides a data format for exchanging data between programming languages. In particular, JSON can be processed directly by various programming languages (for example, in JavaScript via the function `eval()`).

The specific syntax of format definitions in JSON is—as the name already indicates—based on JavaScript, but there are no identifiers for objects or data fields:

- An object definition starts with a curly bracket (`{`) and ends with a closing curly bracket (`}`). Such an object block can contain a subordinate list of properties, separated by commas.

- A property consists in turn of a key and a value. Both are separated by a colon (`:`). The key is a string and the associated value can be any data type (an object; array; string; number; or one of the expressions `true`, `false`, or `null`).

- An array in JSON simply starts with an opening square bracket (`[`) and ends with a closing square bracket (`]`). An array can also contain a list of values separated by commas, this time an ordered list.

- A string in JSON starts and ends as usual with quotation marks (`"`). It can contain any Unicode characters and escape sequences. A string in JSON is very similar to a string in C or Java.

- A number is simply a sequence of the digits 0–9. You can use positive and negative signs, decimal points, and exponents via e or E. A number in JSON is also very similar to a number in C or Java. But a fundamental difference applies. In JSON, you cannot use octal or hexadecimal numeric forms.

- A Boolean value is represented as usual with the expressions `true` or `false`.

Here is an example for a simple JSON document whose information content and structural basis[4] corresponds to the preceding XML file (rjs.json).

Listing 3.10   **A JSON Structure**

```
01 {
02   "business" : {
03     "name":"Ralph Steyer",
04     "company":"RJS EDV-KnowHow",
05     "occupation":"Dipl Math",
06     "location":["Eppstein","Bodenheim"]
```

4. The structure is not 100% identical, but largely it is. The attributes in the XML file would have to have been represented differently to make the structure 100% identical. But we are not really interested in the finer points.

```
07  } ,
08  "websites" : {
09    "url":["www.rjs.de","blog.rjs.de","www.ajax-net.de"]
10  }
11 }
```

The good thing with JSON is that the language is really simple and already mostly explained with these few explanations. If you require further information, take a look at http://json.org/index.html.

More Details on Processing JSON for JavaScript Pros

For those readers who have a good knowledge of JavaScript, the following example will demonstrate how JSON is parsed via JavaScript. Let's assume that we already have a JSON object in JavaScript and that we get a string that contains a JSON structure but has to be converted into a JSON object first. This is the case, for example, if we request JSON data via AJAX (which we do not do in this example).

> ### Caution
>
> Without appropriate knowledge of JavaScript, you will find it very difficult to fully grasp this example. But do not let this discourage you. The advantage of a framework such as jQuery is precisely that when using it you do not have to work as deeply on the JavaScript level. So if you think that you lack the required amount of JavaScript knowledge or you find the listing worrying, just ignore this passage.

Listing 3.11   The HTML Page Where JSON Data Is to Be Displayed (ch3_1.html)

```
...
06    <script type="text/javascript"
07        src="lib/ch3_1.js">
08    </script>
09  </head>
10  <body>
11    <h1>Processing JSON</h1>
12    <script type="text/javascript">
13      process_json_text();
14      process_json_object();
15    </script>
16  </body>
17 </html>
```

The HTML page is harmless. Apart from the reference to the external JavaScript file and calling the functions declared in it, `process_json_text()` and `process_json_object()` in lines 13 and 14, nothing particularly interesting happens. We simply write the two functions straight into the web page.

Let's look at the referenced JavaScript file ch3_1.js.

Listing 3.12 **The Referenced JavaScript File**

```
01 function process_json_text(){
02   var JSONText = '{ "business" : {' +
03    ' "name" : "Ralph Steyer",' +
04    ' "company" : "RJS EDV-KnowHow",' +
05    ' "occupation" : "Dipl Math",' +
06    ' "location" : ["Eppstein","Bodenheim"] } ,' +
07    ' "websites" : { "url" : ["www.rjs.de",' +
08    ' "blog.rjs.de", "www.ajax-net.de"] }}';
09   var JSONObject = eval('(' + JSONText + ')');
10   output_all(JSONObject);
11   output_specific(JSONObject, name);
12 }
13
14 function process_json_object(){
15   var JSONObject = {
16     "business": {
17       "name": "Ralph Steyer",
18       "company": "RJS EDV-KnowHow",
19       "occupation": "Dipl Math",
20       "location": ["Eppstein", "Bodenheim"]
21     },
22     "websites": {
23       "url": ["www.rjs.de", "blog.rjs.de",
24               "www.ajax-net.de"]
25     }
26   };
27   output_all(JSONObject);
28   output_specific(JSONObject);
29 }
30
31 function output_all(JSONObject){
32   document.write("<table><tr><th>Key</th>" +
33       "<th>Value</th></tr>");
34   for (i in JSONObject.business)
35     document.write("<tr><td>" + i +
```

```
36          "</td><td>" + JSONObject.business[i] +
37          "</td></tr>");
38   for (i in JSONObject.websites)
39     document.write("<tr><td>" + i + "</td><td>" +
40          JSONObject.websites[i] + "</td></tr>");
41   document.write("</table>");
42 }
43
44 function output_specific(JSONObject){
45   document.write("<table><tr><th>Key</th>" +
46       "<th>Value</th></tr>");
47   document.write("<tr><td>Name</td><td>" +
48   JSONObject.business.name +
49   "</td></tr>");
50   document.write("<tr><td>Company Website</td><td>" +
51   JSONObject.websites.url[0] +
52   "</td></tr>");
53   document.write("<tr><td>Blog</td><td>" +
54   JSONObject.websites.url[1] +
55   "</td></tr>");
56   document.write("</table>");
57 }
```

In one of the functions in the example, the integrated JavaScript function eval() is used to create a JSON object (line 3—var JSONObject = eval('(' + JSONText + ')');) from a string that contains a JSON structure corresponding to the file rjs.json (line 2—note that the string has to be in one line in the file; otherwise, it has to be split and connected via chained strings). In the second function, you find the direct declaration of the JSON object in lines 18–26 via an array literal. Both functions then behave in the same way; two output functions are called that operate on the JSON object. The JSON object created via eval() from the string is completely identical to the object created natively via array literal.

In both cases, the functions dynamically write an HTML table. In the function output_all(), a loop iterates over the JSON object and the key and the contained value are output via a mixture of dot notation and array notation. The beauty in processing JSON objects under JavaScript is that the JSON structures are represented as nested objects. If there are several objects of one type on a level in the object hierarchy, these are made available as object fields. You could hardly make such structures available in an easier and more logical way.

In the function output_specific(), specific values from the structures are addressed.

Key	Value
name	Ralph Steyer
company	RJS EDV-KnowHow
occupation	Dipl Math
location	Eppstein,Bodenheim
url	www.rjs.de,blog.rjs.de,www.ajax-net.de

Key	Value
Name	Ralph Steyer
Company Website	www.rjs.de
Blog	blog.rjs.de

Key	Value
name	Ralph Steyer
company	RJS EDV-KnowHow
occupation	Dipl Math
location	Eppstein,Bodenheim
url	www.rjs.de,blog.rjs.de,www.ajax-net.de

Key	Value
Name	Ralph Steyer
Company Website	www.rjs.de
Blog	blog.rjs.de

Figure 3.2   Processing JSON data via JavaScript.

3.4   DOM and Objects

The previous examples with JavaScript have already confronted you with objects. JavaScript is partly an object-oriented language. Strictly speaking, it is referred to as object based because certain qualities that are required for a true object-oriented language are absent.

The term *object* in programming refers to a software model that is intended to describe an object from the real world with all its properties and behaviors. For example, a printer, a monitor, or the keyboard is an object. Parts of the software itself can also be an object: the browser, for example, or a part of it—such as a frame, the status line in the browser or the browser window, or just part of a document—a heading in a web page, a paragraph, a graphic, and so on. The object-oriented approach sees everything as an object that can be independently grasped, described, and addressed.

Object-oriented programming can be defined by the fact that related statements and data form a related, self-contained, and independent unit (an object) that provides properties and methods (abilities) and can have a certain state. Properties and methods form what is referred to as members of an object.

Central to object-oriented programming is that the methods and properties (attributes or data) are always assigned to an object together. This means that there are no methods or properties without an associated object.

Class elements are special properties and methods that are not available via a specific object but already via the class. You can use these without first creating an object.

3.4.1 DOM and Accessing the Elements of a Web Page

It will happen very often that you create an object in JavaScript itself or use class elements. Practically always you will use objects in your JavaScript codes that have been made available to you automatically by the browser. And these objects are based on an object model that does not count as part of JavaScript or (X)HTML, but instead describes the structures of almost any treelike structured documents—the already repeatedly mentioned DOM concept. Or to put it even more drastically, without using the DOM, JavaScript programming is pointless!

You can use this object library via various techniques, both from within programming or script languages and applications. With DOM, accessing a web page under this object aspect is based on a concept that designates a cross-platform and operating language-independent interface.

In this concept, an (X)HTML site (or generally a document with a treelike structure—so, for example, an XML document as well) is not perceived as a statically structured, finished, and indistinguishable unit, but as a structure that can be differentiated, whose individual components are dynamically accessible for programs and scripts. This approach enables treating components of a web page individually even if the web page has already been loaded into the browser. This treatment goes far beyond the simple interpretation through the browser on loading a document from top to bottom.

The DOM concept comprises several partial aspects. For example, it causes a browser to read an (X)HTML site like a normal text file and execute the corresponding (X)HTML statements. But beyond this, the browser will also index on loading all those elements of a web page that are known within the concept (and individually identifiable) regarding their type, their relevant properties, and their position within the web page.

This a kind of tree in the computer's main memory that is constructed on loading the web page and deleted again when the user leaves the site. The elements in the tree are referred to as nodes.

Similar elements are managed together in a field when the browser indexes them. So on loading the site, the browser has exact knowledge of all relevant data of the elements it can independently address in the web page. But which ones they are and what the browser can do with them can differ greatly between various browsers.

Each addressable element (for example, a specific (X)HTML tag) can also be updated while the web page is loaded in the browser (for example, if a script is used to edit the position of an element in the web page or style sheets are used to dynamically change the layout of an element after the web page fully loads). That is what we did in the examples in Chapter 2, "First Examples with jQuery."

Many objects in the DOM concept are available in the form of an object hierarchy. If an object is subordinate to another object, you write this in the DOT notation by first writing the name of the top-level object and then the name of the object below it.

For example, if you take the example of a web page, it is accessible via the `document` object from within JavaScript. Because the web page is located in a browser window and this can be addressed as `window`, it can be accessed via `window.document`.

These access options for DOM objects are strictly oriented along the object nesting, but there are other syntactic options that ultimately always reference the same object and offer the same properties and methods independent of the type of access. For example, there are the access methods `getElementById()`, `getElementsByTagName()`, and `getElementsByName()`, or you can specify the name directly. But as already discussed, all standard methods for accessing the DOM involve certain problems, and jQuery standardizes the access via a superior syntax such as `$()` and various other techniques.

> **Tip**
> The appendix contains a list of the available DOM objects.

3.5   Style Sheets and DHTML

For many websites, it is a central aspect that a web page is changed after it has been loaded in the browser. That is basically exactly the definition of DHMTL. Though DHTML is often also described as the combination of HTML or XHTML, JavaScript, and style sheets.

Format templates or style sheets consist of pure plain text that describes rules for formatting elements. Modern websites reduce the meaning of HTML and XHTML almost entirely to the pure structuring of the site, whereas the layout is wholly taken care of by style sheets. In particular, style sheets offer the option of removing the mixing of layout commands and information carriers. You can achieve a clear separation of structure and layout. And via JavaScript and style sheets, you can also change the layout or position properties of an element in the web page in a targeted way, after it has already been loaded into the browser.

3.5.1   CSS: The Web's Standard Language

Style sheets do not constitute a separate language, but merely a concept. There is not just one single style sheet language, but various approaches or different languages. The exact rules and syntax elements for style sheets differ slightly from language to language, but they look fairly similar. On the Web, you will find mainly CSS.

Generally, when style sheets are applied, data is present in raw form or presented in an undesirable form that you want to change in a specific way. The representation of the data then takes place in a different form, whereby the information itself remains mostly intact. Under certain circumstances, data of the source may be suppressed or completed with additional data in the output document. The description of the transformation or formatting usually occurs in the form of an external file but can also in some situations be written directly in the file with the data (for example, a web page). So, style sheets simply give a new look to information that is already present. To achieve this, the data and formatting information is processed by an interpreting system and then presented differently.

Basically, style rules in web pages can be applied to any HTML or XHTML elements. But some elements are specifically suited for applying style sheets, and their entire benefit is that they are formatted via style sheets.

Style sheets generally consist of various rules for formatting elements. To use style sheets such as CSS in a web page, you need to add them to an HTML, XHTML, or XML site. This can be done by embedding style sheets into a document or importing them from an external file. If and how this can be done depends on the type of the date to which you want to apply the CSS formatting.

Embedding an internal style sheet into a web page is done via the `<style>` tag, a pure HTML container. In it, all style rules are defined. In HTML, you can write such a style area anywhere in the web page.

A style sheet in HTML is schematically integrated as shown in Listing 3.13.

Listing 3.13   **Schema of a Style Container in HTML**

```
<style type="text/css">
  ... any CSS formattings ...
</style>
```

> **Note**
>
> You often find HTML comments in containers. But these are not necessary (as in the case of integration via JavaScript).

In a web page, you add a reference to an external style sheet via the `<link>` tag. As in the case of JavaScript, referencing external files is practically always the preferred option. In case of style sheets, this is the only way of achieving the usually desired separation of structure and layout.

Listing 3.14 shows the schema for referencing an external CSS file.

Listing 3.14   **Integrating an External CSS File**

```
<link type="text/css" rel="stylesheet"
  href="[URL of CSS file]" />
```

If you want to specify individual style information for just one element of a web page, you can use a style sheet instruction as inline definition of an element. This means that you set an attribute value via an additional `style` parameter within the tag, and the style rule then applies only within the defined container. You also have the option of importing style sheets.

3.5.2   The Specific Syntax of CSS Declarations

Let's turn briefly to the specific syntax of CSS declarations and the options of specifying formatting rules. The syntax of a CSS declaration always follows the same structure. You specify a name, a colon, and the property to be formatted.

The schematic representation of the syntax of a CSS declaration looks like this:

Listing 3.15   **Schema of a CSS Declaration**

```
[name] : [value]
```

3.5.3   Selectors

The element to be formatted (referred to as selector) is placed before such a rule. Several formatting rules for an element are separated via semicolons and usually enclosed by curly brackets. There are different forms of selectors:

- Element selectors
- Attribute selectors
- Generation selectors
- The universal selector
- Pseudo classes

In the area of selectors, jQuery offers one of its most practical highlights.

Summary

In this chapter, you have encountered the central basics and particularities of modern Internet programming in extremely compact form. The effective application and understanding of frameworks and toolkits such as jQuery is based on elementary knowledge in this area. We have only skimmed over the specific techniques very briefly because a certain experience in this area (or a parallel working with other sources) is a requirement for successful working with this book. But you should now have gained understanding of how the jQuery library works, and you can see the advantages jQuery can offer. In particular, this chapter has shown you how you can combine jQuery with a web page and what you need to watch out for.

4

How jQuery Works

This chapter covers the general functioning of jQuery, particularly the relationship to JavaScript and the Document Object Model (DOM). You also learn how jQuery expands the core functionalities of JavaScript and DOM. Effective programming with jQuery requires your familiarity with JavaScript syntax and concepts. This, in turn, means that you want to understand such elementary things as the following:

- Variables and data types
- Literals
- Expressions
- Objects with their methods and properties
- Functions, function calls, and function references
- Value assignments
- Operators
- Keywords

In this chapter, you also learn some other core terms from programming in general and JavaScript in particular.

> **Note**
>
> This is explicitly not a JavaScript textbook, and we definitely cannot offer an introduction to programming. But the appendix provides a condensed summary of the particularities of JavaScript, in as much as they are elementary to the use and understanding of jQuery. Otherwise, JavaScript is a prerequisite for this book.

In this chapter, we discuss the jQuery core ("core" according to the jQuery documentation). This core concept serves as the basis of the framework and is explicitly based on complex

JavaScript and the DOM. However, this chapter is more expansive than the jQuery documentation and covers more topics associated with the question of how jQuery works.

Early in this book, some readers without sufficient knowledge of JavaScript might be discouraged. But don't worry. You can apply many aspects of jQuery even if you do not totally understand how they work. In any case, work your way through this chapter. After all, it explains the essential technique of how to effectively access the elements of a web page and will help you understand how to apply jQuery methods.

When you are familiar with simple ways of applying jQuery and know all you want to know about that or want to understand why jQuery does certain things in a particular way, this chapter provides the necessary background knowledge that forms the central basis of more in-depth use and understanding of the jQuery library and its functionality. This background knowledge will help you understand most animation/effect applications.

4.1   Accessing Elements of the Web Page

A web page is represented in the browser by elements in the DOM. These often have attributes, text as content, and child elements. As mentioned previously, you can access the components of a web page in various ways via pure JavaScript and native DOM methods. But this way of accessing them is usually either inconvenient or extremely unreliable because different browsers structure the DOM of a web page differently, both in terms of the timing of constructing the DOM (more on this shortly) and the actually present nodes. Correspondingly, access methods that iterate only the DOM tree can lead to different results in different browsers.

To make it clearer: Suppose that you want to address a specific image in a web page. Now you describe the path to get to it. This means that you go to the root of the DOM tree and from there along the nodes to the node of the desired image.

Let's use the primitive web page in Listing 4.1 as an example (ch4_1.html).

Listing 4.1   **A Simple Web Page with Two Images**

```
01 <!DOCTYPE HTML PUBLIC
02   "-//W3C//DTD HTML 4.01 Transitional//EN"
03   "http://www.w3.org/TR/html4/loose.dtd">
04 <html xmlns="http://www.w3.org/1999/xhtml">
05   <head>
06     <meta http-equiv="Content-Type"
07       content="text/html; charset=utf-8" />
08     <title>DOM Nodes</title>
09   </head>
10   <body>
11     <img src="images/b1.jpg" /><br/>
12     <img src="images/i2.jpg" />
13   </body>
14 </html>
```

Here you can see a simple web page with two images. Now try to describe the path in the DOM to the second image in the web page. It's not as easy as just counting off the Hypertext Markup Language (HTML) elements in the visual representation. That is fairly clear. But even the arrangement of references to the images in the source code is not sufficient because the source code is the only working instruction for the browser to create a DOM. You have to describe the path in a tree that corresponds to the DOM. But what does it look like?

You can display the internal structure of the DOM from this primitive web page, so you can see what a browser is actually working with. In Firefox, the add-on DOM Inspector is particularly well suited for this purpose. Newer versions of Internet Explorer offer developer tools that also offer this view.[1] With these two tools, you can already compare the paths in the generated DOM tree and see that these can differ.

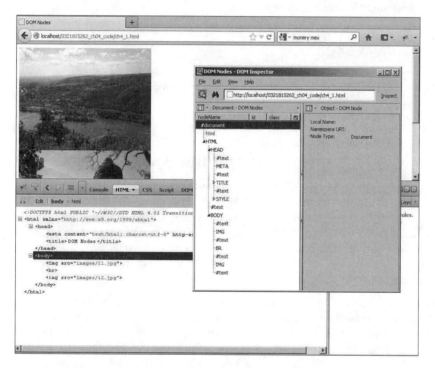

Figure 4.1   The actual structure of the DOM tree that Firefox is working with becomes visible in the DOM Inspector. The developer tools show the DOM tree that Internet Explorer generates from the web page.

As long as all browsers build the DOM tree identically, the description of the path to the second image is universally usable and transferable. But what if a browser creates more or fewer nodes than other browsers from a web page? If the trees have a different number of branches?

1. Most other modern browsers also have similar tools.

Unfortunately, this is indeed the case for many sites (as already in this primitive example); consequently, problems arise with various default methods for accessing the DOM elements. These default methods are based on the DOM structure created in the computer memory by the browser.

As you can see, our simple example already shows the dilemma. If you view the actual DOM tree in the DOM Inspector or the developer tools, a (schematic) description of the path to the second image in the Firefox could sound like this:

> Go from the root down to the element HTML, then from there to the second child node (BODY) and from there to the *sixth* child node. But in Internet Explorer, you would need to go from BODY to the *fourth* child node. Obviously, the number of nodes differs, so a path description of this kind, which gets us to the right point in Firefox, cannot be directly transferred to Internet Explorer.

Note

The access techniques of the jQuery framework shorten and standardize the access to elements of the DOM, compensate for browser-dependent particularities, and add missing functionalities.

4.2   The jQuery Namespace and the jQuery Object

A namespace designates just a scope where a certain identifier is unique. You not only find this in programming but also, for example, in Extensible Markup Language (XML) (and in a file system). Directories can also be regarded as namespaces. Within a directory, a filename must only appear once. It has to be unique. But in different directories, you can have the same filename appearing repeatedly within a file system. This is the benefit of namespaces. You can use certain identifiers repeatedly with different meanings within a context, as long as they are in different namespaces.

This is also useful in programming. In particular, if you want to combine functions and variables from different libraries. How else would you keep programmers on different projects from giving the same names to certain functions or variables, causing a conflict when they are combined? If each project had its own namespace, you could avoid the conflicts.

But JavaScript does not really support the concept of namespaces (in contrast to C# or Java, where namespaces are simply separated via dot notation). This namespace technique is effectively and robustly integrated into the overall concept, and a packet structure ensures a secure separation of namespaces.

In JavaScript, you kind of have to act as if you were in one of the "big" programming languages. So, to implement a namespace concept, you use the dot notation with its separation of object space and property as a template and act as if the components of an identifier separated by the dots are different namespaces.[2] But these are "voluntary" rules, so to speak, that you can adhere to or break with unfortunate syntax structures. It requires a great deal of discipline to avoid wasting the effect of the concept with careless programming.

jQuery attempts to introduce a proper namespace concept in the world of JavaScript and the framework itself. In the framework, all global objects within a namespace are assigned, and the namespace is defined by identifiers starting with the token `jQuery` and separated by a dot following actual names. The identified elements—from the point of view of the framework—are then assigned to the jQuery namespace. And you access it via the token `jQuery` or in an even shorter form via its alias `$`.

> **Caution**
>
> So, with `jQuery` or `$`, you refer in the framework to both the namespace and an object (or more precisely, an array with elements), which constitutes a consistent implementation of a proper namespace concept (if it is upheld in the entire framework).

4.3 Special Data Types and Structures in jQuery

Of course, jQuery is based on the standard data types of JavaScript. These are the types `String`, `Number`, `Boolean`, `Object`, and `Function`; arrays; callbacks; the `XMLHttpRequest` object; the prototyping technique; and several other things. As mentioned before, this discussion assumes that you have basic knowledge in this area and so does not go into much detail here. (The appendix contains a brief summary.) But beyond these, there are some special types or structures (built-in structures) in jQuery that we should remind ourselves of, at least to some extent.

4.3.1 Options

The most important thing should be mentioned right away: In the jQuery framework, you work intensively with **options** in various places. The term *options* in jQuery really refers only to pure JavaScript objects, but in a special notation. These options are usually used declaratively in jQuery via a block indicated by curly brackets. The various options are separated by commas, where applicable, and consist of an option identifier (that you can enclose in quotation marks), a colon, and then the value (in other words, a value pair). A definition with this notation in JavaScript is referred to as an object literal.

Listing 4.2   **Options in the Form of an Object Literal**

```
{
    border: "5px outset",  cursor: "move",
    opacity: 0.5, statusinfo: true
}
```

2. In fact, in JavaScript, the prepended identifier means the specification of an object and the appended identifier a property. This is close to a real namespace concept, but not quite the same.

As mentioned previously, you can enclose the identifiers of the option in quotations marks, as shown in Listing 4.3.

Listing 4.3   **Alternative Notation of Options in the Form of an Object Literal**

```
{
    "border": "5px outset", "cursor": "move",
    "opacity": 0.5, "statusinfo": true
}
```

In some situations, you must enclose the identifiers in quotation marks. For that reason, you should always use the quotation marks. Then you are on the safe side and do not run into problems that might take you a long time to figure out.

In any case, options can give you access to corresponding properties and methods.

> **Note**
>
> You can also assign a callback reference or anonymous function to an option as a value. This is how a large part of the event handling is done in jQuery.

The different value pairs can be either written into several lines (as in the examples) or into just one line. The separator is the comma, not the line break.

4.3.2   Map

One data type explicitly added in jQuery as a special-case option is Map. This type is used, for example, in the AJAX functions of the framework. The data of a request can be delivered in this form. The type can be a string with internal structure, an array with form elements, a jQuery object with form elements, or a general object with key-value pairs. In the latter case, it is possible to assign several values to a key; more specifically, you can assign an array to a key.

4.3.3   The `Array<Type>` Notation

In the jQuery application programming interface (API), you quite often find a notation of the type `Array<Type>`, as shown in Listing 4.4.

Listing 4.4   **Generic Types**

```
dragPrevention Array<String>
```

This notation is motivated by generic types in JavaScript. It indicates that a method not only expects an array as argument, but also of which type (in this example, a string) the elements in it should be. Unfortunately, JavaScript is loosely typed and, purely based on the language, you cannot fulfill these requirements. The framework has to laboriously implement it manually for each situation via internal security measures. In your own programming with jQuery, you are not likely to use this notation.

4.3.4 `jqXHR`

A new data type in connection with AJAX was introduced in jQuery 1.5. The method `$.ajax()` returns a new object of the type `jqXHR`. This is based on the classic `XMLHTTPRequest` object and expands it by adding certain features.

4.4   The Function `jQuery()` and the Alias `$()`

One of the most important functions in the entire framework is definitely `jQuery()`. It is available with various parameters, and you can also use it via the alias `$()`. It is oriented directly on the token for the jQuery namespace or the `jQuery` object. With it, you can reliably select an object or several objects in the DOM and assign it or them to the `jQuery` namespace. So, you are creating a `jQuery` object by cloning the original objects from the DOM, and you then have a new object that refers to the original objects. This means you also have all methods of the framework for such objects available, to apply them via the framework to the embedded elements.

> **Note**
>
> Through the integration of such a powerful and robust framework, a jQuery object makes numerous functions available to you in the background that could easily be overlooked even though they are immensely important. For example, it identifies a browser or an operating system and offers adapted measures in the background. Or in representing a collection of elements,[3] it ensures that certain steps of a called method actually apply reliably to all elements. Many methods of the framework iterate in a kind of loop or recursive form over all elements of a collection to achieve this. Or it ensures invisibly that extensions that adhere to certain rules can be seamlessly integrated into the framework (plug-ins).

As a first parameter, you can pass to the function almost anything that can describe an element or a group of elements in the web page. This includes a CSS selector as a string, an HTML tag as a string, one or several DOM elements, or a callback to a function (including anonymous, of course).

Listing 4.5   **All Elements of the Type `div` in the Entire Web Page**

```
$("div");
```

---

3. For example, several headings or `div` elements.

> **Note**
>
> We discuss the selectors in more detail later.

Let's take a look at a complete example (ch4_2.html).

Listing 4.6   Selection of All Level 1 Headings

```
...
08    <script type="text/javascript">
09      $(document).ready(function(){
10        jQuery("h1").css({
11          background: "red",  color: "white"
12        });
13      });
14    </script>
15  </head>
16  <body>
17  <h1>The hen is wisest of all the animal creation.
18    She never cackles until the egg is laid./h1>
19  <h1>Action speaks louder than words
20    but not nearly as often.</h1>
21  <div>
22    <h1>Do not go where the path may lead,
23      go instead where there is no path
24      and leave a trail.</h1>
25  </div>
26  <h1>No  great genius has ever existed
27    without some touch of madness.</h1>
28  </body>
29  </html>
```

In this example, you see `jQuery()` applied twice, once via the shortened form `$()` in line 9. Here the entire web page is selected via the specified DOM object via `$(document)`.

But in line 10, the long version indicates a selection that also specifies a CSS selector as a string. With `jQuery("h1")`, you get all elements of the type h1 in the web page. These are assigned to the jQuery namespace as a collection. You then also have the methods and properties of the framework available. We are making use of the `css()` method to set certain CSS properties of all headings with the type h1 in the web page for the options via an object literal, but this is of secondary importance here. Note, however, that one of the headings is within a `div` block. We make use of this in the next section. In this example, it is explicitly *not* relevant (which we also want to demonstrate here).

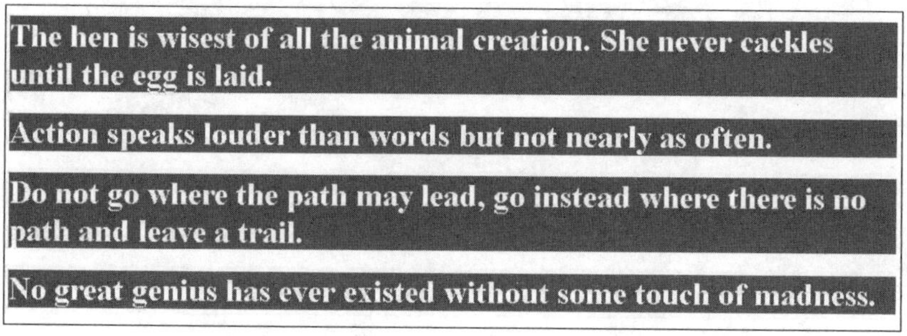

> **The hen is wisest of all the animal creation. She never cackles until the egg is laid.**
>
> **Action speaks louder than words but not nearly as often.**
>
> **Do not go where the path may lead, go instead where there is no path and leave a trail.**
>
> **No great genius has ever existed without some touch of madness.**

Figure 4.2   All level 1 headings have been formatted.

4.4.1   The Context

The second (optional) parameter of `jQuery()` specifies the **context**. The term *context* refers to the context in which an element should be seen. If it is not specified, the context of the entire HTML document is used instead. Otherwise, you can specify a DOM element, document, or jQuery object as context, and then the element will be seen only in this context (for example, a paragraph or a form).

Listing 4.7   **Selection of All Input Elements with the Type Attribute Radio (in Other Words, a Radio Button), but Only in the First Form of the Web Page**

```
$("input:radio", document.forms[0]);
```

Take a look at this slight variation of the preceding example (ch4_3.html—the lines not repeated here are identical to ch4_2.html).

Listing 4.8   **Selection of All Headings with the Type `h1` Within the Context of an Element with the Type `div`**

```
...
09      $(document).ready(function(){
10        jQuery("h1","div").css({
11          background: "red",  color: "white"
12        });
13      });
...
```

Note that the second parameter limits the selection. We only want to select the headings that are within a `div` block. This means that only the third heading is addressed in this specific example.

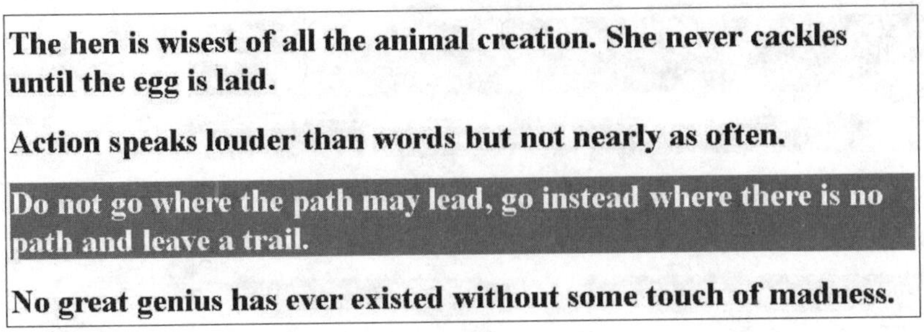

> **The hen is wisest of all the animal creation. She never cackles until the egg is laid.**
>
> **Action speaks louder than words but not nearly as often.**
>
> **Do not go where the path may lead, go instead where there is no path and leave a trail.**
>
> **No great genius has ever existed without some touch of madness.**

Figure 4.3   Only the third heading has been formatted.

4.5   Executing Functions After DOM Has Been Built

Let's approach the topic in a more fundamental way. Already in the course of the first few chapters you have learned why this method and the whole topic is so important. You cannot access the components of a web page reliably via JavaScript in the browser before the DOM tree has been correctly constructed. And because the different browsers behave differently when constructing the DOM, various problems can arise when you try to access the elements of the web page—especially if you try to access elements of a web page too soon, before the browser has correctly constructed the DOM.[4] jQuery offers a reliable method for preventing these problems.

> **Caution**
>
> In principle, you could use the `onload` event handler both in HTML and directly under JavaScript to call a function after the web page is loaded (which is identical to completing the DOM or at least should be). However, this event handler is incorrectly implemented in various browsers. So, using it is definitely not recommended. In jQuery, you are on the safe side.

4.5.1   Callback or Anonymous Function as a Parameter of `jQuery()`

One way of reacting to the completion of the DOM is this: If you pass a callback to a function or an anonymous function as a parameter in `jQuery()` or `$()`, this is executed immediately after the DOM has been completed—not too early.

Let's take a look at an another example (ch4_4.html).

---

4. Which can also be due to a delay in loading the website from the Internet.

Listing 4.9   **A Callback to a Function**

```
...
08    <script type="text/javascript">
09      $(output);
10      function output(){
11          $("#info").html($("img:first").attr("src"));
12      }
13    </script>
14  </head>
15  <body>
16    <div id="info"></div>
17    <img src="images/i1.jpg"/><br/>
18    <img src="images/i2.jpg"/>
19  </body>
20  </html>
```

Note that the images are integrated only in lines 17 and 18. Plus, the `div` area where the output takes place is listed only after the access. The output is the URL of the first image file, which shows clearly that the corresponding tag has already been used to construct the DOM tree.

The crucial place can be seen in line 10. There, you can see the reference to the function `output()`, whose declaration is written down in lines 10–12.

Figure 4.4   At the precise point when the function was called, the DOM tree had been completed.

Let's also look at how the anonymous function is used as an alternative (ch4_5.html—any lines not listed are identical to ch4_4.html).

Listing 4.10   **An Anonymous Function as a Parameter**

```
...
09    $(
10    function(){
11        $("#info").html($("img:first").attr("src"));
12    });
...
```

The two notations are a shorthand form of `$(document).ready()` is a reaction to the DOM loaded event, which indicates that the DOM tree is ready to be traversed and manipulated. A ready event handler is passed as an argument.

> **Tip**
>
> You can use any number of `$(document).ready` events in your site (in any notation). The functions bound to it are executed in the order in which they were added.

Let's explore this in a complete example (ch4_6.html).

Listing 4.11   **Different Variations of the** `ready()` **Methods**

```
...
06    <script type="text/javascript"
07      src="lib/jquery-1.8.2.min.js"></script>
08    <script type="text/javascript">
09      function extern(){
10        alert("Callback: " +
11          $("img:first").attr("src"));
12      }
13      $(function(){
14        alert("Anonymous: " +
15          $("img:first").attr("src"));
16      });
17      jQuery(extern);
18      $(document).ready(function(){
19        alert("Anonymous: " +
20          $("img:first").attr("src"));
21      });
22      $().ready(extern);
23    </script>
24  </head>
25  <body>
26    <img src="images/i1.jpg" />
27  </body>
28 </html>
```

Just go ahead and test the example. You will see that the output windows are called sequentially in the order they were integrated.

4.5.2 Placing `document.ready()` into an External JavaScript File

If you look at the structure of the examples we have used up to now, you will see that the jQuery library was integrated as an external JavaScript file, but calling the functions and methods (including `document.ready()`) took place in an internal script container. For our examples, this is usually convenient in terms of description, but not obligatory. You can separate structure and function completely and remove these calls to an external file as well. In fact, this is highly recommended as a general rule in practice. But then you have to provide the reference to the JavaScript file with the calls *after* the reference to the jQuery library.

> **Note**
>
> All JavaScript files combined within a web page, as well as the internal script containers and inline scripts, form a **common** global namespace. That is why the framework forms its own sub-namespace `jQuery` within it, for its own functionalities. This means that in a script container you can access all components of an external JavaScript file, but you can also access components of another external JavaScript file from within one JavaScript file (provided the order is observed).

Such an external JavaScript file then consists of only one or more calls of `document.ready()` in any permitted notation. Other calls beyond this should, of course, be avoided in any case if you are assuming a completed DOM. But if required, you can write down additional declarations in the external JavaScript file. I would even remove these to other JavaScript files in larger projects and modularize the project even more; the same with all calls of functions on loading the site that are not (for whatever reason) supposed to be packed into the protected area of `document.ready()`.

> **Note**
>
> If you are using style sheets in your web page, all style sheets should be integrated *before* the scripts. In particular, the integration should take place before the `ready()` methods are called. If you do not do this, it can cause problems in some browsers.

4.5.3 Example of Creating a Basic Structure for a Modularized jQuery Web Application

Let's look at a complete example that shows a practical useful web application structure that attempts to work with jQuery consistently (ch4_7.html).

Listing 4.12   An HTML Basic Structure for a Modularized jQuery Application

```
01 <html xmlns="http://www.w3.org/1999/xhtml">
02   <head>
03     <meta http-equiv="Content-Type"
04       content="text/html; charset=utf-8" />
05     <title>Structuring a jQuery Application
06     </title>
07     <link type="text/css" rel="stylesheet"
08       href="lib/ch4_7.css" />
09     <script type="text/javascript"
10       src="lib/jquery-1.8.2.min.js"></script>
11     <script type="text/javascript"
12       src="lib/ch4_7_declarations.js"></script>
13     <script type="text/javascript"
14       src="lib/ch4_7_ready.js"></script>
15   </head>
16   <body>
17     <h1>Replacing an image</h1>
18     <button id="toggle1">Image 1</button>
19     <button id="toggle2">Image 2</button>
20     <hr/><img src="images/i1.jpg"/>
21   </body>
22 </html>
```

This example shows the described HTML basic structure for a completely modularized jQuery application. First, you can see the reference to the CSS file (lines 7 and 8). Here you could include further CSS references if required. Then follows the reference to the jQuery library (lines 9 and 10). Next, the references to additional JavaScript files appear.

The file ch4_7_declarations.js, referenced after the jQuery library, just contains two functions in our example and looks like this.

Listing 4.13   The Declaration of Two Functions

```
01 function image1(){
02   $("img").attr({
03     src: "images/i1.jpg"
04   });
05 }
06 function image2(){
07   $("img").attr("src", "images/i2.jpg");
08 }
```

The two functions change the attribute src of a referenced object.[5] (You know this example from Chapter 2, "First Examples with jQuery." Note that the file explicitly uses jQuery syntax!

---

5. More precisely, all elements of the type, but that is not relevant here.

> ### Caution
>
> Let there be no misunderstanding: Access to an image element *does not* takes place before its description in the web page and yet outside of `document.ready()` (which can only be found in the JavaScript file referenced later). Here, you only have the **declarations**; these are not **calls**.

The file ch4_7_ready.js looks like this.

Listing 4.14   **Using** `document.ready()`

```
01 $(document).ready(function(){
02   $("#toggle1").click(image1);
03 });
04 $(function(){
05   $("#toggle2").click(image2)
06 });
```

Here you see two[6] sequentially listed uses of `document.ready()`. Each describes a click event describing a callback to a function that is declared in the other external JavaScript file ch4_7_declarations.js.

Let's now play around with the order of the references. You will see that this can result in errors. Take a look at the following extract with the changed order of the references (ch4_7_error.html).

Listing 4.15   **An Error in the Sequence of Integration**

```
...
09   <script type="text/javascript"
10     src="lib/ch4_7_declarations.js"></script>
11   <script type="text/javascript"
12     src="lib/ch4_7_ready.js"></script>
13   <script type="text/javascript"
14     src="lib/jquery-1.8.2.min.js"></script>
...
```

In this variation, the reference to the jQuery library (lines 13 and 14) is included too late. As a result, the jQuery syntax is not available in the preceding scripts.

However, switching around the references to the files ch4_7_declarations.js and ch4_7_ready.js is not relevant, although you can try if you like with file ch4_7_2.html on the companion web page.

---

6. These are only two method calls for demonstration purposes.

Figure 4.5   The jQuery syntax is not available in time, as you can see in the error console.

4.6   Creating an Element with `jQuery()` and Inserting It into the Web Page

An interesting possibility for `jQuery()` and `$()` is the creation of DOM elements on-the-fly. These can then be dynamically and reliably inserted into a web page. Internally, you use either `.html()` or the property `innerHTML`, depending on the element type. But you need not worry about how exactly this works internally. After all, the essence of a framework such as jQuery is that these things stay hidden from the programmer and above all that they work reliably in all supported browsers and save you the trouble of adapting to various browsers and different element types.

You should not overlook that an element you want to create and insert, of course, has to fit into the context. For example, you cannot insert a `body` element into a `div` container. Also, the entire HTML content has to be well formed. You cannot rely on the principle of error tolerance, as you would usually with pure HTML. In particular, you have to ensure that you correctly close the elements to be created. For example, an instruction such as `$("<span>")` will not work in some browsers, whereas the correct XHTML syntax `$("<span />")` works fine.

> **Tip**
>
> Optionally, you can specify as a second parameter a document where the new element is to be created (the context).

Now, creating an element does not mean that it has already been added to the web page. But you can do this, for example, with the jQuery method `appendTo()`.

Let's take a look at a complete example (ch4_8.html).

Listing 4.16   **Creating an Empty Web Page**

```
...
06    <script type="text/javascript"
07       src="lib/jquery-1.8.2.min.js"></script>
08    <script type="text/javascript"
09       src="lib/ch4_8.js"></script>
10    </head>
11    <body></body>
12  </html>
```

Obviously, the body of the website is empty. But the linked JavaScript file ch4_8.js looks like Listing 4.17.

Listing 4.17   **Dynamically Creating Elements and Integrating Them into the Website**

```
01  $(document).ready(function(){
02    var block= $("<div>A Block</div>");
03    $("<h1>Dynamically Creating Elements</h1>").
04       appendTo("body");
05    block.appendTo("body");
06  });
```

After the DOM is created, a jQuery element of the type `div` is created in line 2. In line 3, a jQuery element of the type `h1` is created and directly added to the website (line 4). Then the first created element that was saved in the variable `block` is added to the website. Correspondingly, you first see the header in the website and then below it the block.

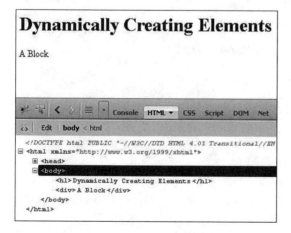

Figure 4.6   The website and Firebug show clearly how the elements were added.

4.6.1   Options for Initializing Attributes

Since jQuery 1.4, you can use this approach when creating elements to specify options as second parameter with which you can set attributes of the created elements. The listing of the following example file ch4_9.html can be omitted here; it is identical to ch4_8.html, apart from the reference to the JavaScript file ch4_9.js. But what is interesting is this file ch4_9.js.

Listing 4.18   **Creating Elements with Options**

```
01 $(document).ready(function(){
02   var block = $("<div/>", {
03     css: {
04       background: "red",
05       color: "white"
06     },
07     html: "A block with parameters<br />",
08     click: function(){
09       $(this).fadeOut("slow");
10     }
11   });
12   var image= $("<img />", {
13     src: "images/i1.jpg"
14   });
15   $("<h1/>", {
16     text: "Dynamically Creating Elements"
17   }).appendTo("body");
18   block.appendTo("body");
19   image.appendTo(block);
20 });
```

In the example, three elements are created on-the-fly that are then added dynamically to the website:

- A block of the type `div`

- An image

- A heading of the type `h1`

All three elements are created as empty elements (the first parameter in each case) but equipped with options via the second parameter. Let's first look at the `div` element.

Listing 4.19   **Creating and Initializing a `div` Element**

```
02   var block = $("<div/>", {
03     css: {
04       background: "red",
05       color: "white"
06     },
```

```
07    html: "A block with parameters<br />",
08    click: function(){
09      $(this).fadeOut("slow");
10    }
11  });
```

The options are written as object literals. The `css` property stands for a correspondingly named jQuery method via which the HTML `style` property of an element is set.[7] With `html`, you are using the jQuery method `html()`, which essentially corresponds to access via `innerHTML` and writes interpreted assigned text into the website. And `click` stands for the event helper `click()`, which basically corresponds to the event handler `onclick`. This part also ensures that the `div` block is filled with HTML content, formatted with CSS and equipped with event handling.[8]

Creating the image in lines 12–14 is obvious. The URL is set as an option. In lines 15–17, the header is created and directly assigned to the `body` element.

Line 19 is also of interest. The object to which the element in the variable `image` is appended is itself addressed via a variable: `block`. This means that the image is written into the `div` area.

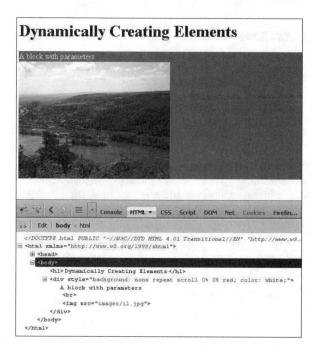

Figure 4.7   The attributes have been set and the elements integrated into the website.

7. You can see this clearly in Firebug.
8. If you click on this area, it slowly fades out.

If you click the `div` area, you will see that the entire area, including the image, is faded out.

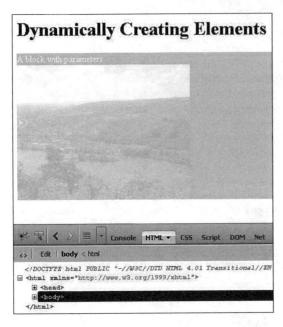

Figure 4.8   The `div` area is dynamically faded out.

4.7   Wrapping Existing Elements with `jQuery()`

Let's reiterate once more: When you are passing an element or a group of elements as parameters to `jQuery()` or `$()`, these elements are wrapped. Therefore, they are then available within the context of `jQuery` and you can apply the properties and methods from the `jQuery` namespace or the jQuery library to them accordingly. This is remarkable because the method accepts not only DOM elements, but also XML documents and `window` objects, even if they are not DOM elements. Of course, you can also specify other jQuery objects as parameters. We have done this in different ways in the last few examples.

Listing 4.20   **The Background Color of the Website Is Set to Blue**

```
$(document.body).css( "background", "blue" );
```

Note that elements are not enclosed within quotation marks.

4.7.1   Direct Access to DOM elements via `get( )`

If you use `jQuery()` to get an element into the context of jQuery, you can use the methods of the framework. But you do pay a price! Because in the context, you do not have direct access to the classic DOM properties and methods. Plus, you cannot place all elements into the jQuery context.

Consider the following example (ch4_10.html).

Listing 4.21   **Attempting Access to a Classic DOM Property**

```
...
06    <script type="text/javascript"
07      src="lib/jquery-1.8.2.js"></script>
08    <script type="text/javascript">
09      $(function(){
10        alert($("img:first").src);
11      });
12    </script>
13  </head>
14  <body>
15    <img src="images/i1.jpg" />
16  </body>
17 </html>
```

In line 10, the first image in the website is addressed and integrated into the jQuery context. Via the now-generated jQuery object, we then try to access a classic DOM property: `src`. But if you load the page, you will see that it is `undefined`.

Figure 4.9   You cannot access the classic DOM properties with this approach.

But with the method `get()`, you have a way of reaching the DOM tree directly from within the jQuery context. In particular, this type of access is also possible for elements that are not directly available via the jQuery object (if there are no suitable properties or methods available). You use this kind of access, for example, if you are operating directly on DOM elements and do not need any jQuery built-in functions (or if none are available).

Let's look at the following modification of our example (ch4_11.html).

Listing 4.22   **Alternative Attempt at Accessing a Classic DOM Property via** `get()`

```
...
10        alert($("img:first").get(0).src);
...
```

Figure 4.10   Accessing the DOM property works.

Without a parameter, `get()` returns all DOM elements that were selected via `$()` in the form of an array (with all options of operating on them as usual). If you specify an index, as in the example, you can select a DOM object as usual and address all available DOM properties.

4.8   Using jQuery in Combination with Other Frameworks

The jQuery library offers a multitude of functions. Generally, these should offer adequate solutions for most problems occurring in web programming. If this is not sufficient for you, there are extensions based on jQuery, such as the jQuery UI or Mobile jQuery, plus the many jQuery plug-ins that are compatible without limitations. But another library or another framework might contain a specific function that is not implemented in jQuery in quite the same way. Or perhaps you prefer the solution offered in another framework. In this case, you may want to use jQuery together with other libraries or frameworks within a website. Then you might want to integrate these together within a page, according to the rules described earlier.

To ensure that several libraries or frameworks cooperate as smoothly as possible, the jQuery library with all plug-ins uses—as discussed earlier—a separate namespace.[9] If you are using several libraries or frameworks in combination, this should ensure that an identifier in one framework does not conflict with a potentially identical identifier in another framework. But, of course, this applies only if all used libraries and frameworks support or implement the namespace technique.

9. Within the limitations arising as a result of the concept of JavaScript.

In jQuery, all global objects are saved within the jQuery namespace. So, you should not run into problems if using it in combination with other libraries such as Prototype, MooTools, or YUI.

4.8.1 The Function noConflict()

But in certain cases, there can still be a conflict. The identifier $ is, as mentioned previously, a shortcut for the jQuery namespace (or more precisely—the variable or object jQuery). Note that $ is also used, for example, in the Prototype framework. So, if both frameworks are used in combination within a website, we have a case where the pure concept of namespaces as they are possible in JavaScript is not going to work to resolve all conflicts. The identifier is not unique if both frameworks are used in combination because the root of the (added on) namespace system in JavaScript will contain both identifiers with different meanings.

For that reason, the core area of jQuery offers the jQuery.noConflict() function, which is intended to provide protection against such conflicts when you are using multiple libraries in combination. If you are using it, the $ variable is assigned the meaning of the library that is first implemented in the website. For the other library, this identifier is then no longer available, but this resolves the ambiguity of meaning and therefore the conflict.

If $ is no longer available in jQuery, you can still address the jQuery namespace via the synonymous variable jQuery. This alias of $ is not turned off by jQuery.noConflict(). With a Boolean parameter, you can remove all jQuery variables, including the synonymous variable jQuery.

> **Caution**
>
> The function jQuery.noConflict() has to be called after the jQuery library is integrated but before integrating and using the additional library that causes the conflict.

The jQuery.noConflict() function returns the jQuery object, and so you can also assign it to a separate variable. This can then be used as your own alias for $, as shown in Listing 4.23 (ch4_12.html).

Listing 4.23   **Defining Your Own Alias for $**

```
...
06    <script type="text/javascript"
07      src="lib/jquery-1.8.2.js"></script>
08    <script type="text/javascript">
09      var $j = jQuery.noConflict();
10      $j(function(){
11        alert($j("img").get().length);
12      });
13    </script>
14    </head>
```

```
15       <body>
16          <img src="images/i1.jpg" />
17             <img src="images/i2.jpg" />
18    </body>
19  </html>
```

Figure 4.11   With $j you can address the jQuery object.

Ultimately, you can also pack all jQuery code into the ready() method. Within this area, you have a separate namespace in which you can use $. Outside it, $ could then represent the Prototype functionality, for example. The trick is that $ is passed as a parameter to the function that is called with ready().

Listing 4.24   **Shifting All jQuery Code into the** ready() **Method**

```
...
  <script src="prototype.js"></script>
  <script src="jquery.js"></script>
  <script>
    jQuery.noConflict();
    jQuery(document).ready(function($){
      // $ here stands for jQuery
      ...
    });

    // Here $ stands for the Prototype variation
    ...
  </script>
...
```

4.9   More About Context

But let's get back to the term *context*. This term appears repeatedly in this chapter. In JavaScript, the variable this always refers to is the current context (in other words, the object that you are currently in).

In the basic setting, `this` refer to the browser window (that is, the DOM object window). But if you are within a function, the context can also point to other objects (subobjects of `window` such as buttons or form fields). This depends on the specific circumstances under which the function is called. Under jQuery, all event handlers reference the triggering element of an event as context.

4.9.1 context, selector, and nodeName

From version 1.3 onward, jQuery offers the property `context`. This gives you the context of the DOM that has been passed along to `jQuery()`. If no context is passed on, `context` will be identical to the document. The property `context` itself is again an object and makes the name of a node in the tree available via `nodeName`.

The property `context` is usually used in combination with the property selector to determine where an action is coming from. This is usually used in developing plug-ins. Since jQuery version 1.3, this property `selector` represents the selector that is delivered by `jQuery()`. With it, you can determine the selector of a request directly and use it further in the script. This information can be used in connection with the property `context` to determine the exact circumstances of a request.

> **Note**
>
> Selectors are discussed in more detail in a later chapter.

Listing 4.25 **Requesting the Context (ch4_13.html)**

```
...

06      <style type="text/css">
07        #output {
08          width: 800px;
09          background: green;
10          color: white
11        }
12      </style>
13      <script type="text/javascript"
14        src="lib/jquery-1.8.2.min.js">
15      </script>
16      <script type="text/javascript">
17        $(document).ready(function(){
18          $("#output").append(
19            "<tr><td>$(\"div:first\").context</td><td> " +
20              $("div:first").context + "</td></tr>")
21          $("#output").append("<tr><td>$(\"div\", " +
22            "document.body).context.nodeName</td><td> " +
23              $("div", document.body).context.nodeName +
24              "</td></tr>")
```

```
25          $("#output").append("<tr><td>$(\"img\")" +
26            ".context.nodeName</td><td> " +
27            $("img").context.nodeName + "</td></tr>");
28          $("#output").append( "<tr><td>$(\"img\", " +
29            "document.getElementsByTagName(\"div\")[0])" +
30            ".context.nodeName</td><td> " +
31            $("img", document.getElementsByTagName("div")
32              [0]).context.nodeName +
33            "</td></tr>");
34          $("#output").append("<tr><td>$(\"img\", " +
35            "document.getElementsByTagName(\"div\")[0])" +
36            ".selector</td><td> " +
37            $("img", document.getElementsByTagName("div")
38              [0]).selector +
39            "</td></tr>");
40        });
41      </script>
42    </head>
43    <body>
44      <div>
45        <img src="images/i1.jpg" />
46      </div>
47      <hr/><table id="output" />
48    </body>
49  </html>
```

The example shows different ways of using `context`. The property `nodeName` returns the name of a node, and the other outputs give the context itself plus the selector.

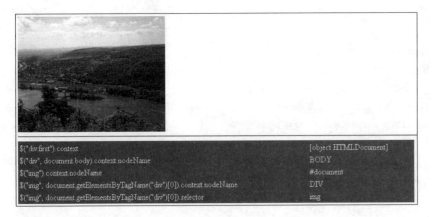

Figure 4.12   The context of different elements.

4.10 Chaining jQuery Objects

A central aspect of jQuery is that most methods of the framework can themselves return a jQuery object (or a collection of jQuery objects) as a return value. Therefore, you can use dot notation to achieve a chaining of method calls. I believe this is one of the highlights of the framework, in that it allows you to implement an extremely condensed notation. You will see this more clearly in animation techniques, but even simple appending content to an area can be done quite compactly and logically with this approach.

Listing 4.26   **Chaining jQuery Methods (ch4_14.html)**

```
...
06    <script type="text/javascript"
07      src="lib/jquery-1.7.2.js"></script>
08    <script type="text/javascript">
09      $(document).ready(function(){
10        $("#output").append("First this. ").
11          css({background:"red",color:"white"}).
12          append("<hr />").
13          append("And then this.");
14      });
15    </script>
16  </head>
17  <body>
18    <div id="output" />
19  </body>
20 </html>
```

In line 10, you can see that text is added to a `div` area via the `append()` method. As a return value, it again returns a jQuery object. Correspondingly, you can in turn apply jQuery methods to this object. In our case, in line 11 we apply the `css()` method for formatting the preceding object with CSS. As is most commonly the case in object-oriented programming, the linkage is the dot (which applies under JavaScript anyway). The return value of `css()` is once more a jQuery object that represents the selected area that has been processed to this point. To this object, you can in turn apply a jQuery method (and so on).

Figure 4.13   Chaining jQuery methods.

4.10.1   Executing Function Calls Sequentially: The jQuery Queue

In connection with self-calls, chained calls, or generally delayed calls of functions in jQuery, delayed calls are held in a **queue**. This term is also part of the name of several methods in the framework that take care of the queuing task.

If several function calls are to be executed sequentially, they have to be managed in a queue. Strictly speaking, such a queue is an array of function references. The jQuery framework manages this queue automatically in the background (for example, in case of call chaining), or you can use various methods to manually access this queue (for example, the `queue()` and `dequeue()` or `delay()` methods). With the `queue()` method, you get a reference to the first element (the first function) in the queue. As a parameter, you can specify a string via which you can identify the queue. The default is `fx`. If you specify a second parameter, this is a call-back. Then you add a new function at the end of the queue, which is executed when all previous functions have been completed. If you specify the name of another queue as a second parameter, the existing queue is replaced with the new one. You can also specify an array with functions.

With the `dequeue()` method, you take a function from the beginning of the queue and execute it. An optional parameter is the name of the queue from which you want to take the function. The `delay()` method that was added in jQuery 1.4 enables you to delay the execution of methods that follow in the queue. Another method added in version 1.4 is `clearQueue()`, used to remove all calls to not-yet-executed functions from the queue. As with `queue()`, you can either access the default queue `fx` by omitting a parameter or specify the name of the queue as string.

4.11   New Core Techniques Since Version 1.5

In version 1.5,[10] a few new techniques were added to the core area of the framework. For the sake of completeness, we briefly mention them here, without going into too much detail.

> **Note**
>
> You will not find many new features in version 1.5.x in comparison to version 1.4.3. Most changes in version 1.5.x take place more in the background (the exception being AJAX). In the release change from 1.3.x to the various 1.4 variants, there were many more extensions that facilitated different programming.

4.11.1 `jQuery.sub()`

The method `jQuery.sub()` creates a new copy of the `jQuery` object whose properties and methods can be modified without affecting the original `jQuery` object. It was introduced into the framework for two reasons. One, you can conveniently use it to overwrite methods from

---

10. Version 1.8.2 was used for testing the examples in this book.

jQuery without destroying the original methods or preventing access. Two, the namespace for jQuery plug-ins can be encapsulated better.

4.11.2 `jQuery.when()`

The `jQuery.when()` method is interesting. It lets you describe a kind of if condition for one or several objects for which callback functions are to be executed if they occur. This proves particularly useful for asynchronous or generally delayed events as they occur, for example, with AJAX. In combination with a chained `then()` method, you can describe a compact reaction system.

We have to jump ahead a bit to describe such a delayed event in an example. We send an AJAX request and react when the answer arrives.[11]

In the official documentation, you will find the following code fragment.

Listing 4.27   **The Official Code Fragment for Using `when()` in an AJAX Request**

```
$.when( $.ajax("test.aspx") ).then(function(ajaxArgs){
    alert(ajaxArgs[1]); /* ajaxArgs is [ "success", statusText, jqXHR ] */
});
```

But, this example causes errors in some older browsers. In principle, something like what is shown in Listing 4.28 should work well.

Listing 4.28   **Several Delayed Events with Common Handling**

```
$.when($.ajax("rjs.txt"), $.ajax("rjs2.txt")).
then(myFunction, myErrorMessage);
```

So, you can create common handling of several delayed events. If only one object of the methods is passed that does not show a delayed reaction, each callback is executed immediately.

4.11.3   Version 1.6: What's New?

The changes and additions in jQuery 1.6 are, as mentioned before, important. However, they are mainly optimizations and largely invisible for the user of the framework. But, the programmer can/must explicitly notice and make use of a few specific optimizations/changes.

If you look at the other new features of version 1.6 at http://api.jquery.com/category/version/1.6/, you will see that these are rather specialist or technical and hardly touch upon "normal" website programming. For example, there are the new `deferred.always()` and `deferred.pipe()` methods for dealing with delayed objects and the method

11. If you are not familiar with AJAX yet, be patient; we get to the details about AJAX later on.

jQuery.holdReady() for influencing the execution of the ready event in jQuery. Plus there is a promise() method that delivers a dynamically generated object that is, so to speak, a promise that all actions for a preceding type (such as animations or content changes) have ended. When triggering this object, you can then assume a guaranteed state. The special feature of this method is that the relevant actions can be chained, or not.

attr(), prop(), and removeProp()

Also, the internal workings of the attr() method have been rewritten. Since jQuery 1.6, the handling of DOM attributes and properties is separated. For the latter, jQuery 1.6 introduced the prop() and removeProp() methods. The new method prop() sets the properties (hence, the name of the method) of DOM elements or returns the corresponding values. Correspondingly, removeProp() removes the properties.

The background is this: In the previous versions, jQuery did not separate DOM attributes and properties clearly. But there are small differences. Generally, DOM attributes represent the status of a DOM information that is delivered by the document (for example, the value of the attribute value in <input type="text" value="abc">). So, this is the **static** value set by the HTML markup. DOM properties, in contrast, represent the **dynamic** status of the document. And this can differ from the static preset value, as the example shows. So if the user in the described case enters a value in the form, the method prop("value") returns the input of the user rather than the preset value. Up to now you should have been working with the val() method anyway in case of form elements, but you could also have used attr("value").

In most cases, browsers return the value of the attribute value as the start value for the corresponding property, but with Boolean attributes such as checked or disabled there are certain problems (yet you need to avoid such Boolean attributes if you want to take XHTML logic into account—and then the problem does not arise).

Prior to jQuery 1.6, attr("checked") returned the Boolean property value true, but since jQuery 1.6, you get an empty string back. (The same happens with other Boolean properties.) And there you can now work with the method prop(), as shown in Listing 4.29.

Listing 4.29   **Applied to Boolean Property Values**

```
$(this).prop("checked")
```

Alternatively (and irrespective of the version), you could also use this for Boolean property values.

Listing 4.30   **Alternatively, You Can Use the is() Method**

```
$(this).is(":checked")
```

data()

Another innovation concerns the `data()` method. With version 1.6, this was adapted to the HTML5 specification of the World Wide Web Consortium. This means more specifically that attribute names connected by dashes are turned into CamelCase names for this method, as well. These are the identifiers where each new word within the identifier is spelled with an uppercase letter (as it is used already in the DOM concept and in various other places in jQuery). This fact is relevant when importing data attributes, because in jQuery 1.5, a feature was introduced in the `data()` method to automatically convert all data attributes set for an element to JavaScript values, using the JSON semantic. The new feature in jQuery 1.6 has about the same effect as if we were to assume an attribute `data-max-value="100"`.

Listing 4.31   **The Result in jQuery 1.5.2**

```
{ max-value: 100 }
```

Listing 4.32   **The Result in jQuery 1.6**

```
{ maxValue: 100 }.
```

In the context of changes in jQuery 1.6, it is also worth mentioning that CSS properties can now be changed relatively. For example, you can use the operator +=. Further improvements concern animations and effects, but these are not particularly noticeable.

Summary

In this chapter, you encountered the most important background information about how jQuery works. This background is based explicitly on JavaScript and the DOM concept because jQuery makes extensive use of their possibilities. The advantage for a user is that he gets highly powerful techniques presented on a silver platter with this framework (and across many browsers). Admittedly, the statement that you do not need to know JavaScript to be able to use jQuery is explicitly incorrect. But you get methods for programming your website in the easiest way possible, and pure JavaScript or the native DOM object simply cannot offer these in the same way. Of course, you could also program these functionalities yourself if you are a JavaScript expert, but this would mean reinventing the wheel (with a huge amount of effort).

This chapter has covered specific objects in jQuery. An important aspect was accessing elements of the website, which is reliably possible via the jQuery namespace and the `jQuery` object plus the functions `jQuery()` and `$()`, as well as via various additional methods in jQuery.4.8   Using jQuery in Combination with Other Frameworks

5

Selectors and Filters

This rather extensive chapter covers how you can use jQuery to select specific components of a web page. This is the basis of all dynamic processes in a web page, but also of the targeted formatting of individual web page areas. The classic approach is selecting via names, object fields, or native Document Object Model (DOM) methods because every web page is represented as DOM in the browser.[1] Object fields are—as the name indicates—available via an array notation (and limited to it) and only work for a few elements.[2] Access via the name from within JavaScript is also only possible to a limited extent.[3] And with regard to conceivable options, the native DOM methods only permit very limited selection options (for example, only selecting an ID or a class, a few relationship specifications, or just specifying the name of a Hypertext Markup Language [HTML] element). The conclusion is that in the classic DOM access, many conceivable selection options are absent altogether, have different effects, or are only supported by a few browsers.

Undoubtedly, one of the biggest strengths of the jQuery framework is that you can use it to select elements in a web page in an easy, reliable, extensive, and universal way across all common browsers. Essentially, you are determining a selection of elements via the `jQuery()` method or its alias `$()` and parameters that select the elements.

Note

The significance of such a targeted selection is also indicated by the name of the framework that contains the term *query*. When selecting an element or a group of elements in a web page, you are specifying a query based on selectors and filters. The extensive options for specifying selection criteria are, I think, among the most important features of the entire framework. Not

1. Although it can differ from browser to browser, as we have seen in the previous examples.

2. But historically, these are among the first options of accessing the components of a web page. The limitation is the restriction to elements that were included in the first draft of an object model by Netscape—the basis of today's DOM concept—around 1995 (for example, forms, applets, links, or images). Incidentally, some sources also use the term HTMLCollection instead of object fields.

3. It is only really reliably possible with those elements for which Netscape had intended object fields as well. Essentially, the access via names in the classic DOM access is limited to images and forms or form elements.

least, they are the basis for dynamically manipulating a web page via style sheets. Here, too, jQuery offers a range of interesting methods that we use for visual demonstrations in this chapter but discuss in more detail in a later chapter.

5.1   The Basics

Let's first clarify what exactly is meant by the term **selector**. The whole chapter revolves around selectors.

> **Note**
> In this chapter and the following chapters, we repeatedly use Firebug for our explanations. After you have installed this Firefox add-on, you can open Firebug via the Tools menu or go to the context menu and choose Inspect Element with Firebug.

5.1.1   What Is a Selector?

In jQuery, the term *selector* refers to a specification for selecting one or several elements in the tree of a web page. You are probably familiar with it from Cascading Style Sheets (CSS), and in Extensible Markup Language (XML) there are also several techniques for selecting an element or a node.

> **Tip**
> If selectors are specified as argument type in any functions or methods in jQuery, you can write down anything that the jQuery constructor accepts, for example strings, elements, or lists with elements.

On the one hand, selectors in jQuery are easy to apply. Plus you as reader probably already have knowledge of CSS, so you will know the basics of selectors already. On the other hand, the specific selectors in jQuery are extremely powerful. This makes them a bit more complex, or more appropriately, more extensive. For that reason, discussing them in a separate chapter is appropriate.

5.1.2   What Are Filters?

In addition to selectors, jQuery works with **filters**. These are used to limit an already selected group of elements with regard to further conditions. For example, if you have used a selector to select all images of the web page as elements, you can then filter the set so that you only get every second image. In older versions of the framework, a clear distinction existed between selectors and filters, but in newer versions, the term *selector* is used almost throughout, and *filter* appears only in the form of several methods. We follow suit and use the specific term filter only when it seems appropriate.

5.1.3 XPath as Basis

To understand how selectors and filters in jQuery work and comprehend the various tokens for describing the selectors and filters, it makes sense to take a closer look at the basics of navigating in trees. Let's take a *brief* look at XPath without going into too much detail with this rather complex XML technique.

The term *XML Path Language (XPath)* refers to a query language developed by W3C for addressing components in an XML document (or a tree/DOM in general). XPath is often seen for XML as what SQL is for databases—a universal query language that can be used in many situations.

> **Note**
>
> In jQuery, selectors and filters are a composition of classic CSS selectors and XPath. An extension of CSS (version 1.3) with an added subset *based on* XPath is perhaps a good description. True XPath selectors are available as plug-in in jQuery.

Basically, you can use XPath expressions[4] to address specific content in a document with a tree-like structure. The central concept involved in these selections is the tree or DOM.

Trees, Nodes, and Elements

Such a tree consists of nodes and axes that develop from a single root. The nodes of the tree are all elements[5] contained in it. The subelements contained in an element are child elements. The element superior to the child in the tree hierarchy is referred to as parent element.

All other node types belong to the same hierarchy level of the tree as the node that contains them. These are referred to as siblings.

Axes are seen as the trunk or the branches of the tree and also take into account the order of the element declarations (seen sequentially from the root of the tree). Accordingly, there are ancestors and descendants in the tree.

Let's take a look at some selected terms of XPath that refer to the elements in this way.

Table 5.1 **Selected XPath Terms**

Token	Addressed Nodes
Ancestor	All superior nodes. Refers to all ancestors of the current node in the tree, up to the root.
Child	All nodes that are directly subordinate to the current node.
Descendant	All nodes that are directly or indirectly subordinate to the current node.

4. As well as similarly structured selection techniques.

5. We are not going into the fine details of XPath regarding attributes, comments, namespaces, PIs, and so on. We are using the term elements in a universal sense.

Token	Addressed Nodes
Following	All nodes that follow the current node in the sequence of the tree.
Following sibling	All nodes that are on the same hierarchy level of the tree structure (siblings of the same parent node) and that follow the current node in the tree sequence.
Parent	The node directly superior to the current node.
Preceding	All nodes that precede the current node in the sequence of the tree.
Preceding sibling	All nodes that are on the same hierarchy level of the tree structure (siblings) and precede the current node in the tree sequence.

XPath also offers a mechanism with the name node test. A node test consists of an axis expression followed by two colons and then a test node. This designates all nodes that occur on the preceding axis. You can specify how to further limit a set of selected nodes (a filter). You find the same logic in jQuery, but only one colon is used as separator there and—as mentioned before—we then generally talk of a selector in newer versions for expressions that are composed of an (optional) preceding selector, a colon, and then a following filter. Ultimately, it is the effect that's important, and the uniform term emphasizes this.

In jQuery, selectors and filters are distinguished by type, although this distinction is also becoming increasingly less significant in the documentation. We are still going to introduce the selectors in the following section separated by topics, by first describing a group of selectors that logically belong together in one or two tables, followed by examples.

> **Note**
>
> Note that the grouping of the selectors used in this book is not standardized and there can be overlaps or some selectors may be sorted into other categories elsewhere. Our grouping arises from didactic rules and partly also my personal categorization. For the effect and application, it is irrelevant how the selectors are grouped.

5.2 The Basic Selectors and the Hierarchical Selectors

> **Note**
>
> You might need to use special characters in the jQuery selectors. In that case, the characters have to be masked via a preceding backslash (\), as usual in JavaScript.

The selection options grouped under **basic selectors** in jQuery correspond to the classic CSS selectors. Via an element, an ID, and so on, you access the components of a web page and as a result you get an element or array with elements.[6]

As mentioned in the context of XPath, you can also describe the position in a tree in terms of parent-child relationships, siblings, and ancestors or descendants. These relationships also occur in CSS.

This type of selection allows a very comfortable description of a group of elements that belong together in hierarchy levels. Some sources therefore refer to these selectors as **hierarchical selectors** and functionally distinguish them from the basic selectors. We do not examine the exact distinction between basic selectors and hierarchical selectors further in most cases; for their application, this is not necessary in any case.

Table 5.2   **Basic Selectors and Hierarchical Selectors**

Name	Description
`#id`	Specify an ID to get the specified element. Note the preceding #. Usually, you get exactly one element, as an ID should be unique within a document. But because of the error tolerance of the browsers, this uniqueness is not ensured in a document. Although jQuery can handle this situation, the page is full of errors, and then you cannot program properly. In that case, you might have to correct the document.
`element`	Specify a specific element as selector to get an array with all elements that match that name.
`.class`	An array with all elements whose class (the `class` attribute or a dynamically assigned class) matches the given class. Note the dot preceding the selector.
`*`	The universal selector. Selects all elements.
`selector1, selector2, ..., selectorN`	A combination of different selectors. You get an element or an array with all elements that match one of the specified conditions.
`ancestor descendant`	This hierarchical selection returns an element or an array with all elements that are descendants of the preceding ancestor in the tree. The elements selected via the second selector have to be descendents of the result of the first selector. This is also referred to as context-sensitive selectors because an element is selected if it lies within another element (context). In terms of notation, the descendant simply follows the ancestor element, separated by a space.

---

6. Strictly speaking, an array can also be only one element or even be empty.

Name	Description
`.class1 .class2`	This selection returns an element or an array of elements whose classes (the `class` attribute or dynamically assigned classes) match the given group of classes. The list of hits consists of the elements that were assigned both (or several) classes simultaneously. Note the preceding dot that indicates the class chaining. But this statement is somewhat tricky because it does not mean that an element has been assigned two or more classes as individual attributes, but that there is descendant nesting, so that the parent elements have been assigned the preceding classes. This is a special case of the hierarchical descendant rule.
`parent > child`	This variation of a hierarchical selection returns an element or array of all elements that are child elements of the selected parent element.
`prev + next`	In this case the element specified by the second selector has to be *immediately preceded* as sibling by the element that the first selector specifies. So, you get an element of the type `next` that is next to the element specified with `previous`. This is also a hierarchical selection.
`prev ~ siblings`	This further hierarchical variation of the selection returns an element or array of elements with *all* sibling elements following after the first specified element that correspond to the filtering of the second selector.

5.2.1   Examples

Note

Note that in the following examples, we mainly set CSS properties of elements in a web page because the effect is most clearly visible in the printed screenshots. But applying selectors and filters is by no means limited to these!

In each of the following examples, we work with the following HTML file that contains the main structures for allowing us to demonstrate the basic selectors and hierarchical selectors. To that purpose, the HTML files contain class assignments, IDs, child elements, descendants, and so on (ch5_1.html).

Listing 5.1   **The Basic Structure**

```
...
06   <script type="text/javascript"
07       src="lib/jquery-1.8.2.min.js"></script>
08   <script type="text/javascript"
09       src="lib/ch5_1_ready.js"></script>
10   </head>
11   <body>
12     <h1 class="c2">Basic Selectors</h1>
13     <div class="c1">
14       <span class="c1">
15         The example shows the effect of
16         <span class="c2">basic selectors</span>
17         in jQuery</span>
18       <div>
19         To demonstrate this, different
20         <span class="c1" class="c2">structures</span>
21         are nested.
22       </div>
23       <div>
24         <img src="images/i1.jpg" id="i1" />
25       </div>
26     </div>
27     <p class="c1">
28       <span class="c1" class="c2">First variant</span>
29     </p>
30     <img src="images/i2.jpg" id="i2"/>
31   </body>
32 </html>
```

Note that we are working with IDs and assigned classes in the HTML tags but are consciously not using any style sheets. Formatting with CSS is done dynamically with jQuery so that you can see the effect of the different selectors.

> **Note**
>
> Note the double use of the `class` attribute for two tags. This is generally not a good idea and in most browsers it would result in only the first class being used for CSS formatting[7] (the second class would be ignored). We are using the double notation in order to demonstrate the effect of a selector more clearly.

7. Which we are consciously avoiding here.

Basic Selectors

The example shows the effect of basic selectors in jQuery
To demonstrate this, different structures are nested.

First variant

Figure 5.1   The web page without any formatting.

> **Note**
>
> For the sake of clarity, we test only the effect of one selector at a time, so we are working with
> many little examples. The HTML files only change with regard to the name of the referenced
> JavaScript file that is structured corresponding to the name of the HTML file and a small text
> change. We are therefore not going to look at the HTML file any more or mention it explicitly.

So here is the first JavaScript file (ch5_1_ready.js).

Listing 5.2   **Selecting an ID**

```
01 $(function(){
02   $("#i2").css({
03     position: "absolute", top: "100px", left: "400px"
04   });
05 });
```

The listing should be self-explanatory. In this example, we are selecting the second image in the web page via its ID (as we have done several times already in this book). As an example, the jQuery code applies absolute positioning to the element.

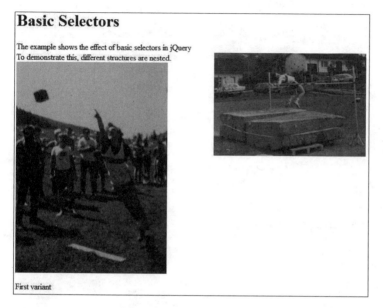

Figure 5.2   The second image has been selected and positioned.

Now let's take a quick look at selecting an **element type** (ch5_2_ready.js).

Listing 5.3   **Selecting an Element**

```
01 $(function(){
02   $("img").css({
03     width: "100px"
04   });
05 });
```

In line 2, all elements of exactly one type (in this case, img) are selected. Here, we precisely specify the width of both images in the web page as 100 pixels.

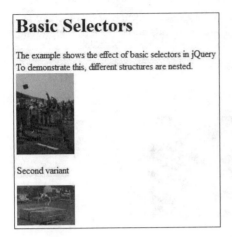

Figure 5.3   The images have been reduced.

Let's move on to selecting via a **class** (ch5_3_ready.js).

Listing 5.4   **Selecting a Class**

```
01 $(function(){
02   $(".c2").css({
03     background: "black", color:"white"
04   });
05 });
```

In the example, all elements in the HTML file that are marked with the class c2 are selected. In our HTML code, that is the header and a span container.

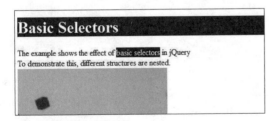

Figure 5.4   The elements marked with c2 have a black background and white text.

Up to now, it all fairly trivial. The next example has two classes as selector, separated by a space (ch5_4_ready.js).

Listing 5.5   **Specifying Two Classes**

```
01 $(function(){
02   $(".c1 .c2").css({
03     background: "black", color:"white"
04   });
05 });
```

At first glance, the example appears simple because there are several elements in the HTML file that are assigned the classes c1 and c2.

```
..
20      <span class="c1" class="c2">structures</span>
...
28      <span class="c1" class="c2">Fourth variant</span>
...
```

But the formatting is *not* applied to these. You could suspect this because a double use of an attribute for a tag is not recommended—as mentioned above—because it is not supported. But you may think that jQuery offers other possibilities in this respect. But this is not the case. So, it is not as trivial after all in this case. Instead, the selection selects the following text:

```
...
14      <span class="c1">
15         The example shows the effect of
16         <span class="c2">basic selectors</span>
..
```

Do you understand why this has to be the case? In the first two cases (lines 20 and 28), the two classes have been assigned for a tag, but this is not a descendant specification. In the second case, the span element is a descendant of the P element. The P element has the class c1, and the span element as descendant of the P element has the class c2. That is why this area is selected.

Let's demonstrate the **descendant rules** once more by specifying elements. To that purpose, we make an exception and also apply a second selector—the **universal selector.** This is fairly obvious, but the example includes it for the sake of completeness (ch5_5_ready.js).

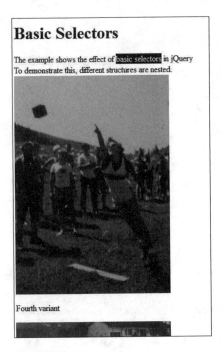

Basic Selectors

The example shows the effect of basic selectors in jQuery
To demonstrate this, different structures are nested.

Fourth variant

Figure 5.5   The selection may come as a surprise here.

Listing 5.6   **Universal Selector and Descendant**

```
01 $(function(){
02   $("*").css({
03     background: "gray", color:"yellow"
04   });
05   $("div span").css({
06     background: "black", color:"white"
07   });
08 });
```

First you see the universal selector in use, and there is nothing to explain here. In line 5, you
see the selection of all span areas that are within a div area. To make things clearer, the HTML
file also contains span areas that are not descendants of a div area. These are consequently not
selected.

Figure 5.6   Only the `span` areas within a `div` area have been formatted.

Now you will see a selection for a **parent-child relationship** (ch5_6_ready.js).

Listing 5.7   **Relationship Between Parents and Children**

```
01 $(function(){
02 $("div > img").css({
03   position: "absolute", top: "100px", left: "400px",
04   width:"50px"
05 });
06 });
```

We specify an image that has to be a child in a `div` area. In our example, this is the case with the second image.

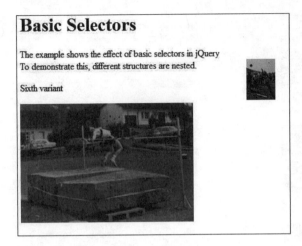

Figure 5.7   The image is the child element of the `div` area.

Our second-last example in this section concerns a **direct sibling relationship** (ch5_7_ready.js).

Listing 5.8   **The `div` Area Has to Follow the `span` Area**

```
01 $(function(){
02   $("span + div").css({
03     background: "black", color: "white"
04   });
05 });
```

In the selection, you specify that the `div` area has to follow the `span` area *directly* on the same level (as sibling).

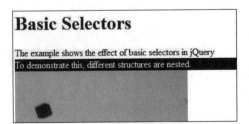

Figure 5.8   The `div` area that follows the `span` area is formatted.

In the last example in this section, you can see an alternative sibling relationship that also selects **indirect siblings** (ch5_8_ready.js).

Listing 5.9   **Sibling Relationship the Other Way Round**

```
01 $(function(){
02   $("span ~ div").css({
03     background: "black", color: "white"
04   });
05 });
```

In the selection, you specify that all `div` areas that follow the `span` area on the same level (as siblings) are selected.

Figure 5.9   The text and the image, in two `div` areas, have been selected and formatted.

5.2.2   Potential Pitfalls

When using all basic selectors and especially all hierarchy selectors, you need to watch out for some potential pitfalls that jQuery cannot fully compensate for.

For example, when specifying selectors, remember that the order of the notation in the source code can be relevant (in particular in connection with CSS value assignments where rules that follow can overwrite the preceding rule if the two contradict each other). But the sequence of notation in the `document.ready()` method can also be significant if you expect things too early that are only declared further down.

More serious when using hierarchy specifications is that you have to be careful because certain things might not work as you would probably expect. And in some cases it is not intuitively clear why. For example, you can specify a selection of a `div` element in a paragraph and basically also rules for a paragraph in a `div` element. But in the latter case it can happen that the selector does not seem to work. Yet strictly speaking, it is not the selector or jQuery that is limited or has an error; instead, you have to watch out for how the browser renders the DOM tree.[8] You can see that very clearly in Firebug.

Take a look at the following file ch5_9_error.html.

Listing 5.10   **A `div` Element in a Paragraph**

```
...
08    <script type="text/javascript">
09      $(function(){
10        $("p div").css("background", "red");
11      });
12    </script>
13  </head>
14  <body>
15    <p>
16      Many thanks.
17      <div>
18        I look forward to hearing from you.
19      </div>
20    </p>
21  </body>
22 </html>
```

If you try the example, the assignment of the CSS rules is not going to work. The reason is that the paragraph and the `div` container are no longer nested in one another in the actually rendered DOM (even though you have nested them in the HTML—but the standard does not permit this). In the paragraph, there is only the text, and the `div` container is arranged outside of the paragraph in the tree. Consequently, the whole descendant rule is no longer correct.

8. Which ultimately means that you can also have problems in pure CSS.

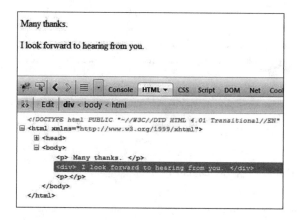

Figure 5.10   The `div` area was rendered out of the paragraph by the browser, and the selector can no longer take effect.

This behavior is not random, but instead is strictly based on the rules of HTML. Yet due to the principle of error tolerance, hardly anyone still adheres to this strict interpretation of the rules. But as you can see from our example, in some cases this laxness can go wrong.

5.3 Filtering Selectors

Filtering selectors in jQuery correspond roughly to the node tests in XPath. With these, you specify further conditions for a preceding group of elements, separated by a colon. In this section, we subdivide this filtering into several categories by their effect.

> **Tip**
>
> You can write down a filter without preceding selector. Then you just start with the colon. This applies the filter to all elements of the web page. You can also chain any filters. Just write them down one after the other, separated by colons.

5.3.1 Basic Filters

These are the basic filter selectors available in jQuery.

Table 5.3 **All Basic Filters**

Name	Description
`:first`	The first selected element from the preceding set of elements.
`:last`	The last selected element from the preceding set of elements.

Name	Description
`:not(selector)`	An array with all elements (that can, of course, also be empty) that do *not* match the selector. The elements that match the selector are filtered out.
`:even`	All elements in an indexed structure such as a table or list with an *even* index (starting at 0).
`:odd`	All elements in an indexed structure such as a table or list with an *odd* index.
`:eq(index)`	A single element that is specified via an index.
`:gt(index)`	An array with all elements that are greater than the specified index (`gt`, greater than).
`:lt(index)`	An array with all elements that are less than the specified index (`lt`, less than).
`:header`	An array with all headers (`h1`, `h2`, `h3`, and so on).
`:animated`	An array with all currently animated elements.
`:focus`	Selects element if it is currently focused.

For the examples, we once again work with the same HTML file as the basis each time and only change the reference to each JavaScript file used and accordingly the name of the HTML file (ch5_10.html).

Listing 5.11   The Basic File for Various Filters

```
...
08    <script type="text/javascript"
09        src="lib/ch5_10_ready.js"></script>
10    </head>
11    <body>
12      <h1>Robert Lee Frost</h1>
13      <h3>(1874-1963)</h3>
14      <h4>US poet</h4>
15      <div>The brain is a wonderful organ.</div>
16      <div>It starts working</div>
17      <div>the moment you get up in the morning</div>
18      <div>and does not stop</div>
19      <div>until you get into the office.</div>
20      <h1>Franz Kafka</h1>
21      <h3>(1883-1924)</h3>
22      <h4>German author</h4>
23      <h2>Life</h2>
24      <div>A continual distraction</div>
25      <div>that does not even allow us to reflect</div>
```

```
26   <div>on that from which we are distracted.</div>
27   </body>
28   </html>
```

In the example, you can see a web page with a few headers and a structure comprising several div areas.

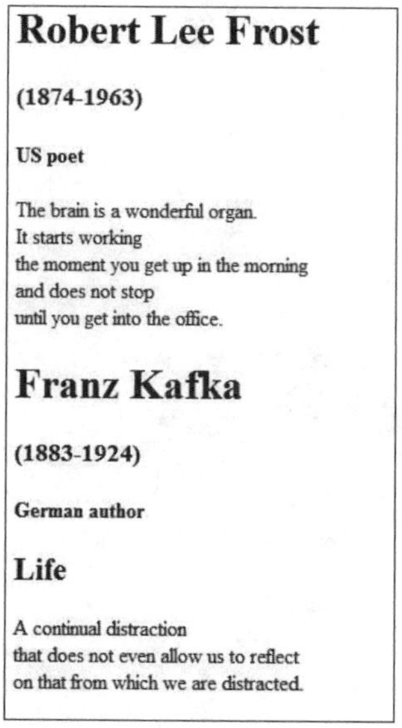

Robert Lee Frost

(1874-1963)

US poet

The brain is a wonderful organ.
It starts working
the moment you get up in the morning
and does not stop
until you get into the office.

Franz Kafka

(1883-1924)

German author

Life

A continual distraction
that does not even allow us to reflect
on that from which we are distracted.

Figure 5.11   The page without formatting.

To keep it simple, we are not going to apply all filters in one example, but only a maximum of three filters at a time.

Let's first look at the filter for selecting **animated elements**. In principle, that is the hardest situation that we are discussing in this section. First we need to animate elements in the web page before we can use the filter. This is also done with jQuery itself (ch5_10_ready.js).

Listing 5.12   **Selecting Animated Elements**

```
01 $(function(){
02   animation();
03   $(":animated").css({
04     background: "black", color: "white",
05     textAlign: "center"
06   });
07 });
```

```
08 function animation(){
09  $("h2").slideToggle("slow", animation);
10 }
```

The example shows several interesting things. For one, the filter in line 3 itself. It is explicitly used *without a preceding selector*. It selects all animated elements in the web page.

Specifically, we animate all elements of the type h2, which in our example is only one element. We center this element and change its background and foreground colors.

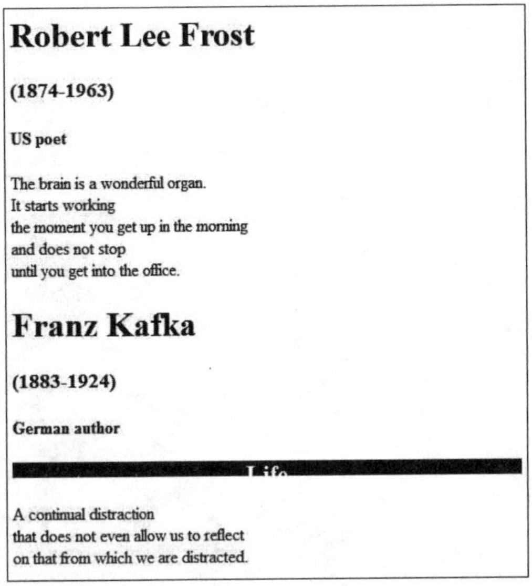

Robert Lee Frost

(1874-1963)

US poet

The brain is a wonderful organ.
It starts working
the moment you get up in the morning
and does not stop
until you get into the office.

Franz Kafka

(1883-1924)

German author

Life

A continual distraction
that does not even allow us to reflect
on that from which we are distracted.

Figure 5.12   The level 2 header is animated and formatted.

To animate the element, we use the jQuery slideToggle() method. Note that we are using a recursive call here, so the animation runs permanently. This causes the header to be incessantly hidden and shown, but this is of secondary importance here.

The important point is that the first call of the animation function must happen *before* the filter is applied. Note line 2. Otherwise, the header will not be perceived as animated at the time when the filter is applied, although it is animated in the web page.[9]

Let's now look at the selectors for selecting the first and last element and also the selection of all headers (ch5_11_ready.js).

9. This kind of situation was mentioned above in the context of potential pitfalls of selectors and filters.

Listing 5.13 **The First and Last Element of the Type** `div` **and All Headers**

```
01 $(function(){
02   $("div:first").css({
03     background: "black", color: "white",
04     textAlign: "center"
05   });
06   $("div:last").css({
07     background: "yellow", color: "blue",
08     textAlign: "right"
09   });
10   $(":header").css({
11     background: "lightgray"
12   });
13 });
```

The effects of the three filters are probably clear. The first and last element of the type `div` and all headers are selected, and each of them is formatted differently.

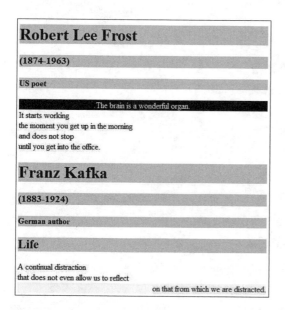

Figure 5.13 The effects are obvious.

Let's look at how you can select elements with an **odd** and **even index** (ch5_12_ready.js).

Listing 5.14　**Selecting Odd and Even Indexes**

```
01 $(function(){
02   $("div:odd").css({
03     background: "black", color: "white",
04     textAlign: "right"
05   });
06     $("div:even").css({
07     background: "yellow", color: "blue",
08     textAlign: "left"
09   });
10 });
```

In the preceding selector, we select all elements of the type div in the web page and then use the filters to distinguish between odd and even indexes.[10]

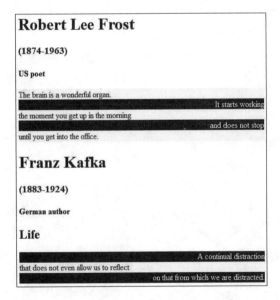

Figure 5.14　Alternating formatting of odd and even indexes.

Now we select by *explicitly specifying* an **index** or **index area** (ch5_13_ready.js).

Listing 5.15　**Specifying an Index Area or Index**

```
01 $(function(){
02   $("div:gt(1)").css({
```

10. Note that the indexes start at 0.

```
03    fontStyle: "italic", textAlign: "center"
04  });
05  $("div:lt(3)").css({
06    textDecoration: "underline"
07  });
08  $("div:eq(3)").css({
09    background: "#9999ff", textAlign: "right"
10  });
11  });
```

As you can see, all div elements from the index 1 onward (excluding it) are displayed in italics and centered (in other words, from the third element onward). Up to index 2 (including it), they are underlined. For the third element, both rules apply, and they only specify additive formatting.

The fourth element gets a background color and is aligned on the right. As the rule is the last rule that is written down, the right-alignment overwrites the centered alignment that would still apply from the gt() filter.

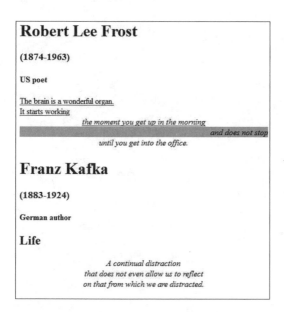

Figure 5.15 Selection via exactly one index or index areas.

Finally, let's look at **negation** via not(), which leads to an exclusion of elements (ch5_14_ready.js).

Listing 5.16   **Exclusion of Elements**

```
01 $(function(){
02   $(":header:not(h2)").css({
03     fontStyle: "italic", textAlign: "center"
04   });
05 });
```

As mentioned earlier, you can also **chain** any filters. You simply write the various filters behind one another, separated by colons, as also demonstrated here. First, we select all headers, and then we exclude all headers of the type h2.

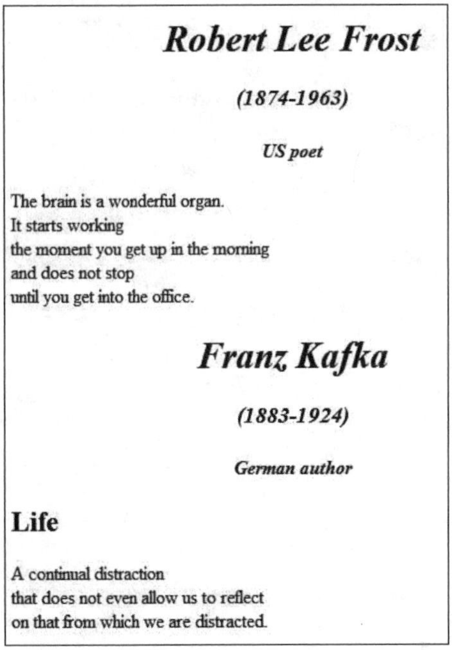

> ### *Robert Lee Frost*
>
> #### *(1874-1963)*
>
> ##### *US poet*
>
> The brain is a wonderful organ.
> It starts working
> the moment you get up in the morning
> and does not stop
> until you get into the office.
>
> ### *Franz Kafka*
>
> #### *(1883-1924)*
>
> ##### *German author*
>
> **Life**
>
> A continual distraction
> that does not even allow us to reflect
> on that from which we are distracted.

Figure 5.16   All headers except those of type h2 are in italics and centered.

5.3.2   Content Filters

For a request, the content of an element can be very interesting. Content filters in jQuery enable you to select an element by assessing content; but only fairly generally.

Table 5.4 **Content Filters**

Name	Description
:contains(*Text*)	An array with all elements that contain the specified text.
:empty	An array with all elements that do not have child elements, including text nodes. These are referred to as empty elements.
:has(*Selector*)	All elements that contain at least one element of the type of the specified selector. The element does not have to be a direct child but can also appear in deeper structures.
:parent	All parent elements. This means the elements have child elements, including pure text nodes. The opposite of an empty element.

Let's apply the content filter for selecting text to the HTML page of the previous examples.

Listing 5.17 **Selection Based on the Word** *You*

```
01 $(function(){
02    $("div:contains(you)").css({ background:'cyan' });
03 });
```

You can see that this selects the div elements that contain the word *you*.

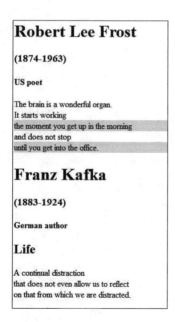

Robert Lee Frost

(1874-1963)

US poet

The brain is a wonderful organ.
It starts working
the moment you get up in the morning
and does not stop
until you get into the office.

Franz Kafka

(1883-1924)

German author

Life

A continual distraction
that does not even allow us to reflect
on that from which we are distracted.

Figure 5.17 The third and fifth div areas contain the word *you*.

For the other three filters we need a slightly different web page structure. It is going to look like Listing 5.18 (ch5_16.html).

Listing 5.18 **The New Basis File**

```
...
08    <script type="text/javascript"
09        src="lib/ch5_16_ready.js"></script>
10    </head>
11    <body>
12      <div>I love deadlines. I like the
13        <span>whooshing</span>sound they make
14      </div>
15      <div>as they fly by.</div><hr/>
16      <div>Douglas Adams</div>
17      <div><span>(1952-2001)</span></div>
18      <span>English writer and dramatist </span>
19    </body>
20    </html>
```

Now we have span areas within div areas, allowing us to demonstrate has(). Plus line 15 contains an empty element of the type hr, to illustrate the effect of empty and parent. We do this in the JavaScript file ch5_16_ready.js.

Listing 5.19 **Different Content Filters**

```
01  $(function(){
02    $("div:has(span)").css({
03      background: 'cyan'
04    });
05    $(":empty").css({
06      width: '200px'
07    });
08    $(":not(:parent)").css({
09      height: '5px'
10    });
11  });
```

In line 2, we select all div areas that contain a span area somewhere. This will be the case for two div areas. In line 5, all empty elements are selected. In our example, that is just the separator line. Its width is specified. In line 8, we select the separator line once more. This additional selection is, of course, unnecessary if we have already filtered out the element with empty. But you can see the effect of parent. We are selecting all elements that are not parents (and those are empty elements). The formatting here adds a height specification to the width specification for the separator line.

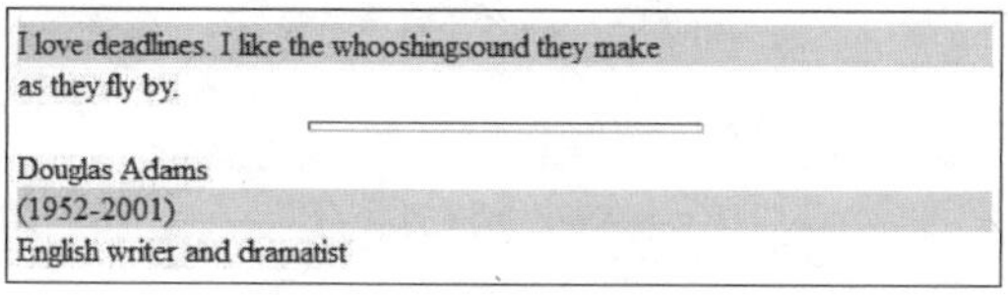

Figure 5.18   Of parents and children.

5.3.3   Visibility Filters

Table 5.5   **Visibility Filters**

Name	Type
:hidden	Selects all hidden elements in a web page. At first glance, this is a rather simple description, but you want to watch out for some finer points. Elements can be hidden within a web page for various reasons: • The CSS property `display` can have the value `none`. • There are hidden form fields (`type="hidden"`). • The width and height are set to the value `0`. • An ancestor element can be hidden, and then all children contained in it are also not displayed. Plus there is the CSS property `visibility: hidden` and setting the transparency via `opacity: 0`. Watch out, these are *not* counted as hidden in jQuery, contrary to what you might expect, because they still take up the same space in the web page as they do in the visible state. An element only counts as hidden in the sense of this filter or jQuery if it does not take up any space in the web page.[11] Then you also need to take into account how elements can be classed if they are hidden via an animation. They are considered visible so long as the end of the animation has not yet been reached. Vice versa, in case of an animation for showing a hidden element: The element counts as visible or no longer hidden immediately after the animation starts.
:visible	All visible elements in exactly the opposite sense of the explanation for `hidden`.

Let's take a look at an example (ch5_17.html).

11. In jQuery versions prior to 1.3.2, it was handled differently.

Listing 5.20 **Four Images and a Button**

```
...
08   <script type="text/javascript"
09       src="lib/ch5_17_ready.js">
10   </script>
11   </head>
12   <body>
13       <img src="images\i1.jpg" />
14       <img src="images\i2.jpg" />
15       <img src="images\i3.jpg" />
16       <img src="images\i4.jpg" />
17       <br/>
18       <button>Switch</button>
19   </body>
20   </html>
```

The example shows a web page with four images and a button. Everything of interest happens in the JavaScript file ch5_17_ready.js.

Listing 5.21 **Working with** :hidden **and** :visible

```
01 $(function(){
02   $("img:odd").css({
03     display: 'none'
04   });
05   $("button:eq(0)").click(function(){
06     $("img:visible").hide('slow');
07     $("img:hidden").css({
08       display: 'inline'
09     });
10   });
11 });
```

In line 2, all images with odd index are hidden. So, they will be selected in the following test for :hidden.

In the reaction method to clicking the button (note the eq filter), the currently hidden images should now be shown and the visible images hidden (in other words, a toggle effect).

Now remember how elements are perceived that are hidden via an animation. They are perceived as visible as long so the end of animation has not yet been reached. You can use this behavior really well in combination with the visibility filters to save yourself lots of programming work.

The deciding factor is the timing. In line 6, the previously visible elements—identified via :visible—are made invisible (but animatedly, and that takes a certain time). If the script flow reaches line 7 and selects the elements that are hidden (identified via `:hidden`), the elements that are visible on triggering the click event are still perceived as visible by jQuery! This saves having to work with queries and decision structures if you want to switch between a hidden and visible state for various elements.[12]

Figure 5.19   The original state of the page.

If you click the button, you will see that the previously invisible images are immediately shown.[13] The visible images are slowly faded out. Once they are fully hidden, the space is taken up by the neighboring images (but only then).

Figure 5.20   Now the other two images are visible.

12. Which is also a possibility.

13. You can also animate this without jeopardizing the functionality of the example.

5.3.4   Child Filters

Child filters always act based on a parent element and filter out the children that match certain factors.

Table 5.6   **Child Filters**

Name	Description
`:nth-child(index/even/odd/` *comparison*`)`	The elements that are the nth child of their parent or have an even or odd index. Note that the indexing does *not* start at 0 (as for arrays) but at 1.
`:first-child`	An array with all first child elements. Unlike `first`, this can select *several* child elements.
`:last-child`	An array with all last child elements. Unlike `last`, this can select *several* child elements.
`:only-child`	An array with all "only children," there are no other children for the parent element apart from one child.

Let's take a look at how selecting child elements works in practice (ch5_18.html).

Listing 5.22   **Nested Containers**

```
...
08    <script type="text/javascript"
09        src="lib/ch5_18_ready.js"></script>
10    </head>
11    <body>
12      <div>
13        <span>I love deadlines. </span>
14        <span>I like the whooshing sound
15          they make as they fly by.</span>
16      </div>
17      <div>
18        <span>Douglas Adams </span>
19        <span>(1952-2001) </span>
20        <span>English writer and dramatist </span>
21      </div>
22    </body>
23 </html>
```

In the example, you can see two `div` areas that are structured with `span` elements. This means that there are child elements in the `div` areas and you can select these children. In the first div area, there are two span areas as child elements, and in the second div area, there are three. We want to select an array with all first children and an array with all last children. By chaining further filters, you can then select individual elements from this, but we just want to format all first children differently from the last children. Other child elements remain unaffected. For example, you could do it as follows (ch5_18_ready.js).

Listing 5.23   **First and Last Children**

```
01 $(function(){
02   $("div span:first-child").css({
03     background: 'red',  color: 'white',
04   });
05   $("div span:last-child").css({
06     background: '#ddd',  color: '#111'
07   });
08 });
```

All first span areas in the various div areas are selected (line 2) or all last span elements (line 5). In the second div area, there are three span areas. The second span area is explicitly not selected because it is neither part of the first nor last child elements.

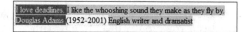

Figure 5.21   The first and last child elements have been selected.

To demonstrate the child filters :nth-child() and :only-child, we slightly change the HTML file structure (ch5_19.html).

Listing 5.24   **Nested Containers**

```
...
12 <div>
13   <span>I <span>love</span> deadlines. </span>
14   <span>I like the <span>whooshing</span
15     sound they make as they fly by.</span>
16 </div>
...
```

In the example, you can see basically the same structures as in the previous example. The only difference is that one word was enclosed in an inner span area within the first two span areas of the first div area. And that means that the surrounding span area has exactly one child element in each case and can therefore be selected via only-child (ch5_19_ready.js).

Listing 5.25   **Selected Children and Only Children**

```
01 $(function(){
02   $("div span:nth-child(2)").css({
03     background: '#000', color: '#fff'
04   });
05     $("span:only-child").css({
06       letterSpacing:'0.8em'
07   });
08 });
```

In line 2, we select the second child in the underlying array. Note, as mentioned earlier, that the indexing does not start at 0 as usual, but at 1! In line 5, you can see the selection of all elements of the type span that contain exactly one child element.

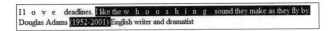

Figure 5.22   The second child in each case and only children.

5.3.5   Attribute Filters

Attribute filters are among the most useful filters in jQuery. You can use them to filter either the presence or the content of attributes for HTML tags or elements. As for most filters, it is surely a highlight that they are easy to apply.[14] You enclose attribute filters in square brackets.

Table 5.7   **Attribute Filters**

Name	Description
[attribute]	All elements that have the specified attribute, irrespective of the value.
[attribute=*value*]	All elements that have the specified attribute and where the value matches the specified test value.
[attribute!=*value*]	All elements that have the specified attribute and where the value does not match the specified test value.
[attribute^=*value*]	All elements that have the specified attribute and where the value begins with the specified test value.
[attribute$=*value*]	All elements that have the specified attribute and where the value ends with the specified test value.

14. In contrast to true regular expressions that tend to cause some people headache. But even XPath is not totally straightforward.

Name	Description
[attribute*=*value*]	All elements that have the specified attribute and where the specified test value is contained in the attribute value in any place.
[attribute~=*value*]	All elements that have the specified attribute and where the value matches the specified test value or where the specified attribute appears as word. A word is a text passage separated from other characters by a space.
[attribute|=*value*]	All elements that have the specified attribute and where the value matches the specified test value or starts with that value followed by a hyphen.
[AttributeFilter1] [AttributeFilter2]... [AttributeFilterN]	The filtered values have to match all conditions of the various filters.

Note

In jQuery versions prior to version 1.3, the token @ used to be written before the attribute name or at least this was still permitted. This was motivated by XPath, but now it is no longer valid.

Let's use two examples to demonstrate the effects (ch5_20.html).

Listing 5.26 **This Site Contains Tags with Attributes**

```
...
08    <script type="text/javascript"
09        src="lib/ch5_20_ready.js"></script>
10    </head>
11    <body>
12      <a href="http://www.rjs.de" target="new">
13        Homepage</a><br/>
14      <a href="http://blog.rjs.de">Blog</a><br/>
15      <a href="http://www.ajax-net.de" target="new-2">
16        AJAX-Portal</a> <br/>
17      <a href="http://fliegerblog.rjs.de" target="new3">
18        Blog 2</a>
19    </body>
20    </html>
```

As you can see, this site contains four tags that have attributes. Specifically, we want to look at the hyperlinks and the target attribute there. The selections in ch5_20_ready.js look like Listing 5.27.

Listing 5.27   **Checking for Attributes**

```
01 $(function(){
02   $("[target]").css({
03     textDecoration: 'none'
04   });
05   $("[target|='new']").css({
06     background: 'gray', color: 'yellow'
07   });
08 });
```

In line 2, we are only checking whether the attribute target is present at all. All hyperlinks where this is the case are no longer underlined. That means all hyperlinks except the second one.

In line 5, we check if the value of the attribute target starts with the token new and if the value string then ends or is followed only by a hyphen (this filter is also referred to as prefix filter). This explicitly *excludes* the link from line 17 of the HTML file (<a href="http://fliegerblog.rjs.de" target="new3">). The value of target does start with new in this case, but the next character is not a hyphen.

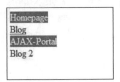

Figure 5.23   Different attribute filters checking for target.

Let's test the other filters with a new web page. We reference images and check them for the alt attribute (ch5_21.html).

Listing 5.28   **Five Images in a Web Page with Specification of Alternative Text**

```
...
08   <script type="text/javascript"
09       src="lib/ch5_21_ready.js"></script>
10   </head>
11   <body>
12   <img src="images/i5.jpg"
13       alt="Sheep in the meadow" />
14   <img src="images/i6.jpg"
15       alt="Different perspective - Sheep in the meadow" />
16   <img src="images/i7.jpg" alt="Football" />
17   <img src="images/i8.jpg"
18       alt="Flying kites on the meadow" />
```

```
19   <img src="images/i9.jpg"
20      alt="I love my kite" />
21   </body>
22 </html>
```

In this web page, you have the references to five images that all have natively the same size. Without formatting, the images are simply displayed next one another.

Figure 5.24   Without formatting, the page looks like this.

Let's now see what happens in ch5_21_ready.js.

Listing 5.29 **Selections Based on Value of `alt` Attribute**

```
01 $(function(){
02   $("img[alt^='Sheep']").css({
03     border: 'solid', borderWidth: '10px'
04   });
05   $("img[alt$='meadow']").css({
06     position: 'relative', top: '100px'
07   });
08   $("img[alt*='Sheep']").css({
09     width: '100px'
10   });
11   $("img[alt~='kite']").css({
12     position: 'relative', left: '-100px'
13   });
14 });
```

In line 2, we are checking all attributes `alt`—limited to elements of the type `img`, which is really not necessary here—for the token `Sheep`. This appears twice. But by using the symbol `^`, we specify that it has to be at the beginning of the value string, and that is only the case in the first occurrence.

The search in line 5 is interpreted as successful if the token `meadow` is at the end of the value string: this is the case in images 1, 2, and 4.

In the search in line 8, the token `Sheep` just needs to appear somewhere in the value string; this is the case in images 1 and 2.

The selection in line 11 requires for a match that the token `kite` appears as single word. This is only the case in the fifth image. In the fourth image, the token is part of a longer word and therefore not a hit.

Figure 5.25   The effect of the selections and the resulting formatting.

5.3.6   Filters for Form Elements and Form Filters

The names of these filters show what we discuss next: With these filters you can set special selection criteria for form elements. In earlier versions of jQuery, the two types of filters were listed separately. This distinction has now been removed in the documentation for the current version, but for the sake of clarity we still discuss them under separate headings here.

Filters for form elements serve to select one element or a group of elements based on the type of the form element, whereas **form filters** filter the element via its state.

Filters for Form Elements

To select a form element, you could, of course, in many cases use a filter on the `input` element and a more precise specification via the attribute `type` and attribute filters. But in jQuery, special filters allow an even more compact notation.

Table 5.8   **Filters for Form Elements**

Name	Type
`:button`	An array with all buttons (the element `button` and input elements of the type `button`)
`:checkbox`	An array with all input elements of the type `checkbox`
`:file`	An array with all input elements of the type `file`
`:image`	An array with all input elements of the type `image`
`:input`	An array with all input elements (all form elements of the type `input`, `textarea`, `select`, and `button`)

Name	Type
:password	An array with all input elements of the type `password`
:radio	An array with all input elements of the type `radio`
:reset	An array with all input elements of the type `reset`
:submit	An array with all input elements of the type `submit`
:text	An array with all input elements of the type `text`

Caution

Watch out for the exact representation of form elements in the DOM of a browser. For example, to format a check box or an option field, you usually need to address the parent element because the descriptive text is another node.

Let's once again test some of the filters in an example (ch5_22.html).

Listing 5.30 **Filters in Connection with Forms**

```
...
08   <script type="text/javascript"
09       src="lib/ch5_22_ready.js"></script>
10   </head>
11   <body>
12     <form>
13       <table width="500">
14         <tr>
15           <td>First name</td>
16           <td><input type="text" name="fn" /></td>
17           <td>Surname</td>
18           <td><input type="text" name="sn" /></td>
19         </tr>
20         <tr>
21           <td>User ID</td>
22           <td><input type="text" name="user" /></td>
23           <td>Password</td>
24           <td><input type="password" name="pw" /></td>
25         </tr>
26         <tr>
27           <td></td>
28           <td><input type="checkbox" name="t&cs" /></td>
29           <td></td>
30           <td><input type="checkbox" name="nl" /></td>
31         </tr>
```

```
32      </table>
33        <input type="submit" /><input type="reset" />
34      </form>
35    </body>
36  </html>
```

In this example, you can see a form that consists of some text input fields, a password field, two check boxes, two buttons, and that it is structured with a table. Here is the external JavaScript file ch5_22_ready.js.

Listing 5.31   **The Specific Form Filters**

```
01 $(function(){
02   $(":reset").css({
03     background: 'red',
04     color: 'yellow'
05   });
06   $(":submit").css({
07     background: 'green',
08     color: 'white'
09   });
10   $(":text").css({
11     background: 'green',
12     color: 'yellow'
13   });
14   $(":password").css({
15     background: 'blue',
16     color: 'white'
17   });
18   $(":checkbox:first").parent().append(
19     "Accept Terms and Conditions").css({
20     background: "yellow", border: "1px red solid"
21   });
22   $(":checkbox:last").parent().append("Newsletter").
23     css({ background: "yellow", border: "1px red solid"
24   });
25   });
```

The filtering regarding the two buttons, the text input fields, and the password field probably does not require any further explanation by now. But let's take a closer look at the filtering of the check boxes in lines 18–22.

As you can see, the filters are chained; there is a filter for form elements followed by a basic filter (:checkbox:first or :checkbox:last).

This selects the desired check box in each case. So far, so good. But it does not make sense to format this element because we have only selected the tiny check box itself. Here, the CSS formatting does not have any visible result. So we go to the parent element via the method `parent()`.[15]

Theoretically, we could now already apply the CSS formatting to this element. But that would only add a frame and background to the empty space after the check box. Up to now, the check boxes are not yet labeled. So, we use `append()` to insert a text node into this area. Now, the whole area gets CSS formatting.

Figure 5.26 The formatted form.

Form Filters

Next, let's move on to the filters via which you can select form elements based on their state.

Table 5.9 **Form Filters**

Name	Description
`:checked`	All elements that are checked
`:disabled`	All disabled elements
`:enabled`	All enabled elements
`:focus`	An array with all input elements that are currently focused
`:selected`	All selected elements

Caution

Note that these filters in particular are only partially suitable for formatting elements with CSS. In contrast, filters such as `:checked` or `:selected` are useful if you want to check the number of elements with a certain state based on a filter or if you want to program a reaction based on a state, without any great programming effort involved.

Listing 5.32 demonstrates these filters (ch5_23.html).

---

15. We could, of course, also have used a filter to achieve such a selection.

Listing 5.32   **Two Check Boxes**

```
...
08    <script type="text/javascript"
09        src="lib/ch5_23_ready.js"></script>
10   </head>
11   <body>
12     <form>
13       <table width="500">
14         <tr>
15           <td>Accept Terms and Conditions</td>
16           <td><input type="checkbox" name="agb" /></td>
17           <td>Newsletter</td>
18           <td><input type="checkbox" name="nl" /></td>
19         </tr>
20       </table>
21         <input type="submit" /><input type="reset" />
22     </form>
23   </body>
24 </html>
```

Here, we have a little form with two check boxes. Note that unlike the previous example the labels have already been written down via HTML in each case in the table cell before the check box. We now want the background color of the corresponding label to change depending on whether a user checks a check box. This is what we do (ch5_23_ready.js).

Listing 5.33   **Filtering Based on Selection State**

```
01 $(function(){
02   $(":checkbox:first").click(function(){
03     if ($(":checkbox:first:checked").length == 1)
04       $("td:first").css({
05         background: "yellow",
06       })
07     else
08       $("td:first").css({
09         background: "white",
10       })
11   });
12   $(":checkbox:last").click(function(){
13     if ($(":checkbox:last:checked").length == 1)
14       $("td:eq(2)").css({
15         background: "yellow",
16       })
17     else
18       $("td:eq(2)").css({
19         background: "white",
```

```
20      })
21   });
22 });
```

In the source code, we register for each check box a reaction mechanism in response to a click by the user (lines 2 and 12). This makes sense because each click switches the state of the check box from checked to unchecked and vice versa. But how can we tell which state the user has switched to?

The solution is this: We check how many elements have the state `checked`. If you look at the selection `:checkbox:first:checked` in line 3, this can only be exactly one element or none (because of `first` and following the same pattern in line 13 `last`). And we can easily check this by comparing to the value 1. The result is what we wanted. If the check box has been selected by clicking it, the label gets a background color. If the check box was deselected via a click, the label's background color is reset.

Figure 5.27   The first check box has been selected.

5.4 Filter Methods

In direct connection with filtering selectors that are passed as parameters to `jQuery()`, the framework also offers various filter methods. The fundamental difference with filters/selectors is in the way they are applied. These are methods, and they are called via dot notation and the preceding object, not passed to `jQuery()` as parameters in the selector. Otherwise, the effect of the filter methods usually derives clearly from the filters listed here. So, we do not provide examples for the majority of these methods.

5.4.1 eq()

Via the method `eq()` you can select exactly one element from the underlying object via an index.

5.4.2 not()

The method `not()` filters those elements out of a group of elements that correspond to the selector. In other words, they are not contained in the found set.

5.4.3 `first()` and `last()`

Similar as with the filter selectors, you use `first()` to select the first matched element and `last()` to select the last matched element from a set of elements. The methods are really simply but were only introduced in jQuery 1.4.

5.4.4   `slice()`

The method `slice()` does not exist as filter of the same name. It filters all elements from a starting value onward (an index). You can also specify an optional end value. In other words, you are specifying an **range of indexes** with this filter method. Let's use an example to make it clearer (ch5_24 .html).

Listing 5.34   **Filtering an Index Range**

```
...
08      <script type="text/javascript"
09         src="lib/ch5_24_ready.js"></script>
10   </head>
11   <body>
12     <div>When I was young,</div>
13      <div>I thought that money</div>
14      <div>was the most important thing in life.</div>
15      <div>Now that I am old,</div>
16      <div> I know:</div>
17      <div>It is.</div>
18   </body>
19 </html>
```

In the example, we want to filter `div` areas according to their filter, as follows (ch5_24_ready.js).

Listing 5.35   **Applying** `slice()`

```
01 $(function(){
02   $("div:contains('I')").slice(2).css({
03     "color": "yellow", background:"red"
04   });
05 });
```

In line 2, all `div` areas that contain the token `I` are selected. They are selected from the index 2 onward (so from the third `div` element of the selector's found set).

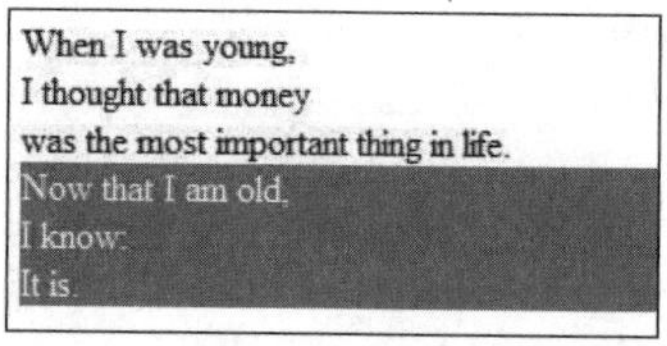

Figure 5.28   Filtering elements corresponding to an index range via `slice()`.

> **Caution**
>
> Do you understand the third hit? As you can see, the token (in our case, `I`) can also be part of a word, not just a word in itself.

5.4.5 `filter()`

The function of the `filter()` method is fairly self-explanatory. It removes all elements that do not correspond to the filter specified as parameter. In addition to a selector, you can specify a function in form of a callback or an anonymous function as parameter.

The `filter()` method also does not exist as a filter with the same name (ch5_25.html).

Listing 5.36   **The Basis of the Filtering**

```
...
08    <script type="text/javascript"
09        src="lib/ch5_25_ready.js"></script>
10  </head>
11  <body>
12    <div>
13      One <span>Ring</span> to
14      <span class="yes">rule</span> them all,
15      One Ring to <span>find</span> them,
16      One Ring to <span class="yes">bring</span>
17      them <span>all</span>
18      and in the <span>darkness</span>
19      bind them
20    </div>
21  </body>
22  </html
```

In the example, we want to filter `span` areas according to their assigned class. We do this as follows (ch5_25_ready.js).

Listing 5.37   **Using** `filter()`

```
01 $(function(){
02   $("span").filter(".yes").css("background", "gray");
03 });
```

In the example, we are filtering from all `span` areas exactly two areas that have the class yes. The following formatting is applied only to these.

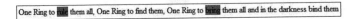

One Ring to rule them all, One Ring to find them, One Ring to bring them all and in the darkness bind them

Figure 5.29   Two `span` areas match the filter.

5.4.6 `is()`

With the Boolean method `is()` you can test if an expression specified as parameter matches the preceding selection. In case of a hit, it returns `true`, otherwise `false`.

Again we want to look at an example, and for a change we are using a slightly different notation—a direct integration of `document.ready()` (ch5_26.html).[16]

Listing 5.38   **Filtering with** `is()`

```
...
08     <script type="text/javascript">
09       $(document).ready(function(){
10         $("button").click(function(){
11           if ($(this).is(":first-child")) {
12             alert("First button");
13           }
14         });
15       });
16     </script>
17   </head>
18   <body>
19     <button>OK</button>
20     <button>Not OK</button>
21   </body>
22 </html>
```

In the example, you have two buttons that both trigger a click event. In the reaction method in line 11, we check via `is(":first-child")` if the triggering element was the first child element. Only then will the message box be displayed.

---

16. Just so you don't forget that you can also work like this in jQuery.

Figure 5.30   The first button was clicked.

5.4.7 map()

With the method map(), you can translate a set of elements in the jQuery object into a set of values in a jQuery array.[17] Then you can apply the specific methods of an array such as get() to it. As a parameter, you specify a callback or an anonymous function.

> **Note**
>
> The method is in direct connection to the jQuery data type Map.

Listing 5.39   **Mapping a jQuery Object into a jQuery Array (ch5_27.html)**

```
...
08    <script type="text/javascript">
09      $(document).ready(function(){
10        $("button").click(function(){
11          var data = $("input").map(function(){
12            return $(this).val();
13          });
14          $("#output").text(data.get().join(" "));
15        });
16      });
17    </script>
18  </head>
19  <body>
20    <table>
21      <form>
22        <tr>
23          <td>Surname:</td>
24          <td><input/></td>
25        </tr>
26        <tr>
```

17. In programming, this is referred to as *mapping* (hence the name).

```
27            <td>First name:</td>
28            <td><input/></td>
29          </tr>
30          <tr>
31            <td>Age:</td>
32            <td><input/></td>
33          </tr>
34        </form>
35      </table>
36      <button>OK</button>
37      <h2>Data you have entered:</h2>
38      <div id="output" />
39    </body>
40  </html>
```

The example describes a web page with a form. If the user clicks the button, the elements that represent the three input fields are mapped into a jQuery array. Strictly speaking, the values contained in the input fields are mapped using the val() method.

Listing 5.40   **Returning the Values in the Input Fields**

```
11 var data = $("input").map(function(){
12     return $(this).val();
13 });
```

Via get(), we get in line 14 the elements (values) from the array data. These are then joined to a string with join() and output.

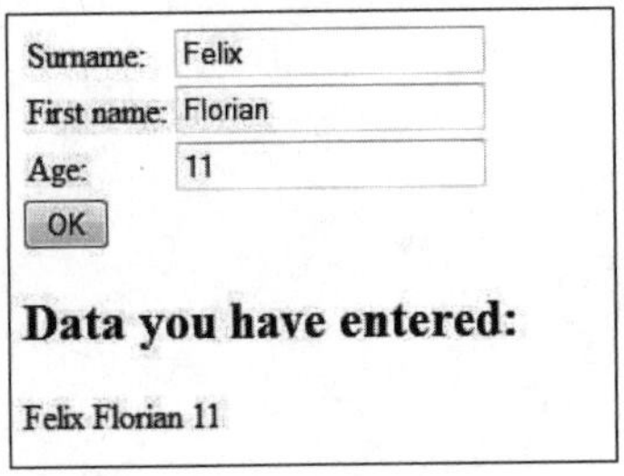

Surname:	Felix
First name:	Florian
Age:	11
OK

Data you have entered:

Felix Florian 11

Figure 5.31   The data has been further processed with Array() methods.

Summary

In this extensive chapter, you have seen how to use selectors and filters plus corresponding filter methods under jQuery that are available in various variations. With these, the framework considerably expands the native possibilities of DOM selections and the historic variations such as object fields and names. Yet the filters and selectors remain browser consistent and easy to apply. With jQuery, the syntax of selectors and filters was conceived as a kind of composition of classic CSS selectors and XPath expressions. The approach of jQuery is rather intelligent for several reasons in my opinion (because many users already know CSS selectors and because the ideas from XPath have been integrated into the concept harmoniously and simplified). Beyond this, there are filter methods that make the selection of elements even more flexible.

6

Accessing the Elements of a Web Page

jQuery offers you numerous methods for accessing the web page or manipulating its content/ structure. *Manipulating* in the context of this chapter means inserting nodes into the site or removing them or changing the content or structure of a node. In addition, you can traverse a web page to find specific nodes and contents quite well in jQuery with various methods. This long and in part somewhat theoretical but immensely important foundation chapter introduces these techniques, which are strongly based on the already discussed navigation on trees plus filters and selectors. After all, accessing the elements of the web page is the basis of all dynamic effects that you want to program in the web page, be it animations, dynamically changing content, or processing user input.

6.1 General Info on Checking, Changing, Adding, and Removing Nodes

As already mentioned in various places, the Document Object Model (DOM) concept interprets a web page as a tree with nodes and axes that develops from a single root. Depending on the type of a node, the DOM concept offers different methods and above all properties for inserting nodes into the tree or removing them from the tree, or for changing nodes (especially their content). However, these access techniques are sometimes not quite straightforward and are potentially unreliable in certain browsers. jQuery makes these processes more abstract or more normal and ensures that they are available across all the browsers in a helpful and secure way.

> **Caution**
>
> If you access elements in the web page via a jQuery object,[1] the normal DOM properties and methods are not directly available. You can use `get()` to get the native DOM node, but then you are explicitly foregoing the advantages offered by the `jQuery` namespace with its homogenous syntax and its protection against browser errors.

1. In other words, via the namespace `jQuery`.

6.2   Checking and Changing Node Contents: `html()` and `text()`

Let's start with two of the most important methods for accessing the web page. Accessing the **contents** of a node, of course, comes under the category of changing a node, because in the DOM concept contents (texts) are also independent nodes. They are text nodes, as you can see quite well in the DOM Inspector. With the method `html()`, you can check the content of a text node that is available in the classic DOM access via `innerHTML`. The method returns the content of the first matched element.

> **Note**
>
> To clarify, we are also talking about the text-based content of elements (for example, headings or `div` areas) because what we usually perceive as content of such container elements is a subordinate, independent node in the DOM (in other words, a text node). The text that you see in a heading or a `div` area has to be retrieved via this subordinate text node. That is exactly what `html()` (or in the DOM concept `innerHTML`) does, via an encapsulated access. But if you operate directly on a node object, you first need to select the text node (for example, via `firstChild`, and then a property such as data for the content).

The method `text()` works in the same way (or more precisely, almost in the same way). Unlike with `html()`, the returned content is not interpreted. In other words, the contained HTML tags are not returned. This corresponds to `innerText` in the classic DOM programming.

If you specify a string parameter for both methods, the content is transferred to *all*[2] matched text nodes. So, it is an assignment of the relevant property or properties, with the usual effects of the corresponding DOM property. For `html()`, the passed content is interpreted in the web page. This means HTML tags are processed. For `text()`, however, the pointed brackets are masked internally, and so the tags are displayed in the web page.

Let's look at the two methods in an example, in which we both get and set content (ch6_1.html).

Listing 6.1   **Getting and Setting Content of Text Nodes**

```
...
06    <script type="text/javascript"
07        src="lib/jquery-1.8.2.min.js"></script>
08    <script type="text/javascript"
09        src="lib/ch6_1_ready.js"></script>
10    </head>
11    <body>
12      <h1>html() and text()</h1>
```

2. Note how conveniently you can assign the same content to several nodes. Instead of having to painstakingly use a loop, you can do it in one statement by cleverly using the right selectors.

```
13    <p> Tiger, tiger, burning <i>bright</i> in the
14      <u>forests</u> of the <b>night</b></p>
15    <button>Get content via html()
16    </button>
17    <button>Get content via text()
18    </button>
19    <button>Set content via html()
20    </button>
21    <button>Set content via text()
22    </button>
23    <div id="output" /></div><div/>
24  </body>
25  </html>
```

In the example, you can see four buttons. With two buttons, we get the content of a paragraph, and with two buttons we set the contents of a `div` container. This is the referenced JavaScript file ch6_1_ready.js.

Listing 6.2   **Using `html()` and `text()`**

```
01  $(function(){
02    $("button:first").click(function(){
03      $("#output").html($("p:first").html());
04    });
05    $("button:eq(1)").click(function(){
06      $("#output").text($("p:first").text());
07    });
08    $("button:eq(2)").click(function(){
09      $("div:gt(0)").html(
10        "<i>What immortal hand or eye\
11        could frame thy fearful symmetry?</i>");
12    });
13    $("button:last").click(function(){
14      $("div:gt(0)").text(
15        "<i>What immortal hand or eye\
16        could frame thy fearful symmetry?</i>");
17    });
18  });
```

If you get and display the content of the paragraph via the method `html()` (line 3), you will see that the HTML tags contained in it are interpreted.

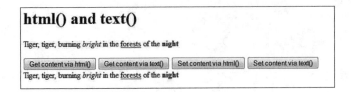

Figure 6.1   Here, we used `html()`.

But if you use the method `text()` instead (line 6), you only get the pure text.

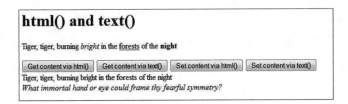

Figure 6.2   No formatting if you are working with `text()`.

If you use the methods with a string parameter, the content is transferred to all matched nodes. To demonstrate this, we use a `div` container that is addressed via the filter `:gt(0)` (in other words, from the second `div` container onward). So in this case, only one element is selected.

If you assign the string `"<i>What immortal hand or eye could frame thy fearful symmetry?</i>"` to the `div` container via the method `html()` (line 9 to 11), you will see that the text is displayed in italics in the output area. This means that the HTML tags it contains have been interpreted.

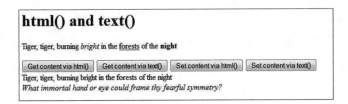

Figure 6.3   The HTML tags contained within have been interpreted; the text is in italics.

But if you use the method `text()` instead, the HTML tags are displayed in the web page.

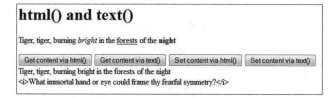

html() and text()

Tiger, tiger, burning *bright* in the <u>forests</u> of the **night**

| Get content via html() | Get content via text() | Set content via html() | Set content via text() |

Tiger, tiger, burning bright in the forests of the night
What immortal hand or eye could frame thy fearful symmetry?

Figure 6.4   The HTML tags are displayed in the web page.

If you analyze the element with Firebug, you will see that the pointed brackets have been masked with entities.

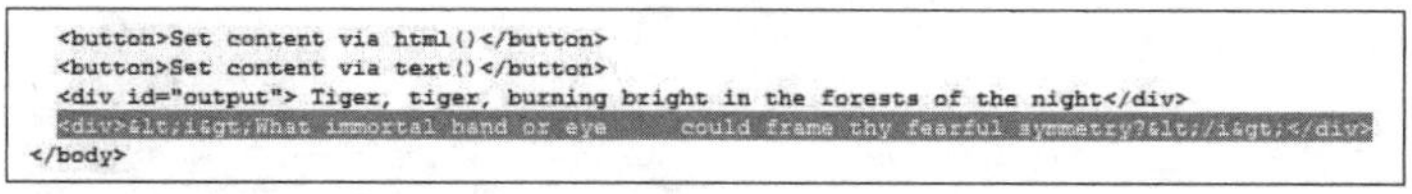

```
<button>Set content via html()</button>
<button>Set content via text()</button>
<div id="output"> Tiger, tiger, burning bright in the forests of the night</div>
<div>&lt;i&gt;What immortal hand or eye     could frame thy fearful symmetry?&lt;/i&gt;</div>
</body>
```

Figure 6.5   The pointed brackets have been masked via `text()`.

6.3   Content of Form Fields: `val()`

In practice, accessing forms is still one of the most important applications of JavaScript. And, of course, jQuery also offers support here, too. With `html()` and `text()`, you can get or set the content of nodes that make values available via `innerHTML` and `innerText`. But this is explicitly not the case with form fields. And in jQuery, too, you have to use a separate method for getting to the content of form fields: `val()`. Passing an argument into `val()`will set the value of the field. If you do not pass an argument into `val()`, then the value of the field is returned.

Listing 6.3   **Accessing Form Fields (ch6_2.html)**

```
...
08    <script type="text/javascript"
09        src="lib/ch6_2_ready.js"></script>
10    </head>
11    <body>
12      <button>Get content</button>
13      <button>Set content</button><hr />
14      <form><input type="text" />
15      </form><hr />
16      <div id="output">
17      </div>
18    </body>
19 </html>
```

Here we have a very simple form with an input field. For the intended access via JavaScript, we need to set neither the method nor the attribute `action`. And here you can see the access in the referenced JavaScript file ch6_2_ready.js.

Listing 6.4   **Using** `val()`

```
01 $(function(){
02   $("button:first").click(function(){
03     var str = $("input:first").val();
04     $("#output").text(str);
05   });
06   $("button:eq(1)").click(function(){
07     var str = $("input:first").val("new");
08   });
09 });
```

With the method `val()`, we get the content of the first input field in line 3 and display it in an output area (addressed via ID). In line 7, we set the value in the input field via a predefined string.

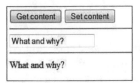

Figure 6.6   The value entered in the form field has been read out and displayed in the output area.

Figure 6.7   The value in the form field has been preset by clicking button 2.

> **Tip**
>
> As an alternative to `val()`, you can also work with the method `attr()` to read out or set the content of form fields. But this is to be taken more generally because with this you can set or read the value of any attribute of an HTML element. In the case of form fields, this would be accessing the attribute `value`. But I find that this approach is more long-winded than using

val(). You should also be aware that as of jQuery 1.6 the method attr() works slightly differently. Static DOM attributes are now separate from dynamic DOM properties. So, if you are
using jQuery 1.6 or later, using prop("value") is the better option. But I still prefer using the
specialized method val().

6.4   Accessing Attributes via attr()

If you want to dynamically change a web page, it is useful to be able to use the values of the
classic HTML attributes from within jQuery. The most general method for accessing attributes
of an element in the web page is attr(), as mentioned earlier. You simply need to enter the
name of the attribute as string (in other words, a parameter) and get the value of the attribute
as return value.

Listing 6.5   **The Value of the Attribute src**

```
var path = $("img:first").attr("src");
```

If you enter a second parameter, the value is set.

Listing 6.6   **The Value of the Attribute src Is Set**

```
$("img:first").attr("src","http://rjs.de/bilder/devil.gif");
```

Note

The method is so easy to use that we are not presenting a complete example. Besides, we are
using the method repeatedly in other examples.

6.5   Inserting Nodes into a Web Page

With the methods html() and text(), you give new content to a text node. But you can also
append content to existing content. This is much more flexible because it is not limited to
pure text contents. And you are working quite closely to the DOM node structure.

Note

Such dynamic manipulations of nodes are convenient if the final structure is not yet clear at
the time when the web page is created. For example, imagine an online shop where you cannot
know how many products a customer is going to select.

6.5.1 `append()` and `prepend()`

First of all, there is the `append()` method that we have already used in the course of the book and that already exists more or less in the same form in the native DOM programming (the method `appendChild()`). The content, passed as a string parameter, is simply added at the *end* of the existing content. So in the selected element, you then have another child node. The method `prepend()` works exactly the same, but the content is added at the *front*. We will demonstrate both methods by again using a form field and adding its content after a click on a specific button to an original text (ch6_3.html).

Listing 6.7 **The Form and the Output Area**

```
...
08    <script type="text/javascript"
09        src="lib/ch6_3_ready.js"></script>
10  </head>
11  <body>
12    <button>Append content</button>
13    <button>Prepend content</button><hr />
14    <form><input type="text" /></form><hr />
15    </form><hr />
16    <div id="output">| Original text |
17    </div>
18  </body>
19 </html>
```

Again, we have the form we had before, with one input field (plus the two buttons via which the actions are to be triggered and the output area to which the nodes will be added as child elements). Initially, the original structure of the site is interesting for us, and we can see it clearly in Firebug.

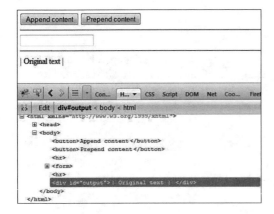

Figure 6.8 The `div` element contains only the original text.

You can see the output area that already contains a certain original text. In this situation, the view in DOM Inspector is more significant to us.

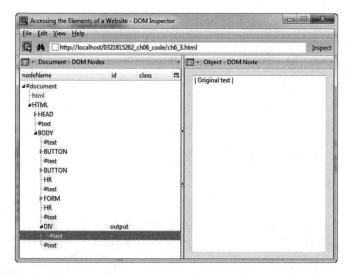

Figure 6.9   In the DOM Inspector, you can see the actual nodes in the `div` container.

In the DOM Inspector, you can see that the content of the output area is a subordinate text node (a child element of the `div` element), as emphasized previously in the context of `html()` and `text()`. You can also see that there are no other nodes in that area. Here you can see the access to the output area in the referenced JavaScript file ch6_3_ready.js.

Listing 6.8   `append()` **and** `prepend()` **in Action**

```
01 $(function(){
02   $("button:first").click(function(){
03     var str = " < " + $("input:first").val();
04     $("#output").append(str);
05   });
06   $("button:eq(1)").click(function(){
07     var str = $("input:first").val() + " > ";
08     $("#output").prepend(str);
09   });
10 });
```

When the first button is clicked, the statement in line 4 appends the content of the form field to the existing content of the output area. In line 8, the content is prepended to the existing content.

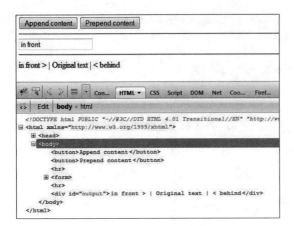

Figure 6.10   Different text has been inserted before or after the original text.

If you take a look at it in the DOM Inspector, you can see clearly how the nodes are now structured in the `div` container. You will see that the `div` container now has a separate text node for each inserted content. Each text node that was added via `append()` is *after* the text node with the original text, and each text node that was added with `prepend()` is *before* the text node with the original text.

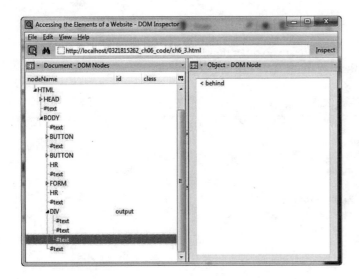

Figure 6.11   In the `div` container, there are now several individual text nodes.

> **Tip**
>
> You can also specify function calls as parameters for `append()` and most other methods for node manipulation. But then you should create these elements first directly (for example, with `document.createElement()`). Or the function returns an HTML string that is to replace the set of matched elements.

With the methods described, you can also *move* objects to another place in the web page. Note that you are then actually removing an object from one place in the DOM and inserting it in another place (ch6_4.html).

Listing 6.9   **Moving an Element to Another Place**

```
...
08 <script type="text/javascript"
09   src="lib/ch6_4_ready.js"></script>
10 </head>
11 <body>
12   <button>Move object</button><hr />
13   <h2>Text in Heading</h2><hr />
14   <div id="output">| Original text |
15   </div>
16 </body>
17 </html>
```

In the example, we want to move the heading of the level h2 to the output area. This is very easy (ch6_4_ready.js).

Listing 6.10   **Moving an Element**

```
01 $(function(){
02   $("button:first").click(function(){
03     $("#output").append($("h2"));
04   });
05 });
```

In line 3, we select the heading h2 (strictly speaking all of them, but in our case, it's just one).

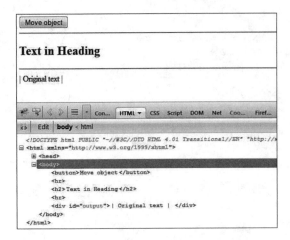

Figure 6.12   The original structure of the web page.

We use append( ) to move it to the output area, as you can see clearly in Firebug.

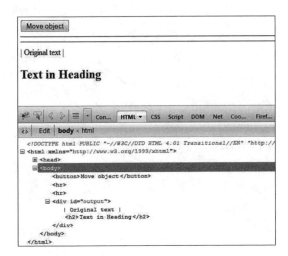

Figure 6.13   In Firebug, you can see particularly well how the heading was moved to the div container.

> **Note**
>
> Please be aware that many jQuery methods for node manipulation (but not all) show this behavior. If you take an already existing node in the web page and insert it in another place in the web page, the original node is removed. But there are some particularities to observe for certain methods in jQuery, as addressed later.

6.5.2 `appendTo()` and `prependTo()`

To append or move nodes, you have other options than just working with `append()` and `prepend()`. There is the alternative method is `appendTo()`. But you have to watch out; this method has a different syntax from the other two methods that are based in their application on the classic DOM method `appendChild()`.

This alternative method appends the nodes selected with a preceding selector to the existing content that is specified with a selector as parameter of `appendTo()`. Or to put it slightly differently, the objects via which the method is called are appended to the objects that are specified as parameters. That is the exact opposite of `append()`. Entirely consistently, the method `prependTo()` inserts the nodes before the existing content.

But now we need to distinguish if the methods are applied to existing elements or if we are looking at elements we need to create first. Because if we apply them to nodes that already exist in the web page, these nodes are moved again. But the issue with moving nodes can be somewhat tricky in certain constellations. To clarify this, let's take a look at `appendTo()` in a situation of a somewhat artificial but expressive example application.

We apply the methods to elements that are already present in the web page and move the appended nodes in the tree. In other words, the appended content is no longer in the same place in the tree where it was before we applied `appendTo()`. And indeed it is not just the text content that is removed and appended in the new place, but the entire node (including specific node properties such as Cascading Style Sheets [CSS] formatting). The behavior can be analyzed very well in Firebug and was also present in the previous example for `append()` (ch6_5.html).

Listing 6.11 **Moving Elements to Another Place with** `appendTo()`

```
...
08 <script type="text/javascript"
09   src="lib/ch6_5_ready.js"></script>
10 </head>
11 <body>
12   <button>append()</button>
13   <button>appendTo() one node</button>
14   <button>appendTo() several nodes</button>
15   <hr/><span id="a" style="color:cyan;background:red">
16     - 1st Node - </span>
17   <span id="b" style="color:white;background:cyan">
18     - 2nd Node - </span>
19   <span id="c" style="color:green;background:yellow">
20     - 3rd Node - </span>
21   <div id="output" style=
22     "color:red;background:lightgray">Target area</div>
23 </body>
24 </html>
```

In the example, we want to move existing elements of the type span to the output area
(ch6_5_ready.js).

Listing 6.12   append() **Versus** appendTo()

```
01 $(function(){
02   $("button:first").click(function(){
03     $("#output").append(" - append() - ");
04   });
05   $("button:eq(1)").click(function(){
06     $("#a").appendTo("#output");
07   });
08   $("button:last").click(function(){
09     $("span").appendTo("#output");
10   });
11 });
```

In the example, you again have three buttons via which we call the methods. As usual, we are
using an output area. The new content is to be appended to it. But if you try the example yourself, you will see that append() and appendTo() behave differently.

Look at the span container in the web page with the specific formatting. If you load the page,
you will see this span container directly after the separator line and before the div container
that we append the content to. Also, take a look at the DOM structure in Firebug. You will see
the corresponding elements in the tree in the same order as you have created them in HTML.

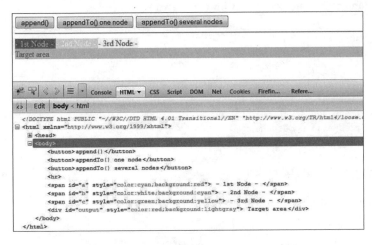

Figure 6.14   The web page after loading.

If you now use the method `append()` to append the text specified as string parameter to the target area, you will see that it is simply added to the existing content. In Firebug, you can see clearly that apart from the new text nodes that there are no changes in the node structure of the tree. Only the content of the target container is being expanded.

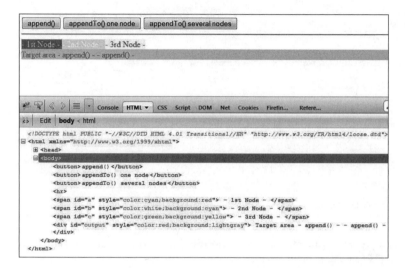

Figure 6.15   With `append()`, the node structure of the tree is not changed (apart from new text nodes).

But if you click the second button, the content of the `span` container with the ID `a` is appended to the target area (the `div` container). More precisely, it is inserted as child element into the parent element of the type `div`.

Listing 6.13   The Node Specified via the ID is Appended to the Target Area

```
06 $("#a").appendTo("#output");
```

In the process, this node is removed from its original place in the tree. Again, you can see this clearly in Firebug. After our explanations on `append()`, you should not find this behavior surprising.

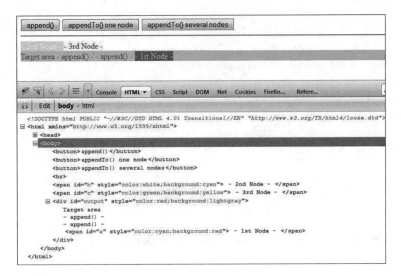

Figure 6.16 The span container with the ID a is now the child element of the div container.

It also gets interesting if you apply the method append() once more to this state. You will see that the specified string is again appended after the content of the div container. But again, you can deduct this from our previous explanations.

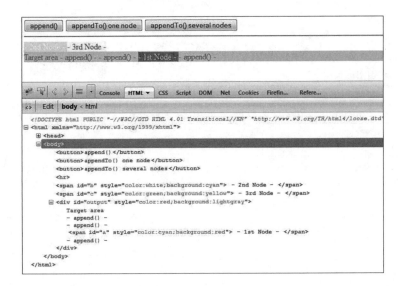

Figure 6.17 With append(), content is again inserted after the last child element.

If you now select several methods with the selector for the method `appendTo()`, these are removed one after the other from the original position in the tree and added to the target area as child elements. Even if these elements are already present in the target area in another place.[3] And then the position where the elements are at that moment in the DOM becomes massively important with regard to the order in which they are inserted again.

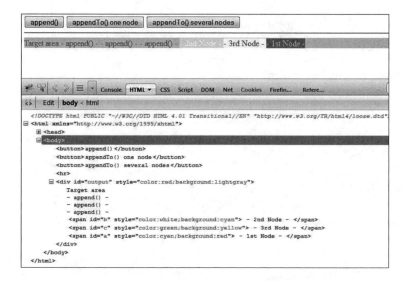

Figure 6.18   Applying `appendTo()` to several elements.

Note

We do not show `prependTo()` in action; it is simply identical.

Now we want to apply `appendTo()` to elements that are not yet present in the web page. We create a jQuery object and then add it to the page (ch6_6.html).

Listing 6.14   **Moving Elements to Another Place with** `appendTo()`

```
...
08    <script type="text/javascript"
09      src="lib/ch6_6_ready.js"></script>
10    </head>
11    <body>
12    <button>appendTo() a new node</button><hr/>
13      <div id="output" />
```

---

3. For example, as a result of a previous action.

```
14    </body>
15 </html>
```

In the example, we now want to create new elements and append them to the output area (ch6_6_ready.js).

Listing 6.15   `appendTo()` **and a Newly Created Element**

```
01 $(function(){
02    $("button:first").click(function(){
03       $("<div>New</div>").appendTo("#output");
04    });
05 });
```

In line 3, you can see that a new `div` element is created, which is then added to the output area.

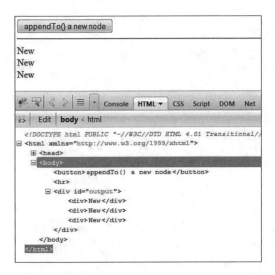

Figure 6.19   Three new nodes have been inserted in the output area.

6.6   Inserting Nodes Before or After

Content and elements are inserted within an existing node, both via `append()` or `prepend()` and `appendTo()` or `prependTo()`. But jQuery also offers methods via which you can add nodes specifically before or after a certain node that you can specify via a selector.

6.6.1 `after()` and `before()`

With the `after()` method , you can add content after each element that matches the selector. The `before()` method behaves accordingly. The content is added before each element that matches the selector (ch6_7.html).

Listing 6.16   **Inserting Elements in a Specific Place**

```
...
08   <script type="text/javascript"
09     src="lib/ch6_7_ready.js"></script>
10   </head>
11   <body>
12     <button>after()</button>
13     <button>before()</button><hr/>
14     <div id="output" style=
15        "color:red;background:lightgray">Target area</div>
16   </body>
17 </html>
```

In the example, we want to create new elements and add them to the output area (ch6_7_ready.js).

Listing 6.17   `after()` and `before()`

```
01 $(function(){
02  $("button:first").click(function(){
03     $("#output").after(
04        '<span style="color:white;background:red">
           After</span>');
05  });
06  $("button:eq(1)").click(function(){
07     $("#output").before(
           '<span style="color:red;background:yellow">
08        Before</span>');
09  });
10 });
```

If you try out the example, you will see that new nodes with the specified content and the appropriate properties (CSS formatting) are inserted before or after the target node, respectively.

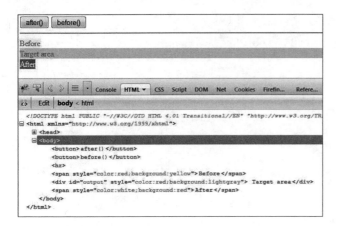

Figure 6.20   Real nodes have been inserted before and after the target node.

Let's again look at how the methods work when they are applied to elements that are already present in the web page (ch6_8.html).

Listing 6.18   **Inserting Elements in a Specific Place**

```
...
08    <script type="text/javascript"
09      src="lib/ch6_8_ready.js"></script>
10    </head>
11    <body>
12          <h2>after()</h2>
13        <h2>before()</h2>
14      <button>after()</button>
15      <button>before()</button><hr/>
16      <div id="output" style=
17        "color:red;background:lightgray">Target area</div>
18    </body>
19    </html>
```

Essentially, you will see the same page as before. But now we have two headings of the type h2.

We want to treat these headings with after() and before() in our example (ch6_8_ready.js).

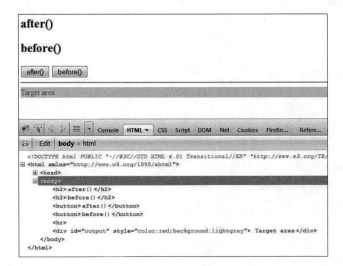

Figure 6.21 The page structure with the two headings at the beginning.

Listing 6.19 `after()` **and** `before()`

```
01 $(function(){
02   $("button:first").click(function(){
03     $("#output").after($("h2:first"));
04   });
05   $("button:eq(1)").click(function(){
06     $("#output").before($("h2:last"));
07   });
08 });
```

If you try the example, you will see that the first heading is moved behind the target area and the second before the target area. So in case of existing elements, the method has the same effect as the related methods did up to now.

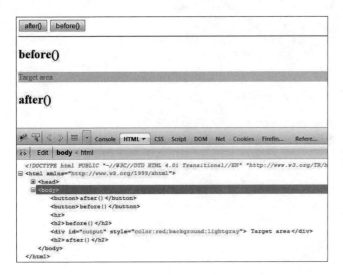

Figure 6.22   Moving the headings.

6.6.2 `insertAfter()` and `insertBefore()`

Then there are also the two methods `insertAfter()` and `insertBefore()`, which work similarly to `appendTo()` and `prependTo()`. The parameter is the target to which they add the specified elements (ch6_9.html).

Listing 6.20 **The Basic Web Page**

```
...
08   <script type="text/javascript"
09     src="lib/ch6_9_ready.js"></script>
10   </head>
11   <body>
12     <button>insertAfter()</button>
13     <button>insertBefore()</button><hr/>
14     <div id="element" style=
15         "color:red;background:lightgray">Text</div>
16   </body>
17 </html>
```

Basically, you can see two buttons and a `div` area that we want to move before and after the first button.

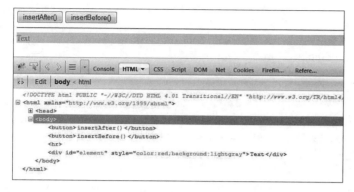

Figure 6.23   The initial site structure.

These are the JavaScript functions (ch6_9_ready.js).

Listing 6.21   `insertAfter()` **and** `insertBefore()`

```
01 $(function(){
02   $("button:first").click(function(){
03     $("#element").insertAfter($('button:first'));
04   });
05   $("button:eq(1)").click(function(){
06     $("#element").insertBefore($('button:first'));
07   });
08 });
```

If you try out the example, you will see that the div area with the ID #element is moved either directly before the first button or after it. If you click the buttons in turn, the process will be alternated.

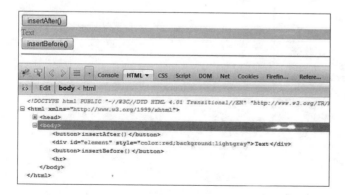

Figure 6.24   The `div` container has been inserted after the first button.

6.7   Wrapping

With jQuery, you can **wrap** existing content with certain structures. The nodes then basically become child nodes of a surrounding structure.

6.7.1   Wrapping Individually with `wrap()`

With the method `wrap()` you specify as parameter either an HTML tag as string or an element. All previously selected elements are wrapped with the corresponding structures and then become their children (ch6_10.html).

Listing 6.22   **The Basic Web Page**

```
...
08   <script type="text/javascript"
09     src="lib/ch6_10_ready.js"></script>
10   </head>
11   <body>
12     <button>wrap() with HTML</button>
13       <button>wrap() with element</button>
14     <hr/><span>Wrapping</span>
15     <span>things</span>
16     <span>up</span>
17   </body>
18 </html>
```

Here in the web page we have three `span` areas on the same hierarchy level that we want to wrap in each case.

Figure 6.25   The site structure at the beginning.

These are the JavaScript functions that we want to use to do the wrapping (ch6_10_ready.js).

Listing 6.23 **Wrapping Content of a Web Page with HTML Structures**

```
01 $(function(){
02   $("button:first").click(function(){
03     $("span").wrap("<h3>");
04   });
05   $("button:eq(1)").click(function(){
06     $("span").wrap($("<div/>"));
07   });
08 });
```

In the example, HTML structures will be wrapped around all span elements in the web page if the user clicks one of the buttons. In line 3, you can see how an HTML tag is simply used as parameter to achieve this. If the user clicks the first button, this event helper is triggered and all span areas are enclosed individually in headings of level h3.

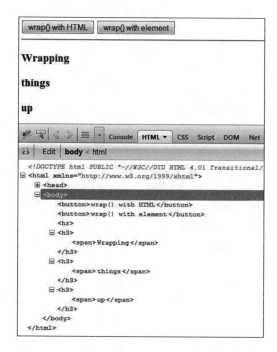

Figure 6.26 Level 3 headings are wrapped around all span areas.

4. You can also write down a function call that returns an object, or you can work again with document.createElement().

In line 6, we explicitly create a `div` element and use it as parameter.[4] As a consequence, it is wrapped around the `span` areas. So, this is another option of wrapping elements in jQuery.

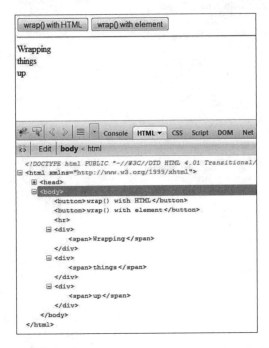

Figure 6.27   Now the `span` areas are wrapped with `div` containers.

Note that this example does not take into account if the user clicks the buttons repeatedly. This is no big deal either. The `span` areas are then only wrapped repeatedly over and over again from the inside out, and the result may be a deeply nested hierarchy structure that could potentially run against valid HTML. In practice, you should not permit this.

```
⊟ <div>
   ⊟ <h3>
      ⊟ <div>
         ⊟ <h3>
            <span>Wrapping</span>
         </h3>
      </div>
   </h3>
</div>
```

Figure 6.28   More and more wrapping and nesting.

6.7.2 Wrapping All with `wrapAll()`

jQuery also offers further methods of wrapping. Via the method `wrapAll()` (related to `wrap()`), all matched elements are enclosed in a *single* wrapping element (ch6_11.html).

Listing 6.24   **The Basic Web Page**

```
...
08   <script type="text/javascript"
09     src="lib/ch6_11_ready.js"></script>
10   </head>
11   <body>
12     <button>wrapAll()</button>
13     <hr/><span>Wrapping</span>
14     <span>things</span>
15     <span>up</span>
16   </body>
17   </html>
```

Again, we have the three span areas, but we want to enclose them completely with a wrapping element (ch6_11_ready.js).

Listing 6.25   **Wrapping with an Element**

```
01  $(function(){
02    $("button:first").click(function(){
03      $("span").wrapAll("<h3>");
04    });
05  });
```

In the example, only one level 3 heading is wrapped completely around all span elements in the web page.

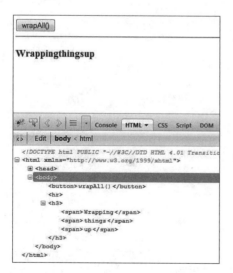

Figure 6.29   You can see clearly that all span areas are now within a heading of the type h3.

6.7.3   Wrapping Inner Areas with `wrapInner()`

jQuery also offers the method `wrapInner()`. It works like `wrap()`, but it wraps an HTML structure around the inner child element of any matched element (including text nodes) (ch6_12.html).

Listing 6.26   **The Basic Web Page**

```
...
08    <script type="text/javascript"
09        src="lib/ch6_12_ready.js"></script>
10    </head>
11    <body>
12        <button>wrapInner()</button>
13        <hr/><span>Wrapping</span>
14        <span>things</span>
15        <span>up</span>
16    </body>
17 </html>
```

Again, we have the three span areas, but this time we do not want to wrap a structure around them. Instead, we wrap it around their content (ch6_12_ready.js).

Listing 6.27   **Wrapping the Inner with an Element**

```
01 $(function(){
02   $("button:first").click(function(){
03     $("span").wrapInner("<h3>");
04   });
05 });
```

In the example, all `span` elements in the web page are selected, and in each case a level 3 heading is wrapped around their content.

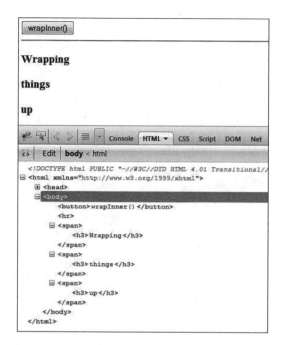

Figure 6.30 This might not be sensible HTML, but all the content of the `span` areas is wrapped with `h3` headings.

6.7.4   Unwrapping with `unwrap()`

With `wrap()`, you can wrap an element. This means that you enclose the target element within a parent element. With `unwrap()`, however, you remove the parent element, which is exactly the opposite. The method is extremely easy to use; you do not even need to specify a parameter.

Listing 6.28   **Removing the Parent Element of All Paragraphs**

```
$("p").unwrap();
```

6.8   Replacing with `replaceWith()` and `replaceAll()`

The topic of this chapter is accessing the elements of a web page. Of course, this also includes replacing the components of a web page. With the jQuery methods `replaceWith()` and `replaceAll()`, you can easily, conveniently, and reliably replace elements in a web page.

6.8.1   Replacing with `replaceWith()`

The method `replaceWith()` replaces all elements selected in the preceding jQuery object with the specified HTML or DOM elements that are specified as parameters.

> **Caution**
>
> Note that the replaced elements are explicitly removed from the existing DOM.[5] You then get these as return values of the method in the form of a jQuery element and you can then use them further accordingly.

Let's take a look at different constellations again (ch6_13.html).

Listing 6.29   **Replacing Parts of a Web Page**

```
...
08   <script type="text/javascript"
09     src="lib/ch6_13_ready.js"></script>
10   </head>
11   <body>
12     <button>replaceWith()</button><hr/>
13     <div>One Ring to rule them all,</div>
14     <div>One Ring to find them,</div>
15     <div>One Ring to bring them all</div>
16     <div>and in the darkness bind them.</div><hr />
17   </body>
18 </html>
```

Here, we have four `div` elements that are enclosed by two separator lines. The replacing process is triggered when the user clicks a button.

We want to replace the `div` elements *successively,* with level 5 headings when the user clicks the button. Each click is to replace the first `div` element in each case with a heading (ch6_13_ready.js).

Listing 6.30   **Replacing the `div` Areas**

```
01 $(function(){
02   $("button:first").click(function(){
03     $("div:first").replaceWith("<h5>" +
04       $("div:first").text() + "</h5>");
05   });
06 });
```

5. In a way, this is comparable to the situations where we have moved existing elements of the web page.

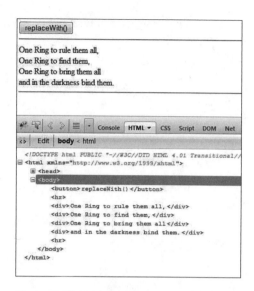

Figure 6.31 Four `div` areas in the original state of the web page.

As you can see, each user clicks on the button in the event helper selects the first `div` element in each case. This is then replaced in the DOM by the parameter from the `replaceWith()` method. In the example, the method's parameter is put together from the text content of the `div` area we are replacing (at this point, it is still available because the replacing has not yet taken place) and HTML tags. The old content is enclosed in a level 5 heading. After the statement in lines 3 and 4 has been carried out, the first `div` area has been removed from the DOM and replaced by an element of the type `h5` with identical text content.

Figure 6.32 The first `div` area has been turned into a level 5 heading.

If the user now clicks again, the `div` area that is now the first one[6] is selected in turn and replaced and so on. After four clicks, all `div` areas will then have been converted to level 5 headings.

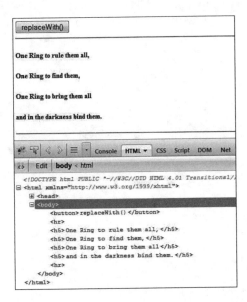

Figure 6.33   The `div` elements are history.

In the last example, we have used the object we were replacing **before it was replaced** by using the method `text()` to read out the content. But the method `replaceWith()` returns the replaced node as jQuery object. So, we can also work with that. Let's take a look at a variant of the example to see how you can process the returned elements further. The underlying HTML file ch6_14.html is identical to the file ch6_13.html—apart from the reference to the JavaScript file. So, let's only take a look at this JavaScript file ch6_14_ready.js.

Listing 6.31   **Processing the Return Value**

```
01 $(function(){
02  $("button:first").click(function(){
03    var element =
04      $("div:first").replaceWith("<h5></h5>");
05    alert(element.text());
06    $("h5:first").text(element.text());
07  });
  });
```

As in the previous example, we successively replace the `div` areas with level 5 headings. But these are all empty. But in lines 3 and 4, we assign the replaced `div` element that was removed

6. On loading the site, this was the second `div` area.

from the DOM of the web page to a local variable `element`. This thereby references a jQuery object that represents the previously removed `div` element. Correspondingly, we can then work with the object in the following steps—provided the variable `element` is available. In line 5, for example, we output the text content in an `alert()`.

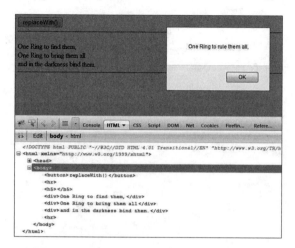

Figure 6.34   The content of the `div` element deleted from the web page is still available and displayed via `alert()`.

In line 6, we access the text content again via the variable `element` and write it into the web page as content of the first heading with the type `h5`.

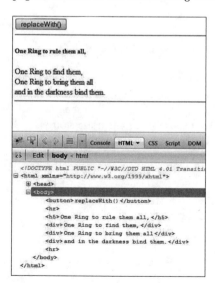

Figure 6.35   The first heading of the type `h5` has been filled with the content of the replaced `div` element.

If we now click the button again, the same process happens. But note that in this variant of the previous example, the content is always written into the *first* heading of the type h5. Consequently, the site in this variant will eventually have only empty headings of the type h5.

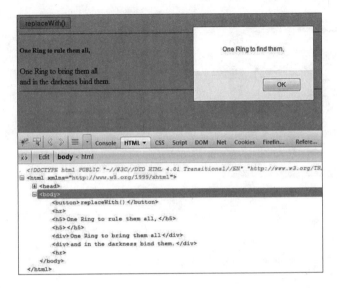

Figure 6.36   The number of filled headings is decreasing.

6.8.2   Replacing All with `replaceAll()`

With `replaceAll()`, you specify a selector as parameter. All elements that match the selector are replaced by the element to which the method is applied. As a return value, you get all *inserted* elements. So, this is the inverted syntax of `replaceWith()`; but when using it, you have to watch out if you still want to use the original elements. As mentioned before, the return value contains the inserted elements. If you need the original elements or their content, you need to save them in a variable before you replace them. This is generally more complicated than working with `replaceWith()`. The method `replaceAll()` is above all useful if you want to replace an element completely with an identical structure or always the same passage with a different fixed structure (ch6_15.html).

Listing 6.32   **Replacing Elements in the Web Page**

```
...
08   <script type="text/javascript"
09      src="lib/ch6_15_ready.js"></script>
10   </head>
11   <body>
12      <button>replaceAll()</button>
```

```
13    <hr />One Ring to rule them all,
14    <hr />One Ring to find them,
15    <hr />One Ring to bring them all
16    <hr />and in the darkness bind them.
17  </body>
18 </html>
```

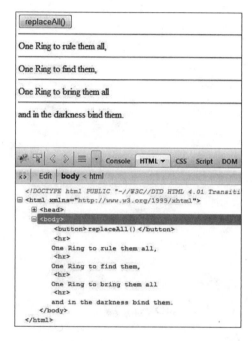

Figure 6.37   Four separator lines.

We are using four separator lines for subdividing the output and we want to replace these separator lines with line breaks when the user clicks the button (ch6_15_ready.js).

Listing 6.33   **Replacing the Separator Lines**

```
01 $(function(){
02   $("button:first").click(function(){
03     $("<br />").replaceAll("hr");
04   });
05 });;
```

Please ensure that the element you want to replace is specified as a parameter and the element you are replacing it with is specified via the preceding jQuery object. And ensure that the element you are replacing is not written as tag syntax.

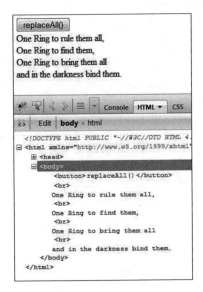

Figure 6.38   The manipulated site. The new structure is clearly visible in Firebug.

6.9   Removing with empty() and remove()/ detach() plus removeAttr()

Fundamentally, both empty() and remove() offer options for removing nodes from a web page. With the empty()method, you simply remove all child elements (including text nodes) from the matched set of elements. But with remove(), you remove all matched elements from the DOM (with child elements).

But there are a few other deep differences between the two methods. For one, remove() does not remove the elements from the jQuery object, and you still use them further, even though all event handlers and internally cached data is eliminated. The advantage is that remove() gives you the elements that were removed from the DOM as return value and you can then use them further. Also, you can optionally specify a filter expression as parameter for remove().

> **Caution**
>
> Using the elements you have removed via remove() is somewhat tricky if the elimination takes place in combination with a filter expression[7] (because the return value of remove() is always

the complete set of elements to which `remove()` is applied). In other words, although the filter expression prevents nonmatched elements being removed from the DOM, the returned jQuery object still contains[8] all elements, even the ones that were not removed! So if you are using the jQuery object further in the following steps, you are operating on the entire set of elements and may need to select individual elements directly once more. The following example demonstrates this behavior (ch6_16.html).

Listing 6.34   **Removing Elements**

```
...
08   <script type="text/javascript"
09     src="lib/ch6_16_ready.js"></script>
10   </head>
11   <body>
12     <h1>Ash nazg durbatulûk,</h1>
13     <h1 id="i1">ash nazg gimbatul,</h1>
14     <h1>ash nazg thrakatulûk</h1>
15     <h1>agh burzum-ishi krimpatul</h1>
16     <button>empty()</button>
17     <button>remove() - all</button>
18     <button>remove() - only once</button>
19     <button>Add one element</button>
20     <button>Add all elements</button>
21     <hr id="i2">
22   </body>
23   </html>
```

In the web page, we are using four level 1 headings that we want to remove in different ways. The elements removed via `remove()` are to be inserted in another place in the tree (ch6_16_ready.js).

Listing 6.35   **Techniques for Removing Nodes**

```
01 var element = null;
02 $(document).ready(function(){
03   $("button:first").click(function(){
04     $("h1").empty();
05   });
06   $("button:eq(1)").click(function(){
07     element = $("h1").remove();
08   });
09   $("button:eq(2)").click(function(){
```

7. And above all, not totally consistent with some jQuery methods that work in a similar way.

8. Or references them.

```
10    element = $("h1").remove("#i1");
11  });
12  $("button:eq(3)").click(function(){
13    $("#i2").after(element[1]);
14  });
15  $("button:eq(4)").click(function(){
16    $("#i2").after(element);
17  });
18 });
```

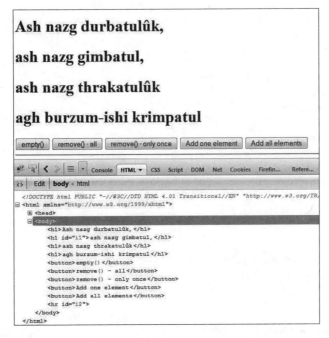

Figure 6.39   The unchanged web page with the relevant part of the tree.

If the user's click on the first button calls the empty() method (line 4), all level 1 headings are emptied. This means that child elements (text nodes) are deleted from the tree.

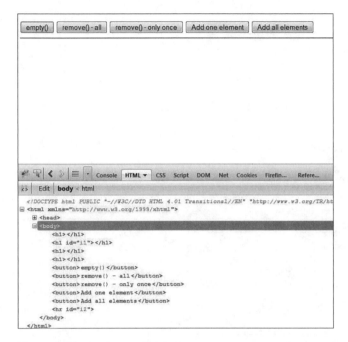

Figure 6.40   The contents of all headings have been deleted after the first button was clicked.

Note that we have created a global variable element in line 1 that will receive the elements removed via remove(). In line 7, you can see how we use remove() without parameter.

Listing 6.36   **Using remove() Without Parameter: All Level 1 Headings Are Removed**

```
element=$("h1").remove();
```

The removed level 1 headings are saved in the variable element and removed from the tree. If the fourth button is clicked, they are reinserted after the separator line with the ID i2 via the method after().[9]

Listing 6.37   **Inserting the Elements Saved in Element in Another Place**

```
23 $("#i2").after(element);
```

9. That we have already encountered earlier.

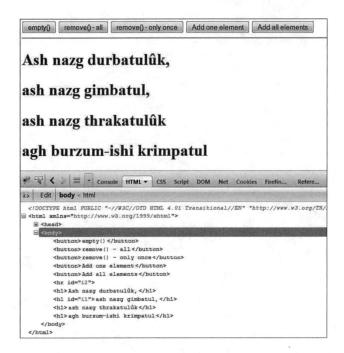

Figure 6.41   The elements have been removed via `remove()` and inserted in a different place with `after()`.

Line 10 is now of particular interest.

Listing 6.38   **Using `remove()` with a Filter Expression**

```
element=$("h1").remove("#i1");
```

Here you can see how we use `remove()` with a filter expression. We only want to remove the heading that has the ID i1. But if you then click the fourth button, **all four level 1 headings** are still inserted in the new place. Plus the not-yet-removed remaining three level 1 headings are removed from the original position in the tree.[10] So, the variable `element` contains all level 1 headings, despite the filter.

So, if you want to insert only the filtered element from the `element` array in another place, you need to address it specifically in the array. And we do this if the user clicks the third button. Note line 13.

Listing 6.39   **Inserting the Second Element from the Elements Array**

```
$("#i2").after(element[1]);
```

10. A logical consequence because we do not want a duplication of the elements.

Synchronized with the filter of the `remove()` method, only the matched element from the array is now inserted and removed accordingly from the original position. The other headings stay where they are.

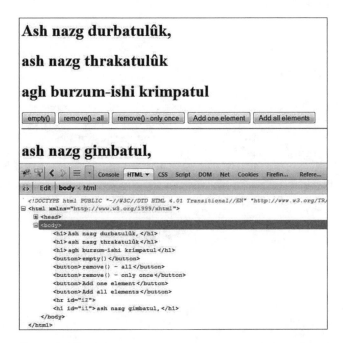

Figure 6.42   An element has been removed from the tree and inserted in another place; the other elements stay in the original place.

6.9.1   The Alternative of `remove()`: `detach()`

Instead of `remove()`, you can also work with `detach()`. The method is almost identical to `remove()` apart from the fact that `detach()` keeps all jQuery data in relation to the removed elements. This can be relevant when you are reinserting them into the DOM tree.

6.9.2   Deleting Attributes

For deleting attributes, jQuery offers the `removeAttr()` method. Using it is fairly straightforward; you only need to specify the name of the attribute you want to remove as a parameter. A complete example is not necessary here.

Listing 6.40   **Removing the Attribute** `disabled`

```
$("input:first").removeAttr("disabled");
```

> **Note**
>
> The `removeAttr()` method directly uses the JavaScript function `removeAttribute()`, but encapsulates it via the jQuery namespace and so prevents problems associated with differently named attributes in different browsers.

6.10   Cloning with `clone()`

Just now we had to deal with a situation where the insertion of elements with `after()` removed the nodes from the original position. This also concerns other methods that insert elements. After all, in most cases you explicitly do not want to duplicate or clone elements. But cloning is, of course, also possible with jQuery (if you want, even including the event handler or event handler assigned to the element). You can do this via the `clone()` method. It has an optional Boolean parameter. If it is `true`, you can also clone the event handler or event helper. The default is `false` (ch6_17.html).

Listing 6.41   **Cloning Elements**

```
...
08    <script type="text/javascript"
09        src="lib/ch6_17_ready.js"></script>
10    </head>
11    <body>
12      <img src="images/b1.png" />
13        <img src="images/b2.png" /><hr/>
14      <button>clone() Image 1</button>
15      <button>clone(true) Image 2</button>
16      <button>clone(false) Image 2</button>
17      <hr/><div id="info"></div><hr id="i2">
18    </body>
19  </html>
```

In the web page, we have two pictures that we want to clone. After cloning, they are reinserted into the tree (ch6_17_ready.js).

Listing 6.42   **Cloning Elements**

```
01  $(function(){
02    $("img:last").click(function(){
03      $("#info").html("Number of images: "
04        + $("img").length);
05    });
06    $("button:first").click(function(){
07      element = $("img:first").clone();
08      $("#i2").after(element);
09    });
```

```
10  $("button:eq(1)").click(function(){
11    element = $("img:eq(1)").clone(true);
12    element.css({
13      border: "solid 1pt"
14    });
15    $("#i2").after(element);
16  });
17  $("button:eq(2)").click(function(){
18    element = $("img:eq(1)").clone(false);
19    $("#i2").after(element);
20  });
21  });
```

In lines 2–5, you can see that the last image in the web page has an event helper assigned to it. If a user clicks the last image in the web page (the second image on loading), the number of images in the web page is displayed. Note that we explicitly use `:last` as filter. This will be significant later on when we are cloning images and then inserting them into the web page.[11] When we are doing so, the question arises how the event helper is assigned (because what was the last image on loading the web page is then explicitly no longer the last image in the web page). And the next question is what happens when we clone the event helper.

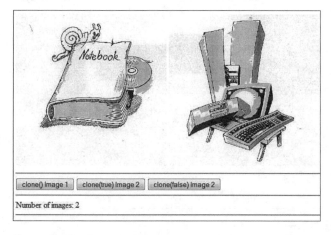

Figure 6.43   The second image in the web page is sensitive to a mouse click after loading; the click generates a message in the web page.

In line 7, you can see how the first image is cloned. The copy is saved in the variable `element` and can then be used further. In the example, we simply reinsert the element in another place in the tree (after the separator line with the ID `i2`).

11. In practice, you could, for example, do this for an online shop with a shopping cart, to select a product represented by an icon. If the product is placed into the shopping cart, a copy of the icon from the online shop is created and displayed in the cart.

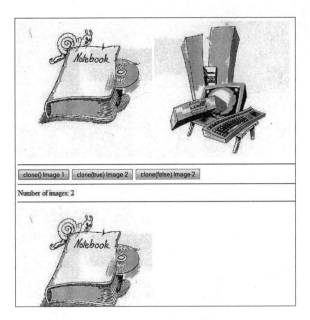

Figure 6.44   The first image has been cloned and inserted after the separator line; the displayed number of images has not yet been updated.

Each click on the button creates a new clone and inserts it into the web page.

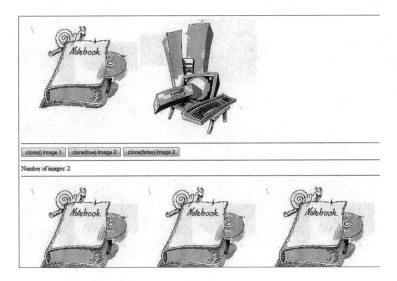

Figure 6.45   Now there are three clones of image 1.

Now we will see what has happened with assigning the event handling. As we have written it down in the source text in line 2 with `$("img:last")`, the last image should be sensitive and write into the web page when clicked. But if you click it, you will see that this is *not* the case. But if you click the second image, the action assigned at the beginning is triggered again.

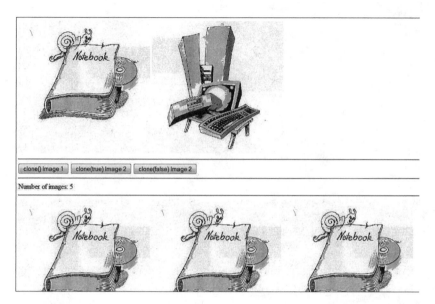

Figure 6.46   When you click the second image, the action is triggered.

Apparently, the framework solves the problem of the originally intended assignment via jQuery selectors and retrospectively dynamically added elements. The framework assigns the original assignment internally—despite the fact that the syntax now no longer fits in the source code—as at the beginning. This is a great relief, on the one hand, and again you can see the advantage of a framework such as jQuery. On the other hand, you need to take this behavior into account, of course, because you might want to explicitly relocate the event handling.

But let's see what happens if we clone the event handling, as well. You can see this in line 11, where we specify the Boolean parameter `true`. The then following added a frame is only intended to visually distinguish a sensitively cloned element from a not-sensitively cloned element and has no other effects.

If you try out the example, you will see that the event helper really does work for the element cloned with this approach. Plus the second element will still remain sensitive. The framework takes care of both the cloning and a correct assignment in the background.

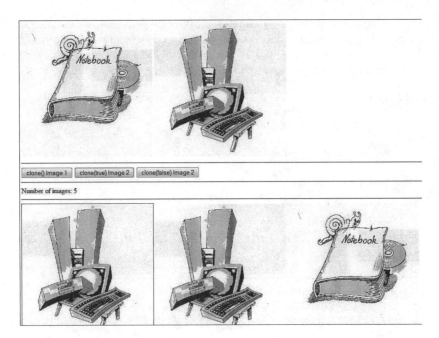

Figure 6.47   The framed image is sensitive, as is the second image.

6.11   Search and Find

jQuery offers a number of powerful methods for searching specific structures in the web page. The special feature in comparison with various other situations of web programming is that there are hardly any equivalent alternatives in pure JavaScript or Dynamic Hypertext Markup Language (DHTML). In this area, using jQuery can add particular value. The jQuery methods are, of course, also based on the typical tree navigation, as you would use it under XPath.

6.11.1   Of Children and Parents: `children()` and `parent()` plus `parents()`/`parentsUntil()`

A very important relationship in the tree of a web page is the relationship between parents and children. With the `children()` method, you can determine all direct children of one or more parent elements and have them returned as jQuery object. The method can also have a filter expression as a parameter. In parallel, the `parent()` method returns the direct parents if the method is applied to a set of elements. The `parents()` method returns all ancestors of an element, except for the root (ch6_18.html).

Listing 6.43   **Elements with Parents and Multiple Children**

```
...
08     <script type="text/javascript"
09       src="lib/ch6_18_ready.js"></script>
10   </head>
11   <body>
12     <div>
13       <img src="images/b1.png" />
14       <div class="c1">
15         <img src="images/b2.png" /><br/>
16         <img src="images/b3.png" class="c1"/>
17       </div><hr/>
18     </div>
19     <button>All children of the first DIV</button>
20     <button>All children in a DIV that has
21       the class c1</button>
22     <button>All children of the parent of the
23       3rd image</button>
24     <button>All parents of the 2nd image</button>
25     <div id="output"></div>
26   </body>
27 </html>
```

In the web page, we have two nested div elements whose parent and child structures we will search (ch6_18_ready.js).

Listing 6.44   **Determining Parent and Child Elements**

```
01 $(function(){
02 $("button:first").click(function(){
03   element = $("div:first").children();
04   $("#output").text("Number of child elements: " +
05   element.length);
06 });
07 $("button:eq(1)").click(function(){
08   element = $("div").children(".c1");
09   $("#output").text("Number of child elements: " +
10   element.length);
11 });
12 $("button:eq(2)").click(function(){
13   element = $("img:eq(2)").parent();
14   $("#output").text("Number of child elements: " +
15   element.children().length);
16 });
17 $("button:eq(3)").click(function(){
18   elements = $("img:eq(1)").parents();
```

```
19    $("#output").text("Number of parent elements: " +
20    elements.length);
21      for (i = 0; i < elements.length; i++)
22        $("#output").append("<br />" + i + ": " +
23           elements[i].nodeName);
24    });
25    $("img").css("width", "150px");
26 });
```

Note that the images in the web page are separated with line breaks (<br />) and horizontal lines (<hr />). Such elements are also independent nodes in the tree and are counted as child elements. Correspondingly, the number of child elements in the first div container is three (two images and one break).

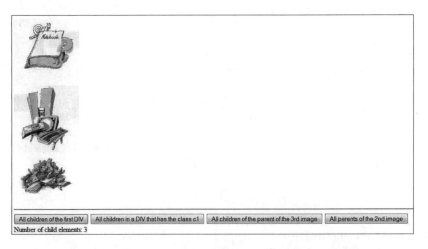

Figure 6.48   In the first div container, there are three child elements.

With children(), we determine all child elements of the div container in line 3 and save them in the variable element. The displayed text proves that there are three child elements. Because the variable element now contains a jQuery object that refers to these elements, we can determine the number via length just as with a normal array.

In line 8, we use a filter expression as parameter for children(). The filter expression ensures that only those elements are in the jQuery object element that actually match the filter. There will be exactly two, as you can try yourself easily.

In line 13, we select the parent element of the third image and then determine the number of its child elements. So, we also have information on the **siblings** of this element. Let's take another look at the block in the HTML file.

Listing 6.45   **From the Third Image to the Parent Element, Then Counting All the Children**

```
<div class="c1">
  <img src="images/b2.png" /><br/>
  <img src="images/b3.png" class="c1"/>
</div>
```

We start from the third image and go to the surrounding `div` element via `parent()`. This then contains three children because once again the line break counts as well.

The fourth situation selects the second image element and from then on returns all parent elements excluding the root (from the inside out, in relation to the index of the data field).

If we look at the DOM tree in Firebug, we can see that from the second image a `div` element is the direct parent. This has another `div` element as parent. And that one's parent is the body. So, we have three parent elements. The body is still contained in the element of the type `html` as child, so there are four (indirect) parents of the second image element.

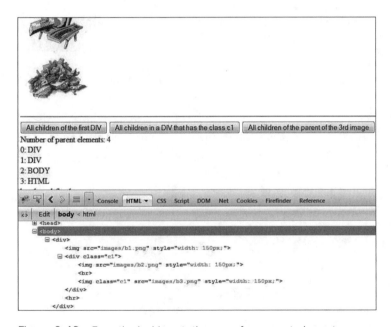

Figure 6.49   From the inside out, there are four parent elements.

> **Caution**
>
> Regarding determining the parent elements via `parents()`, there is a quite strange phenomenon.[12] At least I consider the behavior of the framework when using this method somewhat inconsistent or dangerous. If you iterate with `for (i in elements)` in line 21 over the array that is returned by `parents()`, you also get the root #document and all its DOM properties. You can test this with the example file ch6_18_1.html on the companion website.

Since jQuery 1.4, there is a variation of `parents()` in the form of `parentsUntil()`. This method works exactly the same as `parents()`, but you specify a parameter as selector that specifies a stop of the selection of parent elements. The element specified via the selector is explicitly *no longer* selected. If the selector does not apply at all, all parent elements will be selected, just as with `parents()`.

6.11.2 `offsetParent()` and `closest()`

For parent and child relationships, you also have the `closest()`[13] and `offsetParent()` methods. With `closest()`, you get a set of elements with the next parent element that matches the specified selector (including the start element). The method first checks whether the current element matches the specified expression. If yes, the current element itself will be returned. If not, the method works its way through the tree upward, parent element by parent element, until it finds an element that matches the specified expression. If there is no match, no element is returned.

The method `offsetParent()` returns a jQuery collection with the **positioned**[14] parent element of the first matched element, but the method only works with visible elements (ch6_19.html).

Listing 6.46   **Finding Children and Parents of Elements**

```
...
08    <script type="text/javascript"
09       src="lib/ch6_19_ready.js"></script>
10    </head>
11    <body>
12      <div>
13       <div>
14         One Ring to rule them all,
15              <h6>One Ring to find them, </h6>
16         <h5>One Ring to bring them all </h5>
17         <h5>and in the darkness bind them.</h5>
18       </div><hr/>
```

12. At least in the version of jQuery that the book is based on.

13. As of jQuery 1.3.

14. Via the CSS property `position`, regardless if absolute or relative.

```
19       <table border="1" style="position:absolute">
20         <tr><td>closest("div") von $("h5:eq(0)")</td>
21           <td id="output1"></td></tr>
22         <tr><td>offsetParent() von $("td:eq(1)"</td>
23           <td id="output2"></td></tr>
24       </table>
25     </div>
26   </body>
27 </html>
```

And here is the JavaScript file ch6_19_ready.js.

Listing 6.47 `closest()` **and** `offsetParent()`

```
01 $(function(){
02   $("#output1").text($("h5:eq(0)").
03     closest("div").html());
04   $("#output2").text($("td:eq(1)").
05     offsetParent().html());
06 });
```

In line 3 we search with `$("h5:eq(0)").closest("div")` for the parent element of the type div closest to the first heading of the type h5. If you look at the web page body, you will see that this has to be the inner div container that goes from line 13 to line 18 in the HTML file. We get its content via `html()` and display it uninterpreted with `text()`.

In line 5, we determine the offset parent element of the second table cell. Of course, the table cell is enclosed in a `<table>` element, and this has a `position` property, as you can see in line 19 of the HTML file. Correspondingly, we get the entire content of the table[15] as a jQuery object with `html()`, and we again output this object with `text()`.

One Ring to rule them all,	
One Ring to find them,	
One Ring to bring them all	
and in the darkness bind them.	
closest("div") of $("h5:eq(0)")	One Ring to rule them all, \<h6>One Ring to find them, \</h6> \<h5>One Ring to bring them all \</h5> \<h5>and in the darkness bind them.\</h5>
offsetParent() of $("td:eq(1)"	\<tbody>\<tr>\<td>closest("div") of $("h5:eq(0)")\</td> \<td id="output1"> One Ring to rule them all, <h6>One Ring to find them, </h6> <h5>One Ring to bring them all </h5> <h5>and in the darkness bind them.</h5> \</td>\</tr> \<tr>\<td>offsetParent() of $("td:eq(1)")\</td> \<td id="output2">\</td>\</tr> \</tbody>

Figure 6.50   The effect of `closest()` and `offsetParent()`.

15. In the form in which the browser internally processes the content.

6.11.3   Siblings

Finding elements via relationships in the tree is possible with a few other methods beyond the parent-child relationship. These methods basically can be applied in the same way as children() or parent(), so we discuss them only briefly here. These are sibling relationships; in other words, we are specifically looking for elements that are on the same level as the selector element.

The next() method returns a jQuery object with the next direct sibling of an element or the next direct siblings of a group of elements that follow the basic element. The nextAll() method works almost the same, but all sibling elements after the current element are returned.

You also get the direct siblings preceding the current element with prev() and all sibling elements preceding the current element with prevAll().

With siblings(), you get all siblings before and after the current element or group of elements.

> **Tip**
>
> With an optional filter expression as a parameter, you can limit the selection for all methods, as described earlier.

Listing 6.48   **Sibling Relationships (ch6_20.html)**

```
...
08    <script type="text/javascript"
09       src="lib/ch6_20_ready.js"></script>
10    </head>
11    <body>
12      <div>
13        <h3>Tiger, tiger, burning bright</h3>
14        <h3>In the forests of the night</h3>
15        <h3>What immortal hand or eye</h3>
16        <h3>Could frame thy fearful symmetry?</h3>
17        <h3>In what distant deeps or skies</h3>
18        <h3>Burnt the fire of thyne eyes?/h3>
19        <h3>On what wings dare he aspire?</h3>
20        <h3>What the hand dare seize the fire?</h3>
21      </div><hr />
22      <h2>Relationships of the third
23         heading of the type h1</h2>
24      <table border="1">
25        <tr><td>next()</td><td id="output1"></td></tr>
26        <tr><td>nextAll()</td><td id="output2"></td></tr>
27        <tr><td>prev()</td><td id="output3"></td></tr>
28        <tr><td>prevAll()</td><td id="output4"></td></tr>
```

```
29      <tr><td>siblings()</td><td id="output5"></td></tr>
30      </table>
31    </body>
32  </html>
```

Here we have a web page as an example that contains several headings of the type h3 in the same level. And here is the JavaScript file ch6_20_ready.js.

Listing 6.49   **Siblings**

```
01 $(function(){
02   $("#output1").text($("h3:eq(2)").next().text());
03   $("#output2").text($("h3:eq(2)").nextAll().text());
04   $("#output3").text($("h3:eq(2)").prev().text());
05   $("#output4").text($("h3:eq(2)").prevAll().text());
06   $("#output5").text($("h3:eq(2)").siblings().text());
07     $("h3:eq(2)").css("background","lightgray");
08 });
```

In the example, we determine the siblings of the third heading of the type h3. That is the heading with the content *What immortal hand or eye*. This heading is highlighted in line 7 purely to add visual emphasis. The script is output as described earlier.

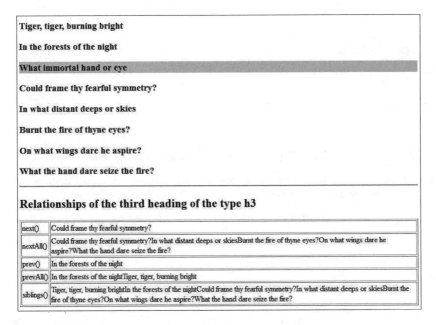

Figure 6.51   The various siblings of the third heading with the type h3.

With next(), you get the directly following heading of the type h3. Via nextAll(), you select all following headings of the type h3 and accordingly with prev() the directly preceding ones. With prevAll(), you get the two headings that are before the selected element. And with siblings(), you select all headings of the type h3 except for the selected element from which you are acting.

The ...Until Variants

Since jQuery 1.4, there are variations of nextAll() and prevAll() in the form of nextUntil() and prevUntil(). These work exactly the same as their two sister methods, but you specify as parameter a selector that indicates a stop of the sibling selection. The element specified via the selector is specifically *not* selected any more.

Listing 6.50   **The Siblings Are Selected Up to the Class k1**

```
$('div').nextUntil('.k1')
```

If the selector does not have a match, all siblings in the specified direction are selected.

6.11.4 Searching Descendants with has()

Since jQuery 1.4, there is the has() method, for which you can specify a selector or a DOM element as a parameter. This element has to be a descendant of the preceding element in the tree, so the element is selected.

Listing 6.51   **A Descendant Rule**

```
$('div').has('p').css('background-color', 'red');
```

In this example, only the div elements that have a descendant of the type p would be selected.

6.12   Finding with find() and contents()

Two interesting methods for finding elements and contents of a web page are find() with a filter expression as parameter and contents().

With find(), you can search descendant elements of an element to see if they match the filter expression.

> **Caution**
>
> The current element is not searched! That is what the method filter() is for.

With contents(), you get all child nodes (including text nodes) within a concerned element. If you apply the method to an inline frame, you get the contained document (ch6_21.html).

Listing 6.52 **The Basic Site**

```
...
08    <script type="text/javascript"
09      src="lib/ch6_21_ready.js"></script>
10  </head>
11  <body>
12   <div>
13    <h5>One Ring to rule them all,</h5>
14    <h6>One Ring to find them, </h6>
15    <h5>One Ring to bring them all </h5>
16    <h4>and in the darkness bind them.</h4>
17   </div>
18   <hr>
19   <table border="1">
20    <tr><td>find("h5") in $("div:eq(0)"</td>
21      <td id="output1"></td></tr>
22    <tr><td>contents() in $("h5")</td>
23      <td id="output2"></td></tr>
24   </table>
25  </body>
26 </html>
```

Here we have a web page as an example that contains several headings within a div area. And here is the JavaScript file ch6_21_ready.js.

Listing 6.53 `find()` **and** `contents()`

```
01 $(function(){
02   $("#output1").text($("div:eq(0)").find("h5").text());
03   $("#output2").text($("h5").contents().text());
04 });
```

In the example, you can see that find() returns the content of the level 5 headings specified in the filter expression, and contents() returns the contents of all child elements that we select via $("h5"). In our case, this returns the same result twice.

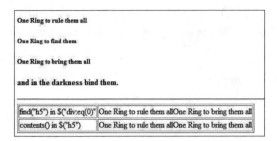

Figure 6.52   The result of `find()` and `contents()`.

6.13   The jQuery Method `each()` for Iterating over Arrays and Objects

We move on to a very fundamental and immensely important section. In JavaScript, you usually use dot notation to access the components of an object, as you know. The alternative is what is referred to as array notation. This involves writing or reading properties or methods via a data field notation, permitting meaningful indices. In JavaScript, objects are implemented completely identical to arrays as lists with value pairs of property and associated value. For methods, the value is a function reference.

Let's look at a little example in native JavaScript where we create an object and access it via array notation.

Listing 6.54   **Accessing an Object via Array Notation**

```
var x = {
  name: "Felix",  age: 11,  occupation: "Student"
};
var index = "name";
document.write(x[index]); // "Felix"
document.write(x[age]); // 11
```

This procedure is also referred to as **associative array**. In JavaScript, in particular when iterating over properties and methods of an object, you can proceed completely consistently as you would for an array. And as the indices are not numbers[16] in case of objects, but names of properties and methods, you just need to use the techniques for an associative array when iterating. A `for-in` loop is well suited for this.

Let's make it clearer by looking at a complete example that for once manages entirely without jQuery and also works with an internal JavaScript (ch6_22.html).

16. Strictly speaking, numeric indices in JavaScript are also strings, just with numbers as content.

Listing 6.55   **Iteration over an Object**

___

```
...
07  <body>
08    <table width="300" border="1">
09      <tr>
10        <th>Property</th>
11        <th>Value</th>
12      </tr>
13      <script type="text/javascript">
14        var x = {
15          name: "Felix",
16          age: 11,
17          occupation: "Student"
18        };
19        for (i in x) {
20          document.write("<tr><td>" + i +
21            "</td><td>" + x[i] + "</td></tr>");
22        }
23      </script>
24    </table>
25  </body>
26 </html>
```

___

Here we have created an object according to our descriptions above and display its properties plus preceding identifier of the properties dynamically in a table whose basic structure was built with pure HTML. We access the properties of the object x with the counter index i of the loop.

Property	Value
name	Felix
age	11
occupation	Student

Figure 6.53   Outputting the properties in a table.

So far, you can work quite well with pure JavaScript. But as complement for the normal iteration with loops, jQuery offers a generic function `jQuery.each()` for iterating over both all properties of objects and elements of an array. It is more flexible than the classic JavaScript technique, plus more robust and quite frequently used within jQuery.[17] There is also a method `each()` that can be applied to a preceding array or object.

___

17. In particular, with almost every plug-in.

6.13.1   jQuery.each()

As first parameter for `jQuery.each()`, you specify the array or object over which you want to iterate. If you specify an (anonymous) function[18] as a second parameter, you get via its first parameter the index of the array or object and via the second parameter the associated value (ch6_23.html)[19].

Listing 6.56   **The Basic Site**

```
...
08    <script type="text/javascript"
09      src="lib/ch6_23_ready.js"></script>
10    </head>
11    <body>
12    <table width="300" border="1" id="tab">
13      <tr>
14        <th>Property</th>
15        <th>Value</th>
16      </tr>
17    </table>
18    </body>
19    </html>
```

Here we have structurally the same web page as in the previous example without jQuery. But the table content is missing, or more specifically the part that we have created there with the internal JavaScript container and the `for-in` loop because we want to generate that part with `jQuery.each()` (ch6_23_ready.js).

Listing 6.57   **Using** `jQuery.each()`

```
01 $(function(){
02   var x = {
03     name: "Felix",
04     age: 11,
05     occupation: "Student"
06   };
07   jQuery.each(x, function(index, value){
08     $("#tab").append("<tr><td>" + index
09        + "</td><td>" + value + "</td></tr>");
10   });
11 });
```

18. Generally, you can write down a callback here.

19. Note that we again start with the standard structure with the first seven source code lines where jQuery is integrated.

We again create the same object as just now. In line 7, you can see the head of the loop with the object x as first parameter and the anonymous function. This has two parameters. The first parameter represents the index of the loop pass and the second parameter the value in the array or the object at this point.

> ## Caution
>
> We have chosen meaningful names for the function parameters, but the names are not relevant. These are not keywords or tokens with any particular meaning. You can choose different names. But this would not be a good decision because it can result in misunderstandings and make the code generally less readable.

Let's look at another example where we explicitly use `jQuery.each()` with a callback and the iterated object represents a collection of objects. Or in other words—in this context, we are not interested in the properties of the individual objects in the collection, but the collection itself.

> ## Tip
>
> Within the callback function, this stands for the currently specified **DOM element** in the iteration. With `$(this)`, you get a corresponding jQuery object.

Listing 6.58   **The Basic Site (ch6_24.html)**

```
...
08     <script type="text/javascript"
09       src="lib/ch6_24_ready.js"></script>
10   </head>
11   <body>
12     <div>An answer for you?</div>
13       <div>Yes. I have.</div>
14     <p>There really is one?</p>
15     <div>There really is one.</div>
16     <p>To Everything?</p>
17       <p>To the great Question of Life,
18       the Universe, and Everything?</p>
19     <div>Yes.</div>
20     <p>And you're ready to give it to us?</p>
21     <div>I am.</div>
22     <p>Now?</p>
23     <div>Now.</div>
24     <div>Though I don't think
25       that you are going to like it.</div>
26     <button>Deep Thought</button>
27     <button>Fool</button>
28   </body>
29 </html>
```

Here you can see a web page with a structure of alternating div and p blocks. We want to format these differently, depending on whether the user clicks the first or second button. For selecting all elements that belong together, we use jQuery.each() (ch6_24_ready.js).

Listing 6.59   jQuery.each() **with Callback Functions as a Parameter**

```
01 $(function(){
02   $("button:first").click(function(){
03     jQuery.each($("div"),function(){
04       this.style.color = "blue";
05       this.style.background = "yellow";
06       this.style.fontSize = "22px";
07     });
08     jQuery.each($("p"),function(){
09       this.style.color = "black";
10       this.style.background = "white";
11       this.style.fontSize = "12px";
12     });
13   });
14   $("button:last").click(function(){
15     jQuery.each($("p"),format);
16     jQuery.each($("div"),function(){
17       $(this).css({
18         color: "black",
19         background: "white",
20         fontSize: "12px"
21       });
22     });
23   });
24 });
25 function format(){
26   $(this).css({
27     color: "red",
28     background: "lightgray",
29     fontSize: "22px"
30   });
31 }
```

In the JavaScript file, you can see two event helpers via which the reaction to the user clicks is implemented. With the selector button:first, we select the first button in the web page and the second via the selector button:last. This works for our specific case because we only have two buttons. Depending on which button a user clicks, either all div areas or all paragraphs are highlighted.

The source code of line 2–13 specifies the reaction to the first button. A click triggers iterations with `jQuery.each()`. The second parameter of `jQuery.each()` is an anonymous callback function in each case, in which various CSS properties of the selected elements are changed. For the first button, we work for demonstration purposes explicitly with the DOM element that is represented by `this`.

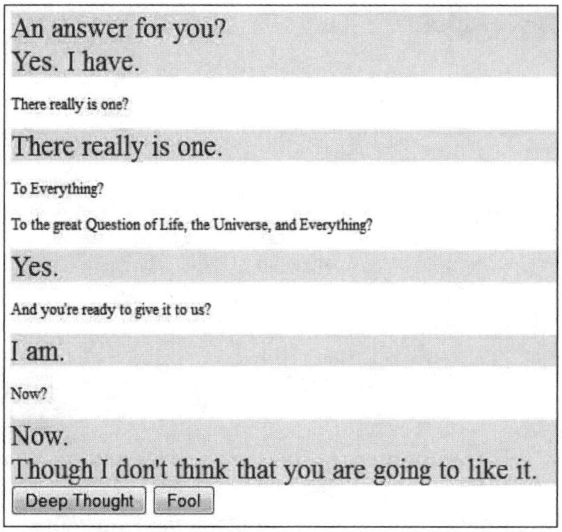

Figure 6.54   After clicking button 1.

For the reaction to the second button, we work slightly differently than with button 1. We only do this for demonstration purposes, because in practice you should avoid choosing different implementation approaches for the same problem wherever possible.

In lines 14–23, you can see that the formatting of the relevant paragraph per each `jQuery.each()` loop pass is done via the jQuery object represented by `$(this)` and via the `css()` method. This is not only more compact, but also less susceptible to browser errors. And note that we here work once (line 15) with a function reference to an external callback function (line 25–30) and the other time with an anonymous callback function that goes from line 16 to 22.[20] Note that we also have `this` or `$(this)` available in the external callback function to be able to access the object currently selected in the iteration.

---

20. As mentioned earlier, we just want to demonstrate the various approaches here.

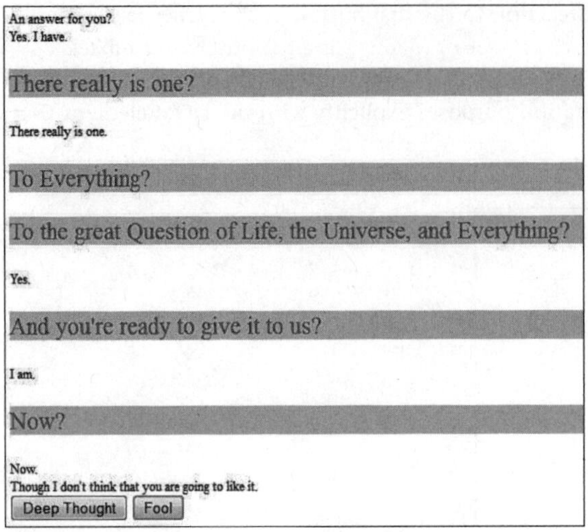

An answer for you?
Yes. I have.

There really is one?

There really is one.

To Everything?

To the great Question of Life, the Universe, and Everything?

Yes.

And you're ready to give it to us?

I am.

Now?

Now.
Though I don't think that you are going to like it.
[Deep Thought]   [Fool]

Figure 6.55   After clicking button 2.

> **Tip**
>
> You can also deliver a return value within the callback. The value `false` stops the loop immediately and corresponds to `break` in a normal loop. The return value `true` corresponds to `continue` and immediately starts the next pass of the loop.

6.13.2   The Method `each()`

In addition to the generic function `jQuery.each()`, the framework also offers an `each()` method that functionally does the same. This is even easier to use because it is applied to a preceding array or object and specifies an anonymous function as parameter whose first parameter is in turn the loop index. Alternatively, a callback is also possible. Inside the anonymous function or the callback, `this` once more stands for the current DOM element of a collection. So, we can directly transfer all explanations on the generic `jQuery.each()` function and only need to simplify the syntax slightly. For the example site ch6_25.html, we use the same structure as in ch6_24.html minus the buttons. Let's look at the JavaScript file ch6_25_ready.js.

Listing 6.60   **Using the `each()` Method**

```
01 $(function(){
02    $("div").each(function(index){
03        $(this).prepend((index + 1) + ": ");
04    $(this).css({
05        background:"lightgray"
```

```
06         });
07    });
08 });
```

In line 2, we select all `div` areas in the web page and iterate over them with `each()`. In the anonymous function, the index of the loop run is available with the parameter. And `this` is the current `div` element that we format with `$(this).css()`. The index is edited slightly and prepended to the text of the `div` element.

> **Caution**
>
> The name `index` of the function parameter is again a meaningful name we selected, but it is not relevant.

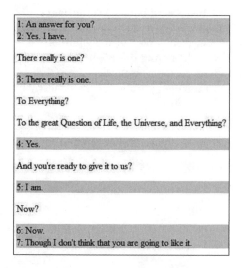

Figure 6.56 The `divs` are formatted and numbered.

6.14 The add() Method

The `add()` method is easy to misunderstand, in my opinion, because its name suggests adding nodes or elements to a web page or the DOM. But this is *not* what the method does. With the `add()` method, you can instead add elements to a set of already selected elements. In other words, you are only expanding a previously made selection. This proves most useful when using chained expressions.

As a parameter, you specify a selector that the additional elements have to match, DOM element, jQuery object, or an HTML fragment. As a second optional parameter, you can specify a context.

Take a look at the example where we use as web page ch6_26.html the same structure as ch6_25.html. Let's look at the JavaScript file ch6_26_ready.js.

Listing 6.61   **Using the** add() **Method**

```
01 $(function(){
02   $("div").css("background", "yellow").add("p").css({
03     "color": "red"
04   });
05 });
```

In line 2, we first only select all div elements and format their backgrounds. Via the css() method, the background color is set to yellow. The method gives us as a return value a jQuery object that contains all selected (and now formatted) div elements. We can apply further jQuery methods to it (in other words, chain several method calls). And this is where add() comes in. By calling it, we expand the selected collection of elements by all elements of the type p. To this *expanded* collection, we then apply the method css() again and set the text color to red.

After this chained sequence of statements, all div elements will have a red font color and yellow background, and all p elements have a red font color but no yellow background.

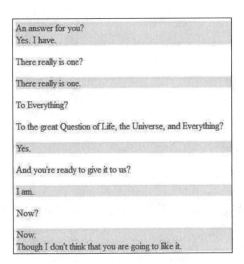

Figure 6.57   The background color applies only for div elements.

6.14.1 The end() and andSelf() Methods

For the sake of completeness, I want to mention two other methods to conclude this chapter, but I do not consider them quite so important. Most methods in jQuery for selecting or filtering elements operate on an instance of a jQuery object and produce a new instance if they encounter a diverging set of DOM elements. In this situation, it is like writing a new set of elements onto a stack. Already existing elements move down in the stack. So, if you still need these older elements, you can use end() to get them back from the end of the stack. But as I said, this method is very specific, and I do not think you will need it very often.

The andSelf() method belongs in the same category. If a jQuery method has written a new set of elements to a stack, you can use this method to fetch back the previous set of elements.

Let's assume you have the following structure.

Listing 6.62   **An Enumerated List**

```
<ul>
   <li>Ice Cream</li>
   <li>Beer</li>
   <li>Candy</li>
   <li>Chocolate</li>
   <li>Peanuts</li>
 </ul>
```

Now we want to format all list entries from the third list item onward. We do it like this.

Listing 6.63   **Formatting from the Third List Item Onward**

```
$(function(){
  $('li:eq(1)').nextAll().css({
    'background-color': 'red',
        'color':'yellow'
  });
});
```

Or this is another alternative.

Listing 6.64   **Formatting from the Third List Item Onward Using** andSelf()

```
$(function(){
  $('li:eq(2)').nextAll().andSelf().css({
    'background-color': 'red',
        'color':'yellow'
  });
});
```

Figure 6.58   The list items have been formatted from the third item onward.

In the first case, we choose the *second* list item as the starting point and then select all descendants. But in the second case, we choose the *third* list item, then all descendants, and then explicitly the third list item itself.

You can see the complete example ch6_27.html on the companion website. I do not consider this method quite as important either because, as you can see from our two examples, you can usually choose a suitable selector to create a situation where you can manage quite well without this method.

6.15   A More Comprehensive Example at the End: A Date Component

To conclude this chapter, we create a more elaborate example and practice using selectors and methods for iterating over and manipulating elements in a more complex context. First we need to skip ahead a little and use CSS techniques that are only discussed in detail in the next chapter. But these should not cause any serious problems here, and we have already worked through the other techniques involved.

More precisely, we create an automatic date component. That is not necessarily a new feature on the Web,[21] but it's good to practice techniques on a very useful application that can be applied in many other situations in that form.

We want to complete the following tasks when creating the component:

1. Determine and display the current month automatically.

2. Depending on the current date, the calendar should start with the appropriate day of the week or highlight the first day of each month.

3. Format the days of the current month differently than the days of the previous and next month, if these need to be displayed to fill up space in the calendar.

4. Apply special formatting for Sundays.

5. Highlight the current day.

6. Use a zebra stripe pattern for the various calendar lines.

---

21. There may already be one or two solutions around (even in the jQuery UI).

7. Display the month and year.

8. Layout adaptable via templates.

As you can see, you have a lot to do. First of all, here is our HTML file ch6_28.html, but not much happens in it.

Listing 6.65   **The Rather Empty Web Page**

```
...
06    <link href="lib/ch6_28_ready.css"
07       type="text/css" rel="stylesheet" />
08    <script type="text/javascript"
09       src="lib/jquery-1.8.2.min.js"></script>
10    <script type="text/javascript"
11       src="lib/ch6_28_ready.js"></script>
12  </head>
13  <body>
14    <h1>RJS Date Component V 1.0</h1>
15    <table/><div/>
16  </body>
17 </html>
```

We want to create the calendar component based on a table structure. That makes sense. Just look at the classic calendars you know. Now the web page is obviously rudimentary. We want to generate the entire structure dynamically. The empty table will be expanded, and we want the div area to show the month and the year.

As you can see in lines 6 and 7, we are using an external style sheet file, ch6_28_ready.css. This is the basis for fulfilling the requirement that the component can be adjusted via templates. By template we simply mean a CSS file in this case. With this, we are already jumping ahead to the techniques and philosophies applied, for example, by the jQuery UI with components (of course, in more elaborate and complex form). There, too, a template is a CSS library. Replacing the CSS file already permits adapting the layout completely, to the extent intended in the component. *Intended* means that we connect certain components of our date component to CSS classes (just as it is the case under the jQuery UI). Here you have a variation of the CSS file that shows a structure that is appropriate to our component.

Listing 6.66   **The Default Template File**

```
01 table {
02     font-size:12px;
03 }
04 tr{
05     background: yellow;
06 }
07 .currentDay{
08     color: red;
```

```
09      border:solid 1pt;
10 }
11 .odd{
12      background:lightgray
13 }
14 .headercells{
15      background:gray
16 }
17 .sunday{
18      background:cyan
19 }
```

In particular, the classes that we are using here will be of significance. If you adapt them (plus the rules for the table elements), you can edit the component's layout without changing the HTML or JavaScript file. But the relevant parts take place in JavaScript (ch6_28_ready.js).

Listing 6.67   The Component's Functionality Is Implemented in JavaScript

```
01 /**
02 * Global variables
03 */
04
05 var currentDay; // Day
06 var currentMonth; // Month
07 var currentYear; // Year
08 var startMonthDay // Start day of the current month
09
10 /**
11 * Initialization function
12 * @param {Object} - a date object
13 */
14 function init(tag){
15   var today;
16   // If no date is passed,
17   // use current system date
18   if (day == null)
19     today = new Date();
20   else
21     today = day;
22   currentDay = today.getDate();
23   currentMonth = today.getMonth();
24   currentYear = today.getFullYear();
25   var startMonth =
26     new Date(currentYear, currentMonth, 1);
27   startMonthDay = startMonth.getDay();
28   if (startMonthDay == 0)
```

```
29    startMonthDay = 7;  // Sunday
30 }
31
32 /**
33 * Generate 6 rows with 7 columns each
34 * Add class to last row
35 */
36 function row(){
37  var z = $("<tr></tr>");
38  for (var i = 0; i < 7; i++) {
39    if (i == 6)
40      z.append($("<td></td>").addClass("sunday"));
41    else
42      z.append($("<td></td>"));
43  }
44  return z;
45 }
46
47 /**
48 * Generate adapted days in table
49 * @param {Object} startMonthDay
50 */
51 function days(startMonthDay){
52  for (var i = 0; i < 42; i++) {
53    $("td").eq(i).append(
54       new Date(currentYear, currentMonth,
55         i - startMonthDay + 2).getDate());
56  }
57 }
58
59 /**
60 * The ready method
61 */
62 $(function(){
63  // Either pass current day date
64  // or any date
65  init(new Date());
66  // Table header rows
67  $("table").append(
68     $("<tr><th>Mon</th><th>Tue</th><th>Wed</th>" +
69       "<th>Thu</th><th>Fri</th>" +
70       "<th>Sat</th><th>Sun</th></tr>"));
71  // Append 6 rows with 7 columns each
72  for (var j = 0; j < 6; j++) {
73    $("table").append(row());
74  }
75  // Fill cells depending on start day
```

```
76   days(startMonthDay);
77   // Format TH cells
78   $("th").addClass("headercells");
79   // Format odd line numbers
80   $("tr:odd").addClass("odd");
81   // All TD cells before start of month transparent
82   $("td").slice(0, startMonthDay − 1).css(
83      "opacity", "0.3");
84   // All TD cells after end of month transparent
85   for (i = 28; i < 42; i++) {
86     if ($("td").eq(i).html() < 15)
87        $("td").eq(i).css("opacity", "0.3");
88   }
89   // Format the current day
90   $("td").eq(currentDay + startMonthDay − 2).
91      addClass("currentDay");
92   // Output month and year
93   $("div:first").append(
94      (currentMonth + 1) + "/" + currentYear);
95 });
```

Now, this is a jQuery book, not a JavaScript book. So, I want to just briefly describe what happens in the pure JavaScript passages in lines 1–30.

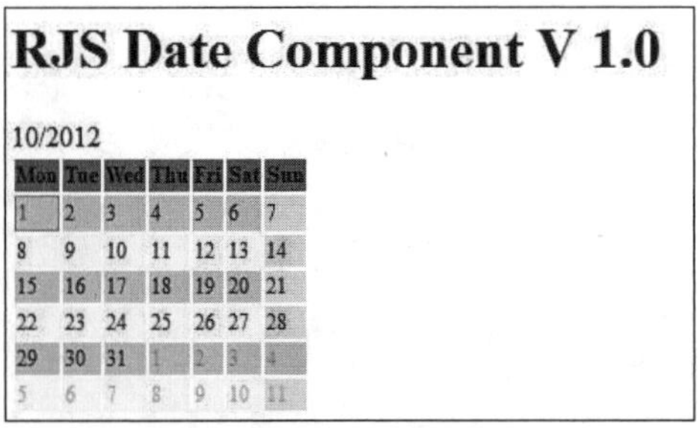

Figure 6.59   The date component with the highlighting for various structures.

The fundamental problem with a date component is having to determine the current day. This, in turn, determines the specific month to be displayed. Really, only the month is relevant, but we also want to highlight the current day.

To determine the current date, we use new Date(). If you do not want to use the current system date, you can also pass any other date to the constructor.[22] The relevant bit is in line 65. If you specify as a parameter for the function call something like new Date(2012,12,2), for example, you are explicitly selecting the second of December[23] 2012. And in this line, an initialization function is called that determines various pieces of date information in lines

14–30 in order to use these as global variables. With this information, we can determine the current day of the month and then format it later. And we can determine what day of the week the first day of the month is (because, of course, it is not always a Monday). So, we need to write the number 1 into the first line of the table with the days, into the column provided for the suitable day. But if the month does not start with a Monday, this row has to be filled up with the last days of the previous month. And these filler days are to be highlighted in a particular way.

In the same way, the last and sometimes next to last line may need to be filled with the days of the next month if the last day of the current month is not a Sunday.

With the months, you also need to take into account that these have different numbers of days. Imagine that there is no leap year and that February starts on a Monday. Then we can manage with just four rows in the table for that month.

If we have a month with 31 days and the first day of the month is a Saturday or Sunday, however, the current month will take up six rows. If you do not want to work with a dynamic number of rows in the date component,[24] you use six rows for the days and use special high-lighting for the days of the current month. This also has the advantage that the size of the component always stays the same.

In the `row()` function in lines 36–45, we create a table row with seven columns that are still empty for now. This structure of `tr` and `td` elements is returned as a string. We use `append()` to append the individual cells in a loop to a `tr` element. Then we add a `class` attribute to the last column via the method `addClass()`.

Listing 6.68   **The Empty Rows for the Days of the Month**

```
36 function row(){
37   var z = $("<tr></tr>");
38   for (var i = 0; i < 7; i++) {
39     if (i == 6)
40       z.append($("<td></td>").addClass("sunday"));
41     else
42       z.append($("<td></td>"));
43   }
44   return z;
45 }
```

The function is called six times in a loop in the `ready` method in line 73, and the return value is appended via `append()` to the table element that we have written as HTML tag in the web page.

---

22. This is pure JavaScript.

23. Remember that the month indexing starts with 0!

24. Which would be uncommon.

Listing 6.69   **The Empty Cells Are Appended to the Table**

```
72  for (var j = 0; j < 6; j++) {
73    $("table").append(row());
74  }
```

Previously, we appended the column headers of the table in lines 67–70 via th elements. The trick is now how to create the content of the up to now empty table cells.

Listing 6.70   **The Days Are Written into the Table**

```
51 function days(startMonthDay){
52   for (var i = 0; i < 42; i++) {
53     $("td").eq(i).append(
54        new Date(currentYear, currentMonth,
55          i - startMonthDay + 2).getDate());
56   }
57 }
```

In total, there are 42 cells of the type td. We use the filter eq() function to address these in a loop. As a start value for filling the table, we use the date of the Monday before the first of the target month. We can calculate its date because we have already determined the day of the week of the first day of the month. Then we can count back the days that we need to specify in the third parameter of the constructor.

For example, if the first of a month is a Thursday, we need to count back to see which day of the month the previous Monday was. That, in turn, depends on what month it is. We solve the problem by taking the day of the week for the first of the month and then counting back in the previous month by the difference between Monday and—in this case—Thursday. The factor 2 is a correction factor that is necessary in the selected algorithm in various places.[25]

> **Tip**
>
> We explicitly make use of how the constructor of Date behaves in case of a spillover. For example, you can specify new Date(2011,2,-8) (this gives you the February 20, assuming it is not a leap year) or new Date(2011,15,66). The days are simply counted backward from the 1ast.

Now let's examine the formatting more closely because selectors are used effectively here.

Listing 6.71   **Different Formatting with Intelligent Selectors**

```
77  // Format TH cells
78  $("th").addClass("headercells");
```

25. Of course we could also rebuild the algorithm, but it works like this, and that's all that matters.

```
79   // Format odd line numbers
80   $("tr:odd").addClass("odd");
81   // All TD cells before start of month transparent
82   $("td").slice(0, startMonthDay - 1).css(
83       "opacity", "0.3");
84   // All TD cells after end of month transparent
85   for (i = 28; i < 42; i++) {
86     if ($("td").eq(i).html() < 15)
87       $("td").eq(i).css("opacity", "0.3");
88   }
89   // Format the current day
90   $("td").eq(currentDay + startMonthDay - 2).
91       addClass("currentDay");
```

In line 78, the column headers are formatted. This is simple because we only use elements of the type th. In line 80, you can see how easily a zebra stripe pattern can be implemented. In both cases, we assign a specific class (and for the current day, too, in lines 90 and 91). So, you can simply change the class definition, or—even better—another CSS file to adapt the layout without having to change the HTML or JavaScript code.

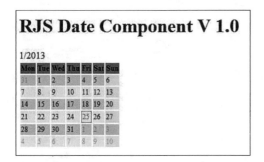

Figure 6.60   Different date and different "template."

Note that we set the transparency for the days in the previous month and following month directly in the source code. This consciously prevents adaptability here (for demonstration purposes). And what you need to watch our for, particularly in connection with transparency, is that Internet Explorer does not support the default property opacity. If you want to set it in the CSS file, you need to additionally work with the filter() function for Internet Explorer. But if you are using the css() method by jQuery, you can use opacity universally because the framework compensates for these problems in the background. In lines 93 and 94, we then output the month and year.

Summary

In this extensive chapter, you have seen how you can traverse a web page with jQuery and manipulate it, and how you can insert, edit, or remove nodes in a web page. Plus you have encountered further options for finding specific nodes and content in the web page. In particular, you should remember the methods `html()`, `text()`, `append()`, `prepend()`, `appendTo()`, `prependTo()` plus `after()`, `before()`, `insertAfter()`, and `insertBefore()` in this context. Wrapping with `wrap()` is also important. But you now also know methods for replacing content and nodes and for removing and cloning, plus iterating over objects and collections of objects. Finally, you now know more about relationships between parents and children, siblings, and the way in which jQuery deals with them.

7

Formatting with Style Sheets Under jQuery

Selectors and filters, plus the corresponding filter methods, are the basis of dynamically creating and changing web pages based on style sheets. On the Web, such style sheets in the form of Cascading Style Sheets (CSS) are the standard. Purely with regard to web pages, other style sheet languages really do not play any important role. And the times when we were using Hypertext Markup Language (HTML) commands to visually enhance a web page are now over. Using tags such as `<font>` or the general specifying of colors or alignment via HTML attributes is now only appropriate for quick and dirty sites that do not have to fulfill any particular expectations. This is not really worth mentioning, apart from the fact that it already applied more than 10 years ago.

However, web designers continued to use HTML tags for the visual design of web pages until recently. In some situations, this persistence may have had its merits because even though CSS has been standardized for many years, there are still problems with it in some browsers for certain effects, even today. You can assume that CSS version 1 is supported by all browsers, but certain rules from CSS 2 still do not work everywhere—even more than 12 years after the 3WC has standardized it. Let's not even mention CSS 3 and certain expanded properties that have actually been around for ages. Just think of the CSS property `opacity` that is still not supported by Internet Explorer, which instead requires a notation that does not conform to the standard.[1] Or the strict refusal of Internet Explorer to support rounded corners for block elements.[2]

> **Note**
>
> As of version 1.4.3 of jQuery, there are `cssHooks`. These are intended for hooking directly into the jQuery framework to overwrite certain CSS properties. Primarily this is intended for creating adapted and browser-optimized properties of the specific CSS3 properties.

1. Microsoft uses the proprietary method `filter()`, but jQuery uses this in the background automatically.

2. Even jQuery fails to succeed regarding support for rounded corners by Internet Explorer. Or rather, jQuery consistently uses CSS3 here, and anyone who chooses not to implement this standard will have to live with the consequences.

In normal jQuery programming, you are unlikely to need this feature very often, if ever.

The formatting with style sheets under jQuery does not mean that you should not convention-ally integrate `style` attributes, internal style containers, or—which is usually recommended—references to external CSS files into the HTML site when using jQuery. On the contrary, you are almost always going to do so. This chapter, however, focuses on dynamically accessing CSS formatting from within JavaScript (in other words, in combination with a certain programming logic).

With pure DHTML, you can access CSS properties easily via the style object, but if you choose this approach you will have to deal with the problems described earlier. Plus you have to deal with the fact that the properties for the `style` object differ from the notation of the CSS prop-erties regarding the use of uppercase and lowercase spelling and usage of the dash. These are only small difficulties, but it all adds up.

By using jQuery, you can normalize the properties, and they are then available in identical form on all supported browsers (including the `opacity`). I believe this constitutes the main benefit. The CSS methods in jQuery allow easy access to style sheets and integrate the access into the general framework philosophy (including the option of chaining).

> **Note**
>
> The jQuery methods are, of course, based directly on the classic applications of CSS or the `style` object.

7.1 The `css()` Method

The most fundamental, most general, and probably most important method for accessing style sheets in jQuery is `css()`.[3]

7.1.1 Getting Style Properties

Via the method `css()`, you can easily get the value of a CSS property. You simply specify the property as a string parameter. For example, you get the specific value of a single property like this.

Listing 7.1 **Getting the Background Color**

```
var color = $(this).css("background-color");
```

For the names of the CSS properties, you can also use the notations offered by the `style` object. The framework is easy going here and simply accepts both notations; for example, you could also write `backgroundColor`. (Note that the words must be written together and that the second word starts with a capital letter; this is required.)

3. We have already used it a few times.

> **Tip**
> This applies to all places where you specify style properties in jQuery.

Listing 7.2 **Alternative Naming of Style Properties**

```
var color = $(this).css("backgroundColor");
```

> **Caution**
> Commonly used shorthand notations of some CSS properties such as `border` are explicitly not supported by `css()` and other similar methods! The degree of support for these methods can vary in the different versions of the framework. For example, older versions did not understand `background`, and you had to write down the complete names of the desired CSS properties. So, for example, `background-color` rather than `background`. In version 1.5, the shorthand form `background` was possible. As of version 1.7.2, shorthand CSS properties are no longer supported. To be on the safe side, it is best to always use the full variation rather than the shorthand.

7.1.2 Setting Properties

Of course, you can also set the values of CSS properties via the `css()` method. CSS properties are set by passing the `name, value` arguments or by passing an object literal with multiple `name: value` pairs into `css()`. Usually, the names of the properties and the values are enclosed by quotation marks, as shown in Listing 7.3.

Listing 7.3 **Setting the Value for a Property**

```
$(this).css("color","red");
```

This notation is used for setting exactly one property. The other option is to only specify a parameter. Then the parameter is not a string, but an option object where you write down a properties list as usual with key value pairs separated by commas, enclosed by pointed brackets. With this notation, you can also set several properties at once.

Listing 7.4 **Setting Several Values with a Properties List**

```
$(this).css({
    'background-color' : 'blue', 'color' : 'white',
    'opacity' : '0.7'
  });
```

> **Caution**
>
> With the property names, you can in some cases manage without the string form and write
> the names without enclosing them in quotation marks. This is usually the case if you are
> using the notation in the object literal for a property of the `style` object (for example,
> `backgroundColor`). But I advise against this and recommend using the uniform notation in
> quotation marks. This is more consistent and easier to manage, and you are erring on the side
> of caution. For the variant with two parameters, you always have to write the names of proper-
> ties in string form and enclose them in quotation marks, even if you use the notation for a
> property of the `style` object.

The `css()` method is very simple and can be applied to any conceivable formatting with CSS
without requiring further explanation. But for the sake of completeness, Listing 7.5 provides a
full example (ch7_1.html).

Listing 7.5   **The Basic File**

```
...
06    <script type="text/javascript"
07        src="lib/jquery-1.8.2.min.js"></script>
08    <script type="text/javascript"
09        src="lib/ch7_1_ready.js"></script>
10   </head>
11   <body>
12     <div>A child of five</div>
13     <div>would understand this.</div>
14     <div>Fetch me a child of five.</div><hr/>
15     <button>Set text color</button>
16     <button>Set text color and
17        background color</button>
18     <button>Get text color</button>
19     <hr/><div id="output"></div>
20   </body>
21 </html>
```

And here is the JavaScript file ch7_1_ready.js.

Listing 7.6   **Getting and Setting CSS Properties**

```
01 $(function(){
02   $("button:first").click(function(){
03     $('div:lt(3)').css("color", "red");
04   });
05   $("button:eq(1)").click(function(){
06     $('div:lt(3)').css({
07       "color": "blue",
```

```
08        "background-color": "lightgray"
09      });
10    });
11    $("button:last").click(function(){
12      $("#output").text($("div:first").css("color"));
13    });
14  });
```

In the example, we set the font color of the first three `div` elements in the web page. You can see this in line 3. We are using the variant with the two string parameters.

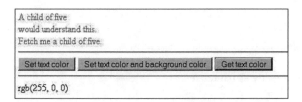

Figure 7.1   Setting font color to red and getting it.

In lines 6–9, you can see the variant with the parameter in the form of options. The font color is set to blue and the background to light gray.

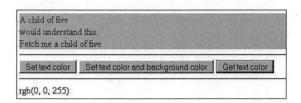

Figure 7.2   Setting font color to blue and getting it.

Finally, in line 12, you can see that we get the property `color`.

Chaining CSS formatting is also easily possible in the framework. You can use dot notation to chain several `css()` methods. But this is rarely necessary because you can almost always manage with a method call with options as parameter.

7.2 Changing Classes of Elements

The jQuery framework offers some interesting methods for accessing CSS classes. These make dynamic handling much easier. Essentially, these methods manipulate the value of the `class` attribute of an element.

7.2.1   Adding Classes: `addClass()`

As the name of the method `addClass()` indicates, calling this method assigns one or several style sheet classes to the previously specified elements. This happens dynamically, but without the web page having to be reloaded or updated in any form. The CSS class must, of course, be available in some form in the web page.

> **Tip**
>
> Via this method and the other methods for accessing CSS classes, you can ensure the separation of layout and functionality. The layout is prepared in the classical way in a CSS file via the static specification of classes and only the specific assignment (the logic) is implemented in JavaScript.

Direct Specification of Classname

The class to be assigned can be specified directly as parameter.

Listing 7.7   **Adding a CSS Class**

```
$("#e").addClass("myClass1");
```

Several classes in the string are separated by spaces.

Listing 7.8   **Adding Three CSS Classes**

```
$("#e").addClass("myClass1 myClass2 myClass3");
```

Using a Callback Function

As of jQuery 1.4, you can also write a callback function as parameter for all methods that manipulate classes. This should (or better, *must*[4]) return one or several classnames, separated by spaces, that are to be assigned to the elements in the previously specified jQuery object.

Listing 7.9   **Specifying a Callback Function That Is Intended to Return One or Several Classes**

```
$("div").addClass(function(){});
```

The callback function has two optional standard parameters. The first optional parameter represents the index position of the currently accessed element in a set of previously specified elements. When the different elements are passed through while the method is processing, you can decide based on the index what you want to do with each specific element (for example, return an individual class, as we will do in our next example).

4. If it is to be useful.

The second optional parameter represents the current value of the attribute `class` at the relevant processing stage—in other words, before the new assignment.

Listing 7.10   **Specifying a Callback Function Where Two Parameters Represent the Index and the Old Class**

```
$("div").addClass(function(index, Class){});
```

> **Note**
>
> We analyze in detail how the method `addClass()` works using the following example. We use Firebug to analyze the situation repeatedly—in particular, the behavior of the callback function because this is rather interesting and fundamentally important. You can then apply these explanations to the other methods for manipulating the `class` attribute and to many other manipulation methods of elements in general. So, the explanations for the other methods are less detailed. Please do not be surprised to find such detailed explanations for a method that is really rather simple.

Let's move on to our complete example. We use it to test the different variations of how you can apply `addClass()` (ch7_2.html).

Listing 7.11   **The Basic File**

```
...
06    <link rel="stylesheet" type="text/css"
07       href="lib/ch7_2.css" />
08    <script type="text/javascript"
09       src="lib/jquery-1.8.2.min.js"></script>
10    <script type="text/javascript"
11       src="lib/ch7_2_ready.js"></script>
12  </head>
13  <body>
14    <div>A child of five</div>
15    <div>would understand this.</div>
16    <div>Fetch me a child of five.</div><hr/>
17    <button>Assign class 1</button>
18    <button>Assign class 2 and 3</button>
19    <button>Assign class 4</button>
20    <button>Assign classes by index</button>
21  </body>
22 </html>
```

The web page contains three `div` areas to which we want to assign classes dynamically. We want to test four constellations, so there are four buttons to trigger these actions.

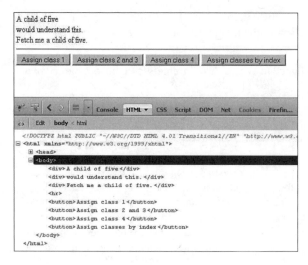

Figure 7.3   The web page before applying the style sheets.

Because we want to work with CSS classes, we have to make these available in the web page, as mentioned earlier. The best way of doing this is, of course, via an external CSS file. In lines 6 and 7, you can see the reference to the external CSS file ch7_2.css. It looks like Listing 7.12.

Listing 7.12   **The CSS File**

```
01 .c1 {
02   background: red;
03 }
04 .c2 {
05   color: yellow;
06 }
07 .c3 {
08   font-size: x-large;
09 }
10 .c4 {
11   word-spacing: 2em
12 }
```

The file is not very exciting. In the CSS file, you can just see four simple classes that will be assigned in several variations to the div elements and set color, font size, and word spacing.

> **Note**
>
> We have already mentioned this in the section on jQuery basics, but here once again note that the references to the CSS files have to be written in the web page *before* the references to the scripts.

Here is the JavaScript file ch7_2_ready.js, in which we make the specific assignments to the `div` elements.

Listing 7.13   **Assigning CSS Classes**

```
01 $(function(){
02   $("button:first").click(function(){
03     $("div").addClass("c1");
04   });
05   $("button:eq(1)").click(function(){
06     $("div").addClass("c2 c3");
07   });
08   $("button:eq(2)").click(function(){
09     $("div").addClass(function(){
10       return "c4";
11     });
12   });
13   $("button:last").click(function(){
14     $("div").addClass(function(index, Class){
15       alert("Value of index: " + index +
16         ", Value of class: " + Class);
17       return "c" + (index + 1);
18     });
19   });
20 });
```

By clicking the first button, we simply specify the classname as string to assign the class `c1` to all `div` elements; see line 3. You can see the result in the web page and even better in Firebug.

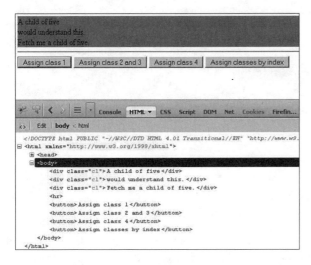

Figure 7.4   In Firebug, you can see that the value of the class attribute has been set.

Clicking the second button, we want to assign several classes at once in line 6. The classes in the string are simply separated by spaces. If you have already assigned another class before, the classes are used additively, as usual in CSS.[5]

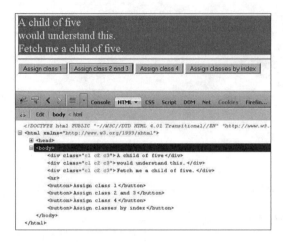

Figure 7.5   Separated by spaces, the elements are assigned several classes.

For the third button you see the situation that a callback function in line 10 simply returns a class. Of course, it could also return several classes. These would just have to be separated by spaces in the string.

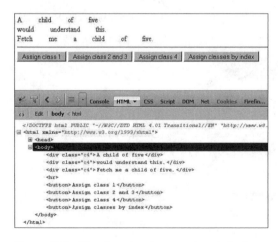

Figure 7.6   The class has been assigned via the return value of a function.

5. With all consequences that apply under CSS. Either the properties from the different classes combine or they contradict one another. In that case, the class that is furthest right in the value of the `class` attribute takes effect (but this takes us into CSS, no longer jQuery).

In practice, the effort involved in using a callback function is only usually sensible if you implement a sensible logic there. You can construct this logic based on various constellations. But two constellations are particularly relevant for manipulating CSS classes:

- The index of the element in the set of elements to be manipulated should be used.

- The previously assigned class plays a role.

The method addClass()[6] with the two optional default parameters of the callback function fulfills these. In other words, in the methods for class manipulation in the jQuery framework, you always have these two pieces of information available in the callback function. You can see how this information is used in the reaction to the fourth button.

In lines 14–19, you can see the specific application that we want to analyze in more detail. Let's take a closer look at it.

Listing 7.14   **Using the Callback Function with Parameters**

```
14   $("div").addClass(function(index, Class){
15      alert("Value of index: " + index +
16         ", Value of class: " + Class);
17      return "c" + (index + 1);
18   });
```

The first parameter index will specify which preceding element from the selected set is currently being processed. The framework processes the method for each item individually. Based on this, you can, for example, assign a particular class to each specific element. Through our logic of indexing the classnames in the CSS file numerically, prefixed by the same letter, we can assemble the returned class from a letter and the value of index. You can see this in line 17.

The second parameter represents the classes that have currently already been assigned to the element. In our example, this information is not processed further into the selection of a class,[7] but we output it together with the value of index before assigning the class in an alert() window.[8] For our analysis and demonstration of how addClass() works as well as many other methods in the jQuery framework, this has the added benefit that the processing of the script is interrupted until the dialog window has been closed. So, we can more easily follow the individual steps and see how they work. You will see that each div element is formatted individually.

After you have clicked the fourth button, you will first see the alert() window. The value of the index in the first pass is, of course, 0. If the element that is being accessed has already been assigned a class, this is available via the value of the second parameter and will be displayed. Note that the new class has not yet been assigned.

6. As well as the following methods for manipulating classes.

7. Which is easy to implement, just as any other conceivable logic.

8. Which shows at least that this information is available and represents in itself also a way of processing the information, albeit a very trivial one.

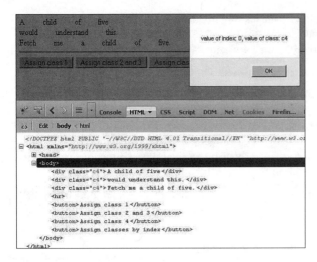

Figure 7.7   After clicking the fourth button; also note Firebug.

If you acknowledge the `alert()` message, the class is assigned and we return its name with `return`. As we generate this name from the token `"c"` and the value of `index + 1`, the class `c1` is assigned to the first `div` element in addition to any existing class. For the other `div` elements, the formatting remains unchanged.

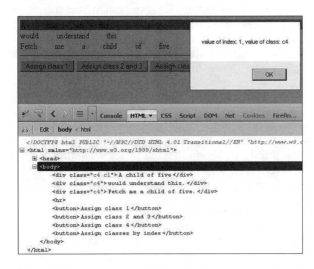

Figure 7.8   After acknowledging the first `alert()`, the class `c1` has been assigned.

After you have iterated over all three div elements following this pattern, you have assigned the class c1 to the first div element, c2 to the second, and c3 to the third.

> ### Caution
>
> Although it should be clear, I want to address the way the callback function works once more. Do not be confused by the return with callback functions of this kind. The statement is a jump statement with which a function or method ends. Here it seems that the method returns a class for an element and then continues running and assigns a class to the next element. But this is not the case, although the effect could be described in these terms. The statement return already ends the callback function, as always with functions or methods. But it is called again directly by the framework for the next element if it is still registered for other elements. So, in our example, the method is called three times and the framework manages the calls.

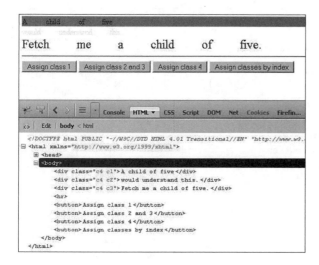

Figure 7.9   Each div element has been formatted individually.

If you now process the class parameter in the callback function again, you will see that several classes are also available through it. It is simply a string with the classes separated by spaces.

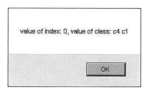

Figure 7.10   The class parameter can also make several classes available.

7.2.2   Removing Classes: removeClass()

Removing classes works in exactly the same way as assigning classes. We use the method removeClass() and pass it the class we want to remove as a string. It works basically in the same way as addClass() and, of course, you can also remove several classes simultaneously.

Listing 7.15   **Removing a CSS Class**

```
$("#e").removeClass("myClass1");
```

And as of jQuery 1.4, you can also use a callback function as a parameter. In the next example, we more or less use the same basic web page for demonstrating addClass(). The CSS file stays unchanged, apart from the new name ch7_3.css (ch7_3.html).

Listing 7.16   **The Basic File**

```
...
10    <script type="text/javascript"
11        src="lib/ch7_3_ready.js"></script>
12  </head>
13  <body>
14    <div>A child of five</div>
15    <div>would understand this.</div>
16    <div>Fetch me a child of five.</div><hr/>
17    <button>Assign class 1</button>
18    <button>Assign class 2 and 3</button>
19    <button>Remove class 1</button>
20    <button>Remove class 2 and 3</button>
21  </body>
22 </html>
```

Here is the JavaScript file ch7_3_ready.js.

Listing 7.17   **Assigning CSS Classes**

```
01 $(function(){
02  $("button:first").click(function(){
03    $("div").addClass("c1");
04  });
05  $("button:eq(1)").click(function(){
06    $("div").addClass(function(){
07      return "c2 c3";
08    });
09  });
10  $("button:eq(2)").click(function(){
11    $("div").removeClass("c1");
```

```
12   });
13   $("button:last").click(function(){
14     $("div").removeClass(function(){
15       return "c2 c3";
16     });
17   });
18 });
```

By clicking the first two buttons, we once more assign classes. With the identical syntax, but using the method removeClass(), we can remove the classes again.

7.2.3 Toggling Classes with `toggleClass()`

With the method toggleClass() we can remove or add a CSS class, depending on the state. If the class specified as parameter is already assigned, it is removed. If it is not yet assigned, it will be assigned. As with the previously discussed methods for class manipulation, you can specify one or several class names as a string or a suitable callback function.

> **Tip**
>
> As of jQuery 1.3, the method has a second optional parameter. This is a Boolean and specifies whether a class should be added or removed. In my opinion, this use contradicts the meaning of the name of the method, and after all, there is explicitly the alternative of addClass() and removeClass().

Listing 7.18 **The Basic File (ch7_4.html)**

```
...
10     <script type="text/javascript"
11         src="lib/ch7_4_ready.js"></script>
12   </head>
13   <body>
14     <div class="c1">A child of five</div>
15     <div class="c3">would understand this.</div>
16     <div>Fetch me a child of five.</div><hr/>
17     <button>Toggle class DIV 1</button>
18     <button>Toggle class DIV 2</button>
19   </body>
20 </html>
```

In the web page, we once again have three div areas. The first div element has already been assigned the class c1 in HTML, and the second div area has been assigned the class c2. The third div area has no explicit formatting via a CSS class. Using the different conditions, we will now take a closer look at how the toggling works.

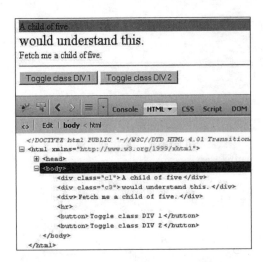

Figure 7.11   The original structure on loading.

Listing 7.19 shows the JavaScript file ch7_3_ready.js.

Listing 7.19   **Assigning and Removing CSS Classes**

```
01 $(function(){
02   $("button:first").click(function(){
03     $("div").toggleClass("c2");
04   });
05   $("button:last").click(function(){
06     $("div").toggleClass(function(){
07          return "c4";
08     });
09   });
10 });
```

The first time we toggle by directly specifying a string with the name of the new class (line 3), the second time we use the variation with the callback function (lines 6-8).

After clicking the first button, you see that all div elements have been assigned the class c2. But no existing class with another name has been removed. Instead, the class specified as a parameter was simply assigned in addition to the existing class.

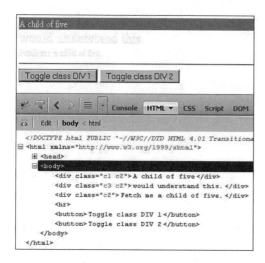

Figure 7.12   All `div` elements have been assigned the class `c2`.

If you click the button again, the class `c2` is removed and the previous condition is reinstated. The same happens accordingly when you click the second button and then click it again.

7.2.4   Testing for a Class: `hasClass()`

With the Boolean method `hasClass()`, you can test whether an element has been assigned a class. If the test is applied to several elements, it is enough if *one* of the elements fulfills the condition.

You simply specify the class as string parameter. Of course, you can also test for several classes if you separate the classnames in the string parameter with spaces, as usual. The return value in case of a match is `true`; otherwise it's `false`.

> **Note**
>
> For `hasClass()`, you cannot currently specify a callback function as a parameter.

Listing 7.20   **The Basic File (ch7_5.html)**

```
...
10    <script type="text/javascript"
11        src="lib/ch7_4_ready.js"></script>
12    </head>
13    <body>
14    <div class="c1">A child of five</div>
15    <div>would understand this.</div>
```

```
16      <div>Fetch me a child of five.</div><hr/>
17      <button>Test 1</button>
18      <button>Test 2</button>
19  </body>
20 </html>
```

The first div element has the class c1 that we want to test for. Here is the JavaScript file with the two test functions (ch7_5_ready.html).

Listing 7.21   **Testing for a Class**

```
01 $(function(){
02  $("button:first").click(function(){
03     alert($("div").hasClass("c1"));
04  });
05  $("button:last").click(function(){
06     alert($("div:eq(1)").hasClass("c1"));
07  });
08 });
```

In the first test, we check all div elements. Because the first div element has been assigned the class c1, the test returns true.

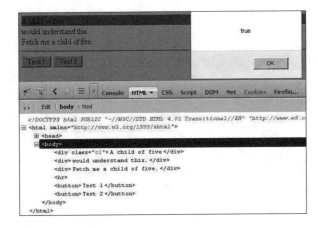

Figure 7.13   The first div element has passed the test.

In the second case, we test only the second div element, and it does not have the class c1 assigned. So, the test will return false.

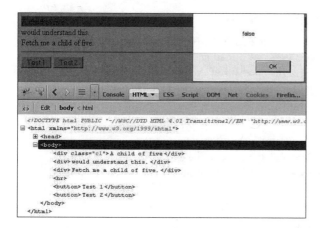

Figure 7.14   The class has not been assigned in the selected set of elements.

7.3   Positioning Methods

One of the biggest problems when designing and dynamically changing a web page is the positioning of elements. Via CSS, you can control the positioning of elements in a web page quite well with the properties `position` in combination with left and top.[9]

> **Note**
>
> The specifications right and bottom are still not supported by various browsers. It is best to avoid working with them.

The positioning data is based on the **offset** of an element. The null point of the coordinate system is placed into the top-left corner of the offset element. The jQuery positioning methods use these properties and coordinates as reference point.

> **Note**
>
> Although we are assuming basic knowledge of CSS in this book, the explanations on positioning, text flow, and the significance of offset will go into a bit more detail than would be necessary for the pure—rather primitive—application of most jQuery methods in this area. From my experience in training seminars, knowledge on these matters is in many cases quite rudimentary, despite otherwise good experience in CSS.

9. Note that elements absolutely positioned via CSS are taken out of the "normal" text flow or element flow of the site. For example, if there are three headings written down subsequently in HTML and the second heading is positioned absolutely via CSS, the normal flow of the site shows the third heading as directly following the first heading. But this should be already familiar to you from CSS.

7.3.1   Determining the Position with `position()`

Via the `position()` method, you determine the `top` and `left` values of an element relative to its offset parent element, both for elements positioned via CSS and those that are simply arranged in the text flow by the browser. This means that the positioning data in pixels is always to be seen in relation to the *top-left corner* of the surrounding offset parent element. In many cases, the offset parent element is the web page itself (in other words, the DOM object `document`), but it can also be a `div` element or another container object that the child element is contained in.

But (as you probably know) first this parent element has to be explicitly turned into an offset parent element;[10] for example, by absolutely positioning it (as shown in the following example, ch7_6.html).

Listing 7.22   **The Basic File with Four Images**

```
...
10      <script type="text/javascript"
11       src="lib/ch7_6_ready.js"></script>
12   </head>
13   <body>
14     <h1>Position of Elements</h1><hr/>
15     <table id="info"></table><hr/>
16     <img src="images/pic1.png" alt="A scanner" />
17     <div id="p1">
18       <img src="images/pic2.png"
19         alt="A portable computer" />
20       <img id="p2" src="images/pic3.png" alt="Mice" />
21     </div>
22     <img id="p3" src="images/pic4.png"
23       alt="Cable mouse" />
24   </body>
25 </html>
```

In the web page, you can see four images. Two of them are in a `div` area that has been assigned an ID p1. Plus you should notice that the third and fourth images have an ID.

Here is the JavaScript file ch7_6_ready.js, where we read out the positioning data of the four images and output it in the web page's info area (a table).

Listing 7.23   **Getting Positioning Data**

```
01 $(function(){
02   var pos = $("img:first").position();
03   $("#info").html(
```

10. Otherwise, the web page remains the reference. This is pure CSS.

```
04     "<tr><td>Image 1</td><td>left:</td><td>" +
05       pos.left +
06       "</td><td>top:</td><td>" +
07       pos.top + "</td></tr>");
08   pos = $("img:eq(1)").position();
09   $("#info").append(
10     "<tr><td>Image 2</td><td>left:</td><td>" +
11       pos.left +
12       "</td><td>top:</td><td>" +
13       pos.top + "</td></tr>");
14   pos = $("img:eq(2)").position();
15   $("#info").append(
16     "<tr><td>Image 3</td><td>left:</td><td>" +
17       pos.left +
18       "</td><td>top:</td><td>" +
19       pos.top + "</td></tr>");
20   pos = $("img:eq(3)").position();
21   $("#info").append(
22     "<tr><td>Image 4</td><td>left:</td><td>" +
23       pos.left +
24       "</td><td>top:</td><td>" +
25       pos.top + "</td></tr>");
26 });
```

In this example, the JavaScript functionality is not particularly complicated. We simply get the positioning data of the four images on loading the site, save it in a variable, and output the values of left and top in each case.

But in our situation, it is interesting how the values change when we position the div area with the images and what happens if we do not do this. These changes are made via CSS in our example. Take a look at this CSS file, ch7_6_1.css.

Listing 7.24 **The CSS File**

```
01 img {
02   height: 150px;
03 }
04 #info{
05   width: 440px;
06   background: yellow;
07 }
08 #p1 {
09   border: solid 1pt;
10 }
11 #p2 {
12   position:absolute;
```

```
13  top:200px;
14  }
15  #p3 {
16    position:absolute;
17    top:200px;
18  }
```

The images are all set to a height of 150 pixels and the info area to a width of 440 pixels. The ID p1 is the formatting for the `div` area that contains the second and third images. This puts a frame around the area, to see which area of the web page it takes up. None of this is very spectacular.

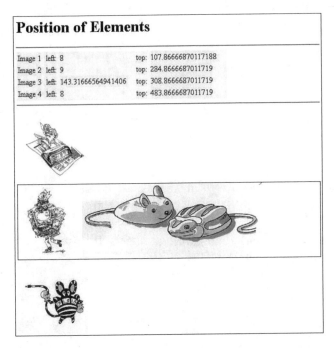

Position of Elements	
Image 1 left: 8	top: 107.86666870117188
Image 2 left: 9	top: 284.8666687011719
Image 3 left: 143.31666564941406	top: 308.8666687011719
Image 4 left: 8	top: 483.8666687011719

Figure 7.15   This is what the web page would look like if no elements were positioned in it.

The first two images are not influenced individually. But the third image that is within the `div` area, together with the second image, is positioned absolutely in the rules for the ID p2. The same with the fourth image that is outside of the `div` area. The specification for `top` is identical for both images! As a consequence, the third and fourth images will partly overlap because they are both pushed to the same `top` position.

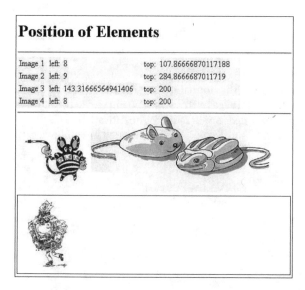

Position of Elements

Image 1 left: 8	top: 107.86666870117188
Image 2 left: 9	top: 284.8666687011719
Image 3 left: 143.31666564941406	top: 200
Image 4 left: 8	top: 200

Figure 7.16   The third and fourth images overlap in the top position.

Note that the offset parent element of the third image is obviously the web page, just as with the fourth image and all other elements in the web page—even if they are not positioned. Now we slightly expand the rule p1 (ch7_2.css).

Listing 7.25   **The Modified CSS File**

```
...
08 #p1 {
09   border: solid 1pt;
10   position:absolute;
11 }
...
```

We now apply absolute positioning to the div area. Note that we are specifying neither top nor left. The assignment as absolute is enough to turn the div element to an offset parent element of its content (in this case of the two images).

This has massive consequences for positioning the third image because the top specification is now counted from the top-left corner of the div element. So, the top positions of the third[11] and fourth images[12] are no longer overlapping, although the values in the CSS file are the same.

11. Counting from the top-left corner of the offset div.

12. Counting from the offset of the web page.

But the consequences go even further. The width of the div element with the two images as content is based on the content that is still directly in the internal text flow of the block element. And this is now only the second image, because, due to the absolute positioning of the third image, this has been taken out of the text flow of its parent element.

And as the div element itself has been taken out of the normal text flow of the overall document because of the absolute positioning, the first image in this text flow immediately follows the fourth image. This has been absolutely positioned, but because the specification left has not been set, it follows the normal text flow in this direction and is positioned next to image 1.

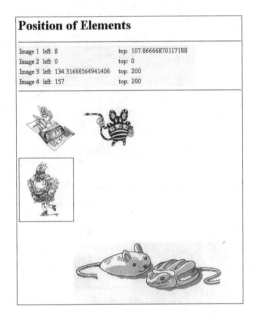

Position of Elements

Image 1 left: 8	top: 107.86666870117188	
Image 2 left: 0	top: 0	
Image 3 left: 134.31666564941406	top: 200	
Image 4 left: 157	top: 200	

Figure 7.17   The effect if the div area is absolutely positioned.

7.3.2   Position in Relation to the Document: offset()

With offset(), you act regarding the position in relation to the document. You can use it to position elements and to get the position.

Getting the Position

The offset() method gives you as a return value the current offset (top and left) of the first matching element in pixels. But always *in relation to the document*, in contrast to position(), even if there is an offset parent element.

The web page ch7_7.html, that we base our new example on, is identical to the file ch7_6.html. But in the CSS file ch7_7.css we have made a few changes.

Listing 7.26 **The New CSS File**

```
01 img {
02   height: 150px;
03 }
04 #info {
05   width: 640px;
06   background: yellow;
07 }
08 #p1 {
09   border: solid 1pt;
10   position: absolute;
11   left: 100px;
12 }
13 #p2 {
14   position: absolute;
15   top: 160px;
16   left: 10px;
17 }
18 #p3 {
19   position: absolute;
20   top: 290px;
21   left: 280px;
22 }
```

We position the third and fourth images completely. In particular, the div area that serves as the offset parent element of the second and third images is positioned in left direction. You will see that this specification works additively to the values delivered by offset().

The JavaScript file ch7_7_ready.js has only changed slightly from the previous example.

Listing 7.27 **The Document Offset in Action**

```
01 $(function(){
02 var offset = $("img:first").offset();
03 $("#info").html(
04   "<tr><td>Image 1</td><td>Offset left:</td><td>" +
05     offset.left +
06     "</td><td>Offset top:</td><td>" +
07     offset.top + "</td></tr>");
08 offset = $("img:eq(1)").offset();
09 $("#info").append(
10   "<tr><td>Image 2</td><td>Offset left:</td><td>" +
11     offset.left +
12     "</td><td>Offset top:</td><td>" +
13     offset.top + "</td></tr>");
14 offset = $("img:eq(2)").offset();
15 $("#info").append(
```

```
16     "<tr><td>Image 3</td><td>Offset left:</td><td>" +
17       offset.left +
18       "</td><td>Offset top:</td><td>" +
19       offset.top + "</td></tr>");
20   offset = $("img:eq(3)").offset();
21   $("#info").append(
22     "<tr><td>Image 4</td><td>Offset left:</td><td>" +
23       offset.left +
24       "</td><td>Offset top:</td><td>" +
25       offset.top + "</td></tr>");
26   offset = $("#p1").offset();
27   $("#info").append(
28     "<tr><td>DIV #p1</td><td>Offset left:</td><td>" +
29       offset.left +
30       "</td><td>Offset top:</td><td>" +
31       offset.top + "</td></tr>");
32 });
```

In addition to processing the offset in relation to the document, you can also see that we get the coordinates of the div area that is positioned absolutely. Note that the positioning of objects contained within, of course, takes into account this positioning of the parent element, and as mentioned earlier this has an effect on the data of offset().

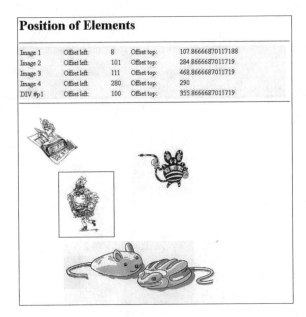

Position of Elements

Image 1	Offset left:	8	Offset top:	107.86666870117188
Image 2	Offset left:	101	Offset top:	284.8666687011719
Image 3	Offset left:	111	Offset top:	468.8666687011719
Image 4	Offset left:	280	Offset top:	290
DIV #p1	Offset left:	100	Offset top:	355.8666687011719

Figure 7.18   The various offset specifications in relation to the document.

Setting Positions

As of jQuery 1.4, you can also specify two coordinates in an option expression to set the position via `offset()` (always in relation to the document). Alternatively, you can use a callback that returns the coordinates you want to set. The callback function has two optional default parameters, as the methods described earlier for similar cases. The first optional parameter represents the index position of the element currently being accessed in a set of previously specified elements. The second optional parameter represents the `left` and `top` values of the element at the time of processing in the pass in the form of a coordinate object.

Listing 7.28   **The Basic File (ch7_8.html)**

```
...
10    <script type="text/javascript"
11        src="lib/ch7_8_ready.js"></script>
12    </head>
13    <body>
14        <h1>Position of Elements</h1><hr/>
15        <button>Image 1</button><button>Image 2</button>
16        <button>Image 2</button>
17    <button>Image 3 and 4</button><hr/>
18        <img src="images/img1.jpg" />
19        <img src="images/img2.jpg" />
20        <img src="images/img3.jpg" />
21        <img src="images/img4.jpg" />
22    </body>
23    </html>
```

In the web page, you can see four images. We want to position them in three different ways via `offset()`. Listing 7.29 shows the JavaScript file ch7_8_ready.js, in which we do this.[13]

Listing 7.29   **Setting Positioning Data**

```
01  $(function(){
02   $("button:first").click(function(){
03    $("img:first").offset({
04      top: 200,
05      left: 30
06    });
07   });
08   $("button:eq(1)").click(function(){
09    $("img:eq(1)").offset(function(index, coords){
10      return {
11        top: 100,
12        left: 300
```

13. The CSS file is not of interest in this example.

```
13      };
14    });
15  });
16  $("button:eq(2)").click(function(){
17    $("img:gt(1)").offset(function(index, coords){
18      if (index == 0)
19        return {
20          top: coords.top + 10,
21          left: coords.left + 30
22        };
23      else
24        return {
25          top: coords.top - 10,
26          left: coords.left - 30
27        };
28    });
29  });
30 });
```

After you load the site, the images are still within the normal text flow.

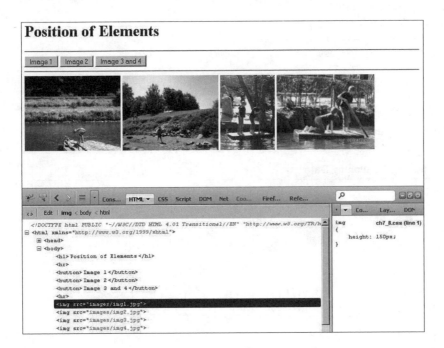

Figure 7.19   The images are still in the text flow as normal.

If a user clicks the first button, the positioning is called via the statements in lines 3–6. We set the data for left and top via an option object. This involves relative positioning, as you can see in Firebug.

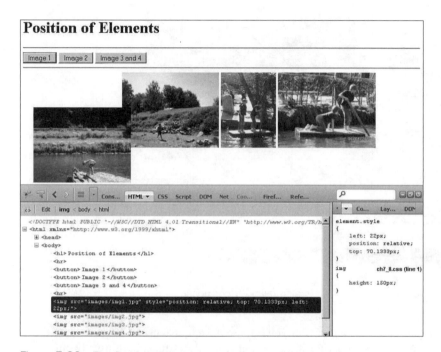

Figure 7.20   The first image has been relatively positioned.

Note that the actual positioning specification is not identical with the values in the source text, but is calculated in the background so that it harmonizes with the offset of the document. This enables the framework to compensate for any browser particularities that may occur.

With the code in lines 19–14 that is executed when the user clicks the second button, we position the second image with a callback function that returns a matching option object.

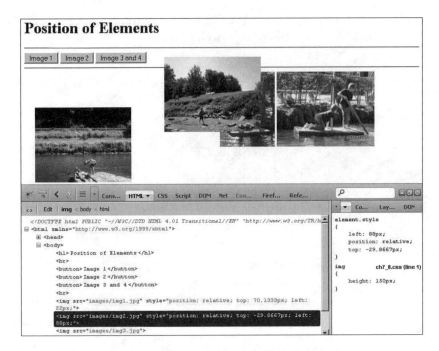

Figure 7.21   Now the second image is also relatively positioned.

When clicking button 3, you can see how you can use the optional default parameters of the callback functions to create a logic for the positioning. A callback function is usually only appropriate in this context if you want to implement a logic. Let's once more take a look at the relevant source code snippet.

Listing 7.30   **The Callback Function for the Third Button**

```
17    $("img:gt(1)").offset(function(index, coords){
18      if (index == 0)
19        return {
20          top: coords.top + 10,
21          left: coords.left + 30
22        };
23      else
24        return {
25          top: coords.top - 10,
26          left: coords.left - 30
27        };
28    });
```

We apply the positioning to images 3 and 4. So, the callback function is called twice. For the third image, `index` has the value 0. In this case, we add 10 pixels to the previous value of the `top` property (available via `coords.top`) and 30 pixels to the previous `left` property (available via `coords.left`).

For all other images (in this case, only the fourth image), we reduce the values accordingly.

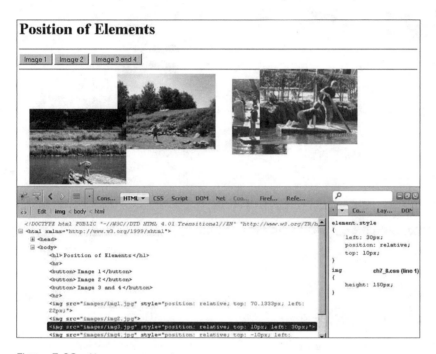

Figure 7.22   New arrangement.

Because the positioning always refers to the current positions, each click shifts the two images farther in the specified directions.

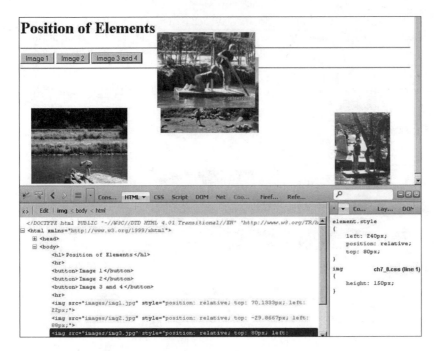

Figure 7.23   Images 3 and 4 have been moved farther along several times.

7.4   Scrolling Methods

With the `scrollTop()` and `scrollLeft()` methods, you can get the values by which an element has been scrolled down from the top or sideways. And if you pass an integer value as a parameter to the methods, you can move the element by the specified value in pixels. The values are, of course, seen in relation to the surrounding offset parent element. So, this is the same effect as if the user was moving content via scrollbars.

Listing 7.31   **The Basic File (ch7_9.html)**

```
...
10    <script type="text/javascript"
11      src="lib/ch7_9_ready.js"></script>
12  </head>
13  <body>
14    <h1>Scrolling elements</h1><hr/>
15    <button>Image 1</button>
16    <button>Image 2</button>
17    <div><img src="images/img1.jpg" /></div>
```

```
18    <div><img src="images/img2.jpg" /></div>
19    <span id="output1"></span><br/>
20    <span id="output2"></span>
21  </body>
22 </html>
```

In the web page, you can see two images that have each been inserted in a `div` area. But this is smaller than the images. Any protruding content is cut off. This is done in the conventional way via CSS (ch7_9.css).

Listing 7.32 **The Images Require More Space Than Is Available in the Web Page**

```
01 img {
02   height: 300px;
03 }
04 div {
05   width: 200px;
06   height: 200px;
07   overflow:auto;
08 }
```

So, the example shows two images, but these are not depicted in full because the `div` areas that are too small have the CSS attribute `overflow` with the value `auto` and a fixed size. As a result, only part of the image is displayed in each case.

Figure 7.24   Only a part of the images is displayed.

We want the user to be able to scroll the images in the relevant area by clicking a button. Here is how (ch7_9_ready.js).

Listing 7.33   **Scrolling**

```
01 $(function(){
02   $("div:lt(2)").scrollTop(0);
03   $("div:lt(2)").scrollLeft(0);
04   $("button:first").click(function(){
05     $("div:eq(0)").scrollTop(190);
06     $("div:eq(0)").scrollLeft(210);
07     $("#output1").text("Image 1 - scrollTop: " +
08     $("div:eq(0)").scrollTop() +
09     ", scrollLeft: " +
10     $("div:eq(0)").scrollLeft());
11   });
12   $("button:last").click(function(){
13     $("div:eq(1)").scrollLeft(265);
14     $("div:eq(1)").scrollTop(280);
15     $("#output2").text("Image 2 - scrollTop: " +
16     $("div:eq(1)").scrollTop() +
17     ", scrollLeft: " +
18     $("div:eq(1)").scrollLeft());
19   });
20   $("#output1").text("Image 1 - scrollTop: " +
21   $("div:eq(0)").scrollTop() +
22   ", scrollLeft: " +
23   $("div:eq(0)").scrollLeft());
24   $("#output2").text("Image 2 - scrollTop: " +
25   $("div:eq(1)").scrollTop() +
26   ", scrollLeft: " +
27   $("div:eq(1)").scrollLeft());
28 });
```

The div containers, in contrast, get scrollbars based on the value of the property overflow. This, in turn, means that the images in the div container can be scrolled by the user via these scrollbars (and also via jQuery or JavaScript).

After loading the web page, we initially scroll the images to the position (0, 0) in lines 2 and 3. Via scrollTop() and scrollLeft() in lines 21–27, we display the current displacement of the images in the relevant div containers (in pixels).

Via the two buttons, a user can now scroll the first or second image within the div containers by fixed factors to the left or top.[14] We again display the new values in the web page.

---

14. Of course, you do not have to reposition in both directions every time.

Scrolling elements

Image 1 - scrollTop: 117, scrollLeft: 210
Image 2 - scrollTop: 117, scrollLeft: 217

Figure 7.25   The images have been scrolled.

7.5   Height and Width

For many manipulations and representations within a web page, height and width are important. jQuery, of course, also offers suitable methods for accessing the height and width of elements. These methods are based on the corresponding CSS properties.

7.5.1   `height()` and `width()`

The `height()` and `width()` methods simply return the height and width of the first matching element in pixels. If you specify a numeric parameter instead, however, you are setting the height or width of the element.

> **Tip**
>
> As in pure HTML, you often only need to specify either the height or the width of an element. The corresponding property is usually scaled automatically by the browser. And the reduced specification of only one property is by no means uncommon. On the contrary, specifying both values can cause distortions, an effect that you might, of course, want to use intentionally in some cases. If you are manipulating only one property, however, you need to ensure that the other property is really "clear." Certain measures such as applying certain jQuery methods can have specified both the height and the width in the background. Or dimensions may have been

set via CSS. And if you then change only one of the two values, this can result in distortions, or the whole thing no longer works. From this point of view, it is a good idea to specify both the height and width for specifying sizes via jQuery.

Listing 7.34   **The Basic File (ch7_10.html)**

```
...
10    <script type="text/javascript"
11      src="lib/ch7_10_ready.js"></script>
12  </head>
13  <body>
14      <h1>Width and Height of Elements</h1><hr/>
15      <button>More</button>
16      <button>Less</button>
17      <button>Slightly distorted/button>
18      <hr /><img src="images/img4.jpg" />
19      <div id="output1"></div>
20  </body>
21  </html>
```

In the web page, you can see an image that is initially displayed in its native size. In the CSS file, we only specify the web page's background color this time. In particular, we are not specifying the width and height of the image. We determine the position and dimensions of the output area via CSS, so we can also use it as scale for the dimensions of the graphics.

We want the user to be able to scroll the images in the relevant area by clicking a button. Listing 7.35 shows how it works (ch7_10_ready.js).

Listing 7.35   **Accessing Width and Height of an Element**

```
01 $(function(){
02 $("button:first").click(function(){
03   $("img").width(440);
04   $("#output1").text("Width: " + $("img").width());
05 });
06 $("button:eq(1)").click(function(){
07   $("img").width(64);
08   $("#output1").text("Width: " + $("img").width());
09 });
10 $("button:last").click(function(){
11   $("img").width(440);
12   $("img").height(64);
13   $("#output1").html("Width: " +
14     $("img").width() + " Height: " +
15     $("img").height());
16   ;
```

```
17  });
18  });
```

Width and Height of Elements

| More | Less | Slightly distorted |

Figure 7.26   The native image size.

In the example, we access the width and height of an image. By clicking the first button, the width of the image is set to 440 pixels in line 3. The height is adapted automatically. The width is output in the web page via the method `width()` (without a parameter) in line 4.

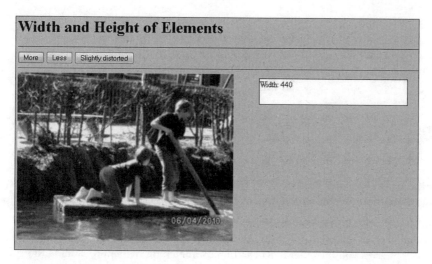

Width and Height of Elements

| More | Less | Slightly distorted |

Width: 440

Figure 7.27   Image, large.

Via the second button, the width is reduced to 64 pixels. Again, the height is adapted automatically.

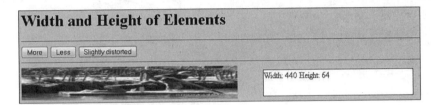

Figure 7.28   Image, reduced.

With the third button, we set both the width and height when the button is clicked. And we make the image distorted.

Width and Height of Elements

| More | Less | Slightly distorted |

Width: 440 Height: 64

Figure 7.29   Distorted image.

> **Caution**
>
> Note that the click on enlarging the image no longer works after you have set the height, as happens when the third button is clicked. Here you can explicitly see a situation where the height is no longer clear and where changing only the other property no longer works.

7.6   Inner and Outer Dimensions

With many visual elements in web pages, certain elements often influence the space the element requires beyond the "natural" size of the element. In particular, this concerns the margin (`margin`), border (`border`), and padding (`padding`).[15] So, you also need to take the inner and outer dimensions of an element into account. This is the classic CSS block model.

With `innerHeight()`, you get the inner height of the first matching element (without the border, but including the padding), and with `innerWidth()` the corresponding inner width. And `outerHeight()` gives you the outer height of the first matching element (including the border and `padding`), and `outerWidth()`, accordingly, gives you the outer width of the first matching element. You can use an optional Boolean parameter for the outer dimensions to specify whether the `margin` should be taken into account. (If yes, specify `true`; no parameter means `false`.)

15. From the outside in.

Listing 7.36   **The Basic File (ch7_11.html)**

```
...
10     <script type="text/javascript"
11       src="lib/ch7_11_ready.js"></script>
12   </head>
13     <body>
14         <h1>Inner and Outer Dimensions</h1><hr/>
15       <div id="block">www.rjs.de</div>
16       <div id="output"></div>
17   </body>
18   </html>
```

In the web page, you can see a block with the ID block, which we format as follows via CSS (ch7_11.css).

Listing 7.37   **Specifying the Dimensions of a Block**

```
01 #block {
02    background: gray;
03    color: #FFFF00;
04    font-size: 24px;
05    width: 200px;
06    height: 100px;
07    margin: 30px;
08    padding: 50px;
09    border-style: solid;
10    border-width: 5px
11 }
```

We want to read out these dimensions with the jQuery methods mentioned earlier (ch7_11_ready.js).

Listing 7.38   **Inner and Outer Size**

```
01 $(function(){
02    $("#output").html("width: " + $("div:first").width()
03    + "<br>innerWidth: " +
04    $("div:first").innerWidth() +
05    "<br>outerWidth: " +
06    $("div:first").outerWidth() +
07    "<br>outerWidth(true): " +
08    $("div:first").outerWidth(true) +
09    "<br>height: " +
10    $("div:first").height() +
11    "<br>innerHeight: " +
12    $("div:first").innerHeight() +
```

```
13   "<br>outerHeight: " +
14   $("div:first").outerHeight() +
15   "<br>outerHeight(true): " +
16   $("div:first").outerHeight(true));
17   });
```

In the example, we get the various size values as set via CSS and output them. For example, you can see that the outer width derives from the width of the div element plus the border width and the padding value.[16] If you include the margin via the Boolean parameter, the value increases accordingly.

Figure 7.30   The various size specifications.

> **Tip**
>
> With Firebug, you can analyze the inner and outer dimensions of elements very easily in the DOM category.

---

16. Of course, multiplied by the factor 2 in each case.

Summary

This chapter showed how you can use style sheets dynamically under jQuery. The dynamic CSS formatting of elements via suitable jQuery methods is an option of the framework that is visually immediately apparent. I believe that the highlight of these methods and concepts lies in the background—in the very easy application and encapsulation of browser-specific particularities and shortfalls.

Event Handling Under jQuery

In this chapter, we move on to event handling with jQuery. In other words, we look at the circumstances in which certain actions are triggers within the web page. This is certainly one of the most important areas of application of a framework such as jQuery because the reaction to events within a web page is not at all trivial with JavaScript instruments, perhaps contrary to what you would expect. And the alternative reaction with Hypertext Markup Language (HTML) event handlers, which even people without any knowledge of JavaScript know from web pages, is supported rather well, apart from a few exceptions, but is less powerful and incomplete. Even worse, structure and functionality are mixed up in it, and that is what we should avoid for more elaborate web applications. With jQuery, you have a very powerful instrument at hand for dealing with this complex topic successfully and safely.

8.1 Basic Information on Events, Event Handlers, Triggers, and Data Binding

You are probably aware that JavaScript statements and function calls are executed simply through loading the web page in the browser if you write these calls directly in a script container or an external script. As soon as the relevant script line is loaded by the browser, the corresponding statement is executed. This is the most primitive constellation in which a JavaScript is executed. But usually it is only used for initializing. And, of course, there are also other situations where you might want to call a function or statement, apart from just loading the web page.

8.1.1 Events

Here, the term **event** enters the stage, referring to anything that can happen while the web page is active in the browser. This can include loading the page into the browser or removing the page from the browser, but also actions executed by a user (for example, clicking a button, sending form data, or moving the mouse pointer over part of the web page). Such events are ideally suited for calls based on statements.

8.1.2   General Information on Event Handlers

So, we need a mechanism via which we can react to such events and that can trigger a statement, function, or object method where appropriate. This mechanism is referred to as an **event handler**. Different event handlers can be used to react to various events that the event handler mechanism identifies via predefined names.

Event handlers are available both in pure HTML and in JavaScript.[1] So, they exist in both worlds and are the most important link between (X)HTML and JavaScript.[2] Essential is also that the triggering events are present both in HTML (version 4 and later) and in JavaScript and are functionally identical. But a few event handlers in the JavaScript environment do not have a direct counterpart in HTML.[3]

8.1.3   HTML Event Handlers

In HTML, event handlers simply constitute attributes of a tag. You can specify such event handlers for most tags.[4]

> **Note**
>
> The W3 consortium has officially included event handlers in the HTML language standard. This is particularly important because it means that uppercase and lowercase spelling does not play a role if event handlers are written as HTML attributes. In JavaScript and XHMTL, however, event handlers always have to be written *entirely in lowercase*.

The name of an event handler generally starts with the syllable on, followed by a self-explanatory description of the event. I am sure that you are familiar with the concept.

Listing 8.1   Different Event Handlers in HTML

```
onmouseover
onload
onclick
```

1. Strictly speaking, in the DOM concept, but let's not split hairs.

2. As mentioned previously, the link can be made from either side.

3. One such case is `onreadystatechange`, which exists only within the JavaScript environment for implementing an AJAX request.

4. Essentially for all tags, but with some it simply does not make any sense.

If you use these event handlers for an HTML tag, you write an equals sign after the name of the attribute. As usual with an HTML attribute, this is followed by a value assignment enclosed in double quotation marks. In this case, this is a JavaScript statement or function call.

Listing 8.2 **Calling a Function with an HTML Event Handler**

```
<h3 onclick="myFunction()">Click me</h3>
```

8.1.4 JavaScript Event Handler

For a strict, highly recommended separation of structure and logic, use JavaScript event handlers rather than HTML event handlers, as you probably know. If you want to react to an event within the JavaScript environment, you can also use an event handler. Event handlers in JavaScript are properties of an object. So, you are not going to write down a function **call** as a value assignment here, but instead bind a **function reference** to an object of the web page. Take a look at the following source code snippet.

Listing 8.3 **Using an Event Handler from Within JavaScript with Function Reference**

```
<form name="myForm">
  <input type="button" name="myButton" value="OK" />
</form>
...
<script language="JavaScript">
  document.myForm.myButton.onclick = myfction;
</script>
```

The syntax used in the example references a `myfction()` function that is called if a user clicks the form button. The example snippet shows a neutral JavaScript syntax for selecting the button. Of course, you can also reference the triggering object with jQuery here.

A function reference does not permit a specification with brackets.[5] But how are you then supposed to pass values for parameters to a function? You already know the answer by now—certainly from the numerous examples in this book. Instead of the direct reference to a function, you can also use the keyword `function` followed by a pair of brackets—perhaps with parameter values—and a function body where you can write down any JavaScript statements (or function calls). Take a look at the following snippet.

Listing 8.4 **An Anonymous Function**

```
document.onclick = function(){
  myFction();
};
```

---

5. It is specifically *not* a call!

Although you could also use a named function here, it is most common to use an anonymous function in practice.[6] In general, you can also use a general callback function here that has to give a function reference as return value.

8.1.5   The Event Object

Behind event handling in JavaScript is a special object: the event object. The user constantly[7] produces such event objects, and you can use them in a targeted way to react to events. The event objects offers a range of interesting properties to that purpose. Let's use as an example the situation that the user clicks anywhere in the web page with the mouse. Each mouse click causes the browser to create an event object that contains, among others, the following information:

- The mouse button used
- Any keys pressed in addition (Ctrl, Alt, CapsLock)
- The coordinates of the click

Other event objects that are created for further events will, of course, contain different information that corresponds to the event. For example, if a key is pressed, you can get information about which key was pressed. Generally, an event object contains numerous pieces of useful information that you can use for creating well-adapted applications.

This leads us to the question of how you can use the event object. The answer is simple and yet complicated at the same time. The simple part of the solution is that to access the properties of an event object, you specify the object as usual via dot notation. The complicated part is that for the name of the event object or its availability, you need to distinguish between the Microsoft world and the concept in other browsers, and there is also a difference regarding the visibility of the object. Microsoft uses a proprietary naming convention for the properties of the event object. jQuery compensates for the differences by encapsulating the event object and permits using the standardized syntax even for Internet Explorer.

> **Caution**
>
> Most events within a web application are supported by almost all modern browsers. But some events are browser specific, and in particular differences exist even with HTML event handlers regarding the tags for which an event is supported. It gets really complicated when dealing with the event object, because on top of all the trouble with the different identifiers and access levels, even identical properties of the event object are named differently in the different browser concepts, as mentioned earlier.[8] Without separating the browser worlds between Microsoft and the rest, nothing will work, but even then the whole thing is extremely difficult.

6. You never need the identifier of this callback function anyway.

7. As you move the mouse pointer over the browser area, you create a multitude of event objects, not just one.

8. These are the results of the unfortunate browser wars of the '90s. "If you are going to name that property `which`, then I definitely won't. What name could I use that is as different as possible? Hmm, how about `keyCode`? That will give your developers something to puzzle over."

8.1.6 Bubbling

In connection with the event object, you will come across the term **bubble events** or **bubble phase**. As mentioned previously, a browser is constantly generating event objects (and not just from those few events such as clicking the mouse). Moving the mouse over the browser area happens more or less constantly, so thousands of event objects can be generated in the shortest period of time, or think of scrolling text. Most of these events are not processed by the application at all but are simply ignored. After all, why would you want to react to each single millimeter of a mouse movement, except in a few special instances?

If an event occurs for a node in the tree (such as an image or a paragraph), the question is which of these objects is responsible for the relevant event. After all, nodes are quite deeply nested in the tree. What should happen if several objects have the same event handler and would therefore be able to react to the event?

The problems are solved via event bubbling. This means the event is always treated in the innermost element first where it occurred—if there is a suitable event handler there. The innermost element is furthest away from the root in the hierarchy. If this element does not have a suitable event handler, the event object is passed on in the tree to the next higher object in the Document Object Model (DOM) and so on. It rises up like a bubble until it reaches the root. It bubbles through the tree. If the event object has still not been handled when it reaches the tree, the event object is destroyed.[9] And this untreated destruction of an event object is the rule, not the exception (simply because of the fact that most events, such as moving the mouse pointer by just a few millimeters, do not force a specific reaction by the application).

8.1.7   Data Binding

To react to events, you can also use the mechanism of **data binding**. With this, you can create a direct relationship between two variables or expressions.[10] You associate the value of a target with the value of a bound expression. Such a bound expression can be a simple value of any type, an object, the result of a function, or an expression. The process is similar to reference relationships between cells in a table or a spreadsheet such as OpenOffice Calc or Microsoft Excel (in particular if these are used in formulas and these formulas relate to other cells).

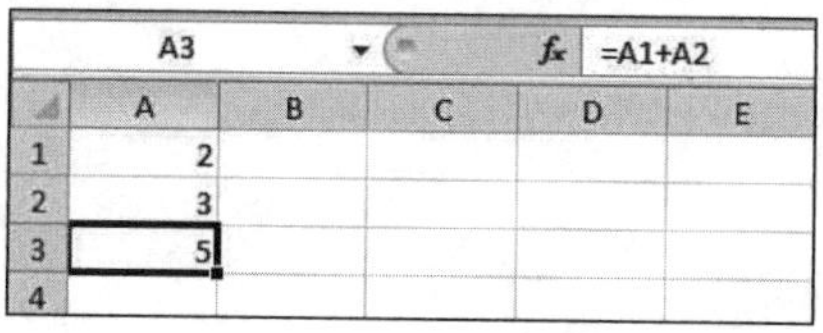

Figure 8.1   Classic data binding in a spreadsheet program.

9. Although there are also models where the event object is returned back to the triggering element and then destroyed only if no handling occurs on the way back.

10. The key for data binding in jQuery is `bind()`, as you will see later.

If the value of the referenced cell changes in any way, all other expressions that are bound to it change in the way that the binding rule (the formula) prescribes. This happens without delay and without the update having to be triggered manually.

8.1.8   Trigger

For reacting to certain events, there is also the mechanism referred to as **trigger**. This is fired for events that result from data modifications. In contrast to data binding, you can also include complex statements in the body of a trigger. This block is executed every time the specified event occurs. Triggers are useful if the code you want to execute for a value change in a variable is flexible or complex.

8.2   The Event Object in jQuery

As the warnings and comments in this chapter have made clear, the native working with the event object is more luck than sensible programming if you want to support more than just one browser. Plus there is a whole range of techniques for dealing with events. Fortunately, jQuery encapsulates the problem and standardizes the syntax. The jQuery event system normalizes the event object via `jQuery.Event` (including the names of the available properties and methods) corresponding to the W3C standards and ensures standardized handling in all supported browsers. In particular, this guarantees that the event object is passed on reliably to the event handlers.

8.2.1   The Constructor of `jQuery.Event`

The constructor of the event object in jQuery is open and can be used in any form by triggers. As a parameter, you specify a jQuery event handler.[11] Remarkably, you can also create an object with the constructor without using the new operator. Or you can use new if you want. The result is the same. You get an event object of the type `jQuery.Event`.

Listing 8.5   **Creating a New Object of the Type** `jQuery.Event` **Without Using** new

```
var e = jQuery.Event("click");
```

The following syntax works exactly the same.

Listing 8.6   **Here, We Use** new

```
var e = new jQuery.Event("click");
```

---

11. Not a classic event handler that starts with on. In jQuery, these are also referred to as event helpers. More on this later.

8.2.2   The Properties of the Event Object `jQuery.Event`

The event object in jQuery has a number of properties that are, of course, based on the attributes of the classic event object.

event.type

With this attribute, the type of the event is described (for example, if a mouse click happened or keyboard input or something similar).

event.target

Via this attribute, you can get the DOM element that has triggered the event. This can be the element that is registered for this event or one of its children.

event.data

This attribute is immensely important because `event.data` offers you optional data if this has been passed on to `bind()` and the current execution handler was bound.

event.relatedTarget

In case of mouse movements, this property contains the DOM element where the mouse pointer was previously if the mouse pointer is moved to another element or away from another element. This is the involved node.

event.currentTarget

Via this property you get the current DOM element within the bubble phase. This attribute is always equivalent to the value of `this` in the function.

event.pageX/event.pageY

The X and Y coordinates where a mouse event has occurred. The coordinates are seen in relation to the document. The properties also fix the divergence of Internet Explorer regarding the standard notation for the coordinates.

event.screenX/event.screenY

The screen coordinates.

event.result

The last value that was returned by an event handler.

event.timeStamp

The time stamp in milliseconds when the event was created.

A practical example will help demonstrate these properties of a `jQuery.Event` object (ch8_1.html).

Listing 8.7   Interpreting the Attributes of the Event Object

```
...
06      <link rel="stylesheet" type="text/css"
07         href="lib/ch8_1.css" />
08    <script type="text/javascript"
09         src="lib/jquery-1.8.2.min.js"></script>
10    <script type="text/javascript"
11         src="lib/ch8_1_ready.js"></script>
12   </head>
13   <body>
14     <h1>Different Properties of the event Object</h1>
16     <table>
17       <tr><th>Triggering object</th>
18         <th>Information</th>
19       </tr>
20       <tr><td><img src="images/pic1.jpg" id="pic1"/></td>
21         <td id="output1"></td></tr>
22       <tr><td><img src="images/pic2.jpg" id="pic2"/></td>
23         <td id="output2"></td></tr>
24     </table>
25   </body>
26 </html>
```

The web page contains two images in the first column of a table. The second column is to be used for displaying event information. In the referenced Cascading Style Sheets (CSS) file, we only specify the column width of the table as 400 pixels. We do not need to look at this further here; of course, we should look at the JavaScript file ch8_1_ready.js.

Listing 8.8   The Specific Evaluation of the Properties of the Event Object

```
01 $(function(){
02    $("#pic1").click(function(event){
03      $("#output1").html("timeStamp: " +
04         event.timeStamp +
05      "<br />screenY: " +
06      event.screenY +
07      ", screenX: " +
08      event.screenX);
09    });
10    $("#pic2").mousemove(function(event){
11      var pageCoordinates = "( " + event.pageX + ", " +
12         event.pageY + " )";
13      $("#output2").html("e.pageX, e.pageY: " +
14      pageCoordinates +
```

```
15    "<br />Triggering node: " +
16    event.target.nodeName);
17  });
18  $("#pic2").mouseout(function(event){
19    $("#output2").html("Related node: " +
20    event.relatedTarget.nodeName);
21  });
22  });
```

In the example, you can see three situations where events are triggered and processed: the click on the first image (`click()`), moving the mouse pointer to the second image (`mousemove()`), and the mouse pointer exiting the area of the second image (`mouseout()`). The parameter of the callback function is the jQuery event object.

> **Note**
>
> In this example, we are using the previously mentioned jQuery event helpers that we discuss in more detail later in this chapter. But they should be fairly clear if you think of the "normal" event handlers of JavaScript/DOM or HTML. And we have already used `click()`, in particular, a few times.

In line 4, you can see how we get the time stamp of an event with `event.timeStamp` and in lines 6 and 8 the screen coordinates with `event.screenY` and `event.screenX`. In lines 11 and 12, we use `event.pageX` and `event.pageY` to determine the page coordinates. The triggering node of an event is determined via `event.target`, and because we want to display its name, we use its property `nodeName`.

Figure 8.2   The user clicked on image 1 and the mouse pointer is on the area of image 2.

In line 20, we get the name of the node that is involved in exiting the second image via `event.relatedTarget.nodeName`.

Figure 8.3   The name of the involved node.

8.2.3   The Methods of an Object of the `Type` `jQuery.Event`

In relation to the event object, there are also some methods. These serve mainly for preventing certain default reactions by the browser.

`event.preventDefault()` and `event.isDefaultPrevented()`

Via the method `event.preventDefault()`, you can prevent the browser from executing the default action that it would normally have to carry out at this point. This might sound a bit strange at first, but it is a very useful and sensible feature. For example, you can prevent triggering a hyperlink that a user clicks. This can be appropriate if you want to use the click for another action, such as starting an animation or loading data via AJAX. Or you can prevent sending form data via submit. But you can also prevent individually specified global default actions for certain elements in a specific situation.

With the Boolean method `event.isDefaultPrevented()`, you can check whether the method `event.preventDefault()` has ever been called for this event object (ch8_2.html).

Listing 8.9   **Evaluating Attributes of the Event Object**

```
...
10    <script type="text/javascript"
11        src="lib/ch8_2_ready.js"></script>
12    </head>
13    <body>
14      <h1>Prevent Redirection</h1>
15      <a href="http://rjs.de">Come to me</a><br />
16      <a href="http://ajax-net.de">Or to me</a>
17    </body>
18    </html>
```

The web page contains two hyperlinks. We want to prevent the associated redirection. In the referenced CSS file, we only specify the text decoration of the hyperlinks. Again, we do not need to examine this further. Here is the JavaScript file ch8_2_ready.js.

Listing 8.10   **Preventing Redirection Upon the Clicking of a Hyperlink**

```
01 $(function(){
02   $("a").click(function(event){
03     event.preventDefault();
04     alert("I am not letting you. " +
05     event.isDefaultPrevented());
06   });
07 });
```

If the user clicks the hyperlink, the browser first attempts to redirect to the URL. The statement in line 3 prevents this. It is within the event helper `click()` method that is called with a click on each hyperlink. In the notification, we show (among other things) whether the method was called (which is, of course, trivial in this case).

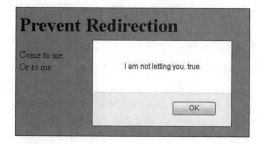

Figure 8.4   The click was prevented and an alternative `alert()` window is displayed.

event.stopPropagation(), event.isPropagationStopped(), event.stopImmediatePropagation(), and event.isImmediatePropagationStopped()

Via the method `event.stopPropagation()`, you can stop the bubble process of an event object through the tree. This means that it will not bubble on to parent elements if there is no suitable event handling for the triggering element. The event handlers that are available for parent elements will not register the event object if it was not handled at a child element.

Caution

Internet Explorer has certain problems with the method `event.stopPropagation()`. In the case of Internet Explorer, the statement `event.cancelBubble = true;` will work.

With the Boolean method `event.isPropagationStopped()`, you can check whether the method `event.stopPropagation()` has ever been called for this event object.

> **Note**
>
> Calling `event.stopPropagation()` does not affect other handlers that are executed for the same element.

The methods `event.stopImmediatePropagation()` and `event.isImmediatePropagationStopped()` work fairly similarly to `event.stopPropagation()` and `event.isPropagationStopped()`. But with `event.stopImmediatePropagation()`, the browser is simply prevented from executing the remaining handlers. The bubbling to parent elements is also prevented because `event.stopImmediatePropagation()` calls indirectly the `event.stopPropagation()` method. Similarly, you can use `event.isImmediatePropagationStopped()` to check whether the method `event.stopImmediatePropagation()` was ever called for this event object.

> **Note**
>
> The methods are specialized and not often required. We are omitting complete examples.

8.3   Ready, Steady, Go: `$(document).ready()`

We use the method `$(document).ready()` in almost all examples in this book! This should make its significance clear enough.[12] But calling the method is also the reaction to an event, and so we should mention the method once more in this chapter. Calling the function is linked to the event that the DOM is ready for traversal and manipulation. Specifically, an argument is passed to the ready event handler: a reference to a jQuery function.

As described previously, you can use any number of `$(document).ready` events in your site if required. The functions bound to it are executed in the order in which they were added.

And all style sheets should be integrated before the scripts. In particular, the integration should happen before calling `$(document).ready()`. If you do not do this, it can result in problems in some browsers.

8.4   Event Helpers

Probably the most important techniques for reacting to events in web pages are based on event handlers. These "normal" event handlers from JavaScript/DOM or HTML are encapsulated in jQuery via what is referred to as **event helpers**. They are completely normal methods that are also linked to specific events. In terms of using them, you can basically just apply your

---

12. So we do not need to use explicit examples here.

knowledge of JavaScript/DOM event handlers directly and simply omit the preceding on from the name of the relevant event method.

> **Note**
>
> Event helpers are all shorthand notations for data binding via `bind()` and specific parameters. All methods return an object of the type `jQuery` as return value.

Table 8.1 describes the event helpers offered by jQuery.

Table 8.1   The jQuery Event Helpers

Name	Description
`blur()`	Without parameters, calling the method means triggering the `blur` event (exiting an element) for each matching element. With a parameter, the event helper binds a function to the `blur` event for each matching element.
`change()`	Without a specified parameter, calling the method represents triggering the `change` event (changing an element; for example, a form input field) for each matching element. With a parameter, the event helper binds a function to the `change` event for each matching element.
`click()`	Surely one of the most important event helpers supports the click on an element. Without a parameter, this means triggering the `click` event for each matching element. With a parameter, the event helper binds a function to the `click` event for each matching element.
`dblclick()`	Although the double-click does not have any tradition with classic web applications, the double-click will probably play a bigger role in future Rich Internet Applications (RIAs). After all, it is desirable for RIAs to behave like desktop applications. And these traditionally work with double-clicks. This jQuery helper for an event serves for triggering the `dblclick` event for each matching element. With a parameter, the event helper binds a function to the `dblclick` event for each matching element.
`error()`	Without a parameter, calling the method represents triggering the `error` event for each matching element, so it represents an error that has happened (for example, when requesting data or resources). With a parameter, the event helper binds a function to the `error` event for each matching element.
`focus()`	Without specifying a parameter, calling the method is equivalent to triggering the `focus` event (getting the focus; for example, for a button or an input field in a form) for each matching element. With a parameter, the event helper binds a function to the `focus` event for each matching element.

Name	Description
focusin()	The event that was added in jQuery 1.4 and updated in version 1.4.3 is triggered if an element or any element it contains gains the focus. This is not identical to the focus event because recognizing focus events on parent elements is supported here (in other words, event bubbling is supported). As of version 1.4.3, you can specify an object of the type map as first parameter, via which data can be passed to the event handler.
focusout()	The counterpart of focusin(). The focus is taken off an element or the parent element. This is also not the case with the related blur(). This event helper has also been available since jQuery 1.4 or 1.4.3.
keydown()	Support of keyboard events has also been rather neglected in traditional web programming. Classic web programming used to be based almost exclusively on mouse actions. But in modern AJAX applications, in particular, you rely heavily on support for keyboard events. With this event helper, jQuery offers support for triggering the keydown event (pressing a key) for each matching element. With a parameter, the event helper binds a function to the keydown event for each matching element. The various phases of pressing a key on the keyboard can be skillfully distinguished. Pressing the key is specified via keydown, and correspondingly keyup represents letting go of the key. The events are massively different because the pressed character is not yet in the keyboard buffer on pressing the key and can therefore not be processed yet at this point. But on releasing the key, the character is available via the keyboard code.
keypress()	The keypress event represents pressing any key. If no parameter is specified, the event is triggered for each matching element. With a parameter, the event helper binds a function to the keypress event for each matching element.
keyup()	Without a parameter, this event helper serves for triggering the keyup event for each matching element. With a parameter, the event helper binds a function to the keyup event for each matching element.
load()	Loading an element. This event helper only exists with a parameter for binding a function to the load event for each matching element.
mousedown()	Pressing the mouse button triggers this event helper. This method exists only with a parameter for binding a function to the mousedown event for each matching element.
mouseenter()	This event occurs if the mouse pointer is moved onto the area of a visible element in the web page. The method exists only with a parameter for binding a function to the mouseenter event for each matching element.
mouseleave()	If the mouse pointer is moved off the area of an element, this event is triggered. This event helper exists only with a parameter for binding a function to the mouseleave event for each matching element.

Name	Description
mousemove()	The mousemove event is triggered if the mouse pointer is moved in the visible area of an element in the web page. This event helper only exists with a parameter to bind a function to the mousemove event for each matching element.
mouseout()	If the mouse pointer leaves the area of an element, this event is triggered. This event helper only exists with a parameter to bind a function to the mouseout event for each matching element.
mouseover()	If the mouse pointer is moved into the area of an element, this event is triggered. The event helper only exists with a parameter to bind a function to the mouseover event for each matching elements.
mouseup()	This event helper exists only with a parameter to bind a function to the mouseup event for each matching element. The event occurs if a pressed mouse button is released.
resize()	This event occurs when you are resizing an element. This event helper exists only with a parameter to bind a function to the resize event for each matching element.
scroll()	This event helper exists only with a parameter to bind a function to the scroll event for each matching element if the user scrolls in the area of an element.
select()	This sets off the trigger of the select event for each matching element if an element is selected. With a parameter, the event helper binds a function to the select event for each matching element.
submit()	Without a parameter, the submit event is triggered for each matching element. This, of course, only concerns forms. With a parameter, the event helper binds a function to the submit event for each matching element.
unload()	This event helper exists only with a parameter to bind a function to the unload event for each matching element.

I could leave it at that with my explanation of the individual event helpers,[13] but we want to include a few more details on the methods and, of course, illustrate the *basic application* via examples. You can use some of these event helpers offered by jQuery both with a function as a parameter and without a parameter. Others require an obligatory function as a parameter. If you use the methods without a parameter, the default event of an element is specified. This is fired, for example, if a suitable trigger is called.

Listing 8.11   click() **for an image**

```
$("img").click();
```

13. This is, in fact, inverse to their significance.

If you pass a function reference or callback function as parameter to the method, the specified function is executed for each matching element when the event occurs.

Listing 8.12   Executing an Anonymous Function for a Click on a Button

```
$("button:last").click(function () {
  $("img").triggerHandler('dblclick');
});
```

The callback function can have an optional default parameter. And that is probably the most important fact in the jQuery event helper concept (because this represents the jQuery event object across all browsers and can be processed in accordance with the previous examples, with the standardized names of the properties and methods—even in Internet Explorer). The name of the parameter is, of course, arbitrary.

Listing 8.13   Executing an Anonymous Function While Processing the Event Object

```
$("button:last").click(function (ev) {
  $("#output").html(ev.pageX);
});
```

8.5   Expanded Methods for Event Handling

In jQuery, some special techniques enable you to react to events in a qualified, secure, special, and reliable way. These methods are based on techniques for reacting to events that we have discussed earlier in the general discussion about event handling.

8.5.1   The `bind()` and `unbind()` Methods

The `bind()` method uses two or three parameters and returns an object of the type `jQuery`, like almost all methods in jQuery. With this method you have one of the most flexible options for describing a reaction mechanism. You bind a handler to one or several events for each matching element. Currently, the possible values for the events that are to be specified as a first parameter (multiple events are simply separated by spaces) are `blur`, `focus`, `focusin`, `focusout`, `load`, `resize`, `scroll`, `unload`, `click`, `dblclick`, `mousedown`, `mouseup`, `mousemove`, `mouseover`, `mouseout`, `mouseenter`, `mouseleave`, `change`, `select`, `submit`, `keydown`, `keypress`, `keyup`, `error`.

But you can also use custom events you define yourself.

In most cases, you will define your event handlers as anonymous functions passed as the last parameter to the method.

Listing 8.14   Binding an Anonymous Function to the Click on Any Paragraph

```
$("p").bind("click", function(event){
  $("#output").text("... and there was a click!");
});
```

If this is not possible and if you still need values to pass to the callback function, you can specify additional data as the second parameter in the format `event.data` and the handler function as the third parameter.

Listing 8.15   Binding a Named Function to the Click and Specifying Additional Data as Second Parameter

```
function myHandler(event) {
  $("#output").text(event.data.p1);
}
$("p").bind("click", {p1: "... and there was a click!"},
myHandler)
```

The counterpart method of `bind()` is `unbind()`, and it does the exact opposite of `bind()`. Via this method, you remove bound events from each matching element. If you do not specify a parameter, you are unbinding all events. Otherwise, you specify the event you are unbinding as the parameter—or several, separated by spaces.

Listing 8.16 shows a complete example (ch8_3.html).

Listing 8.16   Bound Event Handling

```
...
10    <script type="text/javascript"
11        src="lib/ch8_3_ready.js"></script>
12    </head>
13    <body>
14      <h1>Binding events</h1>
15      <img src="images/pic5.jpg" /><hr/>
16      <button>Unbind</button>
17    </body>
18  </html>
```

The web page contains an image for which we want to show bound event handling. Via the button, we will unbind the event. In the referenced CSS file (not explicitly listed in this book), you will find a class via which we want to place a frame around the image if the user clicks it. If he clicks again, the class and therefore the frame are removed. We use the jQuery `toggleClass()` method. Listing 8.17 shows the JavaScript file ch8_3_ready.js.

Figure 8.5   Original version of the web page after loading.

Listing 8.17   **Applying** `bind()` **and** `unbind()`

```
01 $(function(){
02   $("img:first").bind("click", function(){
03     $(this).toggleClass("frame");
04   })
05   $("button:first").click(function(){
06     $("img:first").unbind("click")
07   });
08 });
```

In the example, the frame around the image is dynamically altered in the `bind()` method if the `click` event is triggered on it.

Figure 8.6   The bound event is triggered.

The click on the button unbinds the click event and the image. Any subsequent clicks on the image will then no longer toggle the class.

bind() and bubble: Default Actions

When processing event objects, you need to take into account the bubble phase and default actions for specific elements such as hyperlinks or the submit reaction for a form, as well as custom global default actions for specific elements. If you do not want to carry out the default action, you can prevent both the current execution of the default action and the bubbling to the parent elements for bind(). To do so, just return the value false in the handler function.

Listing 8.18   **Submitting the Form Data Is Prevented**

```
$("form").bind("submit", function() {
  return false;
});
```

If you only want to prevent the default action, use the event.preventDefault() method in the callback function.

Listing 8.19   **The Default Action Is Prevented, but Bubbling Continues**

```
$("form").bind("submit", function(event){
  event.preventDefault();
  ...
});
```

Pure bubbling, in contrast, is prevented by calling the event.stopPropagation() method (also because of problems with Internet Explorer).

> **Tip**
>
> Even namespaces are supported by jQuery. This enables you to form groups of bound handlers without directly referencing them.

bind() and Multiple Events

You can also pass multiple events as parameters to the bind() method. You just need to separate the various event helpers with spaces in the string.

Listing 8.20   **Reaction to Multiple Events**

```
$('div:first').bind('mouseenter mouseleave', function() {
  $(this).toggleClass('myClass');
});
```

As of jQuery 1.4, you can also use multiple event helpers alternatively with an object of the type `Map`. Then you bind a separate callback function or function reference to each event.

Listing 8.21   **Using an Object of the Type** `Map`

```
$('div:first').bind({
  click: function() {
    // ...
  },
  mouseenter: function() {
    // ...
  },
  mouseleave: function() {
    // ...
  }
});
```

Passing on Data

As of version 1.4.3, there are also the following variations of `bind()`.

Listing 8.22   **Passing on Data**

```
bind( eventType, [ eventData ], handler )
```

The second parameter is an object of the type `Map` with data that can be passed on to the handler. This then becomes a property of the `data` attribute of the event object.

Listing 8.23   **Passing Data on to the Function**

```
$("button:first").bind("click", {name: "Felix"},
  function (event) {
    alert(event.data.name);   // Output Felix
  });
```

8.5.2 The One and Only: `one()`

You have a direct alternative for `bind()`: `one()`. With this method, you can bind a handler to one or several events for each matching element. That is just as we already know it from `bind()`. The special feature of this `one()` method is already in its name: The bound handler is only executed precisely once for each element. Then it is unbound. Apart from this, the method behaves in exactly the same way as `bind()`. So, we do not need to provide an example.

8.5.3   The Method `trigger()`

To the `trigger()` method, you pass as a parameter the event and the desired data that you want to trigger "manually."[14] Using triggers in jQuery is linked to the default reaction of the browser for a specific event that you have specified elsewhere or that is automatically triggered by the browser. If you call the `trigger()` method, this call fires the default reaction of the browser that has the same name if such a reaction exists. For example, if you pass `'submit'` on to `trigger()`, this forces the browser to send form data[15] if you set off the trigger in a form.

> **Tip**
>
> The triggered events are not limited to browser-based events. You can also use adapted events. Remember, though, that with triggers the implementation has changed in the different versions of jQuery. So, if you are changing over from previous versions, take a look at the documentation to see whether any changes have been made. (Mostly these are only very specialized details.)

The event handlers of an element get a normalized event object when a trigger is set off, without any browser-specific attributes such as `keyCode`, `pageX`, or `pageY`.

For triggers, you can specify the type of an event in three different ways:

- You can specify the name of the event as string.

- You can use an object of the type `jQuery.Event`. If you do this, you can pass data to this object and this data will reach the triggered handlers.

- You can pass a literal object with data. This is copied into a real object of the type `jQuery.Event`. In this case, you need to specify a type attribute.

Listing 8.24   **Trigger for Event Handling (ch8_4.html)**

```
...
10    <script type="text/javascript"
11        src="lib/ch8_4_ready.js"></script>
12  </head>
13    <body>
14      <h1>Trigger</h1>
15      <h2>Click an image to enlarge.
16        Double-click to shrink the image.</h2>
17      <img src="images/pic3.jpg" />
18      <img src="images/pic4.jpg" /><hr/>
19      <button>Enlarge all images</button>
20      <button>Shrink all images</button>
```

14. For example, due to a data change.

15. Unless you prevent triggering by one of the bound functions returning the value `false`.

```
21  </body>
22 </html>
```

The web page gets two images for which we want to launch an event helper via a trigger. That is what the buttons are for. Listing 8.25 shows the JavaScript file ch8_4_ready.js.

Listing 8.25   **Click and Double-Click Handlers**

```
01 $(function(){
02   $("img").click(function(){
03     $(this).css({
04       width: "400px"
05     });
06   });
07   $("img").dblclick(function(){
08     $(this).css({
09       width: "80px"
10     });
11   });
12   $("button:first").click(function(){
13     $("img").trigger('click');
14   });
15   $("button:last").click(function(){
16     $("img").trigger('dblclick');
17   });
18 });
```

In the example, you can see two images that are scaled to a lower or greater width via the method css(). In lines 2–6, a default event for a click on an image is specified. Each time the user clicks an image, its width is expanded to 400 pixels via the method css(). Correspondingly, you can see shrinking an image by double-clicking it in lines 7–11.

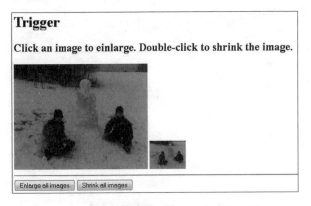

Figure 8.7   Only the image on the right has been reduced.

Up to this point, there are still no triggers involved. But in the clicks on the buttons, we work with triggers. If the user clicks the first button, the click trigger of all elements of the type `img` is triggered in line 13.

For all images, a click on this button sets off the default event that is bound to a click on the relevant image. In other words, if you click this button, both images in the web page are enlarged. That is exactly as we specified in the default event.

Correspondingly, the trigger in line 16 sets off the action that is assigned to a double-click for each image. The image width is set to 80 pixels. This means that the user will reduce all images in the web page by clicking the second button.

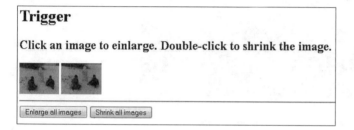

Figure 8.8   The second button sets off the trigger of `dblclick`.

> **Tip**
>
> Because jQuery supports namespaces for events, as mentioned earlier, you can create groups of bound handlers and use them for triggers.

8.5.4 `triggerHandler()`

The `triggerHandler()` method is very similar to the `trigger()` method. It, too, executes all connected event handlers of an element for a specific event type. The important difference with `trigger()` is that this method executes neither the default action of the browser nor passes the event object on to parent elements via the bubble phase, nor executes any live events (see next section).

A second and basically fundamental difference with `trigger()` is that the event is triggered only for the *first element* within the jQuery collection. And this method gives you as a return value the value of the triggered handler rather than a chainable jQuery object. So, if the jQuery collection is empty, the method returns the value `undefined`.

As an example, let's look at a variation of ch8_4.html, where we now just replace the method `trigger()` with `triggerHandler()`. You can find the listing of ch8_5.html and the CSS/JavaScript files on the companion website. If the user clicks one of the two buttons, the action will affect only the first image (because, as described, the event is triggered only for the first element within the jQuery collection). So, only the first image is reduced or enlarged in each case.

Figure 8.9   The trigger affects only the first image.

8.5.5   Live Events: The `live()` and `die()` Methods plus `delegate()` and `undelegate()`

The `live()` method expects as a parameter the type of the event and a callback function. The method that is referred to as a **live event** in jQuery was introduced in version 1.3 of the framework and binds a handler to an event such as `click` for all current and also *future* matching elements.

The possible event values have changed several times in the last few versions of the framework, so it is a good idea to check if a specific event is available in the version of jQuery you are using. For example, only the following events were supported in jQuery version 1.3: `click`, `dblclick`, `mousedown`, `mouseup`, `mousemove`, `mouseover`, `mouseout`, `keydown`, `keypress`, and `keyup`.

In the various versions of jQuery 1.4.x, all missing JavaScript events were successively added that undergo the bubble phase (such as `mouseenter` or `mouseleave`), then `blur` and `focus`, and at some point `hover`. So, almost all events are now supported. Plus you can define custom events. The method basically works in the same way as the `bind()` method. But there are some differences:

- If you bind an event to an element via the `live()` method, the reaction is available not only with all elements currently present in the DOM, but also with elements of the same type that are integrated into the DOM in future. Suppose, for instance, that you have a list with a certain number of items and use `live()` to link a reaction to the click on such an item. The reaction is then assigned automatically to all items in the list that are added later dynamically.[16] This is not the case if you use `bind()`. There, you need to explicitly relink all newly added elements.

- Live events do not bubble in the traditional way and cannot be stopped by calling `event.stopPropagation()` or `event.stopImmediatePropagation()` either. To stop further processing of a live event, the callback function has to return the value `false`.

- Live events only work with a selector in older versions of jQuery. As of version 1.4.1, you can also specify multiple selectors.

Let's look at an example where a reaction function is bound to an image via `bind()` and a second reaction function via `live()`. Then we dynamically create several new images in the web page and see which of the two reaction functions are available for these new images (ch8_6.html).

Listing 8.26 Live Events for Event Handling

```
...
10    <script type="text/javascript"
11        src="lib/ch8_6_ready.js"></script>
12    </head>
13    <body>
14      <h1>Live Events</h1>
15      <button>New image</button><hr />
16        <img src="images/pic1.jpg" />
17    </body>
18  </html>
```

The web page contains an image and a button. We want the image to react to three events:

- **The click by the user:** This reaction is implemented via `bind()`.
- **The mouse pointer moving onto the image area:** This reaction is implemented via `live()`.
- **The mouse pointer exiting from the image area:** This reaction is also implemented via `live()`.

Listing 8.27 shows how we do it (ch8_6_ready.js).

---

16. This involves a concept referred to as delegation. You probably know it from powerful programming techniques such as Java. It is also available in jQuery with a correspondingly named method that you will learn shortly.

Listing 8.27   **Using Triggers**

```
01 var imageno = 2;
02 $(function(){
03   $("img").bind("click", function(){
04     $(this).toggleClass("frame");
05   });
06   $("img").live("mouseover mouseout", function(){
07     $(this).toggleClass("gross");
08   });
09   $("button:first").click(function(){
10     if (imageno < 6)
11       $("body").append($("<img />").attr("src",
12           "images/b" + imageno++ + ".jpg"));
13   });
14 });
```

We show the reaction by changing CSS classes. One class places a frame around the image; the other changes the size.

Figure 8.10   The web page after loading.

Via the `bind()` method, the reaction to a user click is linked to all elements of the type `img` that are listed in the DOM at that point (lines 3–5).

And with `live()`, an anonymous function that toggles the class, is linked to the entering and exiting of the image area.[17] The interesting point is that this reaction is also available for elements of the type `img` that have been dynamically added retrospectively.

17. Note that we explicitly specify two selectors here.

Figure 8.11   After clicking and resizing.

Via a button, a user can add additional images if required.[18] The jQuery `append()` method is used for this. The user can add a maximum of four new images. You will see that the images change size if the mouse pointer is moved onto the images and then off again. But the reaction to a user click is not available for the retrospectively added images.

Figure 8.12   The reaction function is still available even if the input field was added afterward; the third image is enlarged.

delegate()

The technique referred to as **delegates** can be found in powerful language concepts such as Java, as mentioned earlier. In jQuery, you can simply consider the `delegate()` method as an alternative to the `live()` method for binding the execution of a function to an event; it works even for elements that are dynamically added later.

Listing 8.28   `delegate()` **Instead of** `live()`

```
$("table").delegate("td", "hover", function(){
      $(this).toggleClass("myClass");
 });
```

18. In our specific case, this can be done by choosing the image names via an algorithm.

die( ) and undelegate( )

To remove a live event from the event system, you should use the die( ) method. This method was also introduced in jQuery 1.3 as a counterpart to the method live( ), and it simply removes a bound live event. As optional parameters, you again specify the type and the call-back function. Without a parameter, all bound live events are removed. If the type is specified, all live events of the specified type are removed. If you specify a function as a second param-eter, only the specified event handler is removed. If you are working with delegate( ) instead of live( ), you can unbind correspondingly with undelegate( ).

8.5.6   Auxiliary Functions for Interaction

The jQuery framework offers two interesting auxiliary functions to support common interac-tion techniques.

The hover( ) Function

As the name indicates, the hover( ) function mimics the usual hover effect that enables a reaction to reaching the area of an element with the mouse pointer and exiting this area. As a parameter, you specify two function references. This gives you more options than just changing the CSS properties of an element (which you can, of course, do as well).

Whenever the mouse pointer moves over a matching element, the first specified function fires. If the mouse pointer then exits that area, the second specified function fires (ch8_7.html).

Listing 8.29   **The Hover Effect**

```
...
10    <script type="text/javascript"
11        src="lib/ch8_7_ready.js"></script>
12   </head>
13   <body>
14     <h1>Hover</h1>
15     <img src="images/pic1.jpg" alt="The snowman"/>
16     <img src="images/pic2.jpg" alt="and"/>
17     <img src="images/pic3.jpg" alt=
18       "the proud builders"/>
19     <div id="output"></div>
20   </body>
21 </html>
```

In the example, you can see three images for which a value for the HTML attribute alt is speci-fied. You can naturally access this attribute via a jQuery object (ch8_7_ready.js).

Listing 8.30 **Applying the** `hover()` **Method**

```
01 $(function(){
02  $("img").hover(function(){
03    $("#output").text(this.alt);
04  }, function(){
05    $("#output").text("");
06  });
07 });
```

Via the `hover()` method, we get the value of this attribute and write it into the output area of the web page. The function specified as first parameter does exactly that. Behind `this` is the image that is currently underneath the mouse pointer. The second function in lines 4–6 does nothing more than emptying the output area for the message.

Figure 8.13   Outputting a message via `hover()`.

toggle()

The `toggle()` method is used in almost the same way as `hover()`. It just reacts to a click and toggles with each click between two or more functions that are passed to the method as parameters. If a matching element is clicked, the first specified function is fired. A second click on the same element fires the second function. If there are other function references, this goes on accordingly. Then it is back to the first function. All subsequent clicks result in a rotation through the specified function calls. This method is in principle very similar to `hover()`, so we are not providing a complete example.

> **Tip**
>
> Apart from function references as parameters, the `toggle()` method can also be used entirely without parameters. In this case, the visibility of each matching element is toggled on and off. This involves calling the `hide()` and `show()` methods indirectly. You can also use the method with a Boolean value as a parameter. Depending on the value of the parameter, all elements are shown (`true`) or hidden (`false`). If you bear in mind that the numeric value 0 in JavaScript represents `true`, you can also use numeric algorithms for setting the parameter.

Another variation of the method uses as a first parameter a speed specification and as a second optional parameter a function reference or an anonymous function. Let's take a look at this in a complete example (ch8_8.html).

Listing 8.31 **The Hover Effect**

```
...
10    <script type="text/javascript"
11         src="lib/ch8_8_ready.js"></script>
12   </head>
13    <body>
14      <h1>Toggle</h1>
15      <button>Toggle DIVs</button><hr />
16      <div>1</div><div>2</div><div>3</div>
17      <div>4</div><div>5</div><div>6</div>
18   </body>
19 </html>
```

In the example, you can see six div areas that we format via CSS (ch8_8.css).

Listing 8.32 **The Formatting of the div Elements**

```
01 div {
02   width: 80px;
03   height: 40px;
04   margin: 5px;
05   padding: 5px;
06   float: left;
07   background: red;
08   border: 10px outset;
09   cursor: pointer;
10   text-align: center;
11   font-size: 22px;
12 }
```

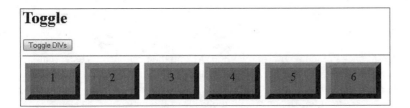

Figure 8.14   The six div elements all have the same formatting.

You can naturally access these div areas via a filter. But we go to every other div container and make these vanish animatedly (ch8_8_ready.js).

Listing 8.33 **Applying the hover() Method**

```
01 $(function(){
02   $("button:first").click(function(){
03     $("div:odd").toggle("slow");
04   });
05 });
```

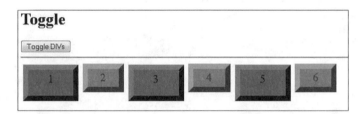

Figure 8.15   Every second div area will animatedly disappear.

As value for the speed you can use a jQuery default token such as "slow" or specify a time interval in milliseconds. See line 3. The click on the button toggles the visibility corresponding to the specified time interval in an animation.

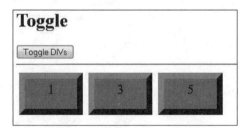

Figure 8.16   Now only the divs with an even index are visible.

Summary

In this chapter, you have learned the basics of event handling and seen how jQuery facilitates this event handling and standardizes it across browser boundaries. Now you are familiar with the general facts about event handlers, the bubble phase, data binding, and triggers. The event object in jQuery provides the basis for being able to use event handling over the entire bandwidth of options without any problems. The various special jQuery methods such as `bind()`, `live()`, `die()`, `one()`, `triggerHandler()`, and `trigger()` provide a solution that you can target precisely to specific tasks. But you should also keep in mind the auxiliary functions such as `hover()` and `toggle()`. And last but not least, there are the specific event handlers in jQuery that represent an improved version of the JavaScript/DOM event handlers.

Effects and Animations

This chapter discusses the effects and animations that jQuery offers for your web applications. Essentially, animations are based on a change of the web page or a part of the web page happening evenly or following a certain algorithm over a defined time period. This means that all the jQuery techniques for creating animations are time dependent. To just create a special effect, however, you can also use some non-time-dependent methods. The effect (for example, displaying an element) then occurs immediately when calling the method. You have already come across various effects and animations in the course of this book.

9.1 Basic Use

jQuery animations and effects are impressive (particularly for laypeople), but they belong in the category of simple techniques once you understand the basic functioning of jQuery. So, we just need to examine the various methods briefly without too many examples. For this reason, this chapter is one of the shorter ones in this book, contrary to what you might expect, and it is also one of the easiest ones, at least from my point of view.

9.1.1 Speed Is All You Need

Essentially, jQuery animation techniques are based on the fact that the style sheet events of components of the web page are changed in a time-controlled way. For a time-independent effect, the change happens immediately, but here, too, Cascading Style Sheets (CSS) properties are changed in a targeted way. From this point of view, you can easily program all animation techniques of the framework manually by recursively manipulating the `style` object. But the jQuery methods simplify the whole thing significantly and encapsulate the underlying processes. As usual, the jQuery techniques are compatible with all browsers.

If you want to use effects in form of animations, you usually need to specify a time period for the length of these animations. In jQuery, there are three **default tokens** (strings) for that purpose, with predefined time values that you can use whenever such a time specification is necessary (generally as parameter of methods):

- `"slow"`

- `"normal"`

- `"fast"`

In each case, the effect on the animation speed after assigning these is obvious. However, because the number of milliseconds behind these tokens is predefined in jQuery and depends on the underlying platform, you do not have direct control over the time period when using the default tokens. You simply have to accept these predefined behaviors.

Alternatively, you can specify the milliseconds directly for the animation and thus set the time period yourself! Although that is not totally precise either.

Tip
The default time period value for animation methods is usually `normal`.

The Animation Rate: `jQuery.fx.interval`

As of jQuery 1.4.3, you can influence the rate (in milliseconds) at which the animation events fire. This means that you can specify the number of frames per second. The default value is 13 milliseconds. If you want to use another value, you can do so; you do not have to use the default value. A lower value causes the animation to run more smoothly on powerful platforms and suitable browsers because of the higher number of individual steps per time unit and the resulting smaller incremental changes. But a higher value takes up a lot of resources and can negatively affect less-powerful platforms and browsers.

Caution
The rate is not identical to the specification of how long an animation should run.

9.1.2   Specifying a Callback

Almost all animations and effects in jQuery allow specifying a callback function or anonymous function. This is executed after the relevant animation has ended, as shown in Listing 9.1.

Listing 9.1   **Specifying an Anonymous Function That Will Be Executed After the Animation Ends**

```
$('img:first').fadeIn('slow', function() {
  alert("Done");
});
```

9.1.3 Chaining

For animations, in particular, you can chain them via dot notation because, of course, animation and effect methods also give you jQuery objects as return values, as shown in Listing 9.2.

Listing 9.2 **Chaining via Dot Notation**

```
$("img").fadeOut('slow').fadeIn('fast').toggleClass('c1');
```

Remarkably, animations and effects are also chained if they are *not* joined via dot notation but simply applied to the same object and called in parallel while one of the animations or effects is running, as shown in Listing 9.3.

Listing 9.3 **Chaining Without Dot Notation**

```
$("button:first") {
  $("img").fadeOut('slow');
}
$("button:eq(1)") {
  $("img").fadeIn('fast');
}
$("button:eq(2)") {
  $("img").toggleClass('c1');
}
```

If a user now clicks the various buttons while an animation is still running, the current animation is not stopped; instead, the new animation is placed into the queue (just as with chaining via dot notation) and is then processed later.

9.1.4 Queues

As discussed earlier,[1] delayed calls of functions in jQuery are generally managed in a **queue**. And usually you need not worry about how it is processed and managed. But the previously introduced methods queue(), clearQueue(),dequeue(), and delay() enable you to manually intervene if it seems necessary. With the method queue(), you get a reference to the first element (the first function) in the queue, and with dequeue(), you can remove a function from the beginning of the queue and execute it. Where appropriate, you can delay the call with delay(). With clearQueue(), you can clear the queue. But thanks to the very powerful and highly configurable standard methods of jQuery, you'll rarely need to use these methods. The method animate(), in particular, already enables you to control the queue via various options.

---

1. So we will just give a quick summary as a reminder here.

9.1.5   Stopping via `stop()` and `jQuery.fx.off`

If you want an animation to stop, you call the method `stop()`, as shown in Listing 9.4.

Listing 9.4   **Stopping an Animation**

```
$("button:first") {
  $("img").fadeOut('slow');
}
$("button:eq(1)") {
  $("img").stop();
}
```

With two optional Boolean parameters, you can influence whether any chained subsequent animation should also be stopped (first parameter, the default is `false`) and whether the current animation should be stopped immediately[2] (second parameter, the default is `false`).

Alternatively, you can use the value of `jQuery.fx.off` to disable all animations. Setting the value of `jQuery.fx.off` to `true` is a global setting with which all animations are disabled. This causes all elements in the web page to be set to their final state immediately. You do this, for example, if the platform is too weak or if there are access problems with animated elements. If you set the value of `jQuery.fx.off` to `false`, the animations are enabled again.

9.1.6 Endless Animations

Creating endlessly[3] running animation with jQuery is extremely easy, simply thanks to the fact that the calls can be chained as described. You just need to use recursive calls in the callbacks. In particular, toggling effects and animations are suitable for this, but if you control the required logic with global variables or parameters, you can easily use other effects, as well, as shown in Listing 9.5.

Listing 9.5   **A Recursive Endless Animation**

```
function ani(){
  $("div.k1").slideToggle(5000,ani);
}
```

9.1.7   Types of Animation

With various jQuery animation methods, you can also specify an easing function in more recent versions of the framework[4]. The easing function defines the amount of the effect that is applied over time. For example, you can specify a linear effect, or one that slows down at

2. So the target value of an animation or effect is applied, or all CSS values are set back to the original state (depending on the situation).

3. Of course, you can also use a counter to limit the number of repetitions.

the end, or one that speeds up at the beginning or end, or a swinging effect. Here are some currently valid strings as values for special effects:

- easeInBack
- easeInBounce
- easeInCirc
- easeInOutBounce
- easeInOutCirc
- easeInOutQuint
- easeInOutSine
- easeInSine
- easeOutBounce
- easeOutCirc
- easeOutQuint
- easeOutSine
- linear
- swing

Note

If you want to apply specific effects, check the jQuery documentation to find additional information about how these effects work. (The documentation describes common standard algorithms for animation techniques.)

9.2   Showing and Hiding: The show() and hide() Methods

Time-controlled showing and hiding of elements on a web page are elementary animation techniques. With jQuery, you can do so easily.

The show() method, without a parameter, shows all matching elements directly if they are hidden. If they are already visible, calling the method changes nothing. Alternatively, you can also use the method with parameters, just as with almost all methods in this category. In this case, you specify as the first parameter the speed with which this effect should happen; the last optional parameter is a callback function. As of jQuery 1.4.3, you can use a second optional parameter, easing, to influence the change rate of the animation. Correspondingly, you use

4. In jQuery 1.3 as extension/plugin, as standard as of 1.4.3.

the `hide()` method to hide visible elements. If the elements are already invisible, calling the method changes nothing.

9.3 Sliding Effects: `slideDown()`, `slideUp()`, and `slideToggle()`

With the three methods `slideDown()`, `slideUp()`, and `slideToggle()`, you can achieve a sliding effect for hiding and showing elements via time-controlled changing of the element's height. You can use the parameters in the same way as with `show()` and `hide()`.

The effect is that elements get bigger (`slideDown()`) or smaller (`slideUp()`). Correspondingly, `slideDown()` represents animated displaying of elements, and `slideUp()` represents hiding.

The type of this development from top to bottom or bottom to top depends on the type or formatting of the element to which the displaying or hiding relates. For example, for a `div` element, only the height is generally changed in animation (not the width). However, the methods have been expanded from jQuery 1.3 onward so that the vertical padding and the value of the vertical `margin` distance are also animated to create a smooth animation effect. For a picture, the width is also changed animatedly in the default setting, unless the image width has been specified (for example, via the style sheet property `width`). Note that whether you specify this property for a `div` element is irrelevant. As you can see, the behavior is a little bit difficult, but essentially it is the height of an element that is changed animatedly.

As the name `slideToggle()` implies, the third method takes care of showing or hiding elements, depending on the state. For all three methods, you can specify as optional parameters the time period, easing behavior, and a callback function.

> **Caution**
>
> The methods manipulate the Document Object Model (DOM) tree of a web page, and in some cases the original structure of the tree can get moved around. In certain circumstances, new nodes for line breaks and so on are inserted.

Listing 9.6   **Applying the Sliding Methods (ch9_1.html)**

```
...
06    <link rel="stylesheet" type="text/css"
07        href="lib/ch9_1.css" />
08    <script type="text/javascript"
09        src="lib/jquery-1.8.2.min.js"></script>
10    <script type="text/javascript"
11        src="lib/ch9_1_ready.js"></script>
```

```
12  </head>
13  <body>
14    <button>Show rectangles</button>
15    <button>Hide rectangles</button>
16    <button>Show images</button>
17    <button>Hide images</button>
18    <button>Toggle images and rectangles</button><hr/>
19    <div class="c1"></div>
20    <div class="c1"></div><hr/>
21    <img src="images/pic1.jpg" class="c2" />
22    <img src="images/pic2.jpg" />
23  </body>
24  </html>
```

In this listing, you can see two rectangles and two images. With the five buttons, you can display and hide the rectangles separately, the same with the images, or you can display or hide all objects simultaneously.

As you can see, we are again using a CSS file (ch9_1.css).

Listing 9.7 The CSS File

```
01  .c1{
02    width: 80px;
03    height: 40px;
04    margin: 5px;
05    background: green;
06    border: 5px outset;
07    display:inline-block;
08  }
09  .c2{
10        width:300px
11  }
```

The first class serves for formatting the `div` elements, and with the second class we explicitly specify the width of one image.

Figure 9.1   Different objects for animating.

Listing 9.8 shows how we apply the methods (ch9_1_ready.js).

Listing 9.8   **The Sliding Methods**

```
01 $(function(){
02  $("button:first").click(function(){
03    $("div.c1").slideDown("slow");
04  });
05  $("button:eq(1)").click(function(){
06    $("div.c1").slideUp("fast");
07  });
08  $("button:eq(2)").click(function(){
09    $("img").slideDown("slow");
10  });
11  $("button:eq(3)").click(function(){
12    $("img").slideUp("slow");
13  });
14  $("button:eq(4)").click(function(){
15    $("div.c1").slideToggle(5000);
16    $("img").slideToggle(10000);
17  });
18 });
```

If you hide the rectangles, you can see that the width of the rectangles does not change. You can try it if you want and remove the width specifications for the rectangles. Even then, the width will remain unchanged when hiding and showing them with the methods.

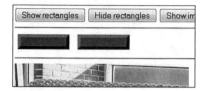

Figure 9.2   The height of the rectangles is changed animatedly.

But for the images, it plays an important role if the image width has been specified. For the first image, we have specified the width, and correspondingly only the height is changed animatedly. For the second image, we have not specified the width; so when hiding and showing, both the height and width are changed animatedly.

Figure 9.3   Different results from hiding or showing the images.

9.4   Opacity Effects: `fadeIn()`, `fadeOut()`, and `fadeTo()` (Plus `toggle()`)

With the methods `fadeIn()`, `fadeOut()`, and `fadeTo()`, jQuery offers options for animatedly changing the opacity of elements. This does not remove an element from the DOM. However, if the opacity is set to the value 0, the element no longer occupies its previously specified place in the web page (the CSS property `display` is set to `none`), which can result in a shift in the site structure.

> **Note**
>
> The jQuery methods compensate for the standard deviation of Internet Explorer with regard to the CSS property `opacity` and manipulate for this browser the opacity in the background with the non–standard-conforming `filter()`.

With `fadeIn()`, you can make an element visible, and with `fadeOut()` you can make it invisible. Again, you can use the same optional parameters as with `show()` and `hide()`. In addition, you can specify as a second parameter for the method `fadeTo()` a target value for the opacity between 0 and 1 to which you want to set the opacity of the elements concerned. Correspondingly, the optional callback function in this case would be the third or fourth parameter (depending on whether you specify a parameter for easing).

Listing 9.9   **Applying the Fading Methods (ch9_2.html)**

```
...
10    <script type="text/javascript"
11         src="lib/ch9_2_ready.js"></script>
12    </head>
13    <body>
14      <button>Image 2 at opacity 0.2</button><br />
15      <img src="images/pic3.jpg" />
16      <img src="images/pic4.jpg" />
17    </body>
18    </html>
```

Listing 9.10 shows the JavaScript file (ch9_2_ready.js).

Listing 9.10   **Animatedly Changing the Opacity**

```
01 $(function(){
02   $("button:first").click(function(){
03     $("img:eq(1)").fadeTo("slow", 0.2, function(){
04       alert("Done");
05     });
06   });
07 });
```

In this listing, we change the opacity of the second image with one of the methods previously described.

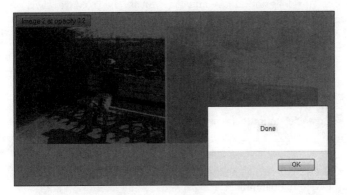

Figure 9.4   The target opacity of the second image has been reached, and the callback function has been triggered.

The `toggle()` method falls into the same category as the three previous methods. You use it to simply toggle the visibility of elements (without parameters). There are two special variations of the method. With a Boolean parameter, you can specify whether the visibility should be enabled or disabled. These are then simply equivalents of `show()` and `hide()`. The variation with three optional parameters, added in jQuery 1.4.3, is more interesting. In addition to the usual time data parameter and the callback as a second optional parameter, it specifies which type of opacity reduction or increase should be used.

9.5 Individual Animations with `animate()`

The default methods in jQuery for firing an effect or time-controlled animation are already powerful and impressive. But you can easily imagine different situations that are not covered by these and that you still want to animate. Imagine, for example, moving the position of an element.

In direct programming, you would probably work with `window.setTimeout()` to control the time periods in animations and use it to change certain CSS properties dynamically. And very probably you would optimize the animations via recursive calls. This kind of effort is not necessary in jQuery because it offers the `animate()` method. This method is available in several variations with different (optional) parameters. The general version looks schematically like Listing 9.11.

Listing 9.11 **Pattern for Applying `animate()`**

```
animate(style object with properties, [time factor], [easing], [callback])
```

An alternative variation works with two parameters, as shown in Listing 9.12.

Listing 9.12 **Pattern for Variation with Two Parameters**

```
animate(style object with properties, options)
```

For the options, you can set the following specifications described in Table 9.1.

Table 9.1 **Options for the More Precisely Specified Call of `animate()`**

Option	Description
duration	Specifies the duration via the usual tokens `"slow"`, `"normal"`, or `"fast"` or period in milliseconds.
easing	Specifies a specific effect when ending the animation as string. The default is `"swing"`.
complete	Specifies a function that is to be executed once the animation ends. The function is called for each affected element.

Option	Description
step	Specifies a callback function that is to be called in each step of the animation.
queue	A Boolean value with a default value `true`. This specification has an effect if animations are to be added to a queue of animations. If the value is set to `false`, the animation skips the queue and starts immediately. This is the same as if you were to start several `window.setTimeout()` calls simultaneously.
specialEasing	An object of the type `Map` with CSS properties and assigned easing functions for the relevant property.

Like the other animation methods, the `animate()` method is based on the fact that style sheet properties can be changed in a time-controlled way. In particular, you need to specify a target value for a specific style sheet property. You also do so, for example, with the `fadeTo()` method. But by calling the `animate()` method, the whole process is much more flexible because basically you can change any style sheet properties in this way. You specify this style sheet property in the form of an object as a first parameter, where each key in the object represents a style property that you want to animate (for example, `height`, `left`, or `opacity`).

The value assigned to a property represents the target in relation to which the property is changed animatedly, setting out from a certain state. In case of a numeric value, the animation adjusts the value using the easing function. If the target value for a property is specified via a string such as `"hide"`, `"show"`, or `"toggle"`, jQuery automatically constructs a default animation for reaching this target state of the property. However, remember that all supported properties have to be represented in one form or another by numeric values. Properties such as `backgroundColor` (or also foreground colors) are not represented in such a numeric form and are therefore not supported in the current version of jQuery.[5]

As of jQuery 1.2, however, you can work with units for some properties (for example, the unit em for font sizes or %). You can also work with relative animations from that version of jQuery onward. You have to precede a property value with the JavaScript tokens += or -= to change it relative to its current value in positive or negative direction.

jQuery 1.3 has new features, as well. If you specify a time period for an animation, the animation will synchronously set the elements concerned to their final state.

The last comment hints at the fact that you can, of course, also specify a time period for the animations with this method. The second optional parameter enables you to do this in the usual way (in milliseconds or via the token `"slow"`, `"normal"`, or `"fast"`). Let's take a look at a few variations of the method in practice.

---

5. The expanded method `animate()` from jQuery UI, on the other hand, permits animating even colors!

Listing 9.13   **Different Ways of Using** `animate()` **(ch9_3.html)**

```
...
10    <script type="text/javascript"
11        src="lib/ch9_3_ready.js"></script>
12  </head>
13  <body>
14    <button>Animate DIV 1</button>
15    <button>Animate DIV 2</button>
16    <button>Animate image 1</button>
17    <button>Animate image 2</button>
18    <button>Animate images and DIVs
19    </button><hr/>
20    <div class="d1" id="i1"></div>
21    <div class="d1" id="i2"></div>
22    <img src="images/pic5.jpg" id="i3" class="img1" />
23      <img src="images/pic6.jpg" class="img1" id="i4"/>
24  </body>
25  </html>
```

In the example, you can see two rectangles and two images. In the referenced CSS file, we first specify properties for the images and `div`s. Among others, we specify the height and position plus some data for a frame and the color. This is not very complicated, but some of these CSS properties are changed animatedly (ch9_3.css).

Listing 9.14   **The Initial CSS Specifications**

```
01 .d1 {
02  width: "80px";  height: 40px;
03  margin: 5px;
04  background: green;  border: 5px outset;
05  position: absolute
06 }
07 .img1 {
08  width: 200px;
09  position: absolute
10 }
11 #i1 {
12  width: 200px;
13  left: 100px;  top: 50px
14 }
15 #i2 {
16  width: 200px;
17  left: 400px;  top: 50px
18 }
```

```
19 #i3 {
20   width: 200px;
21   left: 100px;   top: 150px
22 }
23 #i4 {
24   width: 200px;
25   left: 400px;   top: 150px
26 }
```

Figure 9.5   The web page after loading.

Listing 9.15 shows the JavaScript file (ch9_3_ready.js).

Listing 9.15   **Defining Custom Animations**

```
01 $(function(){
02   $("button:first").click(function(){
03     $("div#i1").animate({
04       width: "50%",
05       opacity: 0.4,
06       borderWidth: "1px"
07     }, 1500);
08   });
09   $("button:eq(1)").click(function(){
10     $("div#i2").animate({
11       width: "-=20",
12       opacity: 0.2,
13       borderWidth: "15px"
14     }, 1500);
15   });
16   $("button:eq(2)").click(function(){
```

```
17    $("img#i3").animate({
18       width: "30%",
19       opacity: 0.3,
20       top: "200px"
21    }, 5000,"swing");
22  });
23  $("button:eq(3)").click(function(){
24    $("img#i4").animate({
25       width: "40%",
26       opacity: 0.3,
27       top: "+40px",
28       left: "-50px"
29    }, 1500);
30  });
31  $("button:eq(4)").click(function(){
32    $("div").animate({
33       width: "5%",
34       opacity: 0.1,
35       top: "100px",
36       left: "100px"
37    }, "slow");
38    $("img").animate({
39       width: "5%",
40       opacity: 0.3,
41       top: "100px",
42       left: "100px"
43    }, "slow");
44  });
45 });
```

With the five buttons in the web page, you can trigger different animations. The click on the first button animates the first rectangle, the second button changes the second image, the third button changes the first image, the fourth button animates the second image, and the last button animates all elements together.

The first rectangle is changed in its width and opacity. Plus, the width of the frame is animated. The second rectangle also changes in width. However, the width is reduced via the token -= by 20 pixels. The opacity and frame width are also animated again.

The first image is enlarged, the opacity reduced to 30%, and the position shifted to 200 pixels from the top. The second image is also moved in its position (both horizontally and vertically) and animated in size and opacity. Here, we also specify an easing factor as a third parameter.

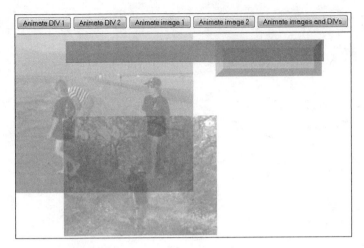

Figure 9.6   All elements have been animated in turn.

A click on the fifth button starts two animations simultaneously. Note that the selectors specify elements this time. In particular, all elements are pulled together in one position.

Let's also look at an example with the second variation of `animate()` (ch9_4.html).

Listing 9.16   **Another Way of Using** `animate()`

```
...
10    <script type="text/javascript"
11        src="lib/ch9_4_ready.js"></script>
12  </head>
13  <body>
14      <button>Start animation</button><hr />
15    <img src="images/pic4.jpg" id="i1"/>
16  </body>
17 </html>
```

Listing 9.17 shows the referenced CSS file (ch9_4.css).

Listing 9.17   **The Initial CSS Specifications**

```
01 #i1 {
02   width: 200px;
03   position: absolute;
04   left: 100px;
05   top: 150px
06 }
```

It gets interesting in the JavaScript file (ch9_4_ready.js).

Listing 9.18 **Chaining and Control for Starting Several Chained Animations Simultaneously**

```
01 $(function(){
02   $("button:first").click(function(){
03     $("img#i1").animate({
04       width: "20%",
05       opacity: 0.4
06     }, {
07       duration: 1500,
08       queue: false
09     }).animate({
10       top: "+40px",
11       left: "-50px"
12     }, {
13       duration: 1500,
14       queue: false
15     }).animate({
16       height: "100%"
17     }, {
18       duration: 5000,
19       queue: true
20     });
21   });
22 });
```

In the source text, you can see that several animations are chained. So, they should really be executed *after one another*. But because we specified `queue: false` here, the three chained calls of `animate()` are started simultaneously. As you can see, the value of `queue` in the last method is set back to `true`. A subsequent call of the `animate()` method would be placed back into the queue.

Summary

This chapter covered the central animation techniques and effects in jQuery. Animations are essentially based on the temporal change of components in the web page. The generally simple jQuery methods in this area support this temporal manipulation. Primary methods for animations and effects include `show()`, `hide()`, `slideDown()`, `slideUp()`, `slideToggle()`, `fadeIn()`, `fadeOut()`, and `fadeTo()`, plus `animate()` for creating custom animations.

10

AJAX

Around the year 2005, AJAX revolutionized the Web. Since then, hardly anything is as it used to be on the Web. AJAX hit like a bomb, although it is in fact just a fashion term. Many frameworks for developing applications on the Web occasionally explicitly referred to themselves as AJAX frameworks, although the pure AJAX functionalities often consisted in only a few percent of their performance range. But this small part is immensely important because it forms the basis for modern Rich Internet Applications (RIAs). Just think of the many special Google features that are almost all based on AJAX. Of course, a high-end framework such as jQuery also offers all required functions for simplifying the creation of AJAX applications. And these AJAX functions in jQuery are what we focus on in this chapter.

If you compare the source code of handwritten AJAX applications with the source code you need to create for an application of the same functionality and quality by using jQuery, you will see that your code is much simpler and therefore of better quality. Above all, the required code is massively reduced. You do not constantly have to reinvent the wheel for many repeated required steps in the AJAX communication, but can instead make use of the sophisticated jQuery techniques. This makes AJAX applications with jQuery much clearer and more compact. At the very least, you can prevent many complications you might otherwise have to deal with if you manually create AJAX applications.

10.1 AJAX and `XMLHttpRequest` (XHR) Basics

Let's first briefly introduce the basics of AJAX. As mentioned previously, you use AJAX to describe a method to ensure a web application reaction in (almost) real time even though the web server is requesting new data. This happens without reloading the entire web page in the browser—only the new required data is loaded and inserted into the web page. The previously loaded web page remains intact in the browser.

AJAX specifically refers only to an interaction of technologies that have long been established on the Web; starting from HTML (Hypertext Markup Language) or XHTML (Extensible HTML) and HTTP (Hypertext Transfer Protocol) via JavaScript and CSS (Cascading Style Sheets) up to XML (Extensible Markup Language) or JSON (JavaScript Object Notation). Even the asynchronous requesting of data to be integrated in a web page is not all that new. It has been around in slightly different form since about 1998. Only the term *AJAX* is relatively new; it became established around 2005, together with the buzzword *Web 2.0*. For supporting this asynchronous communication between client and web server, all modern browsers offer the object XMLHttpRequest (integrated as an extension of the JavaScript object model), an integrated interface for controlling HTTP transactions from client-side programming languages (mainly JavaScript). These transactions take place independently[1] of the "normal" data request by the web browser. These XHR or XMLHttpRequest objects are based directly on the internal structure of HTTP and form the backbone of any AJAX request. And they are made available in one form or another in all frameworks and toolkits that claim the title AJAX.

For the asynchronous communication between browser and web server, the XHR object permits the registration of callback functions via function references. These callback functions are assessed with every change of the transaction state. Plus, you can also access all HTTP header fields of an AJAX request or response via an XHR object.

10.1.1 Creating an XMLHttpRequest Object Manually

To be able to work with an XHR object, this has to be created in accordance with the rules of the programming language used. In JavaScript, you do so via a suitable constructor method. An object of the type XMLHttpRequest then makes available all relevant methods and properties for asynchronous communication via AJAX. Based on the common transfer methods,[2] data can be sent or information can be requested, plus the request header can be set and evaluated.

> **Note**
>
> Note that for security reasons you can generally only use AJAX requests to request data from the same domain as the requesting web page. This is a commonly used **sandbox principle**. Otherwise, you would have what is referred to as cross domain access, and this entails the risk of potential misuse and manipulation. But this sandbox principle constitutes a considerable limitation, and both web designers and browser manufacturers are working hard to find solutions to remove these limitations without endangering security. In Internet Explorer 8, for example, Microsoft offers a proprietary XDomainRequest object, whereas Mozilla and related W3C conforming browsers attempt to expand the XHR object. In jQuery, the method getScript() offers a solution that allows you to load a script from another domain. The basis is an extension of JSON with the name **JSONP** that we will come back to later and with which JSON data can be loaded from any address.

The various browser incompatibilities force us to create the XHR object in different ways to ensure that the procedure works in all relevant browsers. The basic approach looks like Listing 10.1

---

1. Most asynchronously, which as mentioned earlier, explains part of the AJAX abbreviation.

2. In practice, only POST or GET are generally used. Other methods such as PUT or DELETE are theoretically possible, but they are not supported by all browsers, and there is hardly any need to use them.

Listing 10.1   **Creating an** XMLHttpRequest **Object with a Constructor**

```
resObject = new XMLHttpRequest();
```

Unfortunately, older versions of Internet Explorer cannot cope with this. They require using an ActiveX control, and even with different parameters, depending on the browser version. So, you need to program an automatic distinction between the different ways to create the communication object.[3] With jQuery, the rather complex steps in the background are encapsulated in a form that is compatible across all browsers, which makes them much simpler.

10.1.2   The Methods of an XHR Object

An object of the type XMLHttpRequest offers several methods, as discussed briefly here. They form the basis for understanding the AJAX methods of jQuery:

- The method abort() stops the current browser request. More precisely, the client no longer responds to a later response from the web server after this method is called.

- Via getAllResponseHeaders(), you get all header fields sent by the server as string.

- The method getResponseHeader("headerLabel") returns the value of the header field that you have specified as a parameter as a string.

- The method open("method", "URL"[, asyncFlag[, "userName"[, "password"]]]) is one of the most important methods of AJAX communication. With it, you specify the connection data for the contact to a web server. The first two parameters are required—the data transfer method (GET or POST) and the URL. The third argument specifies if a request is processed synchronously (false) or asynchronously (true). If you specify synchronous processing, the then-following sending of the data via the send() method blocks the execution of the script until the response from the server has been completely received.[4] With an asynchronous data request, the blocking behavior of the browser waiting for a response is avoided. The script simply goes on running after the request is sent. The other optional parameters are a potentially required username and the associated password.

- The method send(content) is used for sending a request. It is called after calling the method open(). The parameter content is either null (for GET) or a query string for POST. For POST and a value for the parameter content, the focus is on sending data such as user input from the client to the server. Because the parameter has the value null in case of GET, the question is how any required data can be sent to the web server

3. As a general rule, you work with the concept of **exception handling**. You simply try to create the XHR object, and if it goes wrong, you go an alternative way. By integrating the attempts in an exception handling, the script can carry on running stably despite the fact that the object failed to be generated (jQuery works in the background with this approach). Alternatively, you can also work with browser sniffing, but that is not reliable.

4. This is necessary, for example, if several AJAX requests are meant to follow one another and a following AJAX request has to operate with the result of a previous request.

in this case. Very simple: As always, with `GET`! For the `GET` method, the data is simply appended to the data transfer target (the URL) before sending, with the data separated from the original URL by a question mark (?).[5] You send the data to an evaluating script or program as a set of name-value pairs separated by the token `&`. This set of name-value pairs is transmitted in a partial string of the URL that a web script has to unravel again.[6]

- With `setRequestHeader("label", "value")`, you can set individual header fields.

- Via `setMimeType("mimetype")`, you set the MIME type of the requested data. But the method is not supported by some browsers.

10.1.3   The Properties of an XHR Object

In addition to the methods, an XHR object has a number of properties whose functionality is, of course, also present in jQuery:

- With `onreadystatechange`, you have an event handler that is called whenever the connection state (`readyState`) of an XHR object changes. For the event handler, you normally register a function reference to a callback function.

- The property `readyState` contains the current connection state of a transaction. Possible values are 0 for `UNINITIALlZED`, 1 for `LOADING`, 2 for `LOADED`, 3 for `INTERACTIVE`, and 4 for `COMPLETED`.[7]

- The property `responseText` contains the data sent by the server as text and `responseXML` as XML data (in other words, as a tree that you can navigate). If the data was not sent in XML form, `responseXML` contains the value `null`.

- The property `status` contains a numerical value for the HTTP status of the connection, and the property `statusText` contains the associated text message if one was transmitted.

10.1.4   A Practical Example of Data Request Without Special jQuery Methods

Let's take a look at how to implement a data request via AJAX without using special methods[8] of the framework (ch10_1.html).

---

5. A user will see this resulting pseudo-URL with a classic data request (not with an AJAX request) in the browser address window after a form has been sent.

6. Such a string is structured roughly like this: `name1=value1&name2=value2&name3=value3`. The string has to be divided up into pieces by the processing script or program at the ampersand symbol (`&`) and the equals sign (`=`).

7. Some sources specify 0 as not initialized, 1 as connection established, 2 as request received, 3 as answer in process, and 4 as finished. Both are equivalent.

8. But we are already going to use jQuery for accessing the elements of the web page. However, we could just as well use traditional DOM methods, without any jQuery.

Listing 10.2   **A Web Page in Which Data Is Loaded via AJAX**

```
...
06    <link rel="stylesheet" type="text/css"
07        href="lib/ch10_1.css" />
08    <script type="text/javascript"
09        src="lib/jquery-1.8.2.min.js"></script>
10    <script type="text/javascript"
11        src="lib/ch10_1_ready.js"></script>
12  </head>
13  <body>
14    <button>Request text via AJAX</button>
15    <div></div>
16  </body>
17 </html>
```

> **Note**
>
> In the other examples in this chapter, we usually take the same structure of a web page as a starting point as in our current example. So, to save space, we will not print it again. Instead, you can always find the detailed listings on the companion website.

Clicking the button loads a text file and displays it in the div area. This happens via the following simple script that makes use of the previously mentioned methods and properties of an XHR object (ch10_1_ready.js).

Listing 10.3   **The AJAX Request**

```
01 $(function(){
02   var xhr = new XMLHttpRequest();
03   $("button:first").click(function(event){
04     xhr.open("get", "ajax.txt", true);
05     xhr.send(null);
06     xhr.onreadystatechange = function(){
07       if (xhr.readyState == 4)
08         $("div:first").html(xhr.responseText);
09     }
10   });
11 });
```

In line 2, an XHR object is created. (Note that this explicitly does not work in old versions of Internet Explorer.[9]) In line 4, you can see how the connection is initialized, in line 5 the request is sent, and in lines 6–8 the response is received.

9. Here we would have to work with exception handling, as mentioned earlier, and use different ways of creating the object, one of which we hope will work. But for the sake of simplicity, I am not going to do so here.

In fact, this short script already shows practically everything that constitutes the core of AJAX. However, jQuery offers you the necessary tools, several benefits in simplifying AJAX requests, and avoiding browser compatibility.

10.1.5   The Data Format in an AJAX Communication

If the client requests data from the web server via AJAX, the web server always sends plain text[10] as a response (as you saw in the first example). This plain text can be generated by a server-side script or program (such as in Java, PHP, or ASP.NET) or can already be present as text file on the server.[11] And this plain text can be completely unstructured or have various internal structures. For structured plain text, a specific MIME type is usually specified in the HTTP header, but it is and remains plain text. Even for structured text, it is completely irrelevant whether the plain text is generated by a script or program on the server or already present as a finished file.

In practice, four variations of transfer formats have become established, and these are also reflected in different AJAX methods in jQuery:

- Pure plain text without any structure.
- Plain text with HTML tags; in other words, HTML fragments. These can even contain scripts, although some browsers do not execute the scripts that are loaded with this approach.
- XML.
- JSON.

If pure plain text or plain text with HTML tags is sent by the server, this is usually integrated via Dynamic HTML (DHTML) (or jQuery) into the web page in the server, mostly without further processing of the response in the client. The response by the web server is displayed mostly unchanged and has to be put into its final form beforehand on the server—in other words, the form you want to be used in the client. In many AJAX applications, this will suffice.

> **Caution**
>
> If you send HTML via AJAX, this will only be a **fragment**. You should not reload an entire web page via AJAX.

Yet you will be able to create much more demanding applications if you expand the server response by a structured format that can be used in a targeted way in the client. Structuring the transmitted information gives you many more options for distributing business processes. As a structuring format in AJAX, there is usually only JSON or XML, as mentioned previously. So, if the web server sends XML or JSON, you can operate on the response in the client and move business logic to the client.

10. No multimedia data such as images or other binary data; that has nothing to do with AJAX.

11. It does not matter exactly how the web server generates the response.

> **Caution**
>
> Moving logic in a web application to the client can sometimes prove tricky. You should consider very carefully whether this is really the right way to go for your application.

Regardless of whether this distribution of business logic between web server and client is sensible, the processing of XML in the client via pure JavaScript is problematic. XML is only a description of the syntax for elements and structures. In principle, the strict rules for XML allow such documents to be easily validated and processed in an automated way. At first glance, this predestines XML for data exchange. But unfortunately, the implementation of these rules is insufficient in various platforms. Although it is hard to understand why this might be—unless driven by market objectives—there are serious differences in how XML is processed in different browsers. The jQuery methods reduce these problems and at least theoretically make such a distribution of business logic possible. But JSON is still the better choice in practice for a structured response of the web server. Because if pure plain text offers insufficient logic and XML appears too difficult, JSON is an alternative between the two extremes. With JSON, you have a structure for the transfer format that is simpler than XML and above all processed more consistently in different web browsers. Plus the JSON format corresponds to the format of the options that we are permanently using in jQuery—an object literal. Listing 10.4 shows an example of a simple JSON document, which we will use again later (ch10.json).

Listing 10.4   **A JSON Structure**

```
01 {
02   "name" : "Ralph Steyer",
03   "job" : "Masters in Maths",
04   "place : "Eppstein",
05   "websites" : {
06     "url1" : "www.rjs.de",
07     "url2" : "blog.rjs.de",
08     "url3" : "www.ajax-net.de"
09   }
10 }
```

10.1.6   AJAX Request Process

Here you can see a summary of the rules of how every AJAX application works within the system. An AJAX request can differ in various details and be hidden by a framework or toolkit, but in its rules it always follows the same pattern:

1. An XHR object is created via which the communication is to run.

2. A callback function is registered as function reference with the XHR object. This is then called at each state change of the transaction. The specified function is called for each status change in the XHR object. readyState indicates the current status of the transaction when this callback function is called. This enables distinguishing individual

phases of the data transfer. The most important case is reaching the status COMPLETED with the status code 4. Only this status is handled consistently across the various browsers. For that reason, almost all AJAX applications check for it. jQuery does this, too, although the specific steps are hidden through the AJAX methods of the framework.

3. The connection is opened by calling the open() method of the XHR object. But this is not yet the specific request.

4. The AJAX request is sent to the web server via the send() method.

5. The response of the web server—pure plain text with or without structure—is processed. The status change of an XHR object can explicitly be used for this.

10.2   Special AJAX Support in jQuery

Support for AJAX in jQuery is, of course, based directly on the XHR object and its methods and properties plus the general process of AJAX requests. If you have grasped how AJAX works, many of these jQuery methods become intuitively clear. The individual steps of AJAX communication are usually carried out together within the various AJAX methods in jQuery. Plus jQuery has a few special features for supporting AJAX that have been expanded considerably, in particular in jQuery 1.4.3 and 1.5.x. Generally, nothing much has changed on the surface in jQuery 1.5.x, but more in the internal workings of the framework. Version 1.5.x is by no means a milestone in jQuery, as was the case with version 1.3 or 1.4.3. The exception is AJAX. Here, a lot of new features have been added, but in some cases these are rather specialized and of interest in only specific cases and for very advanced users.

10.2.1   JSONP and Remote Requests

With regard to JSON, jQuery offers an extension with the name **JSONP**[12] to permit cross-server scripting and flexible loading of JSON data.[13] As mentioned before, AJAX requests may be sent only to the same domain from which the web page was loaded. But it has always[14] been possible to integrate JavaScript files from any server into a web page completely independently from AJAX. This is where JSONP comes in. On the one hand, you use jQuery and JSONP to create a script. On the other hand, you expect a specified function to then return the contained JSON object. Specifically, in JSONP, a script is loaded via AJAX by using the DOM representation of the <script> tag and executed. All scripts that are not loaded from the same domain are referred to as **remote requests**. You will see a bigger example for this later.

---

12. The *P* stands for padding.

13. The ajax() method permits this.

14. Or at least since JavaScript has come into use.

10.2.2   The `jqXHR` Object

As of jQuery 1.5, the framework offers a special extension of the native `XMLHttpRequest` object. It is called jQuery `XMLHttpRequest` or `jqXHR` for short. The object is, for example, returned as a return value by the most general jQuery method for controlling AJAX activities: `$.ajax()`. It offers all traditional XHR methods and properties—with one important exception because the `onreadystatechange` event handler is not directly offered. This is not a problem as the new `jqXHR` object provides a new interface that permits specific individual mechanisms for reacting to the success or failure of an AJAX request.

Its special capabilities reveal themselves above all when special formats are loaded via AJAX. Specifically, this concerns the `<script>` tag for a JSONP request. In that case, a `jqXHR` object simulates native XHR functionality whenever possible.

10.2.3   Methods in jQuery for AJAX Requests

As mentioned previously, AJAX requests always follow the same pattern. Basically, you need the URL of the server file or the server-side script, the method of data transfer, any data sent to the server such as user input, the information whether it should happen asynchronously or not, and a callback function for the reaction. With this background knowledge, it becomes instantly clear what the methods `jQuery.get(url, data, callback, type)` and `jQuery.post(url, data, callback, type)`[15] together with the parameters mean and how you need to use them.

Both methods give you an XHR object, as do all request methods. The data is optional value pairs with data to be sent to the server. The optional type indicates whether the communication should happen asynchronously (`true`, the default value) or synchronously (`false`). The callback function is executed when the request has been successfully completed. So, all we still need to mention is how you can use the returned data in the callback function specifically. But, you should also find the method `jQuery.getJSON(url, data, callback)` self-explanatory. Still, it will all make more sense if you look at a practical example. Of course, we take a look at several examples related to this in the next few pages.

10.2.4   Specifying the Data Type

Fundamentally, the AJAX methods react intelligently to the type of data that comes from the server. The frameworks attempts to sensibly process the information on the data type that the server provides via the header. But the file extension can also be taken into account. If the information indicates that XML is delivered, you can access the return value of the AJAX methods in the normal way via the XML methods or jQuery selectors. If another type is identified (such as HTML), the data is treated as text.

Sometimes the server does not correctly indicate the type of the plain text, especially if the file extension of data on the server is not linked to a specific format or if an unsuitable MIME

---

15. Or their shorthand forms `$.get()` and `$.post()`.

type is sent.[16] Often, you just need to adjust a setting on the server. And you rarely have access to this unless you happen to be running the server yourself or you can use a script to set the header. Just as likely, you might just want to treat sent data differently.

In both cases, you can explicitly specify the data type for most methods in jQuery and set out how the data should be interpreted by the server. In `$.GET()` or `$.POST()`, you specify as last parameter `xml`, `text`, `json`, `jsonp`, `script`, or `html` as appropriate. In `$.ajax()` you can also specify the corresponding details.

> **Tip**
>
> If you think that the default data types offered by jQuery for AJAX communication are not enough, you can also create custom data types as of jQuery 1.5. But this topic is beyond the scope of this discussion, and such custom-defined types are required in only rare cases. To do so, you use the `converters` option in `$.ajaxSetup()` for this. You can find a brief explanation about this at the end of this chapter, and, of course, you can find out more in the jQuery documentation.

With the data types `text` and `xml`, the data is then not processed at all by the jQuery methods but simply passed on to the handler `success()`. In the background, the methods `responseText` (text) or `responseXML` (xml) are involved.

If the data is marked as `html`, each embedded JavaScript within the received data should be executed before the actual HTML is returned as a string. The same applies correspondingly if the data is marked as `script`, except that nothing is returned after it is executed.

If the data is marked as `json` it is parsed and made available as a JavaScript object. The method `jQuery.parseJSON()` runs in the background if the browser supports this. Otherwise, the constructor of the JavaScript class `Function` is used and not the potentially unsecure native function `eval()`. If the data is marked as `jsonp`, the framework appends a query string parameter `callback=?` to the URL. The server should append the JSON data to the `callback` identifier to send a valid JSONP response.

> **Tip**
>
> If necessary, you can specify an alternative parameter identifier for `callback` via the option `jsonp` in the method `$.ajax()`.

If the AJAX methods of the framework receive data from the server, the `error` callbacks and global events are never fired.

In some cases, it can be appropriate to add the extension .html to a text file you want to load later (even if it is not a complete web page)—in particular, if the text contains HTML tags that

---

16. For example, XML should be sent by the server as `text/xml` or `application/xml` so that the browsers can handle it. But in case of `application/xml`, various problems are known in certain browsers, so that you may have to intervene if necessary.

you want to be interpreted after loading in the browser. In most implementations, however, you can manage without this file extension and simply use the conventional .txt.

10.2.5 Avoiding Caching

With AJAX requests, a fundamental problem exists with regard to **caching** data in a GET request. Unfortunately, it happens quite often that data is not re-requested by the server in an AJAX request, even though this would be necessary. The browser simply fetches the data from the local cache.[17] This concerns above all Internet Explorer. In manual programming, it is therefore a good idea to use the workaround of appending to the query string a random value or time stamp that is simply generated via JavaScript and basically not used further, neither on the server nor on the client. It is just intended to suggest to the browser that the data has to be reloaded. In fact, this trick is currently the only simple yet reliable way of preventing this caching behavior (a behavior that is indeed useful in traditional web data requests). Those frameworks that offer an explicit mechanism for this (such as YUI) do nothing else in the background. In jQuery, you currently have to create an extra parameter manually in this situation for most methods and append this parameter to the URL. Only the ajax() method offers a corresponding option for preventing caching via a special parameter.

10.3 $.get() and $.post()

Let's first look at the two most important[18] methods for loading data via a request. These are $.get() and $.post(). Essentially, both methods are used as shown in Listing 10.5.

Listing 10.5 **Schematic Form of the Methods**

```
jQuery.get( url, [ data], [ success(data, textStatus, jqXHR) ], [ dataType ] )
jQuery.post( url, [ data ], [ success(data, textStatus, jqXHR) ], [ dataType ] )
```

The only compulsory parameter is the URL to which the request is to be sent. The optional data is an object of the type Map or a string with the data that you want to send to the server.

The third parameter is a callback function that is called if successful. Its parameters represent the data that should come from the server, a text with the status and the jqXHR object. The jqXHR object is only used as a parameter with jQuery 1.5 onward—before, it was the traditional XMLHttpRequest object.

10.3.1 Just Requesting Plain Text from the Web Server

Let's look at the easiest case first: You just want to request plain text from the web server. In the following example, this is done via two buttons through AJAX. We are using $.get() and

---

17. You need to take into account that historically the browsers were never designed for asynchronous data requests.

18. Provided you do not want to specify any particular configurations of the AJAX request.

`$.post()` in parallel to demonstrate both methods. Notice that there are no differences in the source code. You can find the web page ch10_2.html on the companion website. Listing 10.6 shows what the JavaScript file looks like (ch10_2_ready.js).

Listing 10.6   **AJAX Requests via GET and POST**

```
01 $(function(){
02   $("button:first").click(function(){
03     $.get("ajax.txt", function(data){
04       $("div:first").text(data);
05     });
06   });
07   $("button:eq(1)").click(function(){
08     $.post("ajax.txt", function(data){
09       $("div:first").text(data);
10     });
11   });
12 });
```

In the example, we request a simple text file without any kind of structure via AJAX from the web server. On clicking the first button, the file is requested via GET, and on clicking the second button, via POST. Functionally, there is not the slightest difference between the two methods of data requests in this simple example. Internally, the HTTP header looks slightly different, and, of course, the server processes the data according to the relevant method.[19] Data from the client is otherwise not sent to the web server in this first example, and so the methods for the AJAX data request only require two parameters each. The first parameter is, of course, the URL; the second parameter is the callback. Here, we use an anonymous callback function that has exactly the same structure in both cases. The parameter for the function contains the response of the web server. It could not be any simpler. The response by the web server is directly integrated into the web page in this first example, without any further actions.

If you now request the data that contains HTML fragments, these fragments are not interpreted as long as you are working with the method `text()`.[20] But instead of the method `text()`, you can, of course, also use the method `html()` as in the first AJAX example, and in that case the browser response is interpreted accordingly. In practice, it is often common to send such HTML fragments and simply integrate them into a web page. Note, as mentioned earlier, that you must not send a complete HTML page, a few exceptions aside. Such an HTML page is already loaded in the browser, and we only want to replace small parts of this page.

19. It is a significant advantage of jQuery that the AJAX request in itself is not only simplified, but the process is also made uniform for the different methods.

20. This has explicitly *nothing* to do with the fact that the file extension is .txt.

> **Note**
>
> An AJAX request requires almost always that you are working with a web server. After all, you want to request data from a web server and integrate it into the existing website. To do this, you are reloading the data via HTTP. For a test, you also have to load both the web page and the requested data via a[21] web server into the browser. Simply opening the web page from the file system is not generally possible. So as soon as you have launched your local web server, it is usually available via the URL localhost. Otherwise, you simply enter in the address line the IP number or name of the computer where the web server is running. If you execute the page as JavaScript Web Application with an IDE such as Aptana, the page is always requested via the web server.

10.3.2 Sending Data to the Web Server via $.get() and $.post()

Let's now look at how data is sent to the web server during an AJAX request. This will mainly be user input, either data that a user enters in a web form or data based on actions that the user carries out with the mouse.[22] You will see that jQuery significantly simplifies and standardizes the sending via objects of the type Map.

> **Tip**
>
> In the default setting, AJAX requests are sent via GET. If you are using POST, the sent data is encoded with UTF-8. If you want to send a query string, the data is converted to a suitable form with the method . If you do not want this to happen, you can set the parameter processData to false. That can make sense if you want to send an XML object to the server. In that case, you should change the contentType option of application/x-www-form-urlencoded to a more suitable MIME type.

> **Note**
>
> The data that is sent from the client to the web server also has to be processed there. Then it no longer makes sense for you to specify a pure text file on the server as a URL. You need to call a script or program on the server that receives and processes the data. This script or program can then, of course, generate pure plain text again in the client, or a response with any structure. It does not matter. We are not going to go into more detail with the server side here (as this is explicitly not our topic), but instead look at a script that represents a black box for us that sends data. (On the companion website, you will find the PHP files used in the example: ch10_3_get.php and ch10_3_post.php.)

21. Strictly speaking, even the same web server as the web page itself (keyword sandbox principle).

22. Mouse actions form the basis for one of the most widely known AJAX applications around: Google Maps. Here, dragging a map or scrolling the mouse wheel is sent to the Google web servers in the background, and based on this data, the user receives new images that show a different map section.

Access Verification as a Specific Example

As a specific example, we want to program the following situation: We are creating an AJAX application that verifies the user login for a closed area of a web application(an access verification or access control). To do this, we use a web form with a one-line input field and a password field. In addition, the web page requires a button so the user can log in. This click is to trigger the AJAX request.

But we do not want to send the data of the web form to the server in the conventional way; instead, we want to use an AJAX request. Depending on whether the access data is correct or not, the user sees a different response in a section of the web page. We want the server response to be displayed without reloading the web page. This is, after all, an essential criterion of AJAX and distinguishes our application from a traditional web application that would display the web server response in a completely new web page.

For the button in the web form, you therefore cannot work with a submit button, but instead you have to use a normal button or a link that does not send the data of the web form via submit. You must prevent this "normal" sending of the form data. Otherwise, a new web page is requested. Also, the normal data for `action` and `method` is written down *not in the form* but instead in AJAX methods.

> ### Tip
> Server-side, you can, of course, store the access data hard-coded in the script or program that you call via AJAX. But a database table with the access data is more sensible. If you are working with XAMPP, you can use MySQL and the administration tool phpMyAdmin. So, you can create such a table with phpMyAdmin in a MySQL database. This table has to contain at least two fields, one field for the user ID and one field for the associated password. You have to check for both pieces of data. Note that the combination of the two values always has to match. You can find the SQL script for creating such a table on the companion website (ch10.sql).

So let's now see what the web page with the AJAX functionality looks like. For this example, we need a slightly different structure than in most other examples in this chapter (ch10_3.html).

Listing 10.7   **Web Page for Verifying User Input via AJAX**

```
...
11          src="lib/ch10_3_ready.js"></script>
12   </head>
13   <body>
14      <h1>Please enter your user name and password</h1>
15      <form>
16        <table>
17          <tr><td>Name</td>
18            <td><input type="text" size="30"></td></tr>
19          <tr><td>Password</td>
20            <td><input type="password" size="30"></td></tr>
```

```
21      </table>
22      </form>
23      <button>AJAX login via $.get()</button>
24      <button>AJAX login via $.post()</button>
25      <div id=output"></div>
26   </body>
27 </html>
```

In the example, you can see a simple table with two input fields that is formatted a little bit via CSS. In one field, the user needs to enter his user ID; in the other, the password. As sending the data via GET and POST does not differ, you can see two buttons via which the user can send the data. This saves us providing two essentially identical examples for GET and POST.

Figure 10.1   The simple input form.

The AJAX functions are largely the same as in the previous example. The only difference is the additional parameter with the entered user data (ch10_3_ready.js).

Listing 10.8   **Sending the Data**

```
01 $(function(){
02   $("button:first").click(function(){
03     $.get("ch10_3_get.php", {
04       username: $("input:first").val(),
05       password: $("input:last").val()
06     }, function(data){
07       $("#output").html(data);
08     });
09   });
10   $("button:last").click(function(){
11     $.post("ch10_3_post.php", {
12       username: $("input:first").val(),
13       password: $("input:last").val()
14     }, function(data){
15       $("#output").html(data);
16     });
17   });
18 });
```

In lines 3–6 and 11–14, respectively, you can see the value pairs that are sent to the server. The value pairs are written in curly brackets, as usual in jQuery. And as usual, we use a selector to access the input fields. The method val() gives us the content in the relevant input field. Because we also need a name for a value pair to be able to get and allocate the passed values server side, we prepend the tokens username and password.

> **Note**
>
> Note that the actual form tag contains significantly fewer parameters in contrast to traditional HTML forms. In particular, the parameter name is not present for the input fields. We are using jQuery selectors to access these fields. Plus the form tag has had its parameters removed altogether. These are also replaced via the parameters of the AJAX functions by jQuery.

If a user now enters the correct access data in the input fields, the response from the web server appears below the form, without the web page reloading.

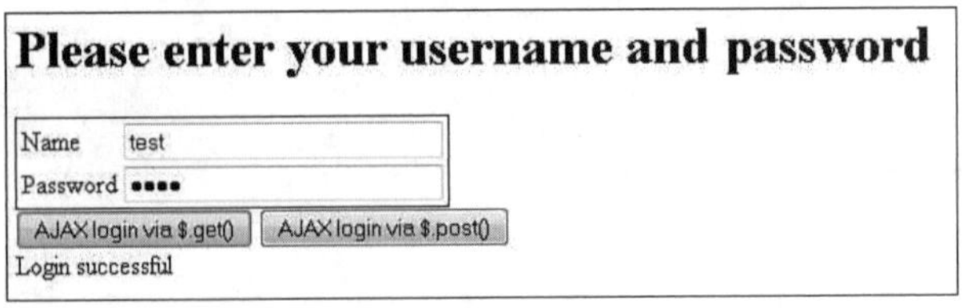

Please enter your username and password

Name	test
Password	••••

AJAX login via $.get()   AJAX login via $.post()

Login successful

Figure 10.2   Successful login.

This applies both for successful login and for a wrong combination of access data.

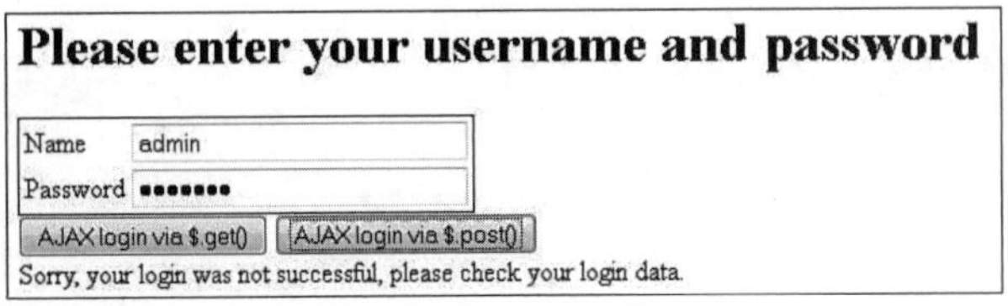

Please enter your username and password

Name	admin
Password	•••••••

AJAX login via $.get()   AJAX login via $.post()

Sorry, your login was not successful, please check your login data.

Figure 10.3   The wrong access data has been entered.

10.3.3   Getting and Parsing XML Data

It is not a big problem if you want to request plain text with an XML structure via AJAX. You just need to put a corresponding URL on an XML file or use a script or program to generate XML code on the server.[23] It only gets exciting on the client because there you have a

---

23. Here you may have to set the correct MIME type, but these server-side specifics are not our concern.

complete Document Object Model (DOM) available as a response if you receive the XML data with `responseXML`! In the jQuery methods, this DOM is available via the parameter of the call-back function.

If you download the example ch10_4.html from the companion website, you will see that we have a button and an output area. Once again, the JavaScript is interesting (ch10_4_ready.js).

Listing 10.9   Requesting an XML File

```
01 $(function(){
02   $("button:first").click(function(){
03     $.get("ch10.xml", function(data){
04       $("#output").text("");
05       for (i in data) {
06         $("#output").append(i + ", ");
07       }
08     });
09   });
10 });
```

We simply request any XML file and iterate in the `for` loop of lines 5–7 over all elements that are available in the response from the web server (`data`). It is irrelevant whether you request the data via GET or POST. And if you look at the output, you will see that the response is a complete DOM object.[24] This means that all the usual properties and methods are available that you can also use in the DOM of a web page, plus the jQuery specialties.

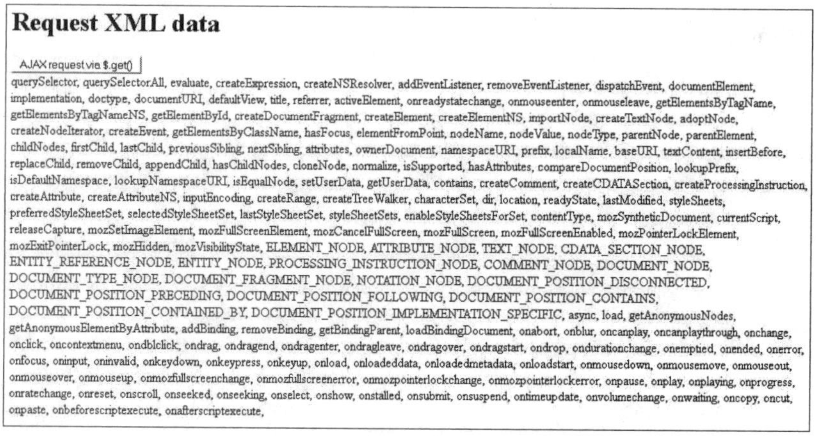

Figure 10.4   The response from the web server is a complete DOM tree.

---

24. The loops output the properties and methods of a DOM object.

In principle, you can now use the DOM further in the client, but that is beyond the scope of this discussion and not very sensible in many cases, because an easier alternative exists with JSON. However, let's still briefly summarize how you can proceed.

For navigating the response from the web server, you can essentially work with the usual methods: `getElementById()`, `getElementsByName()`, `getElementsByTagName()`, or `getElementsByTagNameNS()`; of course, you can also use all jQuery techniques for selecting, traversing, and navigating a tree. In terms of data requests via AJAX, this also enables you to navigate to any parts of the response in a very targeted way.

You just have to be really careful because the DOM is constructed differently in different browsers, as mentioned earlier. The crucial point is always that for selecting an element you try to get as close to the target node as possible via a suitable method. If you traverse the depths of the tree starting from the root of the response, you might get different results in the various browsers.

Let's use the following XML file ch10.xml as a basis.

Listing 10.10   **A Basic XML File**

```
01 <?xml version="1.0" encoding="UTF-8"?>
02 <rjs>
03   <data>
04     <name job="Masters in Maths">
05       Ralph Steyer
06     </name>
07     <place>
08       Eppstein
09     </place>
10   </data>
11   <websites>
12     <url>
13       www.rjs.de
14     </url>
15     <url>
16       blog.rjs.de
17     </url>
18     <url>
19       www.ajax-net.de
20     </url>
21   </websites>
22 </rjs>
```

In principle, we could do something along these lines (we are again only looking at the JavaScript file ch10_5_ready.js).

Listing 10.11   **Targeted Processing of Individual Components of the XML Response**

```
01 $(function(){
02   $("button:first").click(function(){
03     $.get("ch10.xml", function(data){
04       $("#output").text("");
05       y = data.getElementsByTagName("url");
06       for (i = 0; i < y.length; i++) {
07         $("#output").append(y[i].childNodes[0]
08           .nodeValue + "<br />");
09       }
10     });
11   });
12 });
```

In the example, we use the method `getElementsByTagName()` to select specific elements from the server response (`data`). The method returns an array, so we can get the number of contained elements with `length` (line 6).

The text content of an element is itself a node, so we need to take the first child element if we want to get this content. A text node makes this content available via `nodeValue`. In lines 6–9, we iterate over the element array and output the contents of the elements of the type `url`.

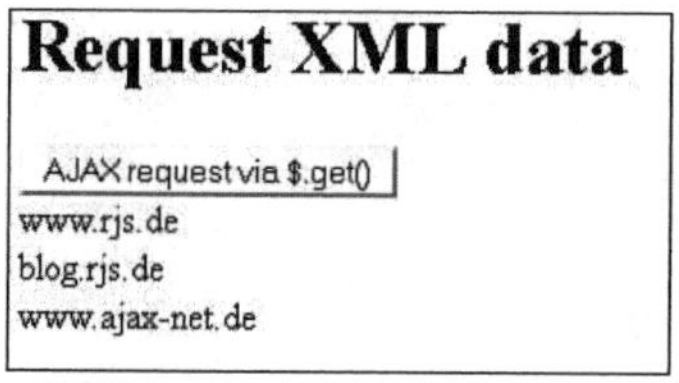

Figure 10.5   The content of elements of the type `url`.

If you now also remember that you can distinguish the different element types via `nodeType` and that you can use all navigation options and filters of the DOM concept plus jQuery, it should be clear how the path toward a targeted use of the XML response will look in principle.

It is definitively even easier to process the XML DOM tree if you fetch it into the jQuery namespace, simply by accessing it via `$(data)`. Then you can work on this jQuery object with the usual selectors. As mentioned earlier, though, this is and remains a laborious task.

10.4   Getting and Parsing JSON Data: `getJSON()` and `parseJSON()`

As mentioned previously, JSON offers almost the same functionality and flexibility as XML, without the latter's complexity and problematic evaluation in various browsers getting in the way. For that reason, JSON has become established as the standard format for AJAX applications if a certain functionality for processing the response in the client is indeed required. In principle, you could use `$.get()` or `$.post()` to request JSON data from the server. But then you would have to process this data further before you can use it. You could, for example, use a native JavaScript function `eval()` to turn JSON into a JavaScript object. But this method is very slow, forces browsers to turn off their just-in-time-compilers, and has the reputation of being extremely unreliable. Alternatively, you can work with the native JavaScript class `Function` or use the method that was introduced in jQuery 1.4.1 and convert a JSON string into a JavaScript object (provided the browser supports this).

But in case of an AJAX request, this effort is not even required. The AJAX method `getJSON()` from the jQuery framework is specialized for this file format and makes dealing with JSON almost child's play.

10.4.1   A Simple Application with JSON

As basis, we use the JSON structure you can see in Listing 10.4 on page 303. The details of how the JSON structure is made available on the web page are again not relevant for our purposes. We are only looking at how it is processed in the client (ch10_6_ready.js).

Listing 10.12   **Requesting and Processing JSON**

```
01 $(function(){
02   $("button:first").click(function(){
03     $.getJSON("ch10.json", function(data){
04       $("#output").append(data.name + ", " +
05       data.websites.url1);
06     });
07   });
08 });
```

We are requesting data in the form of JSON, and the response from the web server is again available via `data` (the first parameter of the callback function). The extremely comfortable situation is such that the method `getJSON()` gives us the data in a form that enables us to use simple **dot notation** to access the names of the individual elements in the JSON structure (of course, also nested, which we make use of in our structure example). This is simple and reliable.

Figure 10.6   Parts of the JSON response have been processed.

10.4.2   Requesting Twitter Tweets via JSONP

Let's now look at how you can use JSON. We turn to Twitter for this. This means we want to use AJAX to access another server, which is initially prevented by the sandbox. JSONP solves this problem.

Twitter is a currently popular social network used by many people to publish a (usually) publicly accessible diary[25] on the Internet. Registered users can enter and publish messages with a length of up to 140 characters (referred to as *tweets*). The social network is based on the fact that you can subscribe to the tweets of other users. The readers are referred to as *followers*.

For our purposes, the file format in which tweets are made available is interesting. The contributions are made available by Twitter both in the form of XML and JSON as well as other formats. This chronologically descending list of entries can also be used from within a program. And that is precisely what we do. We are using JSONP because the tweets are not coming from our own server, but from Twitter (http://twitter.com). So this concept is ideal here.

> **Note**
>
> In the following example, bear in mind that we have to accept the data structure of the tweets as a given fact. You can find further information on the exact meaning and structure of the tweets at http://apiwiki.twitter.com/.

Listing 10.13   **Loading Twitter Tweets via JSONP (ch10_7_ready.js)**

```
01 $(function(){
02    $("button:first").click(function(){
03      $.getJSON("http://twitter.com/status/user_timeline/
         rjsedv.json?count=10&callback=?",
04      function(data){
05        var name = "";
06        var screen_name = "";
07        var profile_image_url = "";
08        var id = "";
09        //Determine user data
```

25. It is also referred to as micro blog.

```
10        for (i = 0; i < data.length; i++) {
11          jQuery.each(data[i].user,
12            function(index, value){
13            if ((index == "name") && (name == "")) {
14              name = value;
15            }
16            if ((index == "screen_name") &&
17              (screen_name == "")) {
18              screen_name = value;
19            }
20            if ((index == "profile_image_url") &&
21              (profile_image_url == "")) {
22              profile_image_url = value;
23            }
24            if ((index == "id") && (id == "")) {
25              id = value;
26            }
27          });
28        } // End for - all user data determined
29        var title = "<h1>The Twitter Tweets of " +
30        screen_name +
31        "</h1>";
32        $("#output").html(title + "<br />" +
33        "Name: " + name + ", ID: " + id + "<hr />");
34        if (profile_image_url != "")
35          $("#output").append("<img src='" +
36            profile_image_url + "' /><hr />");
37        // The specific tweets
38        for (i = 0; i < data.length; i++) {
39          jQuery.each(data[i], function(index, value){
40            if (index == "text") {
41              $("#output").append(value + "<br />");
42            }
43            if (index == "created_at") {
44              $("#output").append("Created: " +
45              value +
46              "<hr />");
47            }
48          });
49        } // End for - Tweets
50      });
51   });
52 });
```

In line 3, we use getJSON() to request the JSON data of an author with the alias name rjsedv.

> **Tip**
>
> Instead of `rjsedv`, you can use any Twitter alias whose tweets are publicly accessible.

This example is somewhat more complicated because we operate explicitly on the structure of the Twitter tweets. We cannot and are not going to discuss this structure in detail here. But, of course, I will explain the specific structures that we are using in this example. These are also the most important keys that occur in the JSON format.

In the JSON format of Twitter, there is a key with the name `text`. As you can probably guess, it contains the text of the relevant tweets. There is also a key with the name `created_at`. This takes you to the creation date of the relevant tweet. In lines 38–49, we use `each()` to iterate over all tweets that we have received via AJAX from the server. Via the parameter `index`, you get the name of the key in the structure and via `value` the specific value. Based on the `if` structures, we only process these two keys and add the relevant value in the output area.

In addition to the tweet texts themselves and their dates, we also want to display some information about the author of the texts in the web page. Each tweet contains this information in the form of an array with the name `user`. So, the information is redundant, provided this data does not change. But a user can also update his profile. For example, he can upload his picture or replace it. The sequential structure of the tweets ensures that the most recent messages appear at the top of the JSON structure. And if you iterate over the tweets with a loop, the first tweet contains the most up-to-date information on the author. We make use of this fact in our program.

We are working with different variables for the author data that interests us. This includes the name of the author, his screen name (an alias), his ID, and his picture. In lines 10–28, we look for the author data for each tweet. I have already pointed out that we would only need to search the top tweet (`data[0]`) because this contains the most recent data on the author. But our universal approach makes it possible to search older tweets, as well, if required and to process any changes of the author data (which we are not doing in our example). But the chronological structure poses a problem: We have to be careful not to overwrite the more recent information with the older information while iterating over all tweets. So, we check whether the value of a variable we are interested in is already filled and, only if it is not yet filled, we assign the specific value of the property from the object `user`.

The whole output is then formatted a little bit via CSS (ch10_7.css).

Listing 10.14   **Formatting the Data Output Area**

```
01 #output {
02   width: 900px;
03   max-height:600px;
04   overflow:scroll;
05   background: yellow;
06   color: blue;
07 }
```

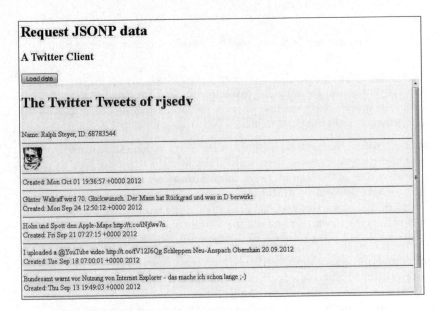

Figure 10.7   Twitter tweets displayed in a web page.

10.5   Loading a Script Later via AJAX: `jQuery.getScript()`

You usually load a JavaScript file immediately along with loading the web page if you are going to require functionality from the library at some point. But you do not generally need all the functionality of the JavaScript library. It would certainly make sense to be able to divide up functionalities between several libraries so that you can load specific functions later if and when required. You can load script instructions later via AJAX easily in almost any browser simply by writing a script statement into an HTML fragment, as shown in Listing 10.15.

Listing 10.15   **A Text Fragment with a Script**

```
This is <i>AJAX</i><script type="text/jscript">alert("Loaded later");</script>
```

If you load the text file via AJAX,[26],\ most browsers will execute the script (but not all browsers). In particular, Internet Explorer acts up,[27] although you can specify the file type in the jQuery methods `$.get()` or `$.post()`, which often solves the problem. But why not use a method straight away that is intended for this purpose: `jQuery.getScript()`?

26. Regardless of whether with manual AJAX or via `$.get()` or `$.post()`.

27. Just as with loading tags that it does not know. These are rendered as empty elements in Internet Explorer, and then you cannot format them via CSS. Plus it takes out the content and inserts it as additional text node in the web page, which also changes the number of nodes.

But what can be done with the jQuery method `$.getScript()`? The method loads a JavaScript library and executes it at the same time. So in its default setting, the method is based on the server explicitly sending JavaScript.

In the case of a function collection, this means that the functions are not only loaded in the global JavaScript namespace of the web page and made available for the call (as in the traditional case), but are also explicitly available in the optional callback function to be executed. This can then also be done with Internet Explorer. Loading the file happens via an HTTP GET request (POST is not possible) as with a conventional AJAX request via GET.

> **Note**
>
> As of version 1.2 of jQuery, you can also load scripts from foreign domains via `getScript()`. Before version 1.2, you could load scripts only from the same domain as the original web page. You learned earlier about the sandbox principle and the JSONP extension of jQuery. The option of loading[28] and simultaneously automatically executing[29] foreign domains obviously expands the functionality considerably. But you should be aware that the option of accessing a foreign domain cancels an elementary security principle of the browsers. The sandbox principle is implemented in the browsers for a very good reason, and the efforts of canceling it invariably reduce the security of web applications. In my opinion, it is indeed possible that this expansion—even though it can be misused to only a limited extent—may damage the acceptance of the basically very secure technology JavaScript. So, I consider this expansion a two-edged sword.

Listing 10.16 **Loading JavaScript Files (ch10_8_ready.js)**

```
01  $(function(){
02    $("button:first").click(function(){
03      $.getScript("lib/random.js", function(){
04        $("#output").text(randomNumber());
05      });
06    });
07    $("button:last").click(function(){
08      $.getScript(
09        "http://rjs.de/jquery/zufall.js", function(){
10          $("#output").text(zufallsZahl());
11        });
12    });
13  });
```

As you can see, the method is very easy to use. As the first parameter, you specify the URL of the JavaScript library and as second parameter is a callback function (if required) in which you use a particular functionality (usually a function) from the library. In our example, we load a

28. Loading is not significant; this has always been possible.

29. This is the special feature.

library from the same domain as the web page (via the first button), or alternatively we load it from another domain.[30]

Listing 10.17 shows the structure of the called library random.js, but it is not really relevant.

Listing 10.17 **The Library random.js**

```
01 function randomNumber(){
02      return Math.random();
03 }
```

For our demonstration purposes, it is sufficient to define a single function in the library. As you can see, the function `randomNumber()` from the library is called in the callback function. The library is loaded if you click the relevant button, and the function is made available for a call.

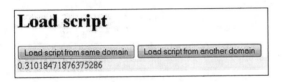

Figure 10.8   Loading and executing external JavaScript libraries.

> **Caution**
>
> In some browsers, various versions have resulted in certain complications with this method. For example, in Safari 2 and earlier versions, it was not possible to execute scripts synchronously in a global context. For this reason, calling a function from a library loaded via `getScript()` has to happen with a slight delay (for example, via the DOM method `window.setTimeout()`). Check the documentation if you are using this method to determine whether you face any potential problems with your target browsers

10.6   The General Variation for Loading Data: `load()`

With the method `load()`, you load data from the server and insert it into the web page's DOM. The special feature of this method is that it works in a very general way. Yet in practice, you are mostly going to load HTML fragments via this method. However, you can also request XML. That works quite well in most browsers. Only Internet Explorer has problems once again because of the basic processing of unknown tags if Internet Explorer is in interpretation mode for a normal web page. In principle, you can also request pure text and JSON via this method, but the main advantages of this method—filtering, which we discuss next—are not working

---

30. Without loss of generality, this is the same library in our example in both cases (no difference at all).

then. That is why loading HTML fragments is the usual way of using it. The pattern of the method signature looks like Listing 10.18.

Listing 10.18   **Pattern of** `load()`

```
load( url, [ data ], [ complete(responseText, textStatus, XMLHttpRequest) ] )
```

In the basic setting, using the method sends a GET request to the server.

Listing 10.19   **The Default Setting: Loading HTML via** GET

```
$("#output").load("rjs.html");
```

But if you use an extra parameter in the form of Object/Map (key-value pair), the request automatically happens via POST.

Listing 10.20   **Sending Data via** POST **for a Value Pair**

```
$("# output ").load("processvalues.php", { names[]': ["Felix", "Florian"] } );
```

An extra parameter as a string, however, is executed as GET request.

As you can see from the schematic representation of the method signature, you can specify a callback function as an optional third parameter. This has three standard parameters with the values of responseText, textStatus, and XMLHttpRequest.

10.6.1   Specifying Filters

Let's turn to what is probably the most useful way of using the method. As of jQuery 1.2, you can specify a jQuery selector in the URL for load(). If you do this, the loaded HTML fragment[31] is seen as DOM and filtered. This means that only those elements that match the selector in the **DOM of the response** are integrated into the web page's DOM. The selector is then simply separated from the URL by a space.

Listing 10.21   **Loading via a Filter**

```
$('#info').load('ajax/rjs.html #myID');
```

> **Tip**
>
> The option for specifying a filter for load() is a simple alternative to using XML or JSON. You can use pure HTML for structural information in the transmission format and logically select it

---

31. And also an XML file, unless Internet Explorer is used as the browser.

in the client. And in this case, you could even load a complete HTML file[32] if you filter out the framework structures.

```
...
10    <script type="text/javascript"
11        src="lib/ch10_9_ready.js"></script>
12  </head>
13  <body>
14    <h1>Filtering with load()</h1>
15    <button>Load whole table/button>
16    <button>Load data cells</button>
17    <button>Load header cells</button>
18    <button>Load XML</button>
19    <button>Load structure with custom tags</button>
20    <div id="output"></div>
21  </body>
22  </html>
```

And here is the JavaScript file (ch10_9_ready.js).

Listing 10.23   load() **with Filters**

```
01 $(function(){
02   $("button:first").click(function(){
03     $("#output").load("load.html").css({
04       background: "red",
05       color: "yellow",
06       width: "300px"
07     });
08   });
09   $("button:eq(1)").click(function(){
10     $("#output").load("load.html td");
11   });
12   $("button:eq(2)").click(function(){
13     $("#output").load("load.html th");
14   });
15   $("button:eq(3)").click(function(){
16     $("#output").load("ch10.xml url").css({
17       background: "red",
18       color: "yellow",
```

---

32. If you wanted to do so for whatever reason.

```
19      width: "300px"
20    });
21  });
22  $("button:eq(4)").click(function(){
23    $("#output").load("load2.html").css({
24      background: "red",
25      color: "yellow",
26      width: "300px"
27    });
28  });
29 });
```

In lines 13 and 16, you can see filters that of are, of course, based specifically on the structure of the HTML file that is loaded later. This is the loaded HTML file load.html.

Listing 10.24   **The HTML Fragment Loaded Later**

```
01 <table>
02    <tr><th>Name</th><th>Age</th></tr>
03    <tr><td>Felix</td><td>11</td></tr>
04    <tr><td>Florian</td><td>11</td></tr>
05 </table>
```

The loaded HTML fragment is a small table with header and data cells. Clicking the first button loads the entire HTML fragment and integrates it into the web page. Note that we have the return of load() available as jQuery object and can also format it as usual.

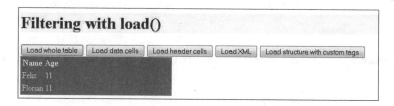

Figure 10.9   The entire table has been loaded and formatted.

Clicking the second button only loads the contained data cells, the third button only the header cells. We are explicitly applying the filters th and td. For the formatting, it is relevant whether a button has been triggered first that has already formatted an output area or if this is not the case; the formatting remains intact if applicable.

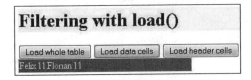

Figure 10.10   Only the data cells have been filtered out of the HMTL fragment and inserted into the DOM of the web page.

Of course, in practice, extracting part of a linked structure such as a table is appropriate only to a limited extent. At least, though, it demonstrates quite well how the filter works.

Now you can see that clicking the fourth button requests an XML file and formats it via `css()`. This works well in all relevant browsers.

Figure 10.11   The filtered elements of the XML file.

It does not work well in Internet Explorer, though, which means this approach is not useful in practice if you want to support this browser.

Interestingly, an alternative works quite well, where you simply break the rules for valid HTML and use elements that are ignored under the principle of error tolerance. Take a look at the following file load2.html.

Listing 10.25   **A Structure with Tags That Do Not Exist in HTML**

```
01 <tab>
02   <row>
03     <headercell>Name</headercell>
04     <headercell>Age</headercell>
05   </row>
06   <row>
07     <cell>Felix</cell>
08     <cell>11</cell>
09   </row>
10   <row>
11     <cell>Florian</cell>
12     <cell>11</cell>
13   </row>
14 </tab>
```

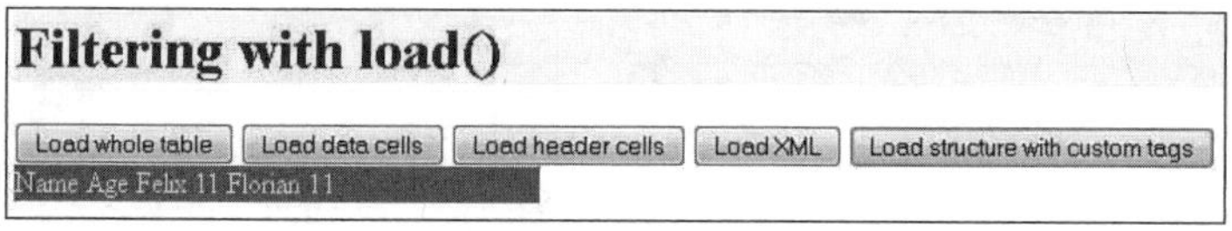

Figure 10.12 Now it works even in IE.

So if you manage to get Internet Explorer to consider the data loaded later as HTML,[33] you can integrate this data into the web page via load() and format it as well. This is remarkable in as much as this trick does not work in Internet Explorer if you load manually via AJAX. The jQuery framework evidently intervenes in the background, as described earlier in the context of data types in jQuery. This trick also works in all other relevant browsers.[34]

10.7 Serializing Data

jQuery also offers methods for **serializing** data. Normally, jQuery uses serialization for preparing user input so that it can be sent to a server without any problems.[35] This is necessary primarily for certain special characters, such as the question mark, the percent symbol, and some other symbols and special characters (for example, foreign characters such as umlauts in German; here, even the jQuery methods act differently). The file format of the serialization is standardized and consequently compatible with most server-side programming languages and frameworks—referred to as URL encoding.

10.7.1 The serialize() Method

The framework offers the serialize()method for serializing a set of input elements in a data string (in other words, a web form). Each form element to be serialized has to have the attribute name for the method to work properly.

The method that operates on a jQuery object representation of a form generates a text string in the standard URL-encoded notation. In principle, you can also apply the method directly to an individual form element, but you would usually use the whole form to combine all input in a string. The method encodes both special characters and umlauts. Let's take a look at an example (ch10_10.html).

33. This can also be done via header information via the MIME type on the server; the file extension .html is only a simple approach. And in other jQuery methods, you can even specify the file type directly.

34. Manually loading also usually works.

35. Especially in the case of manually sending data via AJAX, you will usually have to do this yourself, whereas most AJAX methods of jQuery take care of it automatically in the background.

Listing 10.26   **A Form with Data to Serialize**

```
...
10    <script type="text/javascript"
11          src="lib/ch10_10_ready.js"></script>
12    </head>
13    <body>
14      <h1>Serializing Data</h1>
15      <form>
16        <p>
17          <input type="text" name="name" />
18            <input type="text" name="firstname" /><br />
19            <input type="button" value="Send data" />
20        </p>
21      </form>
22    </body>
23  </html>
```

All data entered by a user into the form is to be serialized. This is easily done, as shown in Listing 10.27 (ch10_10_ready.js).

Listing 10.27   **Serializing the Form**

```
01 $(function(){
02  $("input:button:first").click(function(){
03    alert($("form:first").serialize());
04  });
05 });
```

As you can see in line 3, we apply the method to the first form in the page. In this simple case, we then simply output the serialized input in the callback function.

Figure 10.13   You can clearly see that the special characters have been encoded.

In the case of AJAX or a traditional web form, you now just take the serialized form data and pass it on to the server.

10.7.2   The `serializeArray()` Method

The `serializeArray()` method also serializes all forms and form elements (just as `serialize()`), but it returns a nested JSON data structure that you can operate on. With the parameter name, you get the name of the form field, and with `value`, the corresponding value (just as in any form). In contrast to `serialize()`, special characters are encoded, but umlauts are not. Take a look at the script ch10_11_ready.js.

Listing 10.28   **Using** `serializeArray()`

```
01 $(function(){
02   $("input:button:first").click(function(){
03     var data = $("form:first").serializeArray();
04     $("div:first").html();
05     $(data).each(function(index, v){
06       $("div:first").append(index + ": " + v.name
07         + ": " + v.value + "<br />");
08     });
09   });
10 });
```

As return value, we get a JSON object and we iterate over it. Via it, we iterate the individual form fields. As described, we get the name of the relevant field via `name` and its serialized value via `value`.

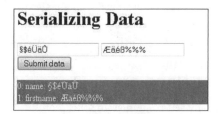

Figure 10.14   The German umlauts have not been encoded.

10.7.3   The General Version: `param()`

With this method, which is also used internally by the two methods mentioned previously, you can serialize an array or object in general. You pass the object or array as the first parameter. As of version 1.4, you can specify via a second Boolean parameter how the data should be serialized, either recursively (`false`, default) or traditionally (`true`).[36]

36. You can also set this globally via `jQuery.ajaxSettings.traditional = true;`.

10.8   Default Values for AJAX

If you do not like the default setting of jQuery for dealing with AJAX requests, you can adjust the values globally. You can do this via the method `jQuery.ajaxSetup()` that has as a parameter an option object where you can make the global adjustments. These are valid so long as they are not overwritten by individual settings of methods. The possible combinations correspond to the commonly used options.

Listing 10.29   **The Default Method for Sending Is** POST

```
$.ajaxSetup({
   type: "POST"
});
```

Listing 10.30   **Another Example for Centrally Initializing an AJAX Request**

```
$.ajaxSetup({
   url: "test.php", global: false, type: "GET"
});
```

All settings are optional.

> **Caution**
>
> You should not set handlers for `complete`, `error`, or `success` with this method, but instead use the global AJAX events.

10.9   AJAX Events and AJAX Event Handlers

The various methods for sending AJAX requests are generally self-contained. In other words, in many cases you only call the corresponding AJAX methods, and your request is done. Sometimes, however, you will want to react in a targeted way to specific events that occur within an AJAX request. AJAX requests generate a number of different events to which you can react specifically. A distinction exists between local and global events.

10.9.1   Local Events

The term *local events* refers to callbacks where you can specify a reaction within the XHR object. This includes, for example, the functions that are to be called in the event of an error or in the case of success. Later in this chapter, you will see a description of the `$.ajax()` method, where using the local events takes place (although that's jumping ahead a bit here).

Table 10.1 describes the local events.

Table 10.1   **The Local AJAX Events in jQuery**

Event	Description
beforeSend	A local event that is triggered before the AJAX request. You can, for example, modify the XHR object in the assigned callback function.
complete	The local event describes the state that a request is complete, regardless of whether the request was successful or not. In either case, you get a complete callback, even for synchronous requests.
error	The local event fires only if an error occurs. Correspondingly, you can never have an `error` and a `success` callback simultaneously for the same request.
success	The local event happens in the case of success, and only then. Any form of error message sent by the server or any errors in the data structure will prevent this event from occurring.

The `jqXHR` object that was introduced in jQuery version 1.5 offers an interface for reacting to the server response that makes the methods `error()`, `success()`, and `complete()` available. These methods use a function reference as an argument. This callback function is called whenever the request triggered by `$.ajax()` ends. The callback functions use the same parameters as the correspondingly named `$.ajax()` callbacks.

Chaining Local Callback Events

As of jQuery 1.5, you can even attach several callbacks to a single AJAX request (for example, as in Listing 10.31, if you are using dot notation).

Listing 10.31   **Chaining Callbacks**

```
var jqxhr = $.ajax({ url: "ajax.txt" })
  .success(function() { $("#output".html("All okay")); })
  .error(function() { $("#output".html("Gone wrong")); })
  .complete(function() { $("#output".html(
    "All done")); });
```

The Callback Queue

As of jQuery 1.5, the error, success, and `complete` callbacks are managed as first-in, first-out (FIFO) queues. If you register several callbacks for a request, they are processed in a corresponding order (if they are specified):

1. beforeSend

2. error

3. dataFilter

4. success

5. complete

10.9.2   Global Events

The framework offers events in the form of objects that you can use in various ways. These events are passed to all elements in the DOM. This enables you to react to them in any place if you listen to these events. And this listening for global events works more or less as shown in Listing 10.32.

Listing 10.32   **Binding to Global Events**

```
$("#output").bind("ajaxSend",
  function(){
    $(this).show();
  }).bind("ajaxComplete", function(){
    $(this).hide();
});
```

So, you can see traditional binding of functions to specific events that are in this case bound via AJAX.

> **Tip**
>
> As you have seen, you can disable global events. To do so, you need to set the option global to the value false. Methods such as ajaxSend() or ajaxError() are then not fired if a request would normally trigger them.

You can also write the events as methods in a node and specify as parameter a callback function or anonymous function (for example, as shown here).

Listing 10.33   **Reaction to an Error**

```
$("#output").ajaxError(function(event, request, settings){
    $(this).text("Error: " + settings.url + "!");
});
```

Listing 10.34   **Reaction to Ending the AJAX Request**

```
$("#loadindicator").ajaxStop(function(){
    $(this).hide();
});
```

Here is a list of AJAX events that can occur in an AJAX communication. Apart from `ajaxStart` and `ajaxStop`, all events are triggered for all AJAX requests (unless a global option was set). The events `ajaxStart` and `ajaxStop` refer to all AJAX requests together.

Table 10.2   **The Global AJAX Events in jQuery**

Event	Description
ajaxComplete	This global event behaves in exactly the same way as the `complete` event and is triggered whenever an AJAX request completes.
ajaxError	This global event behaves analogue to the local `error` event. It is triggered if an error occurs.
ajaxSend	This global event is triggered *before* the request is sent.
ajaxStart	The central global event on starting an AJAX request. The event is triggered when the AJAX request starts and no other AJAX requests are currently running.
ajaxStop	The global event is triggered if no other AJAX requests are carried out.
ajaxSuccess	This global event only occurs if the call has been successful.

You can see complete examples for the `$.ajax()` method in the jQuery documentation at jquery.com.

10.10   Complete Control

The previously discussed jQuery methods for AJAX requests are generally very helpful and often easy to use; they handle much in the background that we need to take care of in AJAX. They are also seen as abstraction on a higher level in the jQuery documentation and keep the details of an AJAX communication mostly away from the programmer. However, you might sometimes be interested in these details of an AJAX communication, and jQuery offers a suitable method for this, as well: `jQuery.ajax()`.

10.10.1   `jQuery.ajax()`

The `jQuery.ajax()` method gives you complete control over the AJAX communication process if required, with all details that specify this data exchange in any form. With `jQuery.ajax()`, you get as a direct return an object of the type `jqXHR` with all the properties and methods discussed thus far.[37] It represents the jQuery low-level AJAX implementation. Among other things, you get qualified error callbacks, but also access to character sets and MIME types. Most of the AJAX methods discussed so far are nothing more than shorthand notations of a specially configured variant of this method.

37. In earlier versions of jQuery, an object of the type `XMLHttpRequest` was returned.

> **Note**
>
> Remember that the `$.ajax()` method is not entirely easy to use and above all requires elementary knowledge of AJAX. Also, some settings require you to observe various server-side rules for the method to achieve proper results. In particular in the context of this method, jQuery 1.5 has added some serious extras that are quite special in their application, the details of which go beyond the scope of this book. We still cover some parts of them, though.

As parameters, you can pass to the method an object of the type `Map`. This represents key-value pairs that are used for initializing the XHR object and handling the request. Of course, the options are based on the properties and methods of an XHR object, but as of jQuery 1.5 in particular, they go far beyond the possibilities of a native XHR object.

As of jQuery 1.5, there is also a variation of the method where you specify as first parameter the URL to which you want to send the request. The optional second parameter is the `Map` object with the settings.

Here is a list of the possible options that you can specify for the method. You are only going to specify the options for the `ajax()` method if its values diverge from the default values or if you simply want to specify them explicitly.

Table 10.3   The Options That You Can Specify as Parameters for `ajax()`

Name	Description
`accepts`	An object of the type `Map`, via which you can tell the server which type of answer to accept.
`async`	A Boolean value to determine whether the data request is synchronous or asynchronous. The default is `true` (asynchronous). Access to other domains, as possible, for example, in JSONP, cannot be synchronized. Generally, synchronous AJAX requests are not entirely unproblematic because they can temporarily lock the browser while the request is active. As of jQuery 1.8, the use of `async: false` is deprecated. Instead use the `complete`, `success`, and `error` callbacks.
`beforeSend`	A local event that fires before the AJAX request and is associated with a corresponding callback function. As a parameter, you can use a `jqXHR` object and an object of the type `Map` for settings.
`cache`	Via the Boolean parameter,[38] you can master the caching problem. If the parameter is set to `false`, sites that are requested via AJAX are not cached in the browser. The default is generally `true`, but `false` for the special cases with the values `script` and `jsonp` for the option `dataType`.

38. As of jQuery 1.2.

`complete`	The function assigned here is called once the request has completed. This is only the case after the success and error callbacks have been completed. As parameters, you pass the XHR object and a descriptive string (`"success"`, `"notmodified"`, `"error"`, `"timeout"`, `"abort"`, or `"parsererror"`). As of jQuery 1.5, you can also specify an array with functions for the settings. Each of the specified functions is executed when the callback is called.
`contents`	As of jQuery 1.5, you can use this option to specify an object of the type `Map` with strings and a regular expression as a value pair via which you determine the way in which the response should be parsed.
`contentType`	When you send data such as user input to the server, certain characters are not transmitted unchanged (for example, German umlauts or special characters, as described earlier[39]). Before the data is sent, the process referred to as URL encoding generally occurs. This involves replacing all spaces with plus symbols, and critical characters such as German umlauts (sometimes) or, above all, special characters are converted to hexadecimal equivalents. Such a converted symbol is then preceded by the percent sign followed by the hexadecimal code.
	In the traditional sending of form data, this conversion is done automatically by the browser. But when sending data manually via AJAX, the URL encoding is not carried out automatically by the browser or the AJAX communication object. You have to do it manually. Thankfully, the jQuery AJAX methods[40] make life much easier for you. They carry out URL encoding automatically. In case of the `ajax()` method, you can intervene if required regarding the specific encoding, but this is rarely necessary. The default value of the encoding is `application/x-www-form-urlencoded`. This is also the most appropriate setting in most cases.
`context`	We have already commented on the significance of the context in the basics on jQuery. This object specifies the context of all AJAX-related callbacks. For example, you can specify a DOM element like this:

```
$.ajax({

    ...

    context: document.body,

    ...

});
```

`converters`	As of jQuery 1.5, there are conversion features for data types in jQuery. Via an object of the type `Map`, you essentially specify how existing data types should be handled. Default:

---

39. Among others, when serializing.

40. And other AJAX frameworks.

```
{"* text": window.String, "text html": true, "text json": jQuery.
parseJSON, "text xml": jQuery.parseXML}
```

Every value in the converter is a function that returns the transformed value of the response of an AJAX request.

`crossDomain`	As of jQuery 1.5, you can specify if you want to allow cross-domain access. The default is `false`, which only permits access to the same domain.
`data`	The data that is sent to the server in form of a query string. This query string is a string with a special structure, as you have already seen earlier several times. The data is transmitted to a processing script or program on the server as a set of name-value pairs. The name represents a variable, and the value is the value that the variable should transmit to the server. This can, for example, be a user input. Such a query string is structured roughly like this:
	If an array is passed, jQuery serializes multiple values with the same key. So, for example
	`{names:["Steven", "Phil"]}`
	is turned into the following query string:
	`info%5Bnames%5D%5B%5D=Steven&info%5Bnames%5D%5B%5D=Phil`
`dataFilter`	With this option, you can specify a function for directly dealing with the reply data of an XHR object. As parameters, the function accepts the data from the server and a parameter of the type `dataType`.
`dataType`	If you receive a response from the server in an AJAX request, the data type will determine how the client deals with the reply. The response is sent twice, as mentioned earlier. Or more precisely, it is available in two properties of an XHR object. The property `responseText` contains the data sent by the server as text and `responseXML` as XML data (in other words, as a tree that you can navigate on). This `dataType` parameter enables you to control how the client should make the assignment. As mentioned before, the default setting in jQuery is `"intelligent"`. In this case, jQuery will decide based on the recognized MIME type of the response whether to use the value of `responseText` or `responseXML`. You are now already familiar with the available types (`xml`, `html`, `script`, `json`, `jsonp`, and `text`) and how to use them.
`error`	Here you specify a special callback function that is called in case of an error (in other words, if the AJAX request has failed). As a parameter, you specify three arguments: the XHR or now `jqXHR` object, a descriptive string for the error that has occurred, and an optional exception object if one occurs. Possible values for the second argument are `null`, as well as `timeout`, `error`, `notmodified`, and `parsererror`. As of jQuery 1.5, you can also specify an array with functions for the settings. Each of the specified functions is executed when the callback is called.

`global`	A Boolean value with default `true` for specifying whether global AJAX event handlers are to be fired for a request. If the value is set to `false`, such global event handlers as `ajaxStart()` or `ajaxStop()` are not triggered.
`headers`	As of jQuery 1.5, you have the option of specifying an object of the type `Map` with supporting header information. As usual, you specify a key-value pair that is then sent with the request. These settings should be entered before calling the `beforeSend()` callback function.
`ifModified`	A Boolean value with the default `false`. Via this, you can specify that a request is counted as successful only if the response has changed since the last request. To control this, the HTTP header `Last-Modified` is assessed. If the value is `false`, the header is ignored.
`isLocal`	With this option, you can identify the current environment as local even if jQuery does not do so as default setting.
`jsonp`	With this option, you can override the callback function in a JSONP request. This value is used instead of `callback` in the `'callback=?'` part of the query string of a `GET` request or the data of a `POST` request. For example, the specification `{jsonp:'onJsonPLoad'}` causes the value `'onJsonPLoad=?'` to be sent to the server via the query string. This option has also changed in jQuery 1.5. If you set this option to `false`, `"=?"` will be used rather than the `"?callback"` string. In that case, you should explicitly specify `jsonpCallback`. For example: `{ jsonp: false, jsonpCallback: "myCallback" }`
`jsonpCallback`	With this option you specify the name of the callback function that you want to trigger in a JSONP request. This value is used instead of the unique name that the framework randomly generates. As of jQuery 1.5, you can also set the name via the return value of a function.
`mimeType`	As of jQuery 1.5.1, you can override the MIME type in the XHR object with this option.
`password`	A password in an HTTP access.
`processData`	A Boolean value (default `true`) for influencing the way in which data is sent to the server. In the default setting, data that is sent via the option data property as a query string that is content type `application/x-www-form-urlencoded`. If you want to send DOM documents or other data structures, set this option to `false`.
`scriptCharset`	If you use `jsonp` or `script` as the value for `dataType` and `GET` as the method (value of `type`), this option forces the interpretation in a certain character set. You only need this if the character sets of the local and remote content differ.

statusCode	Another new feature as of jQuery 1.5 is a map with numeric HTTP codes and functions that are called when the server response contains the corresponding code. You can use this to react individually. For example:

```
$.ajax({

  statusCode: {

    200: function() {

      $('#output').html("All okay");

    },

    404: function() {

      $('#output').html("Gone wrong");

    }

});
```

success	Here you specify the callback function that is called in an AJAX request in the case of success. As parameters, you specify three arguments: the data that is delivered by the server corresponding to the value of dataType, a descriptive string for the status, and the jqXHR object (before jQuery 1.5, the XMLHttpRequest object). As of jQuery 1.5, you can also specify an array with functions for the settings. Each of the specified functions is executed when the callback is called.
timeout	Via this option, you can specify in the client a period in milliseconds for how long it waits for a response by the web server. This specification overrides the value of the global variable timeout if this has been set via $.ajaxSetup().
traditional	With this, you specify the type of serialization. For true, this is carried out in the traditional way; otherwise, recursively.
type	The type (the method) of the request as string. The default is GET.
url	A string with the address for the request. The default value is the current page.
username	A username as a string for an HTTP request with access restriction.
xhr	A callback function for creating an object of the type XMLHttpRequest.
xhrFields	As of jQuery 1.5.1, you can specify a map in which you specify value pairs that expand a native XHR object.

As you can easily see from this extensive table, the $.ajax() method is a Swiss army knife. You will certainly never have to configure most of these options individually nor access this low-level function at all. But it is certainly a good thing that this option exists, in case the default techniques of jQuery should ever fail to work. Let's take a closer look at a few examples.

10.10.2   A JSONP Request

Listing 10.35 shows an example for using JSONP (ch10_12_ready.js).

Listing 10.35   **A JSONP Request with** `ajax()`

```
01 $(function(){
02   $("button:first").click(function(){
03     $.ajax({
04       dataType: 'jsonp',
05       jsonp: 'jsonp_callback',
06       url: 'sendJSONP.php',
07       success: function(data){
08         $("div:first").text(data.website);
09       }
10     });
11   });
12 });
```

You can see the basic way of using `$.ajax()` with the declarative specification of options. In line 4, the data type is set to JSONP; the following line specifies that it is a JSONP callback. In lines 7–9, you can see the anonymous callback function that is called in case of success.

Now you also need to consider certain things server side that would take us beyond the scope of this book. But in case of PHP, we want to indicate the most important point that is required so that the JSON code for a JSONP request is packed into a function and sent to the client in a way that enables the client to deal with it. Listing 10.36 shows the structure of the requested PHP file sendJSONP.php.

Listing 10.36   **Sending JSON Data in the Appropriate Form**

```
01 <?php
02   $data = json_encode(Array(
03     "website => "www.rjs.de"));
04   echo $_GET['jsonp_callback'] ."(". $data .");";
05 ?>
```

The most important part is the `json_encode()` function, which is available as of PHP 5.2.

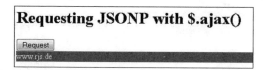

Figure 10.15   The JSON data is has arrived.

10.10.3   Loading and Executing a JavaScript File

You have already seen with `getScript()` how a JavaScript file can be loaded and executed. Listing 10.37 is the low-level equivalent with `ajax()`.

Listing 10.37   **Loading and Executing a JavaScript File (ch10_13_ready.js)**

```
01 $(function(){
02   $("button:first").click(function(){
03     $.ajax({
04       dataType: 'script',
05       type: 'GET',
06       url: 'lib/random.js',
07       success: function(data){
08         $("#output").text(randomNumber());
09       }
10     });
11   });
12 });
```

The important parts are the data type, the specification of the JavaScript library, and the method of the data request. There is no more to be said about this example.

10.10.4   Sending Data Plus Evaluating the Success

Let's take a look at how you can send data via `$.ajax()`. We are using the POST method, but this is irrelevant. For GET, it would look just the same. As a basis, we use the web form ch10_3.html, whose new version ch10_14.html really only differs in the referenced JavaScript file ch10_14_ready.js.

Listing 10.38   **Sending Data via POST**

```
01 $(function(){
02   $("button:first").click(function(){
03     $.ajax({
04       data: {
05         username: $("input:first").val(),
06         password: $("input:last").val()
07       },
08       type: 'POST',
09       url: 'ch10_3_post.php',
10       success: function(data){
11         $("#output").html(data);
12       }
13     });
```

```
14  });
15  });
```

Via the option `data`, you simply specify either the query string with the data you want to send or a `Map` object, as in our example.

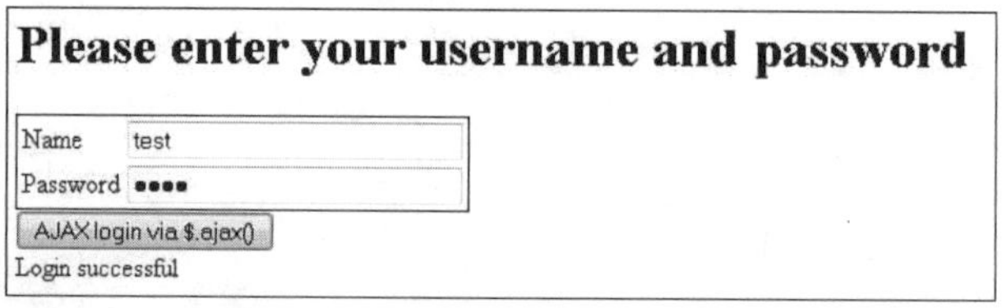

Please enter your username and password

Name	test
Password	••••

AJAX login via $.ajax()
Login successful

Figure 10.16   The data has been received on the server and processed; then a response has been sent to the client.

10.10.5   Extended Techniques for `$.ajax()`

In jQuery 1.5, three interesting extended functions for `$.ajax()` were introduced (mentioned briefly earlier and discussed in more detail here).

Prefilters

The term *prefilter* refers to a callback function that is executed before any AJAX request is sent and before any option is handled by `$.ajax()`.

It usually looks something like Listing 10.39.

Listing 10.39   **The Prefilter Callback Function**

```
$.ajaxPrefilter(
  function( requestOptions, originalOptions, jqXHR ) {
    /* Modify options, control the original options, store jqXHR object etc */
});
```

Converters

Converters also refer to a new kind of callback function. A converter is called when the server sends response data in another data type than is expected. You can then take corresponding countermeasures within the callback function; either convert a data type or introduce your own data types. Converters are stored in the `ajaxSettings` and can be added globally, as shown in Listing 10.40.

Listing 10.40   **A Typical Converter**

```
({
  converters: {
    "text mydatatype": function( textValue ) {
      if ( valid( textValue ) ) {
        // some logic
        return mydatatypeValue;
      } else {
        // indicate parse-error
        throw exceptionObject;
      }
    }
  }
});
```

As already mentioned in the section on data types, you can create custom data types with converters. (The data types must be written in lowercase.)

If you look at the representation of a typical converter in the preceding listing, you can then request data of the type `mydatatype`, as shown in Listing 10.41.

Listing 10.41   **Using a Custom Data Type**

```
$.ajax( url, {
  dataType: "mydatatype"
});
```

Transports

A *transport* in jQuery is an object that offers two methods:

- `send()`
- `abort()`

Both are internally used by `$.ajax()` and can be used to extend `$.ajax()`. But the jQuery documentation also points out that transports should only be the last resort in influencing AJAX requests if even prefilters and converters are not enough.

Because every request requires its own instance of the transport object, these cannot be directly registered. Instead, you should provide a function that returns such an object. Such functions that generate objects are referred to as *factories*. Transport factories are registered as shown in Listing 10.42.

Listing 10.42   **A Typical Transport**

```
$.ajaxTransport( function( requestOptions, originalOptions,  jqXHR ) {
  if( /* conditions for transport */ ) {
    return {
      send: function( header fields as map, callback ) {
        /* code for sending */
      },
      abort: function() {
        /* code in case of abort*/
      }
    };
  }
});
```

Summary

This chapter covered both the basics and particularities of modern RIA programming based on AJAX and alternative data formats. The whole topic is extensively covered by jQuery and made even more useful than AJAX already is by adding interesting extensions such as JSONP and getScript(). High-profile methods of jQuery such as jQuery.get(Url, Data, Callback, Type) and jQuery.post(Url, Data, Callback, Type) make dealing with AJAX very easy, while $.ajax() gives you complete control if required. jQuery 1.5, in particular, has added powerful features for controlling the AJAX requests. You also learned in this chapter how you can evaluate and process the server response in the client if this data is sent in a structured format. In addition to XML, JSON is well suited for this purpose.

jQuery UI

In this chapter, we discuss the visual control elements that the jQuery framework (or more precisely—an extension based on it) offers. These are summarily referred to as the **jQuery UI**.[1] These features are a range of powerful interaction plug-ins that supplement jQuery, plus widgets for building a graphic interface that are additionally expanded by a Cascading Style Sheets (CSS) library with predesigned themes. On top of that, the jQuery UI offers various extensions of the jQuery default effects. Most of these components are widely configurable.

> **Note**
>
> On the one hand, the components of jQuery UI are powerful and impressive. On the other hand, this library only offers the features currently available in all major web frameworks. In this respect, the familiar frameworks such as Dojo, YUI, or jQuery are very similar.

But even though the features of jQuery UI are so powerful, using these predesigned structures is really simple and often self-explanatory.

Plus within the framework there are some web-based tools that make it even easier to use. I like to put it this way: The more you get, the less you need to pay for. In this light, we do not need to discuss every single component in detail in this chapter, but instead just take a brief look at the most important elements in addition to the basic use of jQuery UI, and then we take a closer look at a few selected components and approaches.

11.1   What Is jQuery UI?

The library that is summarily referred to as jQuery UI offers you a level of abstraction for interaction (such as drag and drop, sorting, and selecting) and animations on a low-level basis. Plus you will find extended effects and adaptable widgets on a high level here; these are explicitly based on the normal jQuery JavaScript library. The features under jQuery UI are highly configurable and supported in most modern browsers. Interestingly, at the time of this writing, the browser requirements for jQuery UI (1.8.24) are lower than for the current version of jQuery

---

1. UI, user interface.

itself[2] (explicitly supported are Internet Explorer 6.0+[3], Firefox 3+, Safari 3.1+, Opera 9.6+, and Google Chrome).

jQuery UI is not present in the normal jQuery JavaScript library, as jQuery UI is managed as a separate project within the overall jQuery framework. You can find the home page of the project at http://jqueryui.com.

11.1.1 Components for Supporting Interaction

The framework comprises a number of **components** for supporting complex interaction behaviors such as drag and drop (the methods `draggable()` and `droppable()`), resizing (`resizable()`), selection (`selectable()`), and sorting (`sortable()`). This makes these processes significantly easier. Generally, you need just one line of source code to implement the desired support for an element or a group of elements, as discussed shortly.

11.1.2 Widgets

Widgets are generally more complex elements that you can use to compose a graphical user interface (GUI). With Hypertext Markup Language (HTML) or Extensible HTML (XHTML), you can easily generate simple elements such as buttons, text input fields, labels, headings, forms, and tables. But particularly in the area of desktop applications, there are more complex UI elements that are not supported by a browser without using CSS/JavaScript or additional libraries (for example, input fields for qualified date and time input, dialogs, sliders, and progress bars). All these UI components have to be rendered into pure HTML and CSS and can implement the logic based exclusively on JavaScript. This is definitely not trivial, especially if you consider the different reactions in various browsers. Via widgets, these more complex elements for Rich Internet Applications (RIAs) are easily made available for web page developers. jQuery UI offers, among other things, the following widgets:

- `Accordion`
- `Autocomplete`
- `Button`
- `Datepicker`
- `Dialog`
- `Progressbar`
- `Slider`

2. Which used to be the other way round previously. But this can and will probably change again when new versions of jQuery UI are released.

3. Yet Internet Explorer is not fully supported (in particular, in the CSS themes of the framework). For example, the present CSS themes do not support rounded corners for Internet Explorer nor the tools for creating custom CSS themes.

- `Tabs`

- `Tooltip` (jQuery UI 1.9 and later)

In addition, the relatively recent utility script Position enables you to position each widget in relation to the window, document, a specific element, or the mouse pointer.

> **Note**
>
> You might be surprised by the small number of widgets in jQuery UI. From other frameworks, you might know many more components. Just think of navigation trees. In jQuery, however, there is the concept of plug-ins, and many widgets are extended via these external plug-ins. You will see this in the following chapter.

11.1.3 Extended Effects

jQuery itself already offers numerous effects, as you have already seen. With jQuery UI, these **effects** are expanded by several other effect methods, such as `effect()`, `show()`, `hide()`, `toggle()`, `animate()`, `addClass()`, `removeClass()`, and `toggleClass()`. Most of the names of the effect methods should sound familiar to you. In fact, these already familiar methods are usually just extended in their capacity in jQuery UI, but sometimes considerably extended. For example, you can also change colors in animation via `animate()` in jQuery UI, which you cannot do in the basic version. Fundamentally, though, you use the methods in the same way as you use the methods of the same name in the core framework, so they are fairly straightforward.

> **Tip**
>
> You can find the documentation on jQuery UI at http://jqueryui.com/demos/. For extended help and special questions on jQuery UI, take a look in the Support Center at http://jqueryui.com/support.

11.1.4 The Theme Framework and ThemeRoller

Another component of jQuery UI is an extensive **theme framework** based on CSS. It is a pure CSS library. It also has a ThemeRoller tool for selecting, adapting, and using premade designs and a gallery with premade designs for the available components of the framework.

> **Note**
>
> The book is based on the stable version 1.8.24[4] and a beta version 1.9 of jQuery UI. It is unlikely that incompatibilities will arise with the next few versions, but, of course, we cannot rule it out. Much is already known about the future versions. In version 2.0, we will see the introduction of a widget factory with full prototype inheritance, direct instancing without calling

an `init()` method, revised trigger handling, and more. The application programming interface (API) will also be cleaned up.

11.2   Getting Started

The possibilities offered by jQuery UI are easier to grasp if you look at the official demo examples at the URL http://jqueryui.com/demos/. This site offers several *interactive* examples for each available component and above all an extensive description.

Figure 11.1   The live example for `Autocomplete`.

The source code behind each example can also be viewed via the corresponding link directly on the page (View Source).

Tip

Note the Examples column to the right of each example. Below this heading, you can select various variations of a component or widget. You then get an interactive example for this form plus a complete listing. You implement these adaptations via options, events, and methods, as discussed shortly.

4. Basically, you can only rely on stable version numbers and should at most experiment with the not yet fully released versions, but not use them in practice.

11.3   How Is jQuery UI Used?

After taking a look at the examples, you might decide that you want to use the library for your web pages, either all of it or part of it. The following subsections describe the basic way to use jQuery UI.

11.3.1   Downloading and ThemeRoller

jQuery UI is not contained in the normal jQuery library, as mentioned earlier. So, you need to download the extended library separately and make it available for your web pages.

The Download Builder

From the jQuery project's home page itself, you can download the library via the corresponding Download link that you can see as a tab on the top. Alternatively, you can find a Build link custom download on the start page. In both cases, you get to the same download page of jQuery UI: the Download Builder.

Figure 11.2   Selecting the desired resources.

In the main column of the Download Builder, you can see a list of all JavaScript components in jQuery UI, categorized into various groups. Specifically, this includes the UI core, Interactions,

Widgets, and Effects. You can easily see that you can pick the individual components for which you need support. If you are sure that you do not need certain components in your web application, you can deselect these. This makes the library smaller, which is, of course, an advantage in terms of the visitor loading times. You can also use most project components independently from the other components of the library (but not all).[5] So, consider any potential dependencies for a special feature and integrate additional files if necessary. You specify the dependencies in the documentation for each feature. And you get support from the tool itself. If you simply enable the check box next to a component in the Download Builder, all required dependencies are automatically solved during the download and required components of the library are checked. The selected components are combined into a JavaScript library that you then just need to integrate into your web page.[6]

If you later find that you do in fact need components that you have deselected here, you can simply reload the extended library and replace the old JavaScript file with the newly generated one. But to start, I recommend that you download all components.

On the right side of the Download Builder, you can then select which version of jQuery UI you want to download. Depending on the stage the project is in, you might find several stable versions from which to choose. Via the Google CDN[7] (http://code.google.com/apis/libraries/devguide.html#jqueryUI) you can also get other versions if required.[8] Numerous links on the web page point to various other versions, some of them more recent but potentially not yet stable.

On the right side of the Download Builder, you also see the Theme category. From a drop-down window here, you select a CSS theme that your widgets and components can use. Depending on the theme, the look of these widgets and components (and sometimes even their behavior) changes.

Caution

Without a linked CSS theme of jQuery UI, you cannot properly use the components and widgets.

jQuery UI has numerous default themes, but you can also customize the themes. For example, above the drop-down menu a link enables you to design a custom theme. Alternatively, you can reach the specified target via the Themes tab. This takes you to a site where you can visually adapt the CSS themes.

5. As a general rule, you will always need the core components.

6. Plus you get a CSS library that you also need (referred to as theme, as discussed later).

7. CDN stands for Content Distribution Network or Content Delivery Network. It refers to a network of locally distributed servers connected by the Internet via which content is intended to be delivered as effectively as possible. The data is cached on the Internet and enquiries distributed by load.

8. Generally, it is a good idea to work with the newest version, but under certain circumstances you have to support older browsers, and then it can make sense to use an older version of jQuery or jQuery UI.

Figure 11.3   The drop-down menu for a theme.

The ThemeRoller and the jQuery UI CSS Framework

As mentioned previously, the themes in the jQuery UI framework are nothing more than sophisticated CSS libraries without which the components and widgets of the framework are not represented in a web page. This is immensely important, but creating or adapting the underlying files is not difficult if you have basic knowledge of CSS. However, it might involve a lot of effort because you have to specify many details. To simplify this not-difficult but time-consuming task of creating and adapting CSS rules, jQuery UI offers a special RIA with the name ThemeRoller. This is the site you have now reached, so let's take a closer look at it.

If you look around the ThemeRoller web page, you can see a user interface on the left. This enables you to design all elements that can be used by jQuery UI widgets (Roll Your Own). By clicking the tree-like structure, you can expand the branches and set the values for the various CSS properties for the different categories, in some cases even graphically.

Tip

To the right of the column, the examples of the various components show you right away how your changes will affect the current design.

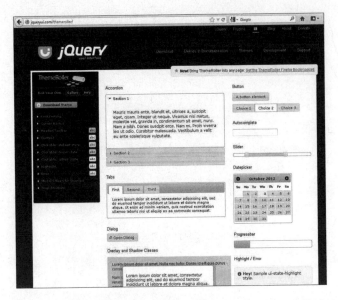

Figure 11.4   Adapting the various CSS properties via a GUI plus preview.

The ThemeRoller Gallery tab shows a selection of predefined themes. These are the same themes that you can also see in the Download Builder. Here you can see directly how a selected theme affects the widgets. (The preview is adapted interactively.)

Figure 11.5   The Gallery enables you to select predefined themes.

> **Tip**
>
> If you select a particular theme in the library, it is then used as the basis for the settings under Roll Your Own. So, if you select a theme from the gallery that is quite close to what you have in mind, you only need to change those details that you are not yet completely happy with. Of course, you can also use a theme without making any changes.

Once your design is finished, you just need to download it, make it available on the server, and integrate it into your web page. For downloading, you will find a button labeled Download Theme in the upper-left corner of the ThemeRoller web page. If you click this button or the Download tab, you go to the Download Builder, and your selected or customized theme will be preselected in the drop-down Theme menu.

> **Tip**
>
> You can adapt the downloaded CSS files manually with an editor any time if this is retrospectively necessary. Or you can reload the file into the ThemeRoller and edit it with the convenient tools offered there. In your CSS file, you will see a line with the text shown in Listing 11.1.

Listing 11.1 Start of a URL in the Comment Area of the CSS File

```
"To view and modify this theme, visit ..."
```

You then just need to copy the long URL that follows this and open it in the browser. This loads your theme into the ThemeRoller for editing, with all settings that you may have customized previously. Make your changes, and then download it again.

11.3.2 Using jQuery UI on a Web Page

When the download completes, you get a compressed Zip file that you can make available in extracted form on your server and then integrate into your web page, just as with the jQuery library.

> **Caution**
>
> Regarding the versions, remember that the jQuery UI versions always cooperate with a specific version of jQuery itself and that compatibility issues may arise if the versions do not match.[9] For example, jQuery UI 1.8.24 is based explicitly on jQuery 1.8 and later versions, whereas you can use jQuery UI 1.6 with the earlier version jQuery 1.2.6. Read the notes on the web page on the specific version of jQuery UI you are using. Fortunately, the download file of jQuery UI also contains a suitable version of jQuery itself.

---

9. But usually only if the version number of jQuery itself is too low.

The extracted library contains the following structures:

- /css/ (the theme; here you also put other themes)
- /development-bundle/ (the demos and documentation; you do not need to deliver this or make this directory available on your web server)
- /js/ (the JavaScript files of jQuery and jQuery UI)
- index.html (the index page for the demos and documentation; you do not need to deliver the file)

As you can also see in the file index.html, you need to integrate three files into your web page to use jQuery UI.

Table 11.1   The Required References

Description	Example
A reference to your specific CSS theme. The link must be integrated *before* the references in the scripts. If you want to change the layout of your application, you just need to reference another CSS theme. You should also integrate this reference before all custom CSS libraries.	`<link type="text/css" href="css/dot-luv/ jquery-ui-1.8.24.custom.css" rel="Stylesheet" />`
The reference to the normal jQuery library. This is made available once more via jQuery UI, but you can, of course, keep your own paths to your normal jQuery file if the version is suitable. The reference must be integrated *before* the reference to the jQuery UI library.	`<script type="text/javascript" src="js/ jquery-1.8.2.min.js"></script>`
The reference to the actual jQuery UI library. Afterward, you can write the references to your own JavaScript files.	`<script type="text/javascript" src="js/ jquery-ui-1.8.24.custom.min.js"></script>`

As mentioned earlier, jQuery and jQuery UI are also made available via various Content Delivery Networks (CDNs). Via these, you can integrate jQuery UI and jQuery into your web pages via the corresponding URLs. This takes pressure off your web server, but you are then relying on the provider of the CDN to ensure that the resources are made available reliably.

> **Caution**
>
> Of course, you have to adapt the paths and names you use to your specific situation, so you need to ensure that the name of the CSS theme is selected correctly and the specific JavaScript libraries you are using are correctly referenced. Unfortunately, the jQuery framework (or rather, a browser that works with it and has a problem) has the tendency to show rather nonspecific error messages if something is wrong. At best, you get an error in the error console, but often the screen simply remains empty, especially if the incorrect references.

11.3.3 A Sample Web Page for jQuery UI

A **sample template** for working with jQuery UI could look like this if we use the jQuery UI default theme and continue using our existing jQuery library and reference structures instead of the jQuery version that comes with jQuery UI.

Listing 11.2 **A Template for jQuery UI**

```
<html xmlns="http://www.w3.org/1999/xhtml">
 <head>
   <meta http-equiv="Content-Type"
     content="text/html; charset=utf-8" />
   <title>jQuery UI</title>
   <link type="text/css" href=
     "lib/css/ui-lightness/jquery-ui-[...].custom.css"
     rel="Stylesheet" />
   <link rel="stylesheet" type="text/css"
     href="lib/[...].css" />
   <script type="text/javascript"
     src="lib/jquery-[...].min.js"></script>
   <script type="text/javascript" src=
     "lib/js/jquery-ui-[...].custom.min.js"></script>
   <script type="text/javascript" src=
     "lib/[...].js"></script>
 </head>
 <body>
 </body>
</html>
```

11.4 Using the Components in jQuery UI

As soon as the libraries in your web page are referenced, you can use the components and widgets in the source code, in the same way as you have been using the normal jQuery functionalities already.

> **Tip**
>
> The components and widgets of jQuery UI work properly only if you use a theme with the matching CSS classes. The classes are explicitly geared toward these components and widgets. But this does not stop you from using the classes of the CSS framework in any way you like. This means you simply assign one of the classes that use specific components or widgets as standard to any elements in the web page. You could, for example, do it as shown in Listing 11.3.

Listing 11.3   **Applying a Class from the CSS Framework to an Element of the Type** h1

```
<h1 class="ui-corner-all">A heading</h1>
```

> **Tip**
>
> You are using a class from the available jQuery UI CSS library and assigning it to a normal level 1 heading, even if it is not a component of jQuery UI. This class gives you rounded corners.
>
> This approach, where you use classes from the available CSS library of jQuery UI when possible, is highly recommended. You achieve a uniform design even across "normal" HTML elements of your application.

11.4.1   The Default Setting

Generally, using even complex components under jQuery UI is only a one-liner, especially if you are using the **default version** of a component that is also displayed as default in the documentation.[10] Just take a look at how easily you can make an object in the web page moveable via drag and drop.

> **Note**
>
> Note that the components we use as examples in this section are purely intended to be seen as placeholders. You can, of course, use other components as well.

Listing 11.4   **Making an Image Draggable (ch11_1.html)**

```
...
18   <body>
19     <h1>Above</h1>
20     <img id="draggable" src="images/pic1.jpg" />
21     <h1>Below</h1>
22   </body>
23 </html>
```

10. All other variations are initially hidden and you have to select them on the right side.

On the companion website, you can see that the lines we have not printed here contain the references from the sample template and the usual references to our external JavaScript and CSS file, whose names are as usually based on the name of the HTML file. Here is the JavaScript file ch11_1_ready.js with the programming logic.

Listing 11.5 **The Image Becomes Draggable**

```
01 $(function(){
02   $("#draggable").draggable();
03 });
```

Could we make it any shorter?[11]

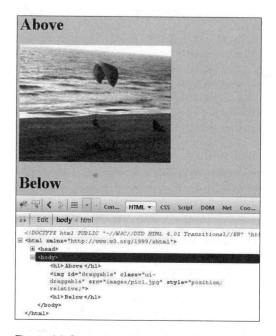

Figure 11.6   In the original, the image is between the two headings. Note the relative positioning in Firebug.

Line 2 is all you need to make an element or a group of elements draggable with the mouse in the web page. You simply write down the method `draggable()` for the desired elements. It is interesting if you analyze the web page with Firebug. Although no CSS positioning is specified in the source text, the method `draggable()` has generated a `style` attribute and specified `position:relative` in the background.

11. Massive functionality of dragging elements is provided in a simple statement.

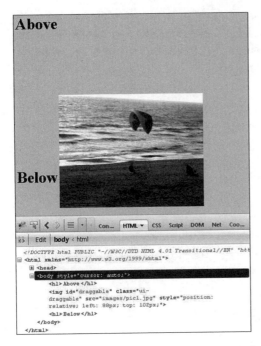

Figure 11.7   The image has been moved with the mouse.

> **Note**
>
> At first glance, it seems child's play to make an element in the web page movable with the mouse. As you know, you can read out the mouse coordinates and the pressed mouse buttons via the event object. The position of an object can be easily specified and changed via CSS with `position`, `left`, and `top`. So, you just need to combine the two aspects and there you go, job done. Or not, because if you try the example you will see that the headings above and below the image remain in their original positions when you drag the image. In addition, note that the original source text does not contain any CSS positioning for the image. With many other widgets, components, and effects, it is also the case that a method in jQuery UI ensures that various CSS formatting is done automatically in the background. So, a lot happens in the background, which obscures how extremely easy the methods are to use and is easily overlooked when you consider the seemingly simple manual programming.

11.4.2   Some Basic Rules on Components and Widgets

Some fundamental rules almost always apply to using jQuery UI components and widgets. If you are aware of them right from the start, you will find it easy to get along with jQuery UI:

- Unlike methods of jQuery, methods for creating components and widgets *cannot* be chained via dot notation. The individual objects are too complex and in general it would make little sense.

- When creating a component or widgets with the default setting, you use the corresponding method for creating without parameters.

- Several jQuery UI widgets should be applied to `div` elements. This will result in as few spillover effects from HTML[12] as possible. Where necessary, the methods adapt the elements in the background. Usually, however, you can use other basic elements, although this is not recommended.

- Widgets explicitly use the default theme CSS files. You generally create the corresponding CSS files on download with the ThemeRoller tool. But if you do want or need to make individual changes,[13] there is a CSS file for each widget that starts with jquery.ui followed by the name of the relevant widget (for example, jquery.ui.slider.css). In it, you will find the classes that you can customize with an editor and that start with `ui-[name of widget/super-class]` (for example `ui-slider`, `ui-slider-horizontal`, `ui-widget`, `ui-widget-content`, and `ui-corner-all`). You can also view these classes explicitly in Firebug if you analyze the generated code of a widget.[14] For more details, refer to the description of each widget under the Theming tab. But, of course, you can also influence the widgets and components with custom CSS rules.

11.4.3 Properties/Options of Components

As you have already seen in the first example, using the UI components of jQuery is often easy. If you are happy with the default settings, you can often manage with just a single line of code. If you want to adapt components, you just need to override the desired properties or options. This gets us to the fact that you need to know which options a specific component offers. We could now list and describe these properties for all UI components, but I consider this superfluous because you can find this list and description via the documentation for each component if you select it at http://jqueryui.com/demos/. You just click the *Options* tab and then you can see at a glance which options can be specified for a component or widgets. You just need to specify the desired options for the relevant component or widget when you create the component.

---

12. For example, for a dialog, button, progress bar, or slider.

13. But this should rarely be necessary.

14. There you will also find the information required for identifying those classes that you might want to apply to nonwidgets to achieve a more uniform design.

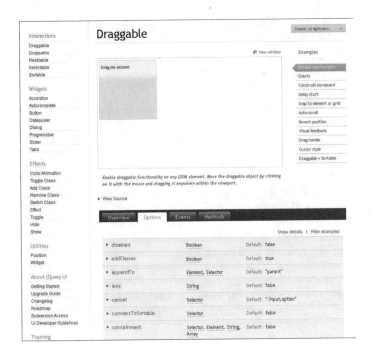

Figure 11.8   The options of `draggable`.

You just need to know what a particular option does and, of course, how to apply it. But each of the specified options in the documentation is sensitive, and if you click one of the options there, you will see a drop-down menu with an explanation of its effect, how to use it, permitted values, and a listing example.

Here you can also see the default value of each option. This takes effect if you do not specify the option further. Then the last question is how to use options. You can set options or get their values.

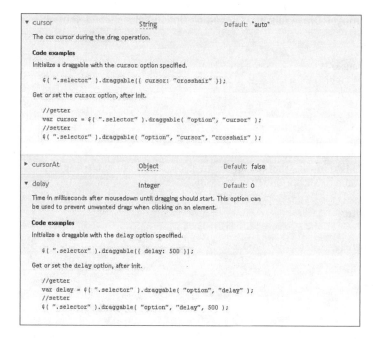

```
▼ cursor                    String              Default: "auto"
The css cursor during the drag operation.

Code examples
Initialize a draggable with the cursor option specified.

    $( ".selector" ).draggable({ cursor: "crosshair" });

Get or set the cursor option, after init.

    //getter
    var cursor = $( ".selector" ).draggable( "option", "cursor" );
    //setter
    $( ".selector" ).draggable( "option", "cursor", "crosshair" );


► cursorAt                  Object              Default: false

▼ delay                     Integer             Default: 0
Time in milliseconds after mousedown until dragging should start. This option can
be used to prevent unwanted drags when clicking on an element.

Code examples
Initialize a draggable with the delay option specified.

    $( ".selector" ).draggable({ delay: 500 });

Get or set the delay option, after init.

    //getter
    var delay = $( ".selector" ).draggable( "option", "delay" );
    //setter
    $( ".selector" ).draggable( "option", "delay", 500 );
```

Figure 11.9   Details on `cursor` and `delay`.

Setting Option Values

You can use options when *creating* components or widgets if you want to modify the default. Generally, you just declare the options on generating the component object with a parameter such as Map as usual in jQuery (particularly if you want to specify several options).

Alternatively, you can work with three parameters. As the first parameter, you specify "option", the second parameter is the name of the desired option as a string, and the third is the desired value. This notation makes sense as a setter when specifying only one option.[15]

Getting Option Values

The getter is structured in a similar way as the setter with three parameters; you simply omit the third parameter, and as return value you get the value of the specified option.

> ### Tip
> Alternatively, some methods give you return values of option values or current values of properties for some components and widgets. We take a closer look at this next.

15. The notation with three parameters showed a strangely unreliable behavior in my experiments, but I was not able to determine the reasons, so it may only occur in certain constellations. I would advise you to set options always as Map (even if you only have one option).

Listing 11.6   **Making Two Images Draggable and Outputting Option Values (ch11_2.html)**

```
...
18  <body>
19    <h1>Two draggable images</h1>
20    <img src="images/pic1.jpg" />
21    <img src="images/pic2.jpg" />
22    <div></div>
23  </body>
24 </html>
```

On the web page, you can see two images that are made draggable and modified in a few parameters. Plus we get the value of an option (ch11_2_ready.js).

Listing 11.7   **Setter and Getter**

```
01 $(function(){
02   $("img:first").draggable({
03     "opacity": "0.35"
04   });
05   $("img:last").draggable({
06     cursor: 'crosshair',
07     delay: 500
08   });
09   $("div:first").html(
10     $("img:last").draggable("option", "cursor"));
11 });
```

Moving the first image is initialized with one option, and moving the second image with two options. In line 10, you can see how we read out the value of an option and use it further.[16]

Figure 11.10   Using getters and setters.

16. In this case it is just primitive outputting.

11.4.4 Methods of Components

For each component, there are also **methods**—because a component can, of course, also be seen as object, and objects usually offer methods in addition to properties. Specifically, these methods are used in jQuery UI for constructing (without parameters or with options), enabling, disabling, configuring, or destroying the object. The term *methods* has a slightly different meaning in the context of components and widgets in jQuery UI than in "normal" objects. In the framework's documentation, the Methods tab always describes only one method for components and widgets. But via default values for a parameter, different behaviors of this method can be achieved, and these **default values of the parameter** are listed there.[17] These parameter values specify the execution and behavior and where appropriate the return value of the method concerned (ch11_3.html).

Listing 11.8 **Making an Object Draggable and Disabling Again**

```
...
18  <body>
19    <h1>Making an image draggable and then
20        disabling it again</h1>
21    <img src="images/pic3.jpg" /><br />
22    <button>Enable</button>
23    <button>Disable</button>
24  </body>
25 </html>
```

In the web page, you will find an image that is made draggable on loading. Via the two buttons, we can either enable or disable this behavior dynamically[18] (ch11_3_ready.js).

Listing 11.9 **Dynamically Enabling and Disabling Draggability**

```
01 $(function(){
02   $("img:first").draggable({
03     cursor: 'crosshair',
04     "opacity": "0.35"
05   });
06   $("button:first").click(function(){
07     $("img:first").draggable("enable");
08   });
09   $("button:last").click(function(){
10     $("img:first").draggable("disable");
11   });
12 });
```

17. It would be more appropriate to name this area Default Values for the Parameters of the Component Method (that would, of course, be too long, but more appropriate).

18. Which, of course, only makes sense if a state can actually be toggled.

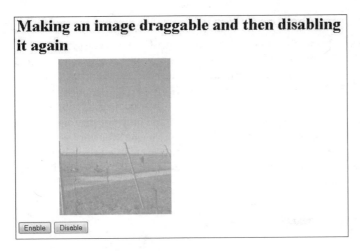

Figure 11.11   The image is being dragged.

In lines 7 and 10, you can see how the method `draggable()` is called with certain parameters. Clicking the first button enables draggability, and clicking the second button disables this again.

Figure 11.12   Both the opacity and the cursor indicate that the image cannot be dragged.

Let's take a look at another example where we process the value of a widget's property via a method. For example, we use an object of the type `Slider` (ch11_4.html).

Listing 11.10   **A Slider**

```
...
18  <body>
19    <h1>A slider</h1>
20    <div id="sl"></div>
21    <form>
22      <input type="text" /><br/>
23      <input type="button" value="Set value" />
24    </form>
25    <div></div>
26  </body>
27 </html>
```

In the web page, we want to turn a `div` element into a slider. You will see that this again a one-liner in the basic setting. But we make it a bit more "elaborate" and set a few options. We want to change the value of the slider via the button and set the slider to the value that is entered in the input field (ch11_4_ready.js).

Listing 11.11   **Processing Property Values**

```
01 $(function(){
02   $("#sl").slider({
03     orientation: 'horizontal',
04     min: -50, max: 50, value: 0
05   });
06   $("input:button:first").click(function(){
07     $("#sl").slider("value",
08       $("input:text:first").val());
09     $("div:last").html($("#sl").slider("value"));
10   });
11 });
```

In lines 2–5, we create the slider with a certain alignment plus a minimum and maximum value and a default setting for where the slider value should be. In line 9, we read out the value of the property `value` and simply display it on the page.

In lines 6–10, you can see the reaction to a click on the button. First you can see in lines 7 and 8 how the `slider()` method and two parameters set the value of the slider to the value that a user enters into the input field.

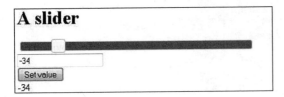

Figure 11.13   Setting and getting the value of a slider.

If this value is bigger or smaller than the minimum or maximum value, the slider is simply pushed to the end point on the left or right, although the assigned value exceeds the limit.

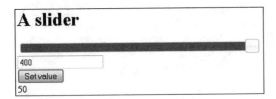

Figure 11.14   The entered value is too big, and the value is set to the maximum.

Now you should notice that a slider is not normally used in this way with the value of the slider being manipulated from the outside.[19] Instead, you want to react to certain changes made to the slider. This is, of course, done via events that are also available for components and widgets.

11.4.5   Events in Components and Widgets

The events supported by components and widgets are also listed in the documentation and described in the Events tab.

For an element that is draggable with the mouse, you can, for example, react to the start of the drag action, the end, and the specific dragging phase. In all three situations, an event is triggered to which you can bind a callback function. This is completely normal jQuery event handling. Or you can react to displaying a tab in a component, perhaps as shown in Listing 11.12.

Listing 11.12   **Reacting to Displaying a Tab in a Tabs Widget**

```
$('.selector').tabs({
    show: function(event, ui) { ... }
});
```

19. Although that is, of course, possible, as you can see here.

You can also make use of data binding via `bind()` (for example, as shown in Listing 11.13, if you want to react to a slider being dragged).

Listing 11.13 Reacting to Dragging a Slider, with Data Binding

```
$('.selector').bind('slide', function(event, ui) {
  ...
});
```

Let's illustrate this with a complete example where we make an image draggable in the web page and react to the various states of the dragging action. In addition, we want to react to the slider being moved (ch11_5.html).

Listing 11.14 Reacting to Events

```
...
18  <body>
19    <h1>A slider</h1>
20    <div id="sl"></div><br />
21    <img src="images/pic3.jpg" id="image" />
22    <div id="info1"></div><div id="info2"></div>
23    <div id="info3"></div>
24  </body>
25  </html>
```

We make the image draggable and turn the first `div` element into a slider. In the last three `div` areas, we then output status information (ch11_5_ready.js).

Listing 11.15 Reacting to Events of the Components

```
01  $(function(){
02    $("#sl").slider({
03      min: -50,max: 50, value: 0,
04      slide: function(event, ui){
05        $("#info1").html("Value of the slider: " +
06        $("#sl").slider('value'));
07      }
08    });
09    $("#image").draggable({
10      start: function(event, ui){
11        $("#info2").html("Dragging starts: " +
12        event.timeStamp);
13      },
14      stop: function(event, ui){
15        $("#info2").html("Dragging stops.<br />" +
16            "Positions in relation to original position:" +
```

```
17            "<br />Top: " + ui['position'].top + ", Left: "
18            + ui['position'].left);
19    }
20  });
21  $('#image').bind('drag', function(event, ui){
22    $("#info3").html("Dragging in progress: " +
23        event.timeStamp + ", X/Y: " +
24        event.pageX + "/" + event.pageY);
25  });
26  $('#image').bind('dragstop', function(event, ui){
27      $("#info3").html("Dragstop triggered");
28  });
29  });
```

In lines 2–8, we create a slider and directly specify a few options. Of interest for our purposes is above all the option slide in line 4. It designates an event that fires every time the slider control is dragged. We assign an anonymous function and process the value of the slider in line 6 via the slider() method and by specifying the 'value' parameter. We output the return value permanently[20] in the web page.

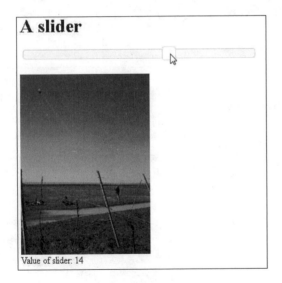

Figure 11.15   Getting the value of a slider.

In the example, we also specify options on creating the object of the type Draggable. In addition, you can again see function references for the time when the action starts (line 10) and for the time when the action ends (line 14). These are classic event handlers. Inside the

20. In other words, every time the slider control is dragged.

anonymous function, we use the jQuery event object and assess in line 12 the moment when the event occurred. Specifically, this is the reaction to the start of the slider dragging action.

In lines 21–25 and lines 26–28, you can also see how we use data binding via `bind()`. For the `drag` event, we assess with the event object the X and Y coordinates of the mouse pointer and the time when the event was created. You will see that dragging the image continuously generates events of the type `drag` and that the displayed value in the web page is consequently constantly updated.

Figure 11.16   The mouse button is pressed, and dragging the image is enabled (the state drag).

Accordingly, we react to `dragstop` and output a message for the event. Simultaneously, lines 14–19 specify the reaction to the `stop` event. Here, we use the second parameter of the anonymous callback function—the triggering visual object. We output the new coordinates in relation to the original position before dragging.

> **Note**
>
> Using data binding in parallel to the reaction via the events of a component is rarely useful in practice. We are only mixing the two approaches for didactic purposes here.

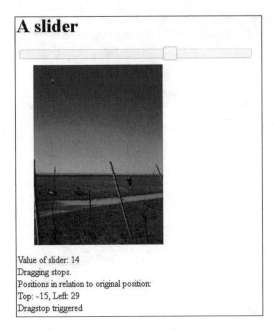

A slider

Value of slider: 14
Dragging stops.
Positions in relation to original position:
Top: -15, Left: 29
Dragstop triggered

Figure 11.17   After the end of the drag action.

11.5   An Overview of the Components and Widgets

As mentioned previously, you only basically need to take a closer look at one component and one widget, and then it should be fairly obvious how to use the other components and widgets in jQuery UI. Let's still at least briefly introduce the available components and widgets in jQuery UI.

11.5.1   The Interaction Components

Let's first take a quick look at the available interaction components.

Draggable

With the `Draggable` component, you enable elements of the web page to be dragged via the mouse. We have already discussed it in detail in the context of the examples.

Droppable

With the `Droppable` component, you can designate an element as a potential target of a drag action. So, such a component only makes sense if you use it in combination of an element of the type `Draggable`. You can trigger specific actions if a dragged element is dropped in a target area marked as such.

Listing 11.16   **Example for a Sensitive Area**

```
$("#targetarea" ).droppable({
  hoverClass: "ui-state-active",
  drop: function( event, ui ) {
    $( this ).html( "Element dropped" );
  }
});
```

Resizable

Some components are connected to certain requirements to function properly (for example, those of the type `Resizable`). With the method `resizable()`, you can make such objects resizable. But these components are only resizable if they have previously been assigned a width/height via CSS and if the area to be resized was specified with a few more CSS rules.[21] But this is not difficult and will hardly complicate the matter. Let's look at a complete example (ch11_6.html).

Listing 11.17   **The Method** `Resizable` **in Action**

```
...
18  <body>
19    <h1>A resizable DIV area</h1>
20    <div id="resizable" class="ui-widget-content">
21      <h3>www.rjs.de</h3></div>
22  </body>
23  </html>
```

We make the `div` element resizable and format it a little bit via CSS (ch11_6_ready.js).

Listing 11.18   **The** `div` **Container Can Be Resized**

```
01 $(function(){
02   $("#resizable").resizable();
03 });
```

---

21. In particular, with `class="ui-widget-content"`.

Figure 11.18   The cursor shows that the `div` container is being enlarged via the mouse.

Selectable

If you tag elements with the `selectable()` method, they can be selected. Because the method does not use parameters, there is not much else to say here.

Sortable

By marking elements with the `sortable()` method, you make them sortable within a group. This makes sense, for example, with list items.

11.5.2   The Widgets

Let's now take a look at the widgets that jQuery UI offers.

Accordion

An `Accordion` component enables you to arrange overlapping contents vertically. These contents can be shown and hidden interactively, so that one area with content is visible at a time and the other content is hidden. The widget is a bit more complex because it is based on a nested structure with `div` elements. But it is still clearly structured. Let's first look at the HTML structure (ch11_7.html).

Listing 11.19   **The Basic Structure**

```
...
18   <body>
19     <h1>An Accordion Component</h1>
20     <div id="accordion">
21       <h3><a href="#">Section 1</a></h3>
22       <div>
23         Two things are infinite:
24         the universe and human stupidity;
25         and I'm not sure about
```

```
26          the universe.
27      </div>
28      <h3><a href="#">Section 2</a></h3>
29      <div>
30          You can lead a horse to water
31          but you can't make it drink.
32      </div>
33      <h3><a href="#">Section 3</a></h3>
34      <div>
35          Be not afraid
36          of going slowly,
37          be afraid only of standing still.
38      </div>
39    </div>
40  </body>
41  </html>
```

The outer structure is a div element (lines 20–39). The individual content areas inside this consist (in the default version) in each case of one heading of the type h3, in which we write down a link (made inactive via a hash sign) with the label. The following div area contains the content for this area. Then this inner structure is repeated again to specify another content area and so on. We now use a one-liner to turn the div element into an Accordion component (ch11_7_ready.js).

Listing 11.20 **The div Container Turns into an Accordion**

```
01 $(function(){
02   $("#accordion").accordion();
03 });
```

We now have an Accordion component with three sections. The top section is displaying on loading the web page; the other two are hidden.

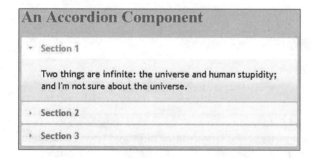

Figure 11.19   The top section is visible.

If the user clicks the title of a hidden section, the text is animatedly displayed.

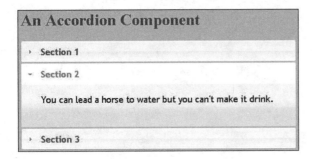

Figure 11.20   Now the middle section is visible.

> **Note**
> In jQuery UI 1.9, this component is internally redesigned, but it is still used in the same way.

Autocomplete

A fairly new and AJAX motivated widget is made available via the `autocomplete()` method. It is used to display a list of suitable suggestions below the input field when a user enters characters into an input field.

In the default version, the method works with a JavaScript array that provides the acceptable values to be automatically suggested. However, the widget is highly configurable and can manage with various data structures. These can also be loaded via AJAX from the server and be offered both in JSON and XML. We are only going to take a brief look at a variation in the default configuration (ch11_8.html).

Listing 11.21   **The Basic Structure**

```
...
18  <body>
19    <h1>An Autocomplete Component</h1>
20    <input id="tags" />
21  </body>
22 </html>
```

As you can see, we specify only one input field in the web page. Note that there is no `div` area, no list, or anything similar where the list of suggested terms will be displayed later. These structures are generated entirely dynamically. Here is the script ch11_8_ready.js with the data array.

Listing 11.22 **The Autocomplete Component with an Array as Local Database**

```
01 $(function(){
02   var db = ["Accordion", "Autocomplete", "Button",
03     "Datepicker", "Dialog", "Draggable", "Droppable",
04     "Progressbar", "Resizable", "Selectable", "Slider",
05     "Sortable", "Tabs"];
06   $("#tags").autocomplete({
07     source: db
08   });
09 });
```

The crucial point is the link between the local array and the Autocomplete component in the options of the method via source (line 7).

If you look at the generated structure in Firebug, you will see that a hidden list has been created based on the array.

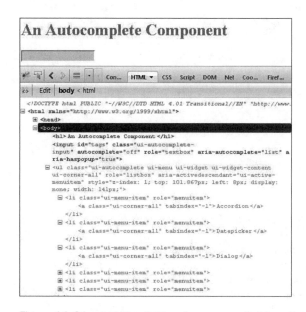

Figure 11.21   A hidden list has been generated from the array.

If a user now enters letters into the input field, a list of suggestions that get more precise with each letter is displayed, and by clicking one of the suggested list items, the user can enter the relevant term into the input field.

Figure 11.22   With each letter the user enters, the suggestions become more precise.

Button

Elements of the type Button provide—you guessed it—buttons. Functionally, such buttons offered by jQuery UI are nothing special. The advantage of the widget version is that they are widely and easily configurable and can be visually adapted. Essentially, you can influence the appearance by assigning icons (the option `icons`) that are supplied in the CSS theme of jQuery UI. You mainly need to pick out the right class and then assign it to an element in the web page (usually a `div` element or an element of the type `button`), as shown in Listing 11.23.

Listing 11.23   **A Button with an Icon**

```
$( "#play" ).button({
  text: false,
  icons: {
    primary: "ui-icon-play"
  }
})
```

Datepicker

A `Datepicker` widget is a date component that offers the user visual support for entering a date and fully checks its plausibility. This visual support is already complex, but the logic in an interactive date component (or a calendar) is even more elaborate.[22] The widget of the type `Datepicker` in jQuery UI turns even using this date component into a one-liner, provided you are satisfied with using the default setting (ch11_9.html).

Listing 11.24   **The Basic Structure**

```
...
18  <body>
19    <h1>A Date Component/h1>
20    <p>Date: <input id="datepicker" type="text"></p>
21  </body>
22 </html>
```

22. Remember our own calendar?

As you can see, we only specify one input field in the web page. There is no `div` area or anything similar where the calendar is to be displayed later. These structures are generated purely dynamically. Listing 11.25 shows the script ch11_9_ready.js.

Listing 11.25   **An Interactive Calendar for Selecting a Date**

```
01 $(function(){
02    $("#datepicker").datepicker();
03 });
```

To integrate such a qualified option for selecting a date into your web page, you need nothing more than an input field for text. A simple call of the `datepicker()` method for this element ensures that the calendar is opened animatedly below the input field if the user clicks the field.

Figure 11.23   Selecting a date via a calendar.

If the user clicks a date in the calendar, this date is automatically entered into the input field, and all of that happens without necessitating you writing a single line of proper programming.

Dialog

Dialog elements are becoming more and more important in RIAs. They increasingly take on the task that used to be fulfilled by pop-ups in the past. Because these represent new window instances of the browser and are frequently blocked by pop-up blockers, web page designers now tend to use dialog elements instead that are based internally purely on dynamically generated and formatted `div` structures and do not really represent new windows (so that they are not blocked by pop-up blockers).

In jQuery UI, you can also create a dialog window with a one-liner that corresponds to the appearance and behavior of modern desktop environments.[23] In that case, you just use the default configuration as usual. The "simulated" window then already fulfills all requirements that a user would have for a modern dialog window (nonmodal in the basic setting) in desktop applications. It can be closed by clicking the X icon (usually at the top-right corner, but you can change this in the theme), enlarged, or reduced with the mouse or dragged.

A dialog can also be widely configured with options—not just in its size, but also whether it is draggable, modal, which title line the dialog should show, and so on. We will try this in an example to make it a bit less primitive. We also want to show you how to use a method. Specifically, we want to have the option of opening the two dialogs in the following example via a button each (ch11_10.html).

Listing 11.26   **The Basic Structure**

```
...
18   <body>
19     <h1>Different Dialogs</h1>
20     <button>Open modal dialog</button>
21     <button>Open dialog</button>
22     <div id="b1" title="My webpage">
23       www.rjs.de</div>
24     <div id="b2" title="My blog">
25       blog.rjs.de</div>
26   </body>
27 </html>
```

In lines 22–23, you can see a `div` container with some random text content (the same in lines 24–25). This content can have normal HTML tags in it. Note that this container is ultimately invisible in the web page on loading or modified to a dialog. (This is done dynamically by the framework if it is turned into dialog components.) The two buttons also reopen the relevant dialog if it is closed.

Listing 11.27 shows the script ch11_10_ready.js.

Listing 11.27   **Dialog Elements**

```
01 $(function(){
02   $("#b1").dialog({
03     autoOpen: false,
04     modal: true,
05     buttons: {
06       "Ok": function(){
07         $(this).dialog("close");
```

---

23. Not just a primitive `alert()`.

```
08      }
09    }
10  });
11  $("#b2").dialog({
12    position: [150, 200],
13    height: 100,
14    width: 400
15  });
16  $("button:eq(0)").click(function(){
17    $("#b1").dialog("open");
18  });
19  $("button:eq(1)").click(function(){
20    $("#b2").dialog("open");
21  });
22 });
```

In the first case, we work with a modal dialog (line 4) that is not displayed on loading the web page[24] (line 3) and for which a specific button with a callback function is displayed (lines 5–9). The dialog is opened by clicking the first button (line 17).

Figure 11.24   The modal dialog blocks the web page.

The second dialog is defined in lines 11–15. Here, we specify the position in X- and Y-coordinates, the height, and the width. This dialog is already open automatically when the web page is loaded, but it can also be reopened via the second button if the user has closed it.

Because the dialogs are independent from one another, they can also both be open at the same time (at least if the modal dialog is opened second).

24. The default is for the dialog to be displayed.

Figure 11.25   Both dialog elements are visible.

Progressbar

The name says it all: This widget is a progress bar. The widget itself is straightforward. The crucial point for the progress bar is the option `value` or the corresponding parameter of the method. This value should be connected to some kind of process in practice for the progress bar to make sense. Data binding is ideal for this. We take a look at an example later, in combination with the slider.

Slider

You have already seen sliders in practice, and there is not really anything interesting to say here. However, the following example combines an object of the type `Slider` and an object of the type `Progressbar` and ensures that the displayed value is synchronized in the progress bar with the value of the slider (ch11_11.html).[25]

Listing 11.28   **Synchronization of a Slider and Progress Bar**

```
...
18   <body>
19     <h1>A Slider and a
20       Progress Bar</h1>
21     <div id="sl"></div>
22     <div id="progressbar"></div>
23   </body>
24 </html>
```

We turn the first `div` element into a slider and the second into a progress bar (ch11_11_ready.js).

25. Although a progress bar actually makes more sense for a continuous process, such as a loading process or similar.

Listing 11.29 **Progress Bar and Slider**

```
01 $(function(){
02   $("#progressbar").progressbar();
03   $("#sl").slider({
04     min: 0, max: 100, value: 0,
05   });
06   $('#sl').bind('slide', function(){
07     $("#progressbar").progressbar("value",
08       $("#sl").slider("value"));
09   });
10 });
```

In line 2, we create a progress bar and in lines 3–5 a slider. The latter is configured with a few options.

More interesting is the data binding that you see in lines 6–9. To drag the slider control (the event slide), we bind calling the following callback function. Inside the function, we assign in lines 7 and 8 the value property of the slider to the value property of the progress bar. This ensures that both are synchronized.

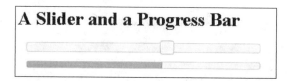

Figure 11.26 The slider and progress bar show the same value.

Tabs

Currently, you see many web pages with pages that are subdivided via tabs. This structure is also easy to implement via jQuery UI. Interestingly, it is even easier if you load the content with AJAX. Of course, you can also configure this widget widely, but in particular in connection with AJAX, the basic setting is already so powerful that you will rarely need to configure it further.

Similar to the Accordion component, tabs are based on a nested div structure. Inside it, you will first find a list. This takes care of labeling the tabs and interactively displays the content so that the user can switch between contents simply by clicking the tabs. This involves hyperlinks that are specified as content of the list items. There are two situations to distinguish:

- We want to display content that is already present in the web page and currently not visible. This content is located within an inner div area that is marked with an ID. This link uses an anchor reference to refer to this ID.

- We want to load new content via AJAX. So, we just need to specify the URL of the new file. As a MIME type, you should send text/html (ch11_12.html).

Listing 11.30   **The Basic Structure**

```
...
18  <body>
19    <h1>Navigation via Tabs</h1>
20    <div id="tabs">
21      <ul>
22        <li><a href="#tabs-1">Home</a></li>
23        <li><a href="#tabs-2">Services</a></li>
24        <li><a href="notice.html">Legal Info</a></li>
25        <li><a href="gallery.html">Gallery</a></li>
26      </ul>
27      <div id="tabs-1">
28        <h3>Welcome to the RJS site for IT KnowHow</h3>
29      </div>
30      <div id="tabs-2">
31        <h3>Training - Consulting - Publishing</h3>
32      </div>
33    </div>
34  </body>
35 </html>
```

The tabs area is from lines 20–33. This is the external structure. In line 22, you can see a link to the ID in line 27 and in line 23 the link to the ID in line 30. These are references to div areas with content already present in the web page. The div area with the ID tabs-1 is already displayed on loading the web page. In the default setting, this is always the first tab, but you can also change it via options.

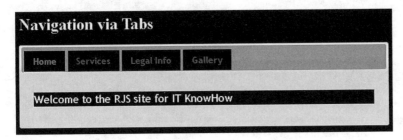

Figure 11.27   The first tab is displayed when the web page is loaded.

You should notice that the links in lines 24 and 25 point to HTML pages, not anchors. Clicking these links loads the referenced file via AJAX, and these files should have the file extension .html but not contain a basic structure.[26]

Figure 11.28   The data has been loaded via AJAX.

Note that there is no div area or similar in the hard-coded structure of the web page where the AJAX content is to be displayed. This is again generated dynamically by the framework.

Listing 11.31 shows the script ch11_12_ready.js.

Listing 11.31   **The div Area Is Turned into Tabs**

```
01 $(function(){
02   $(function(){
03     $("#tabs").tabs({
04       ajaxOptions: {
05         error: function(xhr, status, index, anchor){
06           alert("Error on loading content");
07         }
08       }
09     });
10   });
11 });
```

26. As always when loaded with AJAX.

Basically, we do not really need the whole section from lines 4–9. To turn a div area into tabs, it is sufficient to use tabs(); entirely without parameters, even if we load data via AJAX without refreshing. What you see here is just an error reaction via options. This is, of course, appropriate but not required for the basic functionality.

> **Note**
>
> The tab that is displayed on loading the web page should not be loaded via AJAX. This would not make sense. However, it can be appropriate for all the other tabs, depending on the volume of data. This simplifies the fixed web page structure.

Tooltip and Other New Features in jQuery UI 1.9

With jQuery UI 1.9, we have another interesting component of the type Tooltip at our disposal to display brief context-sensitive text when the user drags the mouse pointer over an element in the web page.

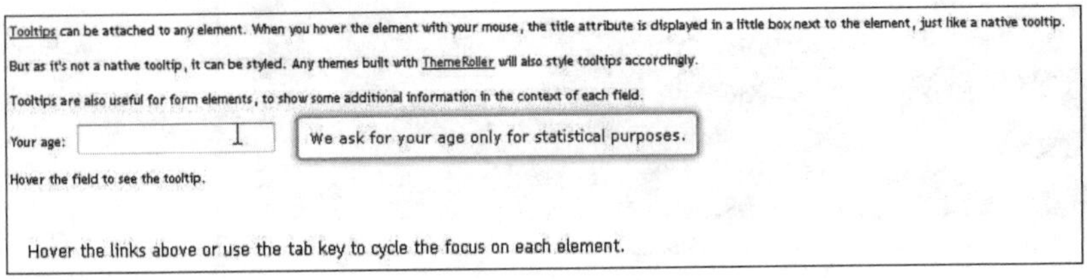

Tooltips can be attached to any element. When you hover the element with your mouse, the title attribute is displayed in a little box next to the element, just like a native tooltip.

But as it's not a native tooltip, it can be styled. Any themes built with ThemeRoller will also style tooltips accordingly.

Tooltips are also useful for form elements, to show some additional information in the context of each field.

Your age: ⌶   We ask for your age only for statistical purposes.

Hover the field to see the tooltip.

Hover the links above or use the tab key to cycle the focus on each element.

Figure 11.29   New in jQuery UI 1.9, a small tooltip.

Listing 11.32   **Creating a Tooltip**

```
$("#myTip").tooltip();
```

The new version also contains a spinner. This is a small component with two arrows to count numeric values up or down. The widget is based on a simple input element.

Select a value: 5

Figure 11.30   A spinner component.

There is also a new Menu widget that is simply based on an unsorted list. If you want to build a nested menu structure, you can simply specify a list item of another list.

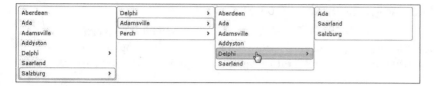

Figure 11.31   A Menu widget.

11.5.3 Utilities

The category Utilities currently comprises only one component of the type `position`. With it, you can reliably position all visible elements of a web page in relation to the window, the document, a specific element, or the mouse pointer. Strictly speaking, it is an auxiliary script with the name `position()`, which you can call without parameters, with a function reference, or with options (for example, within the callback function to a `drag` event).

Listing 11.33   **Positioning**

```
$( "#parent" ).draggable({
  drag: function() { position(); }
});
```

11.6   Effects

The well-documented application of UI components continues with the expanded effects of jQuery UI. Of course, the multitude of effects requires a great number of options and settings. Here, you should definitely turn to the documentation for further advice and information. But you can use most methods directly from your experience with jQuery itself. We just want to expand briefly on two special effects.

11.6.1   The `effect()` Method

The `effect()` method is very impressive. It has at least one parameter that describes the specific effect. Possible values are `'blind'`, `'bounce'`, `'clip'`, `'drop'`, `'explode'`, `'fold'`, `'highlight'`, `'puff'`, `'pulsate'`, `'scale'`, `'shake'`, `'size'`, `'slide'`, and `'transfer'`. As an optional second parameter, you can specify a set of options;[27] the third parameter specifies the duration of the effect, and parameter four is an optional callback function. If you apply these effects to an element, it will—depending on your selection—explode, pulsate, shake, or so forth. You can use the interactive example in the documentation to try it out yourself.

27. Most effects work quite well without specifying options. Only in a few exceptional cases you would specify an option.

11.6.2   Color Animations with `animate()`

Last but not least, let's take a look at the expanded `animate()` method, which can also animate colors via jQuery UI. As the first parameter, you specify a list with CSS properties that you want to animate, and as the second parameter the desired duration of the animation (ch11_13.html).

Listing 11.34   **The Basic Structure with a `div` Area**

```
...
18  <body>
19    <h1>Color Animation</h1>
20    <button>Animate</button><hr />
21    <div id="i1">www.rjs.de</div>
22  </body>
23  </html>
```

The `div` area in the web page is formatted with the external CSS file, and we want it to animatedly change with a click on the button; among other things, we want the color to change.

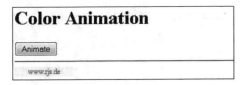

Figure 11.32   The initial appearance.

Listing 11.35 shows how to do it (ch11_13_ready.js).

Listing 11.35   **Animating Colors**

```
01 $(function(){
02   $("button:first").click(function(){
03     $("#i1").animate({
04       backgroundColor: '#aa0000',
05       color: '#fff',
06       width: 500,
07       fontSize: 42
08     }, 1000);
09     return false;
10   });
11 });
```

Figure 11.33   The colors have also been animated.

In lines 3–8, you can see the method `animate()`. The target value for the background color and the foreground color is in line 4.

> **Tip**
>
> Basically, you can animate all conceivable CSS properties by specifying the desired target value.

11.7   A Complete Website Based on jQuery UI

To finish this chapter, we address a basic approach of how you could create a complete web page with jQuery UI. In other words, I am suggesting a possible structure for your web page that uses components and widgets of jQuery UI. The specific layout is only to be seen as a suggestion, and I highly recommend that you put your own ideas into practice.

I want to construct a page that is essentially based on nested tabs with AJAX in the background and the `Accordion` component. As I said, this is only one of many possibilities, but at least an approach that could serve as a starting point for you.

Let's look at a possible complete basic web page (ch11_14.html).

Listing 11.36   **A Basic Template**

```
01 <html xmlns="http://www.w3.org/1999/xhtml">
02   <head>
03     <meta http-equiv="Content-Type"
04        content="text/html; charset=utf-8" />
05     <title>jQuery UI</title>
06     <link type="text/css" href=
07        "lib/css/ui-lightness/jquery-ui-1.8.24.custom.css"
08        rel="Stylesheet" />
09     <link rel="stylesheet" type="text/css"
10        href="lib/ch11_14.css" />
11     <script type="text/javascript"
12        src="lib/jquery-1.8.2.min.js"></script>
13     <script type="text/javascript" src=
```

```
14        "lib/js/jquery-ui-1.8.24.custom.min.js"></script>
15    <script type="text/javascript" src=
16        "lib/ch11_14_ready.js"></script>
17  </head>
18  <body>
19    <div id="header"><img src="images/logo.gif"
20        alt="Logo" /></div>
21    <div id="content">
22      <ul>
23        <li><a href="#home">Home</a></li>
24        <li><a href="sourcecode.html">
25          Examples/Source Code</a></li>
26          <li><a href="notice.html">
27             Legal Info</a></li>
28          <li><a href="more.html">More</a></li>
29      </ul>
30      <div id="home">
31        <h3>Welcome to the RJS site for IT KnowHow</h3>
32      </div>
33    </div>
34    <div id="footer">
35    <a href="http://www.rjs.de/"
36        title="RJS EDV-KnowHow"
37        rel="home">RJS EDV-KnowHow</a>
38    </div>
39  </body>
40  </html>
```

As you can see, the web page has three div areas. The header and footer are structured with pure HTML. In the second div area, we want to manage the actual content of the web page. We turn this area into tabs. Only the start page is already loaded with the web page. The other contents of the tabs are loaded later via AJAX and have in turn interesting structures.[28] But first, here is the CSS file ch11_14.css.

Listing 11.37 **The CSS Formatting**

```
01 * {
02   background: white;
03 }
04 pre {
05  background: lightgray; color: blue;
06 }
07 #header {
08  width: 990px; height: 100px;
```

---

28. If you need additional tabs, you can just expand the structure accordingly.

```
09  margin: auto;
10  }
11  #content {
12    width: 990px; min-height: 500px;
13    margin: auto;
14  }
15  #footer {
16    width: 990px; height: 100px;
17    margin: auto;
18  }
```

Essentially, the three `div` areas in the web page are formatted to the same width and centered. And here is the simple script ch11_14_ready.js with which the tabs are created.

Listing 11.38   **The Second `div` Area Is Turned into Tabs**

```
01 $(function(){
02   $("#content").tabs();
03 });
```

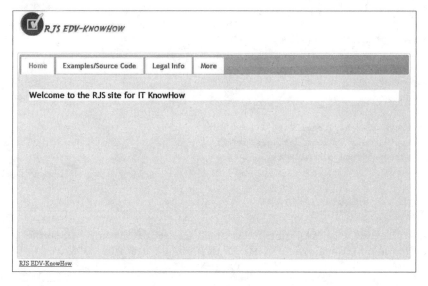

Figure 11.34   The basic structure of the web page.

The content loaded later via AJAX can contain its own structures. As an example, the file sourcecode.html is structured like Listing 11.39.

Listing 11.39   **Accordion Elements from HTML**

```
01 <script type="text/javascript">
02 $(function(){
03    $("#ch2").tabs();
04    $("#ch3").tabs();
05    $("#ch4").tabs();
06    $("#accordion").accordion({
07      "fillSpace": true
08    });
09 });
10 </script>
11 <div id="accordion" style="min-height:400px">
12   <h3><a href="#">Chapter 2</a></h3>
13   <div id="ch2">
14     <ul>
15       <li><a href="ch2/ch2_1.html">ch2_1</a></li>
16       <li><a href="ch2/ch2_2.html">ch2_2</a></li>
17       <li><a href="ch2/ch2_3.html">ch2_3</a></li>
18     </ul>
19   </div>
20   <h3><a href="#">Chapter 3</a></h3>
21   <div id="ch3">
22     <ul>
23       <li><a href="ch3/ch3_1.html">ch3_1</a></li>
24     </ul>
25   </div>
26   <h3><a href="#">Chapter 4</a></h3>
27   <div id="ch4">
28     <ul>
29       <li><a href="ch4/ch4_1.html">ch4_1</a></li>
30       <li><a href="ch4/ch4_2.html">ch4_2</a></li>
31       <li><a href="ch4/ch4_3.html">ch4_3</a></li>
32     </ul>
33   </div>
34 </div>
```

As you can see, the file loaded via AJAX contains essentially an `accordion` component as the outer structure. This, in turn, contains a set of tabs for each content area. This enables you to easily nest contents.

Caution

It is important that you integrate the script with which you generate the jQuery UI widgets into this file that is loaded later and not into the basic file.

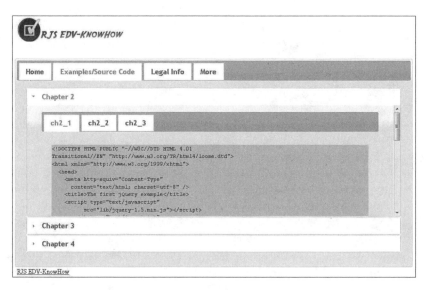

Figure 11.35   In the accordion, there are further tabs.

You can proceed accordingly if you require deeper levels of nesting.

> **Caution**
>
> Remember that the framework reaches its limits at some point, especially with fragments loaded later via AJAX and nested widgets. The framework can then no longer correctly construct components and widgets. But in that case, you could initialize the components or widgets already on loading the web page and simply hide them. When needed, you just reveal them again.

Summary

With jQuery UI, you have encountered the second pillar of the jQuery framework in this chapter. This offers visual control elements in the form of a number of powerful interaction plug-ins and widgets for constructing a graphical interface. Plus it gives you a CSS library with predesigned themes and powerful tools for designing your web application. And not least, jQuery UI expands the default effects of jQuery. Although most of these components are powerful and extremely widely configurable, using the predesigned structures of jQuery UI is relatively simple.

Plug-Ins

The entire jQuery framework consists of the jQuery core and the jQuery UI. Essentially, however, the framework can be expanded as much as you like. The expansions are referred to as **plug-ins**. They are pure JavaScript and Cascading Style Sheets (CSS) libraries, but they have to conform to certain predefined rules. By now, there is a huge number of these plug-ins, which are often available for free (and sometimes commercial) use via the jQuery website. Basically, any jQuery developer can publish plug-ins there. And you, as a website designer or user of the jQuery framework, can use these plug-ins if they offer a functionality that you do not want to create yourself and that the native framework does not offer. In this chapter, we take a closer look at these plug-ins and demonstrate how you can both use foreign plug-ins and write and publish your own plug-ins.

12.1   The jQuery Plug-In Page

To get a better idea about what the topic is all about, you should look at some plug-ins on the Web. At http://plugins.jquery.com/, you will find the official jQuery plug-in page. You can also get there from the normal jQuery website via the Plugins link at the very top of the page. There you will find the published plug-ins by numerous programmers in various categories. And, of course, search functions enable you to search for a specific plug-in.

Figure 12.1   The plug-in page.

12.1.1   Searching For and Using an Existing Plug-In

Let's say you want to use a plug-in that is presumably available via this jQuery plug-ins site. Suppose that you are looking for a navigation menu with a tree structure. Currently, neither the jQuery UI nor jQuery itself offers anything like this. You are probably aware that such an interactive navigation tree should belong in the Navigation category.[1] If you search the plug-ins listed there, you will sooner or later find a suitable plug-in. Or you can search directly via the corresponding input field in the web page.

For example, you might decide to enter the search term *Treeview*.[2] From the list of hits, you then select the most promising plug-in by clicking the corresponding hyperlink.

The next web page describes everything you need for using the plug-in—provided the programmer has made such a useful documentation available; starting with a description of the download, the dependencies, potential license conditions, right up to the required version of jQuery or the jQuery UI. There you will usually also find a preview with a demo for this plug-in (Try Out a Demonstration), at least if the programmer of the plug-in has made such a page available. The documentation of the plug-in is integrated fully into the usual jQuery documentation, so it includes a description in an overview, lists the available options, and so on.

---

1. Strictly speaking, the programmer of a plug-in has to sort it logically into the appropriate category. Otherwise, only a few users will be able to find the plug-in.

2. Search terms should generally be in English.

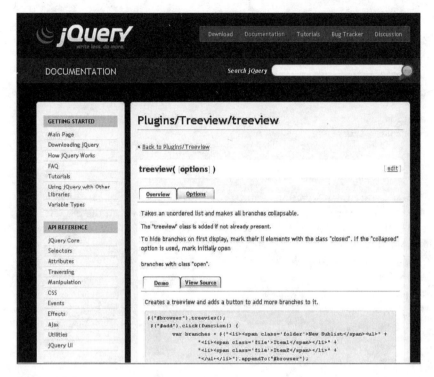

Figure 12.2 The plug-in documentation.

If you have now downloaded the plug-in (the required JavaScript and where applicable CSS files), you usually just have to integrate it into your web page in accordance with the documentation and then call the methods as described in the documentation and the demos—assuming, of course, that the plug-in programmer has made this information available in an extensive and comprehensive form, as is his responsibility).

Let's take a closer look at the Treeview that we have already used as an example. For the following example, we limit ourselves to a simple variation of the navigation tree. But it is the essence of these plug-ins that they often offer considerable functionality. How to use the popular plug-ins is well documented, and so using a more complex variation is easy.

Listing 12.1 **The Web Page That References a Plug-In (ch12_1.html)**

```
...
06    <link rel="stylesheet" type="text/css"
07      href="lib/ch12_1.css" />
08    <link rel="stylesheet"
09      href="lib/jquery-treeview/jquery.treeview.css" />
10    <script type="text/javascript"
```

```
11        src="lib/jquery-1.8.2.min.js"></script>
12     <script type="text/javascript" src=
13       "lib/jquery-treeview/jquery.treeview.js"></script>
14     <script type="text/javascript"
15        src="lib/ch12_1_ready.js"></script>
16   </head>
17   <body>
18     <h1>Navigation menu</h1>
19     <div id="output"></div>
20   </body>
21 </html>
```

In lines 8 and 9, you can see the integration of the specific CSS file for the interactive tree. In lines 12 and 13, you can see the reference to the JavaScript library with which the plug-in is implemented and that you have downloaded and made available on your server, together with the CSS file. In this particular case, these files are located in the directory lib/jquery-treeview. The navigation menu is to be dynamically generated in the div area (ch12_1_ready.js).

Listing 12.2   **A Tree View Based on a Plug-In**

```
01 $(function(){
02   var myTree = $("#output").treeview({
03     animated: "fast",
04     collapsed: true
05   });
06   var newSublist = $(
07       "<li><span class='folder'>Websites</span><ul>" +
08     "<li><span class='file'>" +
09     "<a href='http://www.rjs.de'>www.rjs.de</a>" +
10     "</span></li>" +
11     "<li><span class='file'>" +
12     "<a href='http://blog.rjs.de'>blog.rjs.de</a>" +
13     "</span></li>" +
14     "<li><span class='file'>" +
15     "<a href='http://www.ajax-net.de'>" +
16     "www.ajax-net.de</a>" +
17     "</span></li>" +
18     "<li><span class='file'>" +
19     "<a href='http://www.javafx.cc'>www.javafx.cc</a>" +
20     "</span></li></ul></li>").appendTo(myTree);
21   myTree.treeview({
22     add: newSublist
23   });
24 });
```

Creating the tree view happens simply via calling the method `treeview()`. Which parameters you can specify does, of course, depend on the specific programming, and you will have to look it up in the documentation for the plug-in concerned. In this specific case, we specify the speed with which the tree is opened and collapsed. Here, the plug-in's programmer evidently conformed to the notation commonly used in jQuery for this. The second parameter specifies that the tree is initially shown in collapsed view (lines 2–5).

Navigation Menu

⊞ Websites

Figure 12.3   The collapsed tree.

Up to now, there are no entries in the tree yet. They are added in lines 19–21 by calling `treeview()` again and via the option `add`. But, of course, there has to be substance behind the variable `newSublist`. The specific items in this version of a tree view are based on a list adapted via CSS. The `<li>` elements are assigned specific classes that define a main item (`folder`) and a subitem (`file`). In lines 5–16, you can see how we create four items below a main item.

Navigation Menu

⊟ Websites

 www.rjs.de

 blog.rjs.de

 www.ajax-net.de

 www.javafx.cc

Figure 12.4   The expanded menu.

As you have seen, plug-ins are usually very easy to use if the creator of the plug-in has developed and documented it properly.

12.1.2 Validation Plug-Ins

Validation plug-ins have a special position in my eyes. These are plug-ins that validate a user input following certain rules. The plug-in that you can load at http://jquery.bassistance.de/jquery-plugin-validation/ is even more special. This plug-in is used, among others, by Microsoft in Visual Studio for client-side validation, and in my eyes it is more than just a plug-in; you could even consider it a separate mini framework.

> **Tip**
>
> At http://docs.jquery.com/Plugins/Validation, you will find complete documentation plus numer-
> ous demo applications. Because of space limitations here, this text provides only a very brief
> overview of what this plug-in can offer.

Validation or checking the plausibility of user input is one of the most important ways of using JavaScript. Checking the plausibility of a web form means verifying whether the user input makes sense before the data is sent. If it does not make sense in accordance with the required preset data, measures are taken to correct this. Since Dynamic Hypertext Markup Language (DHTML) and Asynchronous JavaScript and XML (AJAX) are now widely used, the input is sometimes also checked immediately after the user exits an input field or sometimes even directly after entering a character.[3] The whole procedure is rather complicated, and the important point is not the programming itself. Validating a web form is only useful as a global concept that has to also include using the data further after sending and various other factors. When validating a web form, you have to be aware of numerous potential problems. These can be summarized with a few general questions:

- What needs to be validated? This essentially means: Which form fields need to be checked? You need to create rules that will be reflected in the plug-in via options.

- Which dependencies exist between user input and form fields?

- How does it need to be validated? This includes questions such as whether it is sufficient for a field to be filled in (a required field) or if the content has to have a specific form (for example, it must be numeric)? This also needs to be explicitly set out in rules or more precisely assigned methods.

- When will it be validated? For example, do you check the user input directly on an input field or only when the form is sent? Or on leaving a web page, if the data is collected across several web pages before it is sent to the server?

- How and when will it be validated? On the server or on the client? Or redundantly in both places? Mostly, a redundant check is indispensable, but we are concentrating exclusively on the client-side in the context of jQuery.

As you can see, you have much to think about in the context of a validation concept. The task of weighing the required checks against the difficulty of implementing them in practice and the effort involved is not at all easy. In any case, planning a professional web page with user interaction plus a plausibility check invariably takes a lot more time than eventually putting it into practice.

Ultimately, it is up to you how to react when the user enters the wrong information. Usually, you will want to prevent the form data being sent until the error is corrected, and it makes sense to give the user appropriate feedback to that purpose. And for providing this feedback, there are again certain jQuery techniques or jQuery UI widgets that are particularly well suited to the task.

---

3. But the latter is rarely appropriate.

But let's get back to the plug-in itself. Essentially, you need to integrate the plug-in library and mark the form fields you want to check in a particular way. Appropriate preset rules will then already take effect when applying a `validate()` method offered via plug-in. If these do not suffice for your purposes, you can define custom rules that you pass as options to the validation method. Let's first look at a demo application that manages with just the default validations and messages (ch12_2.html).

Listing 12.3   **A Form That We Want to Validate via Plug-In**

```
...
10    <script src="lib/jquery-validate/jquery.validate.js"
11      type="text/javascript"></script>
12    <script type="text/javascript"
13      src= "lib/ch12_2_ready.js"></script>
14   </head>
15   <body>
16     <h1>Form Validation</h1>
17     <form class="cmxform" id="myForm"
18       method="get" action="">
19       <fieldset>
20         <legend>
21           A validated form with default messages
22           and validity checks
23         </legend>
24         <p><label for="sname">Surname</label>
25           <em>*</em>
26           <input id="sname" name="sname" size="25"
27             class="required" minlength="2" />
28         </p>
29         <p><label for="fname">First name</label>
30           <em>*</em>
31           <input id="fname" name="fname" size="25"
32             class="required" minlength="2" />
33         </p>
34         <p><label for="email">E-Mail</label>
35           <em>*</em>
36           <input id="email" name="email" size="25"
37             class="required email" />
38         </p>
39         <p><label for="url">Website</label>
40           <em style="visibility:hidden">*</em>
41           <input id="url" name="url" size="25"
42             class="url" value="" />
43         </p>
44         <p><label for="comment">Comment</label>
45           <em>*</em>
```

```
46              <textarea id="comment" name="comment"
47                cols="25" rows="5"
48                class="required"></textarea>
49          </p>
50          <p>
51            <input class="submit" type="submit"
52              value="OK"/>
53          </p>
54        </fieldset>
55      </form>
56    </body>
57 </html>
```

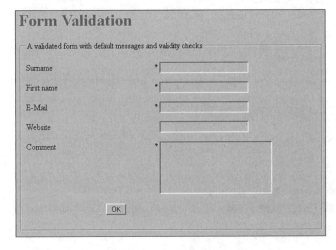

Figure 12.5   The web form. Required fields are marked with an asterisk.

As you can see, we have integrated the central JavaScript file of the plug-in (jquery.validate.js) in lines 10 and 11. Note the classes that are assigned for the individual input fields, plus the attributes for minimum length. These attributes are the basis for the validation via the plug-in. Validation methods are attached to them and called in the background via validate(). The JavaScript code is once again almost obscenely short[4] (ch12_2_ready.js).

Listing 12.4   **Using the Plug-In**

```
01 $(function(){
02    $("#myForm").validate();
03 });
```

4. If you compare it to the effort involved in a manual validation routine.

To fully validate the form, you merely need to apply the method to the form. Thanks to the selection of the classes and length specification, this ensures that all required fields are filled. In case of an error, sending the form data is stopped and a default error message appears behind the input field and describes the problem. After all errors have been fixed, the form is sent.

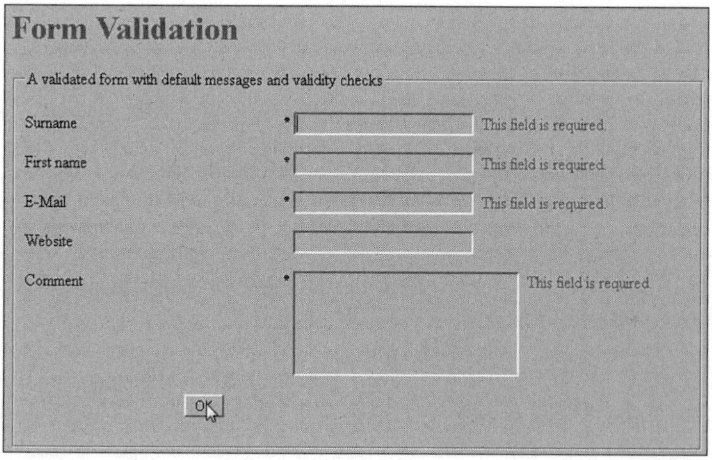

Form Validation

A validated form with default messages and validity checks

Surname   • [   ]   This field is required.

First name   • [   ]   This field is required.

E-Mail   • [   ]   This field is required.

Website   [   ]

Comment   • [   ]   This field is required.

[OK]

Figure 12.6   The fields are required fields.

> **Tip**
>
> The plug-in directory contains a subdirectory localization with JavaScript files with country-specific error messages. If you want to change the error messages to another language, you can open the file for the relevant language (for example, messages_de.js for German) and insert the options listed there (in curly brackets) into the file jquery.validate.js under the option `defaults` as value of `messages`. The error messages will then be displayed in the corresponding language.

If you enter an insufficient number of characters in the input fields where a minimum length is specified, you also get a notification. But the logic goes further because you can even check whether the input is valid in accordance with certain limitations. In our example, we check whether a valid email address and URL have been entered. The corresponding classes for the input fields specify that these need to be validated.

Figure 12.7   The email does not have the @, and the structure of the URL is evidently also incorrect.

Figure 12.8   Now the plug-in is satisfied.

> **Note**
>
> If you want to send the form data and several errors are detected, all errors will be indicated. The first invalid field then usually gets the focus. Incidentally, the validation check occurs only at the first attempt to send the data. So long as a user has not tried to send the form, he can jump around the fields without triggering error notices, even if he enters invalid data. But once errors have been detected and indicated during an attempt to send, each field is checked immediately after a value is entered, and the error message is updated or deleted accordingly once input has ended. This dynamic behavior of the validation check is explicitly intended to offer the user appropriate usability for using a form.

The `validate()` method is the core of the entire plug-in.[5] It works very effectively already in the default configuration—as you have just seen. If you want, you can assign a whole number of options to the method, as described in Table 12.1.

Table 12.1   **A Small Selection of Possible Options for** `validate()`

Option	Description
`rules`	A definition of rules in the form of key-value pairs. The key is the name of an element or a group of check boxes or option boxes. The value is an object with rules or parameter pairs or a string.
`messages`	Key-value pairs with adapted error messages.
Various events	For various events, validations can be triggered. This includes `onsubmit`, `onfocusout`, `onkeyup`, and `onclick`. You assign callback functions in the options as usual.
`errorClass`	Specifying an individual error class.
`highlight`	Specifying how invalid fields should be highlighted.

If you now want to specify the validation further, the plug-in offers two central elements for this:

5. But as we will see a bit later, it is not the only method.

- Validation methods via which the logic for validation is implemented. These can, for example, check the correct structure of an email. There is already a whole set of standard methods, some of which have also worked in the background in our example. But you can also create custom methods that you will then have to assign in rules.
- Rules that associate a validation method with an element.

Table 12.2 describes the most important standard methods for validation that are already automatically available to you and will be automatically applied when specifying a class with the same name for an element.

Table 12.2   **Standard Validation Methods**

Method	Description
`accept(extension)`	Demands a specific file extension.
`creditcard()`	Attempts to ensure credit card format.
`date()`	Valid date.
`dateDE()`	Valid date in German format.
`dateISO()`	Valid ISO date.
`digits()`	Only digits.
`email()`	Valid email format.
`equalTo(other)`	Test with a comparison value.
`max(value)`	Specifies a maximum value.
`maxlength(length)`	Specifies a maximum number of characters.
`min(value)`	Specifies a minimum value.
`minlength(length)`	Specifies a minimum number of characters.
`number()`	Demands a decimal number format.
`numberDE()`	Demands decimal number format in German format. In addition to German, several other language formats are possible.
`rangelength(range)` or `range(range)`	Specifies a value range.
`required()`	Specifies that a field is required. The method is available in several variations.
`url()`	Valid URL.

The plug-in itself currently contains several other methods in addition to `validate()`.

Table 12.3   **Methods of the Plug-In**

Method	Description
`validate(options)`	The already used validation of a form.
`valid()`	Returns a Boolean value indicating whether the checked form is valid.
`rules()`	Returns the validation rules of the first selected element.

`rules("add", rules )`	Adds the specified rules and returns all rules of the first matched element. Such a rule could, for example, be as follows: `$("#name").rules("add", {`
	`  minlength: 5`
	`});`
	The requirement is that the parent form has previously been checked with `validate()`.

`rules("remove", rules )`	Removes the specified rules and returns all rules of the first matched element.
`removeAttrs(attributes)`	Removes the specified attributes of the first matched element and returns these attributes.

Let's output the options that describe the rules for the email fields in the preceding example. To that end, we add a button and a `div` area for the output (ch12_3.html). Listing 12.5 then shows how we output these rules (ch12_3_ready.js).

Listing 12.5   **The Rules for a Field**

```
01 $(function(){
02   $("#myForm").validate();
03   $("button:first").click(function(){
04     var rule = $("#email").rules();
05     for (i in rule) {
06       $("div:first").append(i + ": " + rule[i]
07           + "<br />");
08     };
09   });
10 });
```

As mentioned previously, rules are pure options, so with the loop in the script you will get the key and associated value in each case.

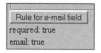

Figure 12.9   The two rules for an email field.

As you can see, the email field in the default configuration is a required field and also requires a suitable format. Corresponding to this structure, you can also create custom rules in option form. Plus, you can link the validation methods listed above with suitable events.

12.2   Creating Custom Plug-Ins

Let's now move on to how you can create your own custom plug-ins. But first you need to understand why you might want to do this in the first place.

12.2.1   Why Create Custom Plug-Ins?

If you require certain functionalities more often, you will usually create a function. In certain circumstances, you would also create classes or objects, provided this is possible within a technology such as JavaScript. The same idea also lies behind plug-ins:

> **Reusability of existing functionalities plus universal application to the widest possible extent**

As you have seen with the foreign plug-ins, highly complex functionalities can be made available in such a way that a potential user can use them easily and simply. Creating plug-ins has much to do with the idea of object-oriented programming or modularization, where inner structures are encapsulated and made available via a call that is as universal and simple as possible.

The jQuery plug-in mechanism enables you to add methods and functionalities to a package (JavaScript file) that can be used directly as part of the framework. Many components of the jQuery framework itself also consist of plug-ins.

12.2.2   Creating Your First Plug-In

Writing a plug-in takes place in two steps. First, you write any methods and functions that you want to make available. The central point is that you assign these functionalities to *a specific namespace*: jQuery.fn[6] for methods and jQuery for functions. Also, this functionality should be offered in a separate JavaScript file that the user later simply needs to integrate and that has to adhere to a fixed naming rule: jquery.[*name of plug-in*].js.

Listing 12.6 shows an example for such a JavaScript file for a plug-in that will have the name DragWithStatusLight (jquery.dragwithstatuslight.js).

---

6. We have already extensively discussed the philosophy of namespaces in jQuery.

Listing 12.6   **The Source Code for a Plug-in**

```
01 jQuery.fn.dragwithstatuslight = function(){
02   return this.each(function(){
03     $(this).css({
04       border: "5px outset", cursor: "move"
05     });
06     $(this).draggable({
07       start: function(event, ui){
08         $(this).css({
09           opacity: 0.5
10         });
11       },
12       stop: function(event, ui){
13         status = "";
14         $(this).css({
15           opacity: 1
16         });
17       },
18       drag: function(event, ui){
19         status = "X/Y-Coordinates: " +
20         event.pageX + "/" + event.pageY;
21       }
22     });
23   });
24 };
```

The idea behind the functionality of this plug-in is simple. Applying the method dragwithstatuslight() makes an element or a group of elements in the web page draggable. So far, the functionality is the same as offered by the method draggable(). You can also see that we use this method in line 6.

But our plug-in will take this functionality further. Each draggable element will be marked with a frame, plus the mouse cursor will change if it moves over a draggable element. It changes to the commonly used cross to indicate that an element in a graphical interface is draggable. We are using the css() method for this.

Another feature of our plug-in is that the dragged element is set to transparent while the position change is active. We implement this by overriding the start option of the draggable() method. If the user drags the element, it becomes transparent. After the element is dropped, the transparency is removed. To do this, we override the stop option of the draggable() method.

In line 13, you can see that the value of the status property is set. More precisely, this property is set to empty when the dragging process ends. You will probably be aware that we address the status line of the browser with this property. But why do we empty the status line here? Well, we want to display continuously updated information there while the user is dragging an object with the mouse; that is, the X- and Y-coordinates of the dragged object. To do this, we override the `drag` option of `draggable()`. So, we are processing an event object with the desired information during the dragging event at even the most minute mouse movement.

> **Caution**
>
> Outputting information via a browser status line is a bit ambivalent. For instance, the status line is absolutely not in the visual field of the user, and most users will completely ignore status line information. So, only optional additional information should be placed into this area. However, the bigger problem is that accessing the status line via JavaScript is disabled in the default settings of some browsers or can be disabled by the user. So, this status information via the plug-in is useful only to a limited extent. But that is not what it is all about here. We want to show you how to create a plug-in.

As you can see in line 2, our plug-in returns an object of the type `jQuery` or a collection of that type.[7] This is a core principle of plug-ins in general!

Because our new function has been assigned to the namespace `jQuery.fn`, it can be used on all jQuery objects via the following syntax.

Listing 12.7 **Using the Custom Plug-In**

```
.dragwithstatuslight();
```

This would happen, for example, like this, if you want to make all images in the web page draggable.

Listing 12.8 **All Images in the Web Pages Are Draggable, Corresponding to the New Functionality**

```
$("img").dragwithstatuslight();
```

Let's use the plug-in as part of a complete example (ch12_4.html).

Listing 12.9 **Using the Plug-In**

```
...
06    <link type="text/css" href=
07      "lib/css/ui-lightness/jquery-ui-1.8.24.custom.css"
08      rel="Stylesheet" />
09    <link rel="stylesheet" type="text/css"
10      href="lib/ch12_4.css" />
11    <script type="text/javascript"
```

---

7. We iterate over all preceding objects with `each()`.

```
12        src="lib/jquery-1.8.2.min.js"></script>
13    <script type="text/javascript" src=
14        "lib/js/jquery-ui-1.8.24.custom.min.js"></script>
15    <script type="text/javascript" src=
16        "lib/jquery-dragwithstatuslight/
          jquery.dragwithstatuslight.js" ></script>
17    <script type="text/javascript" src=
18        "lib/ch12_4_ready.js"></script>
19  </head>
20  <body>
21    <h1>Using the Plug-In DragWithStatus</h1>
22    <img src="images/pic1.jpg" />
23      <img src="images/pic2.jpg" />
24      <img src="images/pic3.jpg" />
25      <img src="images/pic4.jpg" />
26  </body>
27  </html>
```

As you can see, we have to integrate numerous CSS and JavaScript files in the web page. These include resources of jQuery, but also the jQuery UI (because we use one of its components in the plug-in—otherwise, it would not be necessary) and, of course, the plug-in itself.

Figure 12.10   The draggable objects have a frame. The image that has just been dragged is transparent, and the mouse pointer is in the shape of a cross.

In lines 15 and 16, you can see the reference to our plug-in file. Listing 12.10 shows how you apply it to all images in the web page (ch12_4_ready.js).

Listing 12.10   **The Plug-In Method Is Easy to Use**

```
01 $(function(){
02   $("img").dragwithstatuslight();
03 });
```

Figure 12.11   If the browser supports it, the coordinates of the dragged element will be displayed.

12.2.3   The Main Rules for Creating a Simple Plug-In

Here is a summary of the main rules and a few tips for creating a simple plug-in:

- The most important point: Assign your methods to the `jQuery.fn` object and all functions to the `jQuery` object.

- The name of your JavaScript file should follow this pattern: jquery.[*name of plug-in*].js.

- Within methods, you can reference the current `jQuery` object via `this`.

- Each method or function must end with a semicolon; in some cases, `this` is not necessary in normal JavaScript.

- A method must return one or several objects of the type `jQuery`, unless it is explicitly specified differently.

- If you iterate over a set with matched elements, the cleanest way is working with `this.each()`.

- To avoid unsolvable naming conflicts, you should attach the plug-in to jQuery instead of to $. Then the user can define an alias via `noConflict()` if a conflict arises.

12.2.4   Rules for Creating More Complex Plug-Ins

If you want to create more complex plug-ins, adhere to a few more rules to avoid problems. Here is a brief overview of these rules.

Collecting Static Functions in Objects

If you require several public static methods, declaratively collect them in a single object, as shown in Listing 12.11.

Listing 12.11   **Collecting in an Object**

```
jQuery.log = {
  success : function() { ... },
```

```
  error : function() { ... },
  warning : function() { ... },
  debug : function() { ... }
};
```

This avoids splitting the namespace into too many fragments.

Hiding Variables

It is one of the core principles of object-oriented programming to hide variables. When creating plug-ins, you should also make use of this principle. Variables should not be defined globally if possible, but should be hidden in functions (although this is, of course, not done in strict object-oriented programming—there are no functions there) and methods. By passing values and via return values, you can pass on the content of variables if required.

Options jQuery.extend or jQuery.fn.extends for Setting Defaults

More complex plug-ins usually require various setting options. You can pass these setting options to the plug-in via parameters, but the best way is by using options that are initialized with appropriate default values. The best solution is presetting options via extends() or jQuery.fn.extends(), and if options are specified, these are used instead of the preset values. This works, for example, as shown in Listing 12.12 (jquery.dragwithstatus.js).

Listing 12.12   **Optional Settings on Calling the Plug-In**

```
jQuery.fn.dragwithstatus = function(options) {
  defaultvalues = jQuery.extend({
    border: "5px outset",
    cursor:"move" ,
    opacity : 0.5,
    statusinfo:true
  }, options);
  // rest of plug-in (*)
}
```

> **Tip**
> You can also pass parameters to the function with the selected syntax in addition to options. If you do not require parameters, you can also expand the jQuery object itself via jQuery.fn.extends() rather than jQuery.extend().

We can now use the plug-in both with and without options, as shown in Listing 12.13.

Listing 12.13 **Different Ways of Using the Plug-In**

```
$("img").dragwithstatus({border:"50px", opacity:0.1,statusinfo:false});
$("#i1").dragwithstatus();
$("div").dragwithstatus({cursor:"cursor" });
```

Adaptable Animations

If you work with animations in your plug-in for certain events, it is very helpful for the user if you make the type of animation adaptable.

Avoid Provoking Name Conflicts

You should not work with $ within your plug-in, so as to not restrict the use of alias. Within your plug-in, you can also work with an alias yourself if required.

12.2.5 An Example for a Plug-In with Options

Let's now create an extension of our first plug-in. This time, we want to make it configurable with options. To do this, we just need to combine the above template for jquery.dragwithstatus.js with the previous lines 2–23 of jquery.dragwithstatuslight.js and make it possible for the preset values to be used if no options are specified, and for the option values to override the preset values if they are specified.

Listing 12.14 **The JavaScript File for the Modified Plug-In**

```
01 jQuery.fn.dragwithstatus = function(options){
02 // Defining default values and
03   // overriding with options
04  var defaultvalues = jQuery.extend({
05    border: "5px outset",
06    cursor: "move", opacity: 0.5,
07    statusinfo: true
08  }, options);
09  return this.each(function(){
10    $(this).css({
11      border: defaultvalues.border,
12      cursor: defaultvalues.cursor
13    });
14    $(this).draggable({
15      start: function(event, ui){
16        $(this).css({
17          opacity: defaultvalues.opacity
18        });
19      },
20      stop: function(event, ui){
```

```
21        status = "";
22        $(this).css({
23          opacity: 1
24        });
25      },
26      drag: function(event, ui){
27        if (defaultvalues.statusinfo)
28          status = "X/Y-Coordinates: " +
29          event.pageX + "/" + event.pageY;
30      }
31    });
32  });
33 };
```

In lines 4–7, you can see how the preset values for four options are set up. The second parameter is the name for the options that are optionally passed declaratively to the plug-in and in that case override the preset values.

In the relevant JavaScript file, we are working with exactly that `defaultvalues` object and use either the contained properties for presetting property values or the options specified by the user.

Listing 12.15   Using the New Variant of the Plug-In (ch12_5_ready.js)

```
01 $(function(){
02    $("img:first").dragwithstatus({
03      border: "10px inset",
04      opacity: 0.1,
05      statusinfo: false
06    });
07    $("img:eq(1)").dragwithstatus({
08      border: "1px outset",
09      opacity: 0.7,
10      statusinfo: false
11    });
12    $("img:eq(2)").dragwithstatus();
13    $("img:eq(3)").dragwithstatus({
14      border: "5px outset",
15      opacity: 0.2,
16      statusinfo: true
17    });
18 });
```

The method is applied to three images with different options, and for one image we do not specify any options.

Using the Plug-In DragWithStatus

Figure 12.12   The method was called with different options.

12.2.6   Another Example for a Plug-In with Options

To make things clearer, let's take a look at another little plug-in. I had the idea while practicing with my band. We usually start our practice by playing some blues, and after so many years no one wants to be responsible for choosing the key.[8] So, I suggested using a random generator to choose the musical key and set it up as a jQuery plug-in (jquery.keys.js).

Listing 12.16   **Using a Random Generator in a Plug-In**

```
01 jQuery.fn.keys = function(options){
02      // Inner function
03      function keyGenerator(){
04          var key = ["C","C#", "D", "D#", "E", "F",
05            "F#","G","G#", "A", "B", "H"];
06          var index=Math.floor(Math.random()*key.length);
07          return key[index];
08      }
09      var defaultvalues = jQuery.extend({
10          border: "1px outset",
11          width: "150px",
12          opacity: 0.5,
13          height: "60px",
14          fontSize: "42px",
15          textAlign: "center",
16          paddingTop: "5px",
17          background: "black",
18          color: "white"
```

8. I t feels like we have already played in each key a countless number of times.

```
19      }, options);
20      return this.each(function(){
21          $(this).css({
22              border: defaultvalues.border,
23              width: defaultvalues.width,
24              height: defaultvalues.height,
25              opacity: defaultvalues.opacity,
26              fontSize: defaultvalues.fontSize,
27              textAlign: defaultvalues.textAlign,
28              paddingTop: defaultvalues.paddingTop,
29              background: defaultvalues.background,
30              color: defaultvalues.color
31          });
32          $(this).html(keyGenerator());
33      });
34 };
```

Once again, you can see preset options plus the possibility of the user overwriting them. The implemented logic in lines 3–8 simply chooses one key at random from an array with possible keys and returns it. You can then simply output it in a div area that is formatted corresponding to the preset values or options. Listing 12.17 shows the plug-in in action (ch12_6_ready.js).

Listing 12.17   **Using the Plug-In with Options**

```
01 $(function(){
02   $("button:first").click(function(){
03     $("#key").keys({
04       color: "blue",    background: "gray"
05     });
06   });
07 });
```

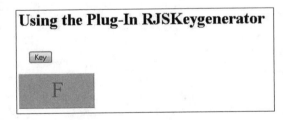

Figure 12.13   Outputting the random value from the array.

12.3   Publishing a Plug-In

Let's now look at how you can publish a plug-in. To publish it via the jQuery site, you need to have an account there. If you have already registered, you need to log in.

Figure 12.14   Before you can publish a plug-in, you first need to log in.

After the login, you will see the Add Plugin link in your personal area.

Figure 12.15   Adding a plug-in.

After you have clicked this link, you can enter all the important details for your plug-in on the right side.

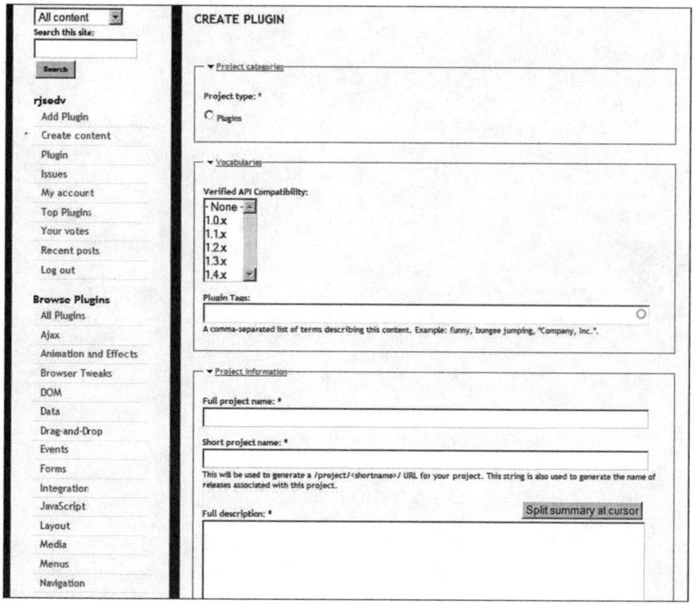

Figure 12.16   The details of your plug-in.

This includes the type, the required version of the application programming interface (API), a description, tags, and a reference to your home page. You can also specify a live demo of your plug-in and provide other information. After you have entered all the information and sent the data, your plug-in will be officially available.

Summary

In this chapter about plug-ins, you have encountered one of the most interesting and most demanding areas of programming with jQuery. In particular, much will happen here in the near future. Plug-ins expand the already very powerful and capable framework almost indefinitely. And you can use these feature without any problems. However, you can also very easily present your own ideas to a wider public via plug-ins within the jQuery web page. As you can see, plug-ins facilitate give and take, which from a programming point of view constitutes the Web 2.0 in the best sense of participating and joining in.

jQuery Mobile

Web technologies on mobile devices are now totally ready to face the competition, not least thanks to Hypertext Markup Language 5 (HTML5), but also due to Cascading Style Sheets 3 (CSS3), particularly in combination with JavaScript and a powerful framework. It is rather charming to transfer traditional Rich Internet Applications (RIAs) for normal web browsers on PC platforms and related worlds to mobile devices or to adapt them accordingly (because most modern cell phones, tablets, and smartphones are Internet capable and have a standard browser). You do not even need to be online to be able to use such apps while on the move. You can simply save the app in the mobile device, load it from there, and use it offline, provided it is set up accordingly. In our environment, there is a framework to facilitate developing such mobile apps based on RIA techniques: **jQuery Mobile**. In this final chapter of our book, we take a closer look at it. The potential is enormous, especially if you consider that you can, of course, also use the numerous jQuery plug-ins in the mobile category as well.

13.1 Basics

You can access the website of the jQuery Mobile framework at http://jquerymobile.com/. You can also find the link to the jQuery Mobile site at the top of jQuery and jQuery UI website.

> **Note**
>
> At the time of writing, the latest stable version is jQuery Mobile 1.2.0. It is not to be expected that there will be any major changes in the near future, but to be on the safe side, you can always check the website for details of the latest version.

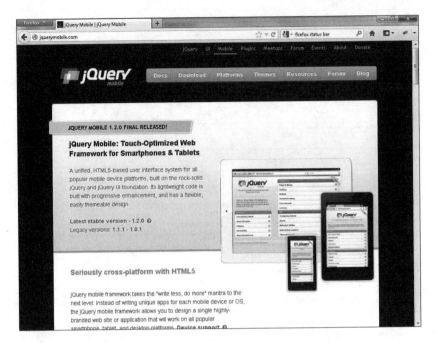

Figure 13.1   The jQuery Mobile website.

Basically, the idea behind the mobile framework is simple and follows the pattern of normal RIAs: Based on JavaScript, a unified user interface (UI) is constructed that works on the most important tablets, cell phones, and smartphones or their browsers. The main problem of jQuery Mobile (and other technologies aimed at mobile devices) is accommodating the huge range of mobile platforms. You need to take into account the smaller screen sizes and lower resolutions plus still low color depth on most mobile devices. On top of that, we face different input options and special effects such as reacting to rotating a device by automatically rotating the screen.

To stand a chance at all with purely standardized web technologies, you need to work with pure, semantic HTML as the basis of mobile RIAs. In terms of logic, only JavaScript will operate on it, whereas CSS takes on all formatting[1] (just as *should* be done with RIAs on desktops). Although you can also create workarounds on the desktop that diverge from this rule or simply do it the dirty way, this would prove absolutely fatal in the mobile world. The Mobile jQuery framework takes a radical approach and explicitly requires support of HTML5 and CSS3 to ensure error-free use. In particular, the web page should be created based on HTML5[2] because the framework uses this standard consistently so that the dynamic features and widgets can be implemented in the first place. And it builds consistently on jQuery itself.

1. Even then, there is still plenty of work to be done for the large number of different platforms; just think of the varying screen sizes or different input and control options.

2. At least you should avoid using obsolete tags, in particular for specifying layout formatting.

13.1.1 The Platforms

jQuery Mobile is a touch-optimized web framework based on graphical widgets that attempts to offer a unified UI across all popular platforms for mobile devices. Instead of developing different applications for different devices and operating systems, the aim is to need just one application. Currently, the following mobile operating systems are supported:

- iOS
- Android
- BlackBerry
- Bada
- Windows Phone/Mobile
- Firefox Mobile
- Chrome for Android
- Opera Mobile
- Kindle 3 and Fire
- Nook Color
- Tizen
- Palm webOS
- Symbian
- MeeGo

With Opera, the browser support includes arguably the most important browser in the mobile area, but also Fennec, Ozone, Netfront, and Phonegap. The fully supported browsers are referred to as A-grade browsers (here, for the mobile domain), and the partially supported versions as B-grade or C-grade browsers; of course, the specific version is relevant. At http://jquerymobile.com/gbs/, you can find a complete list that tells you which platforms are supported and to what degree. Note that new devices offer better support for HTML5 and CSS3, so the framework's widgets are likely to run better on more recent devices than on older versions.

> **Caution**
>
> When creating mobile RIAs, remember that many cell phones and smartphones that are by no means outdated do not meet the required standards. And if a mobile device does not support the required standards or does not use an A-grade browser, the web pages will display according to the principle of error tolerance. In the "worst" case, you will see a web page without the widgets that were intended by the web page creator. This web page will generally still work in part, but the user will have to scroll around a lot and it will not look great. There are still some mobile devices that do not yet fully support CSS3 but otherwise manage quite well with the framework. In that case, rounded corners might not be displayed or animation effects may not run properly, but the widgets will otherwise work fine.

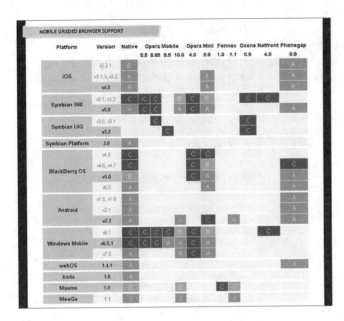

Figure 13.2   The currently supported browsers and operating systems.

In terms of widgets, the Mobile framework offers the familiar components from jQuery UI as long as they are appropriate for mobile devices. They are optimized for use on touch-screens, plus there are some new events. The CSS framework of jQuery UI has been extended and adapted to the Mobile target platform. Mobile jQuery works intensively with CSS3, as mentioned previously. Via special `data-role` attributes, an automatic internalization takes place in the background, which you should not underestimated. Accessibility features such as WAI-ARIA are offered to support screen readers. The performance limitations in the mobile environment are also taken into account throughout the design of the framework. This is reflected by the file size of the files you need to download. The entire framework has a remarkably small file size; the entire mobile functionality is contained in about 24 KB in the compressed version.

13.1.2   Downloading and Integrating the Framework

You can download the current version of the framework from http://jquerymobile.com/download/. The Zip file contains all necessary resources, but jQuery Mobile is also offered via CDN, plus there is now a new Download Builder tool that lets you build a custom bundle with just the components you need.

For a mobile application, you just have to make the CSS file and the JavaScript file available on the web server and integrate it in accordance with the rules for jQuery UI. We will shortly take a look at some application examples.

13.1.3   Alternatives

Of course, there are also alternatives for the Mobile framework. We do not list them all here, but want to briefly mention some of them nonetheless. jQTouch,[3] for example, is a very interesting plug-in for jQuery that is especially geared toward mobile devices with the WebKit browser. This includes the iPhone, Palm Pre, and smartphones with Google's Android, such as G1.

At the time of this writing, the plug-in is still in the beta version, but this already shows where it is heading. With jQTouch and jQuery, the applications based on HTML, CSS, and JavaScript are intended to support in particular specific properties of the WebKit browser and the telephone hardware itself (including motion sensors and smartphone touchscreens, but also loading images in advance and page transitions and new options for full-screen mode). As a result, orientation changes in a web application can be processed just as well as multitouch gestures.

For both, jQTouch also offers suitable events to which you can bind callbacks as usual in jQuery. In addition, special CSS selectors in jQTouch support gestures. For example, such a selector ensures that a link within a list element reacts to the pushing finger gesture. And selectors such as `.back`, `.cancel`, or `.goback` cooperate with hardware components such as the Back button under Apple.

Figure 13.3   The project website of jQTouch.

3. jQTouch is open source under the MIT license and hosted at http://jqtouch.com/.

On the topic of CSS, applications can also be visually adapted via themes in the style of jQuery, and the plug-in contains its own themes.

One interesting aspect of the plug-in, particularly regarding the iPhone, is that you can easily create innovative services without being held back by the hurdle of the App Store.

13.2   The Role System and `data-role`

Let's get back to the framework to which we are devoting this final chapter. In HTML5, you try to concentrate completely on the structure of a page and leave the design entirely to style sheets. In modern pages, you therefore limit yourself to as few tags as possible that only describe the structure. Of crucial importance is, apart from various new elements, the good old `div` element that is supported by new special block elements with specialized tasks or roles in HTML5. And this thought is also consistently reflected by the framework, although it limits itself mostly to established block elements (`div`).

The Mobile jQuery framework works with a role system for elements of a web page to tag widgets. Via the attribute `data-role`, each element that is supposed to fulfill a particular task is tagged via standardized values. For example, as the user you usually do not need to program directly when tagging a widget, as is the case with jQuery UI.[4] You can turn a `div` element, for example, into a button simply by tagging it with the attribute and a specific value. Therefore, you do not need an explicit script area and corresponding statement as you do in jQuery UI. All widgets that you want to use in the framework can be created in this way. You can also create page transitions, links, and pages themselves entirely without manual programming via this approach.

13.3   The Basic Structure of a Mobile Web Page

The basic structure of a web page that you want to profit from jQuery Mobile will generally follow the same pattern. As mentioned earlier, you use the `data-role` attribute throughout the framework and explicitly document in a DOCTYPE statement that you are using HTML as the basis. An entire web page in the vocabulary of the framework can mean one page, but the term *page* generally refers to something else. It indicates a separate segment within the web page. The typical site structure represents either an individual page (if there is not much content) or internally linked pages.

In the body of a single HTML file, each view or element that you want to serve as a page in terms of the mobile screen (normally a `div` element) is assigned the attribute `data-role="page"`. Within this container, you can use any valid HTML statements (except for the statements of the basic framework itself). You would usually structure this page segment with a separate header, content, and footer area, an idea that is also behind several new elements in HTML5. These areas are in turn marked with specific values of `data-role` within the framework (in other words, with attributes, not with separate elements such as `footer` or `header`, in contrast to HTML5).

4. Although largely the same happens in the background as when using a method of jQuery UI.

Listing 13.1   **A Basic Structure for a Page**

```
<div data-role="page">
  <div data-role="header">...</div>
  <div data-role="content">...</div>
  <div data-role="footer">...</div>
 </div>
```

This would be a complete web page that fulfills these requirements, contains only one page, and is integrated into our usual project structure (ch13_1.html).

Listing 13.2   **A Typical Basic Structure**

```
01 <!DOCTYPE HTML>
02 <html>
03   <head>
04     <meta http-equiv="Content-Type"
05        content="text/html; charset=utf-8" />
06     <title>jQuery Mobile</title>
07     <link rel="stylesheet" type="text/css" href=
08        "lib/jquery.mobile-1.2.0/
          jquery.mobile-1.2.0.min.css" />
09     <link rel="stylesheet" type="text/css"
10        href="lib/kap13_1.css" />
11     <script type="text/javascript" src=
12        "lib/jquery-1.8.2.min.js"></script>
13     <script type="text/javascript" src=
14        "lib/jquery.mobile-1.2.0/
          jquery.mobile-1.2.0.min.js"></script>
15     <script type="text/javascript" src=
16        "lib/kap13_1_ready.js"></script>
17   </head>
18   <body>
19     <div data-role="page">
20       <div data-role="header">
21         <h1>The Page Title</h1>
22       </div>
23       <div data-role="content">
24         <p>
25           The normal content
26         </p>
27       </div>
28       <div data-role="footer">
29         <h4>The Footer</h4>
30       </div>
31     </div>
32   </body>
33 </html>
```

In lines 7 and 8, you can see the link to the style sheet file of the framework. You should integrate this file as the first CSS file. If required, you then integrate your own CSS files afterward.

> **Note**
>
> In the examples of this chapter, we include references to our own CSS and JavaScript files, even if we do not explicitly use them in an example.

In lines 11 and 12, we integrate the normal jQuery library. After this, you can see the reference to the mobile JavaScript library in lines 13 and 14. If you are also using jQuery UI,[5] you can place the reference before or after the mobile JavaScript library. Only after this, your own JavaScript files can follow (if required).

If you mark the `div` elements in the HTML file, the framework will ensure on a suitable platform that the areas are formatted according to a chosen theme. And as mentioned earlier, the `page-block` of lines 19–31 is perceived as a page.

Figure 13.4   The page has been formatted by the framework.

13.4   Linking Pages

Fundamentally, the Mobile framework supports all standard link types of HTML. When linking pages, you need to distinguish in the framework between external and internal links, which result from the different interpretation of what constitutes a page.

13.4.1   External Links via Hijax

In the default setting, jQuery Mobile works with an AJAX request (Hijax) in case of links to external pages, as long as the reference is to the same domain. In contrast to a desktop application, the cursor in mobile apps is changed so that you can see when files are loaded later (the rotating egg timer or spinner). If the request was successful, the new data is integrated into the Document Object Model (DOM), and the mobile widgets are reinitialized. Then the new page is displayed in animation.

---

5. In case of mobile apps, this should not really be necessary; this is exactly what you should use the mobile widgets for.

If the link refers to another domain or is marked with `rel="external"` or `data-ajax="false"` or has a `target` attribute, a new page is loaded via the conventional way instead.

The framework also supports Hypertext Transfer Protocol (HTTP) protocols for other link types, some of which are results of the mobile environment. For example, it supports `mailto:`[6] for email and `tel:`, `wtai:` and `dc:` for phone.

13.4.2 Internal Links and the Special Interpretation of a Page

Under jQuery Mobile, a single HTML document can contain several pages in the sense of the framework. This approach makes sense because traditional web pages are simply too large for small cellphone and smartphone screens. In case of a normal web page, the visitor with a mobile device almost always has to scroll to see the content of the whole web page. Subdividing the contents of a web page by the web page creator into fixed segments with logically grouped information is entirely appropriate. And downloading these segments together in advance is also logical in the mobile environment, where bandwidth is still mostly low. These preloaded but not yet displayed segments can then be linked together via special links and be quickly displayed when the user changes from page to page because the different pages are already there.

> **Tip**
>
> You should not transform a web application that was designed for normal PCs to a mobile app in completely identical form. Even linking individual page segments in an HTML file is usually too much for the mobile visitor. It is highly advisable to reduce content and above all compress the multimedia files. To do this, you can, of course, use adapted CSS files if you define custom CSS rules. The best option is to create two separate applications that are separated on loading the start page via a browser sniffer. You can, for example, use the screen resolution. This is likely to be rather low for cellphones and smartphones. If you check the screen width, for example, you should be able to reliably identify a mobile device if the values are under 800.[7] For this check, you use the DOM object screen.

Listing 13.3   A Browser Sniffer to Automatically Identify and Redirect Mobile Devices

```
if(screen.width < 800) {
  location.href="indexMobileApp.html";
}
else {
  location.href="indexPCApp.html";
}
```

6. Including cc:, bcc:, subject, and presetting the body section.

7. Even if a mobile device is wrongly identified here, this does not pose a problem because then it can cope with the normal dimensions.

Of course, other possibilities exist, but this approach should work well. On the companion website, you will find such a simple browser sniffer in form of the file browsersniffer.html, and with the file testresolution.html you can check the resolution of a device.

> **Tip**
>
> If your mobile device supports automatic screen rotation, you can see that the value of screen. Width is also adapted (which makes sense, of course).

So, pages in the sense of jQuery Mobile are simply areas of the web page marked with `data-role="page"` that have already been loaded together (as part of the complete HTML file). Each `page` block now requires a unique ID so that it can be applied appropriately. This ID is used for internal linking, as you have already seen in jQuery (`href="#myId"`). When a link is clicked, the correspondingly marked area is moved on the screen.

> **Caution**
>
> If you link to a page that was loaded via AJAX and contains several `page` segments, you need to add the attribute `rel="external"` or `data-ajax="false"` to the link.

Listing 13.4   **A Link to a Page with Several Page Segments**

```
<a href="multipage.html" rel="external">Link</a>
```

Back in History

You surely know the functionality `history.back()` from JavaScript. This takes you back to the last page in the browser history. With the attribute `data-rel="back"`, you can make use of precisely this functionality. Alternatively, you can use `data-direction="reverse"` if you do not want to use the history (ch13_2.html).

Listing 13.5   **Linking Page Segments and Back in History**

```
...

16    <body>
17      <div data-role="page" id="p1">
18        <div data-role="header">
19          <h1>Page 1</h1>
20        </div>
21        <div data-role="content">
22          <h2>Welcome on the Mobile Page</h2>
23              <a href="#p2">Go to Page 2</a>
24        </div>
25        <div data-role="footer">
26          <h4>(c) www.rjs.de</h4>
```

```
27        </div>
28      </div>
29          <div data-role="page" id="p2">
30        <div data-role="header">
31
32        <h1>Page 2</h1>
33        </div>
34        <div data-role="content">
35          <p>
36            <a data-rel="back" href="#">Back</a>
37          </p>
38        </div>
39        <div data-role="footer">
40            <h4>(c) www.rjs.de</h4>
41        </div>
42      </div>
43    </body>
44 </html>
```

Here, you see an HTML document that contains two pages. If you load the HTML file, only the first page area will initially display, provided the browser correctly supports the framework.

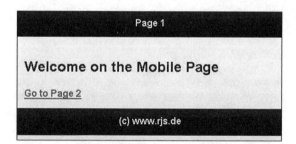

Figure 13.5   On loading the HTML file, only the first page appears.

The hyperlink in line 23 points to an ID and leads to the second page segment that is marked with this ID in line 29.

Figure 13.6   The second page.

On the second page, you will find the link back to first page and an automatically generated graphical Back button. Note in line 37 that the value of `href` was set to #. The link is triggered via `data-rel`, but a # also triggers jumping to the first `page` segment.[8]

13.5   The Transitions

The jQuery Mobile framework currently has nine CSS-based transition effects between pages or objects that you can assign for a page change event or to display a new element. In the default setting, transitions are carried out from right to left. If you want to change this, you can use the attribute `data-transition` for the link that triggers the transition.

Listing 13.6   **Explicitly Specifying the Transition Effect**

```
<a href="index.html" data-transition="pop">Home</a>
```

> **Caution**
>
> Transition effects make massive use of CSS3 and are currently not fully supported by some older platforms. In that case, the new content is simply displayed immediately.

Possible values are `slide`, `slideup`, `slidedown`, `pop`, `fade`, and `flip`. You know these transitions from the animation effects of jQuery itself and jQuery UI.

> **Tip**
>
> You can specify the same transition for the way back via `data-direction="reverse"`.

13.6   Dialogs

Dialogs are also generated in the framework in the simplest way via attributes. You merely need to specify `data-rel="dialog"` in the link to a new page or a new `page` segment. The framework automatically ensures that the new content is displayed in a "dialog window" with rounded corners and appropriate spacing. These dialogs are generally created as modal in the framework and during the display the background is darkened and the application is paused.

Listing 13.7   **Opening a Dialog**

```
<a href="dialog.html" data-rel="dialog">New Dialog</a>
```

---

8. The double notation makes sense because that way you ensure in some not yet fully compatible platforms that jumping back still works.

Once again, to make it clearer, the fact that a page is a dialog is *not* determined in the page, but in the opening link. This is an unusual concept, and you really need to make yourself aware of it.

The transitions between a page and a dialog can be specified in the same way as when changing between standard pages. The framework closes dialogs automatically if a link in the dialog is clicked. This enables you to easily create a Close button; you just need to place a link to the page from which the dialog was opened (for example, via `data-rel="back"` in the link). Alternatively, you can also use the `close` parameter in the `dialog()` method to close the dialog from the outside.

Listing 13.8   **Closing a Dialog**

```
$('#myDialog').dialog('close').
```

13.7 Buttons

While controlling classical web applications on the PC is strongly based on the mouse pointer, mobile apps increasingly use finger controls (keyword touchscreens). These make it much harder or less precise to hit the narrow sensitive area of a classical hyperlink in text form. But even if you can control the cursor on the mobile device with special keys, the control is usually rather fiddly. This means you have to make sensitive elements bigger to ensure comfortable control for the mobile user. Buttons are ideal for this purpose. In addition to the usual tasks these fulfill in PC apps, they can also largely take on the job of text-based hyperlinks.

Buttons are just as easy to create as dialogs. You need do no more than assign the value `button` to the attribute `data-role` in a link.

Listing 13.9   **A button**

```
<a href="index.html" data-role="button">Click</a>
```

Alternatively, the framework also converts form elements of the type `input` with the `type` attribute value `submit`, `reset`, `button`, or `image` into a customized button.

Note

Note the conceptual difference between dialogs and buttons. Although a page that represents a dialog does not have explicit markup, the hyperlink is specifically transformed to a button in the case of buttons. (This is also the case in other widgets.)

13.7.1   Buttons with Icons

You can easily add graphical symbols to the buttons. The jQuery Mobile framework offers a set of frequently used icons for mobile apps. These are optimized in terms of minimal size and maximum contrast. To use these icons, you just add the `data-icon` attribute to a button.

Listing 13.10   **A Button with Icon**

```
<a href="index.html" data-role="button" data-icon=
"delete">Delete</a>
```

The following icons are currently available.

Table 13.1   **Icons for Buttons**

Icon	Description
arrow-l, arrow-r, arrow-u, arrow-d	Arrows pointing left, right, up, and down
delete	Delete
plus, minus	Plus and minus icon
check	Checkmark
gear	Gear icon
refresh	Refresh
forward, back	Forward and back
grid	Hash
star	Star
alert	Alert icon
info	Info icon i
home	Home
search	Search magnifying glass

Tip

You can even define your own custom icons and use them in the framework. You need a unique name as an attribute value, and then the framework generates a new CSS class from it that starts with `ui-icon-`. This is assigned to the button. Then you modify this class body in such a way that it points to an individual image. As the format, you should use 18 x 18 pixels in the PNG-8 format (with alpha transparency).

Position of Icons

The default position of the icons is to the left of the button text. If you want to override this, you can use the attribute `data-iconpos`. Then you can position the icon on the right (`right`), on top of (`top`), or below (`bottom`) the text. With `data-iconpos="notext"`, you can do away with text on the button altogether.

Listing 13.11 **Positioning a Graphic in the Button**

```
<a href="index.html" data-role="button" data-icon="delete"
data-iconpos="right">Delete</a>
```

13.7.2 Block Element or Inline Element

In the default setting, all buttons are generated as block elements (at least in the central content area of the page).[9] Therefore, they take up the whole page width[10] and generate a line break. If you set the attribute `data-inline="true"` for the button, you are creating an inline element that takes up only the space that the content forces. Plus line breaks are prevented. Correspondingly, the value `false` generates a block element.

13.7.3 Grouping

You can also visually combine buttons into groups. They get packed into a container that is assigned the attribute `data-role="controlgroup"`. In the default setting, the buttons are grouped vertically, and all spaces between the buttons are removed. The shadow effects are also redesigned so that the group forms a visual unit.

Listing 13.12 **Grouping Buttons**

```
<div data-role="controlgroup">
  <a href="one.html" data-role="button">Yes</a>
  <a href="two.html" data-role="button">No</a>
  <a href="#" data-role="button">Cancel</a>
</div>
```

> **Tip**
>
> Via `data-type="horizontal"`, you can also arrange the elements horizontally. The buttons are then formatted as inline elements.

9. In the footer of the page, this can also differ in the default setting, depending on the selected theme.

10. Please remember that a page refers to the often quite small screen of the mobile device, and (in case of a touchscreen) this sensitive button has to be operated with a finger. A "large" button is therefore often advisable.

13.7.4   A Practical Example

Now it is time again to provide a complete practical example to illustrate our earlier explanations. Remember our custom plug-in from the last chapter, the musical key generator? Let's use it in a mobile app.[11] This also means that we now bring in JavaScript and jQuery functionality explicitly in addition to the Mobile framework markup. In practice, you are going to offer program logic in a mobile app in addition to widgets and the interface.

Let's first look at the web page ch13_3.html. We want to look at the whole web page, except for the first few lines, because the header structure is also relevant in a few places.

Listing 13.13   The HTML Code of the Mobile App

```
...
15    <script type="text/javascript"
16        src="lib/jquery-rjskeygenerator/jquery.keys.js"
17        ></script>
18    <script type="text/javascript"
19        src="lib/ch13_3_ready.js"></script>
20    </head>
21    <body>
22      <div data-role="page" id="p1">
23        <div data-role="header">
24          <h1>The RJS Key Generator</h1>
25        </div>
26        <div data-role="content">
27          <a id="generator" href="#p2"
28             data-rel="dialog" data-role="button"
29             data-inline="true" data-icon="forward"
30             data-transition="slide">To the key</a>
31        </div>
32        <div data-role="footer">
33          <a href="http://rjs.de"
34             data-role="button">(c) www.rjs.de</a>
35        </div>
36      </div>
37      <div data-role="page" id="p2">
38        <div data-role="header">
39          <h1>The RJS Key Generator</h1>
40        </div>
41        <div data-role="content">
42          <p>
43            <div id="key"></div>
```

---

11. In my case, it was also motivated by personal interest; because the thing is available on my cellphone during our practice sessions, we no longer have to squabble over whose turn it is to choose the key for our band's musical warm-up.

```
44          <div data-role="controlgroup"
45             data-type="horizontal">
46           <a data-rel="back" href="#"
47              data-role="button" data-icon="delete"
48              data-iconpos="right">Close</a>
49           <a data-role="button" data-icon="refresh"
50              data-iconpos="right" id="new">New</a>
51          </div>
52        </p>
53      </div>
54      <div data-role="footer">
55        <a href="http://rjs.de"
56            data-role="button">(c) www.rjs.de</a>
57      </div>
58    </div>
59  </body>
60  </html>
```

At the beginning of the web page (not printed here), you will again find the usual references to the CSS and JavaScript libraries of the frameworks used. In lines 15–17, you can see the reference to the plug-in that we are using here.

Otherwise, the web page again comprises two pages. The start page presents to the user a heading in the header area, the copyright (sensitive in this case) in the footer, and a button in the main content area. The button uses several of the markups described earlier.

In line 27, you can see the link to a page with the ID p2. This is a dialog. But the fact that this linked page is a dialog is, to make it clear once again, not determined at the target page, but here in the opening link. You can see this in line 28. The same line also specifies that the link should be represented by the framework as button.

In line 29, we specify that it is an inline button and that an icon is displayed. The last configuration in line 30 determines the transition effect to the opened dialog window.

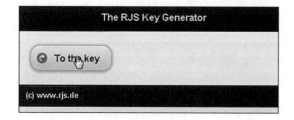

Figure 13.7   The start page.

In lines 33 and 34, we turn the content of the footer of the page into a button that points to an external resource. If you look at the screenshot, you will see that this button is treated as an inline element even though we do not explicitly specify this. The CSS rules of the selected theme for the footer area determine this in this case.

Figure 13.8   A sensitive button in the footer.

In lines 37–58, the second page is described. We have marked it as a dialog in line 27. In line 43, you can see a DIV area. This area is completely "normal". This means the mark-up of the mobile framework does not take effect here. This is the area in which we want to display the musical key selected by the plug-in. So here we have the connection to the "classical" JavaScript or jQuery programming.

In lines 44–51, you can see a horizontal grouping of buttons. This combines two buttons. The button that is defined in lines 46–48 closes the dialog. The second button manages without the attributes `href` and without `data-rel`. It evidently does not use a default reaction of the mobile framework. But of course we can also work with the normal jQuery event handling even in a mobile app. And that is exactly what we will do here (note in line 50 the ID for the button), as you will see shortly when we discuss the JavaScript file ch13_3_ready.js. But first, you should notice that two grouped buttons have icons that are arranged on the right.

Here is the JavaScript file ch13_3_ready.js.

Listing 13.14   **The Custom JavaScript Functionality**

```
01 $(function(){
02   $("#generator").click(function(){
03     ta();
04   });
05   $("#new").click(function(){
06     ta();
07   });
08 });
09 function ta(){
10   $("#key").keys({
11     color: "blue",
12     background: "gray",
13     width: "100px",
14     height: "30px",
15     fontSize: "20px"
16   });
17 }
```

What you can see in the JavaScript file is already familiar jQuery programming. In lines 9–16, you see a function that calls the plug-in with certain options and outputs the return value.

In the `ready` method, the reaction to two click events is assigned; for one, the reaction to the click on the button on page 1 that opens the dialog (ID `generator`). This means that together with opening the dialog, the plug-in is called and a random key is selected and returned. This musical key is then displayed immediately in the dialog window. The click on the button with the ID `new` repeats this selection process for a musical key, except that this button is in the dialog itself. In terms of usability, this means that the user can select a musical key without having to close and reopen the dialog.

Let's complete this section with a quick look at the CSS file ch13_3.css, because here, too, we specify a little detail.

Listing 13.15   **The CSS File**

```
#key {
  margin:auto;
}
```

Here, the `div` area for outputting the musical key is centered. You cannot specify this setting in the plug-in's options.[12]

Figure 13.9   The dialog.

13.8   Toolbars and Navigation Bars

Toolbars are a special form of widgets in the framework. These are used in the header or footer of a page,[13] as we have done in all previous pages. In the header, which is what a page practically always starts with, you occasionally also find one or two buttons in addition to the title

---

12. This would not make sense because it does not concern the plug-in directly, but instead affects how the return value is used.

13. Or with utility bars.

line. The footer concludes the page. It is quite convenient to add a horizontal navigation or subdivision in tabs to these areas. The framework contains a navigation bar widget (`data-role="navbar"`) for this, to change an unsorted list with links to a horizontal bar with buttons. To set one of the links as preselected (active), you add `class="ui-btn-active"` to the anchor element.

Listing 13.16   **A Navigation Bar with a Preselected Register**

```
<div data-role="footer">
  <div data-role="navbar">
    <ul>
      <li><a href="http://rjs.de"
        class="ui-btn-active">Home</a></li>
      <li><a href="http://blog.rjs.de">Blog</a></li>
    </ul>
  </div>
</div>
```

> **Tip**
>
> Navigation bars are also suitable for nesting elements, provided this is appropriate on the small screen.

Positioning of the header and footer areas is done inline in the default setting. This means that these elements are in the normal flow of the web page. The advantage is that they are then visible on practically all devices (because it's independent of positioning via JavaScript/CSS). The elements are simply arranged in accordance with the available space. This is an advantage, particularly in the context of the many different resolutions in the mobile environment.

In some cases, fixed positioning can also be appropriate. In that case, the toolbars stay in their positions at the beginning and end of the screen area when the user scrolls. To have more room for the actual content when required, the framework ensures that tapping/clicking the screen toggles the visibility of the toolbars if necessary. To achieve this behavior, you specify `data-position="fixed"` for the container of the toolbar.

Listing 13.17   **A Fixed Footer**

```
<div data-role="footer" data-position="fixed">
  <a href="http://rjs.de" data-role="button">(c) www.rjs.de</a>
</div>
```

There is also a full-screen position (`data-fullscreen="true"`) that behaves like the fixed position, except that the toolbars are only displayed if the page is clicked.

> **Caution**
>
> Fixing the toolbars and toggling currently does not yet work with some platforms.

Let's take a look at a complete example in form of a small modification of our last example where only the markup in the HTML file changes in accordance with what we have explained above (ch13_4.html).

Listing 13.18 Using Navigation Bars and Especially Formatted Toolbars

```
...
21  <body>
22    <div data-role="page" id="p1">
23      <div data-role="header" data-position="fixed">
24        <h1>The RJS Key Generator</h1>
25      </div>
26      <div data-role="content">
27        <a id="generator" href="#p2" data-rel="dialog"
28           data-role="button" data-inline="true"
29           data-icon="forward"
30           data-transition="slide">To the key</a>
31      </div>
32      <div data-role="footer">
33        <div data-role="navbar">
34          <ul>
35            <li>
36              <a href="http://rjs.de"
37                 class="ui-btn-active">(c) www.rjs.de</a>
38            </li>
39            <li>
40              <a href="http://blog.rjs.de">Blog</a>
41            </li>
42          </ul>
43        </div>
44      </div>
45    </div>
46    <div data-role="page" id="p2">
47      <div data-role="header" data-fullscreen="true">
48        <h1>The RJS Key Generator</h1>
49      </div>
50      <div data-role="content">
51        <p>
52          <div id="key">
53          </div>
54          <div data-role="controlgroup"
55             data-type="horizontal">
56            <a data-rel="back" href="#"
```

```
57                    data-role="button" data-icon="delete"
58                    data-iconpos="right">Close</a>
59                  <a data-role="button" data-icon="refresh"
60                    data-iconpos="right" id="new">New</a>
61                </div>
62              </p>
63            </div>
64            <div data-role="footer">
65              <div data-role="navbar">
66                <ul>
67                  <li>
68                    <a href="http://rjs.de"
69                      class="ui-btn-active">(c) www.rjs.de</a>
70                  </li>
71                  <li>
72                    <a href="http://blog.rjs.de">Blog</a>
73                  </li>
74                </ul>
75              </div>
76            </div>
77          </div>
78        </body>
79      </html>
```

We are formatting the toolbars and creating a navigation bar with two buttons in the footer of the pages.

Figure 13.10   The footer contains a navigation bar with two buttons, and the left button is prese-lected.

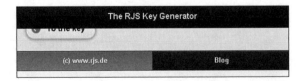

Figure 13.11   The header remains in the same place when the content is moved, provided the browser supports this.

Figure 13.12   Tapping/clicking the screen toggles the visibility of the header.

13.9   Lists

Lists enable clear presentation of data, which is all the more important for the small screens in the mobile environment. The navigation can also be designed with lists. The framework offers a large number of default lists that can be formatted in many ways. The framework supports nested lists, numbered lists, noninteractive (read-only) lists, lists with icons, indented lists, and several other variations.

Essentially, you only need to use the usual HTML tags to build a list and add the attribute `data-role="listview"` to the parent element. The framework automatically adds required styles and the support for events. Entirely in the background, it organizes (when necessary) AJAX requests for new content and integrates it into the Document Object Model (DOM) and so on. A basic list could look like Listing 13.19.

Listing 13.19   **A List**

```
<ul data-role="listview" data-theme="g">
  <li><a href="http://rjs.de">Home</a></li>
  <li><a href="http://blog.rjs.de">Blog</a></li>
  <li><a href="http://www.ajax-net.de">AJAX-Net.de</a></li>
  <li><a href="http://safety-first-rock.de">
    jQuery Examples</a></li>
</ul>
```

Let's expand our mobile reference app again. We add a third page and use another plug-in on this third page, the plug-in rjsTwitter that you will find on the companion website[14] (ch13_5.html).

Listing 13.20   **Using Lists**

```
...
15    <script type="text/javascript"
16      src="lib/jquery-rjstwitter/jquery.rjstwitter_en.js" >
17    </script>
```

14. The plug-in that you will find in the directory jquery-rjstwitter is the plug-in variation of our Twitter client that loads tweets of a tweeter via JSONP and displays them in an output area.

```
18      <script type="text/javascript" src=
19        "lib/ch13_5_ready.js"></script>
20    </head>
21  <body>
22      <div data-role="page" id="p1">
23        <div data-role="header" data-position="fixed">
24          <h1>Mobile RJS PlugIns</h1>
25        </div>
26        <div data-role="content">
27          <ul data-role="listview" data-theme="g">
28            <li>
29              <a id="generator" href="#p2"
30                  data-rel="dialog" data-transition="slide">
31                  RJS Key Generator</a>
32            </li>
33            <li>
34              <a id="generator" href="#p3"
35                  data-rel="dialog" data-transition="slide">
36                  RJS Twitter Client</a>
37            </li>
38          </ul>
39        </div>
40        <div data-role="footer">
41          <div data-role="navbar">
42            <ul>
43              <li>
44                <a href="http://rjs.de"
45                    class="ui-btn-active">(c) www.rjs.de</a>
46              </li>
47              <li>
48                <a href="http://blog.rjs.de">Blog</a>
49              </li>
50            </ul>
51          </div>
52        </div>
53      </div>
54      <div data-role="page" id="p2">
55        <div data-role="header" data-fullscreen="true">
56          <h1>The RJS Key Generator</h1>
57        </div>
58        <div data-role="content">
59          <p>
60            <div id="key"></div>
61            <div data-role="controlgroup"
62                data-type="horizontal">
63                <a data-rel="back" href="#"
```

```
64                data-role="button" data-icon="delete"
65                data-iconpos="right">Close</a>
66              <a data-role="button" data-icon="refresh"
67                data-iconpos="right" id="new">New</a>
68          </div>
69        </p>
70      </div>
71      <div data-role="footer">
72        <div data-role="navbar">
73          <ul>
74            <li>
75              <a href="http://rjs.de"
76                 class="ui-btn-active">(c) www.rjs.de</a>
77            </li>
78            <li>
79              <a href="http://blog.rjs.de">Blog</a>
80            </li>
81          </ul>
82        </div>
83      </div>
84    </div>
85    <div data-role="page" id="p3">
86      <div data-role="header" data-fullscreen="true">
87        <h1>The RJS Twitter Client</h1>
88      </div>
89      <div data-role="content">
90        <p>
91          <div id="twitter"></div>
92        </p>
93      </div>
94      <div data-role="footer">
95        <div data-role="navbar">
96          <ul>
97            <li>
98              <a href="http://rjs.de"
99                 class="ui-btn-active">(c) www.rjs.de</a>
100           </li>
101           <li>
102             <a href="http://blog.rjs.de">Blog</a>
103           </li>
104         </ul>
105       </div>
106     </div>
107   </div>
108  </body>
109 </html>
```

In lines 85–108, the new third page is defined. Its structure is familiar. What we have mainly changed in the application is the navigation on the start page. Instead of a button, we use a list with two items in lines 27–38. Both bring up a dialog and also have the same attributes that the button had previously (except the attributes that explicitly mark a button).

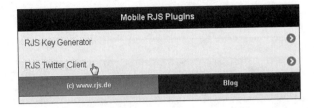

Figure 13.13   The sensitive list.

If a user clicks the first item in the list, he goes to the dialog with the musical key generator. If he clicks the second list item, the new dialog with the Twitter client is called.

Figure 13.14   Page 3 is a dialog with the Twitter client.

Let's look at the JavaScript file ch13_5_ready.js, into which the new plug-in is integrated.

Listing 13.21   **The New Plug-In with a Few Options**

```
01 $(function(){
02   $("#generator").click(function(){
03     ta();
04   });
05   $("#new").click(function(){
06     ta();
07   });
08   twitter();
09
10 });
11 function ta(){
12   $("#key").keys({
13     color: "blue",
14     background: "gray",
15     width: "100px",
16     height: "30px",
17     fontSize: "20px"
18   });
19 }
20 function twitter(){
21   $("#twitter").rjsTwitter({
22     background: "gray",
23     color: "white",
24     fontSize: 12,
25     imageDisplayed: false,
26     idDisplayed: true
27   });
28 }
```

In line 8, the plug-in is called on loading the web page. The function is defined in lines 20–27.

13.10   Form Elements

Essential interaction components in a graphical user interface (GUI) are based on **form elements**. The framework jQuery Mobile offers all common form elements in optimized form for the mobile devices. In particular, it is explicitly geared toward finger control. But basically, all form elements are based on the usual native HTML form elements that the framework initializes and adapts in the background.

> **Tip**
>
> If you do not want the framework to adapt a form element, set the attribute for this element to `data-role="none"`.

The form elements should be enclosed in the usual `<form>` container.

> **Caution**
>
> If you are working with IDs in forms (or other elements), ensure that these are unique in the web page. This rule is somewhat blurry due to the option of structuring several pages within a web page. But even then, the IDs should be unique across the whole web page.

Fundamentally, all form elements are assigned a dynamic width to adapt to varying screen sizes. The arrangement between different elements can also differ depending on screen width (above or next to one another).

13.10.1   Field Containers

To ensure that labels and form elements adapt to wider screens, the documentation recommends enclosing them within a `div` or `fieldset` element and adding the attribute `data-role="fieldcontain"`. The framework then manages the elements together and adds the appropriate design with frames and so on.

13.10.2   The Various Form Elements

As you are already familiar with the various form elements, we are now going to look at a complete example that simply contains all currently available form elements (ch13_6.html).

Listing 13.22   **The Various Form Elements in jQuery Mobile**

```
...
22   <body>
23     <div data-role="page">
24       <div data-role="header">
25         <h1>Form Elements</h1>
26       </div>
27       <div data-role="content">
28         <form action="#" method="get">
29         <div data-role="fieldcontain">
30           <label for="name">
31             Text input:
32           </label>
33           <input name="name" id="name" type="text" />
34         </div>
35         <div data-role="fieldcontain">
36           <label for="textarea">
```

```
37              Text area:
38          </label>
39          <textarea cols="30" rows="5"
40              name="textarea" id="textarea"></textarea>
41      </div>
42      <div data-role="fieldcontain">
43          <label for="search">
44              Search input:
45          </label>
46          <input type="search" name="password"
47              id="search" />
48      </div>
49      <div data-role="fieldcontain">
50          <label for="slider">
51              Slider:
52          </label>
53          <input type="range" name="slider"
54              id="slider" value="50" min="0" max="100" />
55      </div>
56      <div data-role="fieldcontain">
57          <label for="um">
58              Switch
59          </label>
60          <select name="um" id="um" data-role="slider">
61              <option value="off">On</option>
62              <option value="on">Off</option>
63          </select>
64      </div>
65      <div data-role="fieldcontain">
66          <fieldset data-role="controlgroup">
67              <legend>
68                  Options
69              </legend>
70              <input type="radio" name="radio-choice-1"
71                  id="radio-choice-1" value="choice-1"
72                  checked="checked" />
73              <label for="radio-choice-1">
74                  Male
75              </label>
76              <input type="radio" name="radio-choice-1"
77                  id="radio-choice-2" value="choice-2" />
78              <label for="radio-choice-2">
79                  Female
```

```
 80                </label>
 81              </fieldset>
 82           </div>
 83           <div data-role="fieldcontain">
 84             <fieldset data-role="controlgroup">
 85               <legend>
 86                 Checkboxes:
 87               </legend>
 88               <input type="checkbox" name="checkbox-1"
 89                 id="checkbox-1" />
 90               <label for="checkbox-1">
 91                 OK
 92               </label>
 93             </fieldset>
 94           </div>
 95           <div data-role="fieldcontain">
 96             <label for="select-choice-1" class="select">
 97               Selection menu
 98             </label>
 99             <select name="select-choice-1"
100                 id="select-choice-1">
101               <option value="beer">Beer</option>
102               <option value="wine">Wine</option>
103               <option value="coke">Coke</option>
104             </select>
105           </div>
106              </form>
107         </div>
108         <div data-role="footer">
109           <h4>jQuery Mobile</h4>
110         </div>
111       </div>
112   </body>
113 </html>
```

You can see that the entire content area of the app is in fact a form (lines 28–106). In it, you can see the possible form elements within the individual containers marked with data-role="fieldcontain". The switch in lines 60–63 is remarkable; it must be marked with data-role="slider". In addition the fieldset has to be marked as data-role="controlgroup" in line 66 for the radio buttons and in line 84 data-role="controlgroup" for check boxes.

Figure 13.15   The form with all standard elements.

Figure 13.16   The selection menu opens as a pop-up when you enable it.

13.10.3   Plug-In Methods for Form Elements

After jQuery Mobile has generated or adapted the form elements accordingly, you can check them with several integrated methods.

With `.selectmenu('open')` you can open a menu, with `.selectmenu('close')` you can close it again, with `.selectmenu('refresh')` you can refresh it, with `.selectmenu('disable')` you can disable it, and with `.selectmenu('enable')` you can enable it.

Text input can also be enabled with `.textinput('enable')` or disabled with `.textinput('disable')`.

The same applies to check boxes with `.checkboxradio('enable')`, `.checkboxradio('disable')`, and `.checkboxradio('refresh')`: to sliders via `.slider('enable')`, `.slider('disable')`, and `.slider('refresh')`; and to buttons via `.button('enable')` and `.button('disable')`.

13.10.4   Sending the Form Data

In jQuery Mobile, sending form data will be done via AJAX when possible. But the resulting data can be saved as bookmarks through appropriate background actions of the framework if the data is sent via GET. The URL is modified accordingly when the data arrives.

13.11   Special Events

The Mobile framework provides support for a number of special events. These are created based on native events but are not completely available on all mobile devices. The events can be used as usual with `bind()` and `live()`.

13.11.1   Touch Events

Table 13.2 describes the events that are particularly geared toward different kinds of touch on touchscreens.

Table 13.2   **Touch Events**

Event	Description
tap	A tap is a quick, complete touch
taphold	Touch and hold
swipe	Horizontal drag of 30 or more pixels and less than 75 pixels vertically within a second
swipeleft	A swipe event to the left
swiperight	A swipe event to the right

13.11.2   Orientation Change

Many mobile devices react to whether you are holding them horizontally or vertically. This, of course, triggers an event to which you can react.

Table 13.3   **Reacting to the Device Being Rotated**

Event	Description
`orientationchange`	If the device is rotated, you can evaluate the orientation in the callback function via the second parameter and the values `"portrait"` or `"landscape"`.

13.11.3   Scroll Events

You can also react to various events in connection with the content being scrolled.

Table 13.4   **Scrolling Events**

Event	Description
`scrollstart`	Scrolling starts.
`scrollstop`	Scrolling stops.

13.11.4 Page Events

Initializing, showing, and hiding pages are connected to the following events.

Table 13.5   **Page Events**

Event	Description
`pagebeforecreate`	An initialization event that is triggered before creating the page.
`pagebeforehide`	Hiding starts. This describes an event that is triggered before the page is actually hidden.
`pagebeforeshow`	Showing starts (usually in animation). This describes an event that is triggered before the page is actually shown.
`pagecreate`	An initialization event that is triggered after the page has been created.
`pagehide`	The page is fully hidden.
`pageshow`	The page is fully shown.

As an example for the reaction to events, let's take a web page with two page segments and react to hiding and showing the start page (ch13_7.html).

Listing 13.23   **Reacting to Events**

```
...
18  <body>
19    <div data-role="page" id="p1">
20      <div data-role="header">
21        <h1>Page 1</h1>
22      </div>
23      <div data-role="content">
24          <h2></h2>
25              <a href="#p2">To Page 2</a>
26      </div>
27      <div data-role="footer">
28        <h4>(c) www.rjs.de</h4>
29      </div>
30    </div>
31        <div data-role="page" id="p2">
32      <div data-role="header">
33        <h1>Page 2</h1>
34      </div>
35      <div data-role="content">
36        <p>
37          <h2></h2>
38          <a data-rel="back" href="#">Back</a>
39        </p>
40      </div>
41      <div data-role="footer">
42          <h4>(c) www.rjs.de</h4>
43      </div>
44    </div>
45  </body>
46 </html>
```

The specific reaction takes place in the JavaScript file ch17_7_ready.js.

Listing 13.24   **Reacting to Hiding and Showing a Page**

```
01 $(function(){
02   $('#p1').live('pageshow', function(event, ui){
03     $("h2:eq(0)").html(
04       "The first page is now displayed again. " +
05       "Triggering element: " + event.target);
06   });
07   $('#p1').live('pagehide', function(event, ui){
08     $("h2:eq(1)").html(
09       "The first page is now hidden. " +
10       "Triggering element: " + event.target);
```

```
11  });
12  });
```

Figure 13.17   The page after loading.

To the hiding and showing,[15] we bind two events via the `live()` method. After hiding the start page, we display an information message in the second heading of the type h2 (on the second page).

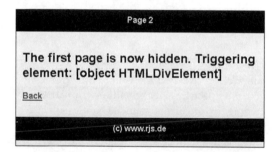

Figure 13.18   The start page has been hidden.

And vice versa, we display a different message on showing it again in the first heading of the type h2 (on the start page).

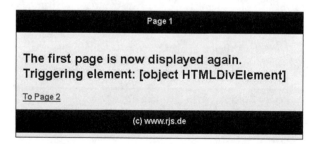

Figure 13.19   The start page is now shown again.

15. Only applies with hiding and showing the elements not when they are initially created.

13.12   The Theme Framework and General Content Design

Fundamentally, you would do best in jQuery Mobile to leave the design of the content largely up to the browser and to transmit as little layout overhead as possible or even force uniform design, wholly in the tradition of the first versions of HTML. In the default setting, the framework uses the standard styles and size specifications of HTML. And as mentioned earlier, you should avoid troublesome design-oriented tags such as `<font>`. Basically, the framework only adds a few styles on this level for tables and field sets to make these a bit more manageable. Anything else is relocated to streamlined CSS classes.

Under jQuery Mobile, there is also a rich Theme framework. The central assignment of CSS rules takes place via the `data-theme` attribute. You can assign this to the header or footer to adapt the display there. You can also assign this attribute to the actual content area of a page, but the documentation of the framework recommends assigning the attribute to individual pages instead—in other words, all containers that are marked with `data-role="page"`. But you can also design other widgets with it individually.

> **Note**
>
> The framework's default theme is aimed at optimal contrast.

The entire concept of the mobile CSS Theme framework is based on the ThemeRoller of jQuery UI but adds a few more extensions that result from the special mobile conditions. In particular, it intensively uses properties of CSS3 (for example, to implement rounded corners and gradients and maximally compressed icons). This considerably reduces the amount of data to be transferred, if you compare it to implementation using graphics. Plus, every theme offers multiple color combinations and various designs.

The mobile theme system separates color and text of structure styles such as dimensions and buffering. So, you can define these rules once and then mix or recombine them at your leisure.

Each theme in the framework contains global settings for font, shadow effects, colors, the radius of rounded corners, and so on.

> **Tip**
>
> jQuery Mobile 1.2 provides a separate ThemeRoller tool that allows you to build a theme and then download the custom CSS file that can be easily dropped into a project.

And although it is not recommended, you can also create grid layouts purely based on CSS using the framework. Separate classes for this start with `ui-grid`. You can find more details in the documentation.

The five default themes in jQuery Mobile are simply "numbered" alphabetically (a, b, c, d, e). The theme a uses the greatest contrast, and e uses the most colors. Let's take a look at a variation of our example ch13_5.html, in which we simply assign the theme e (ch13_8.html).

Listing 13.25   **Using Different Themes**

```
...
21   <body>
22      <div data-role="page" id="p1" data-theme="e">
...
27         <ul data-role="listview" data-theme="d">
...
40      <div data-role="footer" data-theme="e">
..
55      <div data-role="header" data-fullscreen="true"
           data-theme="b">
...
85    <div data-role="page" id="p3">
...
94      <div data-role="footer" data-theme="e">
...
```

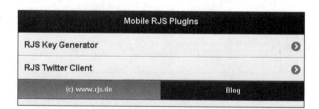

Figure 13.20   The start page gets a new color scheme if you select different themes.

Figure 13.21   You can also nest or mix themes.

> **Tip**
> If you want to create your own custom themes, follow the same naming convention with letters.

13.13　Collapsed and Expanded Content

In jQuery Mobile, you can easily create content that can be expanded and collapsed when the user clicks it with the mouse. You just add `data-role="collapsible"` to a container. Within the container, you can write all HTML headings. The framework designs the headings in such a way that they look like clickable buttons and add a plus symbol while the content is collapsed. If the content has been expanded, you instead see a minus symbol. In the default setting, content is loaded expanded, but if you set the attribute `data-collapsed="true"`, the content is collapsed on loading (ch13_9.html).

Listing 13.26　**A Page with Expandable and Collapsible Content**

```
...
18    <body>
19     <div data-role="page">
20       <div data-role="header">
21         <h1>Famous Quotes</h1>
22       </div>
23       <div data-role="content">
24         <p>
25           <div data-role="collapsible">
26             <h3>Aristotle</h3>
27             <p>
28               The whole is greater than
29               the sum of its parts.
30             </p>
31           </div>
32           <div data-role="collapsible"
33             data-collapsed="true">
34             <h3>Aristotle</h3>
35             <p>
36               Hiding a mistake through a lie
37               means replacing a stain
38               through a hole.
```

```
39              </p>
40            </div>
41            <div data-role="collapsible"
42               data-collapsed="true">
43              <h3>Archimedes</h3>
44              <p>
45                 Give me place to stand,
46                    and I shall move the Earth.
47              </p>
48            </div>
49          </p>
50        </div>
51        <div data-role="footer">
52          <h4>Aristotle and Archimedes </h4>
53        </div>
54      </div>
55    </body>
56  </html>
```

In the example, you can see three areas that can be expanded and collapsed. The first area is expanded on loading; the others are collapsed.

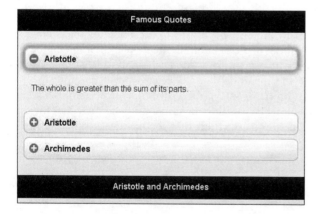

Figure 13.22   After loading the app.

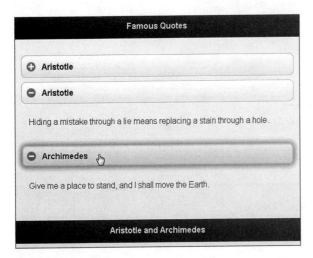

Figure 13.23   Now the first area is collapsed and the other two areas are expanded.

Summary

In this final chapter, you have learned how you can transfer jQuery into the world of mobile apps. The Mobile framework is an extremely promising approach to encapsulating the countless difficulties arising from different platforms and conditions in the mobile environment on a high level. It is easy to apply and (within its possibilities) very reliable and widely supported. And it is practically certain that the level of support on new mobile devices will continue to grow. This means that mobile RIAs based on HTML5, CSS3, and JavaScript are becoming a serious alternative to proprietary approaches. I believe that the future really lies here. But for now, I wish you fun and success with jQuery and everything that you have learned in this book.

Appendix

A.1   Overview of Basic Information on JavaScript

Effective programming with jQuery requires knowledge of the syntax and concepts of JavaScript. This appendix provides a brief introduction to the most important JavaScript techniques so that you can understand how jQuery works and how to use its methods. For a fuller understanding of JavaScript, you should seek additional JavaScript resources.

A.1.1   Case Sensitivity

JavaScript distinguishes between uppercase and lowercase for variables, keywords, function identifiers, and method identifiers.

A.1.2   Variables, Literals, and Data Types

Of course, JavaScript has variables, data types, and literals. However, some particularities in JavaScript differ from most "true" programming languages.

> **Note**
>
> A **literal** is a representation of a clearly defined and unchangeable value, such as a number or text. A **variable**, however, represents a named location in the main memory where values (literals) can be temporarily stored. Both a literal and a variable require a **data type**. This specifies the size of the variable or literal in the main memory, which type of information it is, and how to proceed with it in an operation.

In JavaScript, a data type is not explicitly specified via a keyword in the declaration (meaning the first introduction) of a variable. The data type is specified **implicitly** via the type of value that is assigned to the variable. If a different type of value is later assigned, the data type of the variable even changes during the runtime of the script. The data types are managed internally by JavaScript. So, JavaScript is a loosely typed language that has only a few data types.

But although JavaScript is a loosely typed language, it still has several implemented data types (referred to as built-in data types). These data types do have nearly the functionality of data types available in more powerful programming languages such as Java or C#.

> **Note**
> jQuery extends the scope of data types in JavaScript by adding its own data types. These are referred to as **virtual types** and pseudo-types.

The Classic JavaScript Data Types

Of course, in jQuery you can use all the data types available in classic JavaScript. We do not discuss these in detail, but instead consider them just briefly here.

String

A string is text enclosed in double or single quotation marks. Thanks to the two different variations for specifying a string, you can nest strings within each other. In JavaScript, a string is also seen as an object, and so this object offers some interesting methods (for example, for converting to uppercase letters and for searching text).

> **Tip**
> Beyond the normal methods of a native string, jQuery offers several string-handling methods. The method `jQuery.trim()`, for example, removes superfluous whitespace at the beginning and end of a string.

Number, Integer, Float, and the Math Class

The data type `Number` represents numbers in JavaScript. `Integer` is a subtype that represents whole numbers, and `Float` represents floating-point numbers. You can apply the usual mathematical operations to variables and literals of these types. And the representation also does not require any special explanation here. Beyond the pure data type, JavaScript offers several utilities (properties and methods) in form of the `Math` class for dealing with numbers. With these, you can calculate the sine or generate a random number, for example.

When processing the variables or literals, sometimes the result is either not a number or it represents infinity. For these two cases, JavaScript offers the defined tokens `NaN` (not a number) and `Infinity`.

Object

The data type `Object` represents an object. In JavaScript, such an object can be created with a constructor or declaratively, or it is available based on the environment.

Boolean

A `Boolean` value in JavaScript is represented either by the token `true` or `false`.

> **Caution**
>
> In JavaScript, other data types can also represent Boolean values, in contrast to stable professional or type-secure languages such as Java or C#. For example, an empty string or the numeric zero are interpreted as `false`; correspondingly, other values are interpreted as `true`. But an object can never be interpreted as `false`. It always represents `true`. The latter is often used in messy programming for browser sniffing. (It is used to test whether an object is available; if it isn't available, it is interpreted as `false`.)

A.1.3 Functions and Methods

Functions and methods involve placing one or more instructions into a block (or subroutine) that gets a name or identifier. An important aspect in JavaScript is that forming a subroutine protects certain command steps from being executed when loading a script within the web page. This would otherwise be the case if you simply write statements into a `<script>` area of the web page, due to the sequential processing. Often, this is neither desirable nor appropriate. Only if certain conditions exist (for example, if the user clicks somewhere, leaves the web page, or finishes entering certain data) will the function or method be called via its identifier and the command sequence executed. And last but not least, forming functions enables you to create libraries, which takes us to the jQuery library.

You can define functions and methods by introducing the declaration with the JavaScript keyword `function`, followed by the identifier of the function or method, and finally a pair of parentheses ( ) within which you can pass any required parameters to the function. These are variables that can be used locally in the function. If you need several parameters, they are separated by commas in the brackets. This is followed by the block of instructions enclosed in pointed brackets, *without* a preceding semicolon. Optionally, you can specify a return value of the function via the keyword `return`.

Listing A.1 shows a typical declaration of a function or method in JavaScript.

Listing A.1 **A Typical Function Declaration**

```
function [function identifier]([optional parameters]) {
..any statements
  return [return value];
}
```

> **Note**
>
> For experts, a function in JavaScript becomes a method purely by being anchored via `this` and a function reference in the object declaration of a type or an anonymous notation in the constructor. Note that in the first case it can still be called as pure function (without a preceding object), which is not possible in strictly object-oriented languages.

Function Call Versus Function Reference

Let's move on to the difference between calling a function and function references. If you have declared a function, this has to be called to come to life. But how? One way is through a **function call**. In general, such a function call takes place if you write the identifier of the function followed by a pair or brackets within which you place any required values you are passing as parameters. A function call ends with a semicolon, as usual for a JavaScript statement in a script. When this point of the script is processed, the function is executed.

In contrast to a function call and purely in terms of form, a **function reference** does not have any brackets. This is only a **reference** to the function; it does not call the function. So, the question with function references is this: When is the referenced function executed? The easy answer is this: Function references are usually combined with event handlers that call the referenced function if a specific event occurs.

Function Arguments: `arguments`

As mentioned previously, you can pass any values or parameters to a function. Within a function, there is a special variable with the name `arguments`. This is always available and contains specific information about the parameters. In particular, information about the number, because as for an array there is a `length` property.

Named Versus Anonymous Function

When declaring a function, you can (but do not have to) omit the function name. This is referred to as an **anonymous function** (as opposed to a **named function**).

An anonymous function declaration is appropriate if it only has to be available at this point. Then you do not need a function identifier either. Such an anonymous function can be assigned to a variable or passed to a method.

Listing A.2   **An Anonymous Function as a Parameter of a Method**

```
$("#toggle2").click(function(){
  $("img").attr({src:"http://rjs.de/bilder/ducky.gif"});
});
```

> **Note**
> jQuery works very intensively with anonymous functions. Both in the application programming interface (API) and also if you are creating your own scripts with jQuery.

Callbacks

A callback function, or **callback** for short, is a JavaScript function (with or without return value) that is passed to a method as argument or option. This is exactly what we can see in the preceding example with the anonymous function that is passed to the `click()` method as a parameter. As you can see, some callbacks are simply events that are triggered if a certain state occurs.

Most callbacks offer arguments and a context. For most event callbacks, the argument is an event object, and the context is set to the handling element.

Recursive Function Calls

JavaScript supports recursion, also referred to as recursive calls. This means a function simply calls itself again at some point of execution.

A.1.4   Objects in JavaScript

Almost the entire capacity of native programming with JavaScript is based on the fact that you can use objects with it that offer a certain functionality. Think of the Document Object Model (DOM) concept. The potential of frameworks such as jQuery is based entirely on objects.

To be able to use an object with JavaScript, you can follow different approaches. Objects can be directly available to you in JavaScript. These are either standard objects of the runtime environment or objects that are automatically created and offered by the browser on loading the web page as a result of the (X)HTML structure of the web page. The latter explicitly applies to the DOM concept. Or a library such as jQuery can also offer object in various ways.

The Constructor

The other situation is that you have to create an object explicitly yourself. To explicitly create a new object instance in JavaScript from the description of properties and abilities of an object (class), you usually use the reserved keyword new, followed by the class identifier, and then a pair of brackets (with parameters within them, if applicable). An object declaration or constructor method (or constructor, for short) is also used. Using a constructor to create an object usually looks like Listing A.3 in JavaScript in terms of syntax.

Listing A.3   **Using a Constructor in JavaScript**

```
new [object declaration]([optional parameters]);
```

Declarative Object Creation via an Object Literal

As an alternative to creating an object with a constructor method, you can also create an object declaratively in JavaScript via an **object literal**. You then do not need a constructor method. This simplifies creating objects, in particular for beginners.

Listing A.4   Declarative Creation via an Object Literal Plus Directly Initializing Two Properties

```
var x = {
   name: "Felix", age: 11
 };
```

Note

This variation of creating objects is the preferred option when using jQuery methods.

While you are creating the object declaratively, you simply specify all properties and methods you want the object to have. But because you do not have a constructor in this case, you cannot create another object from an object description, but will instead have to describe another object again, even if it is structurally identical.

Caution

Note that the object literal has a **colon** for assigning the value and a comma for separating the properties. As mentioned earlier, this is declarative syntax, not the classic value assignment.

Accessing Object Components

To access components of an object, you usually use dot notation. Alternatively, you can use array notation. This involves writing or reading properties via data field notation. This enables using meaningful names for the indexes.

Listing A.5   Access via Array Notation

```
var x = {
  name: "Thomas",
  age: 11
};
var index = "name";
document.write(x[index]); // "Thomas"
```

This approach is also referred to as associative arrays. In JavaScript, these are not directly available, but here you can see that this access method can easily be re-created if necessary.

Class Elements

In JavaScript, there are also class elements. You can use these with the preceding class name without first creating an object with a constructor. For example, various properties and methods of the JavaScript Math class are class elements.

Prototyping, Extensions, and Creating New Data Types

JavaScript is not a completely object-oriented language, and there is no provision for writing classes in the strict sense of object-oriented programming and the mechanism of inheritance. However, you can still write your own object definitions and create custom objects with these. Creating your own object in JavaScript effectively requires two steps:

1. You have to create your own object declaration as described earlier.

2. Via this object declaration, you can then create a specific object instance, just as with predefined object declarations.

That this approach is possible forms one pillar of the jQuery framework. With jQuery, the functionality of pure JavaScript is expanded by adding numerous own objects, which in many cases means programming new object declarations.

Plus there is another pillar, what is referred to as prototyping. With it, you create new data types based on existing data types. But what exactly is it, and how does it work? The answer first of all leads us to the mechanism of inheritance, which you should know and understand in order to apply prototyping. The details are beyond the scope of this book. And although you do not really need to completely understand prototyping and creating new data types just to use jQuery, it can still prove helpful if you have a bit more insight into this area.

A.1.5   Arrays

Data fields or arrays refer only to a collection of variables that can be addressed via a name. An array is always a great advantage if you want to save a number of pieces of information of the same type. The special feature is that you can access the contained elements via a name and an index. This is done by placing the index in square brackets after the identifier.

Listing A.6   **Accessing Array Elements**

```
x[0] = 1;
document.write(x[2]);
```

As you have seen earlier, you can also create associated data fields in JavaScript via a text index.

Declaration

In the classic way, an array is created in JavaScript via an instance of the class Array (in other words, using the corresponding constructor).

Listing A.7   **A Data Field Is Created**

```
myDatafield = new Array();
```

Note that in JavaScript you do not usually specify the size of an array because array elements are created "on-the-fly" anyway, if required.

But you can also create arrays by using an array literal.

Listing A.8   **Creating an Array with Array Literals**

```
var x = [];
var primenumbers = [1, 2, 3, 5, 7, 11, 13, 17, 19, 23, 29];
```

Note, as well, the fact that arrays are also to be seen as objects. Most properties and methods for arrays can therefore also be applied to objects or collections of objects. And vice versa, arrays can have the basic properties and methods of any object. In jQuery, this fact is used intensively.

And the fact that in JavaScript objects in general and arrays are recorded in the same way as lists by being listed as key-value pairs means that the declarative object creation with an object literal can be used for an array, as well.

Listing A.9   **Declarative Creation with an Object Literal Plus Direct Initialization**

```
var company = {
    designation: "RJS EDV-KnowHow",
    website: "www.rjs.de",
    contact: "ralph.steyer@rjs.de"
};
```

Accessing Array Elements

You usually access array elements via the identifier and the index in square brackets. A big advantage of arrays is that you can also use them to access the elements via loops. And because arrays are also to be seen as objects, as mentioned earlier, there are implemented methods and properties. The most important property for iterating over the array is `length`, which contains the number of elements in the array. This information can be used as a condition in a loop over an array (or the number of elements in an object).

Tip

The `size()` method provides the same information but is less performant than `length`.

A.2   Available DOM Objects

Under the DOM concept, the following objects are available, among others. Note that not all browsers support all objects and that there are various differences in the type of support, even in the DOM concept.

Table A.1   **Important DOM Objects**

Object/Class	Description
`all`	An object of this type enables in principle directly accessing all elements of a web page. Yet it is not part of the official DOM standard but is a proprietary implementation for Internet Explorer. The object is now replaced almost entirely by the more recent object `node`, which is much better supported in modern browsers. You should avoid using the object.
`document`	This object represents the web page itself and contains the components of the web page as subobjects. In particular, you can write into a web page and select elements via methods of this object.
`event`	An object that is created with events in a web page and can be used for the (central) event handling under JavaScript. But this event handling under JavaScript is implemented inconsistently in various browser worlds. Here, frameworks such as jQuery can provide considerable help.
`element`	An element in a web form is represented via an object of this type.
`form`	The object contains a reference to an object that represents a form in an HTML page.
`frame`	An object representation of a frame below `window`.
`history`	Via `history` (a direct subobject of `window`), you can access the previously loaded pages in the user's browser.
`image`	The object contains a reference to an image in a web page.
`location`	The `location` object (a direct subobject of `window`) represents the complete URL that is linked to a `window` object (in other words, the browser's address line).
`navigator`	Via `navigator`, you can access information on the user's browser.

Object/Class	Description
node	In new variations of the DOM concept, this `node` object offers access to individual elements in a document with tree-like structure. It is a key element for using modern DHTML. Via a `node` object, you can access each component of a web page, although you do not write down `node` directly. To be able to use a `node` object (a node), you use indirect access methods. You can access a node or data field with several nodes, for example, via the methods `getElementById()` and `getElementsByName()` plus `getElementsByTagName()` (or the already rather ancient access via object fields and direct notation of a name, which works in some situations).[1] Ultimately, however, you also get such a node or a whole data field with nodes via jQuery functions and methods such as `$()`, `find()`, or `eq()`.
screen	Via the object `screen`, you can access various platform-specific infos about the user's screen.
style	An object representation of the CSS properties of an object in the web page.
window	This object contains status information about the entire browser window. Each browser window uses its own `window` object. The `window` object is the highest object in the object hierarchy of the objects that affect the browser directly.

1. For example, with forms.

Index

C

M

T

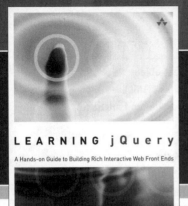

LEARNING jQuery

A Hands-on Guide to Building Rich Interactive Web Front Ends

RALPH STEYER

FREE
Online Edition

Safari
Books Online

Your purchase of **Learning jQuery** includes access to a free online edition for 45 days through the Safari Books Online subscription service. Nearly every Addison-Wesley Professional book is available online through Safari Books Online, along with over thousands of books and videos from publishers such as Cisco Press, Exam Cram, IBM Press, O'Reilly Media, Prentice Hall, Que, Sams, and VMware Press.

Safari Books Online is a digital library providing searchable, on-demand access to thousands of technology, digital media, and professional development books and videos from leading publishers. With one monthly or yearly subscription price, you get unlimited access to learning tools and information on topics including mobile app and software development, tips and tricks on using your favorite gadgets, networking, project management, graphic design, and much more.

Activate your FREE Online Edition at
informit.com/safarifree

STEP 1:   Enter the coupon code: RCPMOGA.

STEP 2:   New Safari users, complete the brief registration form.
            Safari subscribers, just log in.

If you have difficulty registering on Safari or accessing the online edition,
please e-mail customer-service@safaribooksonline.com